Growing Old

Growing Old
a societal
perspective

MARTHA BAUM   **RAINER C. BAUM**

School of Social Work   *Department of Sociology*

University of Pittsburgh

Prentice-Hall, Inc.,
Englewood Cliffs, New Jersey 07632

Library of Congress Cataloging in Publication

BAUM, MARTHA.
    Growing old.

    Bibliography.
    Includes index.
    1. Old age.   2. Retirement—United States.
3. Aged—United States—Economic conditions.
4. Aged—United States—Family relationships.
5. Old age—Political aspects—United States.
6. Death.   I. Baum, Rainer C., joint author.
II. Title.
HQ1061.B38   301.43'5'0973   79-23012
ISBN 0-13-367797-4

Prentice-Hall Series in Sociology
Neil J. Smelser, Editor

Printed in the United States of America

10   9   8   7   6   5   4   3   2   1

Editorial/production supervision: Jeanne Hoeting
Cover design: Lana Giganti
Manufacturing Buyer: Ray Keating

PRENTICE-HALL INTERNATIONAL, INC., *London*
PRENTICE-HALL OF AUSTRALIA PTY. LIMITED, *Sydney*
PRENTICE-HALL OF CANADA, LTD., *Toronto*
PRENTICE-HALL OF INDIA PRIVATE LIMITED, *New Delhi*
PRENTICE-HALL OF JAPAN, INC., *Tokyo*
PRENTICE-HALL OF SOUTHEAST ASIA PTE. LTD., *Singapore*
WHITEHALL BOOKS LIMITED, *Wellington, New Zealand*

contents

Growing Old

theoretical perspectives

INTRODUCTION

This is a book about being old in American society, which also compares the last phase of the American way of life with how that phase is managed in other modern societies. This is not a textbook on aging, though it does cover similar material. We do not attempt to include all known facts and theories of aging. Our objectives are different from, although complementary to, those of a standard textbook. Our approach to the study of older people in modern times has two distinctive features. First, we confine our survey of known facts to six aspects of contemporary old age. Second, we apply three competing theoretical perspectives to each of these aspects.

Most of this chapter is devoted to describing the three theoretical perspectives to be used. In the following chapters, these perspectives will be applied to the six aspects: 1) the income position of the elderly; 2) their political participation; 3) retirement as an institution in modern society; 4) family and kinship ties in old age; 5) dying; and 6) death and its aftermath, the funeral and the status of bereavement in modern times.

The first perspective, abandonment, holds that being old in modern times amounts to a state of relative deprivation. This is so because industrial society has no use for older people. Unlike in other societies, knowledge and skills wear out fast in modernity, and older people are consigned to premature obsolescence. Society casts them out against their will to suffer social isolation and despair.

A second and quite opposite perspective, here called liberation, maintains that being old and therefore freed from the necessity of working amounts to a status of relative privilege. The focus is on retirement as an institution that only industrial societies can afford. In our approach, retirement is also viewed in the broadest sense of the term. It does not just mean relief from work and its constraints but also means release from the responsibilities of the middle years of life generally. Such responsibilities compel the individual to balance the often conflicting obligations to spouse and to self, to children and to career, to friends and to in-laws, and to community and to employer. In short, the liberation perspective directs us to think about two sets of possibilities in retirement and old age generally. First, in modern times this last stage of life may be a genuine release from the pressures of the middle years of life. Second, being old may serve some purpose today after all. Do the elderly teach something important to younger people? Could old age be a reminder that there is more to be asked about humans than what they do or how much money they make? Such questions are prompted by a massive demographic change. All industrial societies are moving into a great gerontological era, in which the proportion of older people in the population is growing to historically unprecedented dimensions. Liberation suggests that this rise of the elderly in modern times may emancipate the middle aged from the shackles of an overblown achievement complex. That complex has narrowed the view of the human personality to mainly *homo faber,* man the maker, with its attendant preoccupation with socioeconomic status. If the elderly actually do have a viable and even privileged place in society when work is over, then the ghost of Karl Marx which rattles around in the closets of contemporary consciousness might be laid to rest.

Our third and last theoretical perspective of old age focuses on diachronic solidarity. We define this as a social identity shared among generations in society and so binding all into an ongoing community, lasting indefinitely. The concept will be described in a later section. Here we note only its use. Diachronic solidarity will be used to investigate whether the aged in modern society, and the mode of caring for them in particular, have another function beyond that suggested by liberation. This function is the production of generalized trust, compensating somewhat for our inability to understand the working of those major institutions of society, such as the economy and the polity, on which our lives depend.

We assume that life in complex modern societies generates unusually high demand for trust. Think, for example, about exposure to the mass media. They tell all of us how deeply we depend, even for everyday routine activities, on highly complex institutions, the workings of which no lay person can understand. News is mostly alarming: Investment rates decline, unemployment looms, stagflation threatens, and the government is declared helpless. To live in the modern world is to live with many threats of uncertainty. Trust also is demanded by the fact that to live in modern times is to expect change as a matter of course, rather than to view it as an exception. Certainly, earlier historical epochs had their crises. We learn from history more about crises than about periods of happiness which, as Hegel remarked (1837/1956), are likely to be blank pages. But only industrial societies have woven the expectation of constant change into the fabric of social life itself. Consequently, only now can one speak of a latent sense of anxiety, of being a "homeless mind," and suffering from "future shock" as constant companions throughout life (Berger & Kellner 1973; Toffler 1970).

Caring for the elderly so as to convince the caretakers that they will be cared for in turn when the time comes may well be one of the last remaining insurance mechanisms against an uncertain future. And, as will be seen, everywhere in industrial society the social security system provides such a mechanism. We will be looking for other mechanisms in relation to the elderly that ensure social continuity over time despite endemic change.

Approaching the subject of old age as just outlined has three purposes. First, we use the three perspectives as an alternative to the pervasive social-problems focus in contemporary social gerontology. This is intended to correct an imbalance in this focus. Up to now, most attention has been to the characteristics of the elderly, and little has been paid to the contrasting features of the nonaged except to mobilize concern with and to find solutions for the afflictions of old age. We suspect that the answers to the question of how industrialized society treats its older people can tell us much about people not yet old, their values, their institutions, and their historical experience with institutions in the twentieth century.

Accordingly we focus as much as we can on the relation between the aged and the nonaged, and on problems of both. Second, many comparative data on the aged in other industrialized countries are added to data on the lives of elderly Americans. This protects us from making unwarranted generalizations about the fate of being old in modern mass society. That fate, as will be seen, is characterized not only by similarities but also by noteworthy differences. Contemporary social gerontology has been quite successful in guarding against stereotyping the elderly. They are, of course, as different from one another as people of all ages are. But gerontology, in our view, has been somewhat less successful in resisting the stereotyping of industrial societies. They too have their differences. Knowledge of these differences is a useful tool for mobilizing moral concern about the fate of old people.

As a third objective, then, cross-national data also will be used to evaluate more realistically how Americans treat their older people. All evaluation requires comparison. But it does matter whether one evaluates what one does compared to some abstract standard of what ought to be done, a procedure quite common in the social problems approach, or whether one judges performance in one country compared to that of other countries. We suggest that the latter approach is more realistic and should, therefore, carry more political weight in debates on reform.

With this overview, the content of this chapter can be outlined. The first section describes our three theoretical perspectives. In the second, we present basic demographic characteristics of modern societies. The distinctive age composition of the population in industrialized societies, more than any other single factor, directly influences the questions raised by most observers about the fate of older people in modern times. Finally, we discuss briefly how our three perspectives pertain to the most widely discussed theories of growing old in contemporary social gerontology.

THE THREE THEORETICAL PERSPECTIVES

A theory is a system of interrelated concepts in which the definitions of each is systematically related to the definitions of the others. In contrast, theoretical perspectives consist of sensitizing concepts (Blauner 1954). The difference is that sensitizing concepts are *not* defined according to their systematic interrelationships. Some may be related, others not; whichever, reliance on sensitizing concepts is an investigative procedure in which the researcher does not start out with any particular concern about the relationships between the concepts used. How the definition of any one may relate to that of the others is left to the theoretical synthesis or interpretation which is considered after gathering the evidence. This also makes describing theoretical perspective a simple task. It is enough to identify its central sensitizing concept and to label it. Then one knows generally the kinds of questions raised and the kinds of facts needed to answer them. Our approach to the study of aging relies on three perspectives. At this point, we also are not concerned with their relationships. The first two perspectives happen to be related. They are, in a common-sense way, opposite perspectives. The third has no immediately discernible relation to the former two. Whether all three have systemic relations we will decide in the last chapter.

Abandonment

As stated earlier, our first theoretical perspective is *abandonment*. It holds that being old in modern society is like being in a condition of generalized uselessness. No one needs older people anymore. They are socially obsolete; there is not and there cannot be any genuine demand for what older people can do for others, and that is why they are abandoned. The themes of obsolescence and consequent abandonment can be traced historically. We shall examine this point in more detail later. Suffice it here to say that the abandonment perspective is based on a number of empirical assertions that in essence claim that preindustrial social orders needed older people, but modern society does not need them.

Let us define abandonment as relative-status deprivation, economic, social, and psychological, a deprivation based on growing old. Further, old age usually begins with the attainment of retirement age. In the United States this usually is at age sixty-five, according to prevailing social security regulations. This deprivation is relative in two ways, involving two distinct comparisons. One compares some specified condition at two points in time. A condition in old age is compared with its corresponding condition earlier in the life course of the same person or group. Another compares some specific condition of older people with the corresponding condition of younger contemporaries at one point in time. Abandonment of the elderly means their suffering some deprivation either relative to what they had before growing old or relative to what the nonaged have, or both. A few illustrations of relative deprivation in economic, social, and psychological terms should clarify this sensitizing concept.

Accordingly, relative *economic* deprivation would be evident, for example, in having an old age income significantly lower than one's preretirement income, say, during the last five years before retirement and/or having a significantly lower income in old age than the nonaged have. Relative *social* deprivation may be indicated by significantly fewer opportunities to participate in society when old than earlier in life, and/or relative to the number of opportunities among the nonaged. For example, any form of reduction in voting participation imposed on the elderly based on age is an indicator of political abandonment. Lacking transportation to go to the polls is one instance; not enough money to keep the TV in repair or to maintain the subscription to some newspaper and therefore not be able to follow the news as well is another. A futile struggle against some mandatory retirement rule indicates abandonment through mandatory retirement. Encountering blatant age discrimination in seeking employment after sixty-five is another. Significantly less, though desired, contact with children or relatives is family abandonment. Dying alone in a hospital, unable to share one's anxiety about impending death because the staff treats terminal patients just like those on the road to recovery is the last abandonment. Suffering the loss of another without the protective umbrella of a recognized bereavement status could be the most frequent form of abandonment into old age widowhood. Relative *psychological* deprivation can be associated with any of these experiences. It would be evident in a diminished sense of self-esteem attributable to them.

Having identified the abandonment perspective, let us return to the empirical assertions on which it rests. If it were true that modern society simply generates no demand for older people, then there are two factors that drastically affect the fate of being old in modern times. First, without being able to generate a genuine demand for older people, industrial society could not adequately reward the performance of the aged, no matter what they do. This would be inherent in the organization of life in modern societies, not just a matter of ill will or indifference among those not yet old. Second, they who are not in demand cannot make others dependent on them. If that were true of the elderly as a group, they would not be able to garner any kind of power. So, the abandonment perspective is that besides being unneeded and powerless, older people in modern society also *must* suffer relative deprivation. The implication is clear: Unless one radically reforms the structure of social life in industrial society, nothing will change the fate of old age from being relatively deprived. One could tinker with public and private pensions perhaps and so vary the level of relative deprivation, but one cannot eliminate it.

Liberation

The second theoretical perspective may be called *liberation*. It is an alternative and competing perspective because it implies the opposite of the abandonment perspective. It also contrasts the fate of older people in preindustrial societies with that in industrial societies and focuses on retirement. But the expectations associated with retirement are rosy rather than gloomy, and older people are seen as serving an important function rather than being condemned to social obsolescence. The premise of this perspective is the observation that retirement from work or full-time participation in the labor force as an emerging institution is an invention of industrial society. By institution we mean that retiring from work becomes an expected stage in life. One retires from work solely because of age or because one has worked long enough, and not because of sickness or any infirmity associated with becoming old that interferes significantly with one's ability to work. No preindustrial social order had retirement as an institution in this sense, simply because no preindustrial social order was capable of producing the sufficient economic surplus to afford it.

The focus here is on retirement as a condition of entitlement to some adequate standard of living for an entire end stage in life, potentially spanning decades, without the obligation to contribute to economic productivity. Being old in modern society is to be liberated from the world of work. Thus, liberation is defined as relative status privilege, economic, social, and psychological, and a privilege attributable solely to attainment of the status of old age. Again, the condition of privilege is relative to some corresponding condition earlier in the life course of the same person or group, on the one hand, and/or relative to the younger people still at work, on the other. Here it is the relative social and psychological privilege of old age that gives rise to speculations about demand for older people. Their privilege, it is held, can teach the nonaged some important lessons. Let us examine them briefly.

For example, relative *economic* privilege is having a retirement income that would allow the maintenance of the life style attained by, say, the five years before retirement, and/or a retirement income adequate compared with that of working people. What is "adequate" is defined in chapter 2. Relative *social* privilege could be any opportunity to participate in society that had to be sacrificed to or significantly curtailed for the sake of work and its previous demands. Similarly, social privilege, compared to that of the working population, is simply enjoying a life style less cramped or constrained. The opportunity for social participation labeled as a privilege is due to freedom from work. Vacationing during the off seasons is one example; finishing a book even though it is past two o'clock in the morning and being able to do so because you need not appear at work seven hours later is another. Any disengagement from work directly connected with new or increased political activity would indicate political liberation. A retired lawyer running for some public office, organizing a neighborhood into a lobby to put pressure on the mayor, or greater participation in letter-writing campaigns to members of Congress illustrate the same. Similarly, acquiring a new family role and doing so because old age has provided a freedom absent during the harried middle years of life would be a form of family liberation. Being a grandparent would be one such role. Enjoying a closer relationship with one's children made possible by giving up further, direct responsibilities for their place in society would be another. Experiencing death as a release from any conceivable form of alienation from self and society would be a form of death liberation. Responding to the death of another by a renewed interest in religion and the ability to share it with relatives and friends would be evidence of bereavement liberation. Relative *psychological* privilege would be manifest in greater self-esteem together with an enhanced sense of personal integrity potentially associated with any of these experiences.

It seems that it may be primarily in psychological privilege that the old and retired have something to teach the younger and still working. Only industrial society has freed its members from increasing toil necessary just to stay alive. It achieved this feat through unparalleled domination over nature accompanied by an equally unparalleled rationalization of the work process, otherwise known as bureaucratization, which subjects people in their work lives to dulling routine in factory or store, in office or outdoors. By contrast, the life styles among the retired may raise some questions which go far beyond the vision of retirement as just the golden years of life. Instead, finding fulfillment and meaning without the need for harsh discipline, becoming important to others without relying on money, and similar accomplishments in retirement may well counteract many forms of social and psychological alienation associated with work in modern society, and not necessary for efficiency. Does retirement as a distinct stage in life signal a liberation from "the iron cage of bureaucracy," as Max Weber once called our modern working lives? Might such liberation not only benefit those in retirement but also teach something to those at work? These are the kinds of questions prompted by the liberation perspective on old age in modern times.

Diachronic Solidarity

Although the themes of abandonment and liberation can be found directly or indirectly in the most prevalent social theories of aging in modern times, our third theoretical alternative is derived from how most industrial countries finance social security. This is a pay-as-you-go procedure in which the younger and still working generate income for the older in retirement. Described further in chapter 2, let us note here only the following. Old age social security is the single most important source of old age income for the largest number of old people in all industrial societies. Everywhere that income is strictly transfer income. It is earned by the young at work but is allocated to the elderly no longer at work. Everywhere also the younger generations provide for the elderly of the nation in the expectation that they will be provided for in turn upon their entry into old age.

That mode of caring for older people in modern society is the basic clue to the concept of *diachronic solidarity*. The term is admittedly cumbersome, but it seems necessary to avoid mistaking it for the related concept of intergenerational solidarity. Diachronic solidarity is a self-perpetuating form of intergenerational solidarity. Simply though abstractly, diachronic solidarity can be defined as a social identity shared with successive generations that always connects the younger with the older in a perpetual chain of community lasting through time, indefinitely.

Clearly then, our focus is on a social identity shared intergenerationally *and* one that is handed on from generation to generation, thus connecting in bonds of loyalty and mutual obligation successive cohorts of parents and children. At any given moment, realizing one's obligation takes the form of a cross-sectional transfer. For example, some cohorts of younger people at work pay their social security tax, and the government distributes old age benefits to a number of cohorts of the elderly in society. But each such transfer is repeated over time. That is why we call these bonds of solidarity diachronic, or holding through time.

As we study the six areas of the fate of old age in industrial society we shall be looking for one particular type of mechanism by which the younger provide for the older. That mechanism of taking care of the elders in society must be able to *create* obligations that form a perpetual chain of mutual care by the expectation that whatever one cohort does for its elderly, it expects to receive in turn from the next younger cohort. The connection between identity and obligation in this formulation is easy to see. Any obligation that takes time to fulfill presupposes permanence in those identities of the contracting partners relevant to the responsibilities assumed at least until the obligation is met. A contractual obligation rests on the expectation that promises made are promises kept, and that in turn rests on the expectation that the partners who made the promises will recognize each other as the same partners over time. The underlying premise of any long-term obligation is that if the promise is not kept, the party accused of breach of promise can defend itself with something like "what are you talking about, I never said that." If we had to be afraid that the response might be "who are you to be talking to me, we have never met before," we would never enter into long-term contracts. It follows that one can use obligations between generations as an indicator of shared identities. The only twist here is that we shall be looking for the kinds of obligations that are self-perpetuating and therefore connect successive cohorts.

The fact that the social security systems of industrial societies rest on trust in diachronic solidarity was partly recognized for the first time by Marcel Mauss (1925/1967) who was investigating a very different subject. In studying economic exchange among primitive and archaic peoples, Mauss characterized these relations as patterns of gift exchange, for three reasons. First, it was groups, not individual persons, that made contracts and created mutual obligations. Second, what was exchanged always was more than material goods, thus expressing diffuse bonds of loyalty and identity. Third, exchange always occurred under the guise of voluntarism and freedom but was in fact a matter of strict obligation and constraint even to the point of enforcement by means of violence, for example, going to war over a dispute of what was purported to be just a gift. Mauss saw in the social security laws of modern states a return to the group morality of earlier times, to "the theme of the gift, of freedom and obligation in the gift, of generosity and self-interest in giving" (1925/1967: 65-66). Was he right? To a great extent he was. Let us see why and how.

To begin with and to avoid confusion, let us keep firmly in mind an insight that we owe to Mauss. Most gift giving never was, is not now, and probably never shall be completely spontaneous and voluntary. Instead, gift giving is highly regulated. Whether we think of birthdays, Christmas, the name days (date of baptism), Valentine's Day or marriage anniversaries, all are occasions when gift giving is expected, when presenting a gift is an obligation and receiving it a duty. Perhaps today failing to give gifts on birthdays or on marriage anniversaries may be a matter overlooked in, say, some marital relationships. But surely, refusal to accept a gift calls forth serious efforts to repair the relation and, if these fail, some drastic alteration in the relation between spouses or even dissolution of the marriage. Therefore, in principle, nothing should deter us from interpreting an exchange relationship as one of gift giving just because it is a duty rather than an expression of pure altruism, somehow free floating and disconnected from social expectations. When we pay social security taxes, we obey the law. But that in itself says nothing about whether or not such taxes are gifts.

Let us also keep in mind that contemporary debates about social security legislation in industrialized countries are debates about public old-age pensions. The proportions of payments going to the nonaged are small enough to be disregarded when considering the significance of social security in the lives of the elderly (Myers 1975; Kaim-Caudle 1973).

Old-age income financed through social security is characterized by three features amazingly similar to Marcel Mauss's analysis of gift giving in preindustrial social orders. First, and to repeat, social security entails group transfers. It is the younger and working who provide for the older and retired in a nation. The contracting partners are groups not individuals, regardless what people, particularly Americans, may believe (Boskin 1977; Kaim-Caudle 1973). Second, even though the name social *insurance* is quite widespread, it is not true that the elderly person usually receives in the form of old age income only what he or she earlier paid into the system. Given the short history of social security, there currently are in all industrialized countries many elderly who receive far more in benefits than they ever paid in. This is not just because the systems have matured. All social security systems are a mixture of welfare elements and equity considerations.

Everywhere old age social security income has become one of the most significant social rights (Marshall 1965). A social right is an entitlement that modern societies grant to their members regardless of whether they as individuals earned it. The welfare element in these systems appear in specifying levels of economic security below which no one is supposed to fall. Although the net balance between the principles of equity (those who paid more shall get more) and assistance (helping the poor or the ill) is exceedingly difficult to judge for any system as a whole in the United States, it seems to work out in favor of redistribution (Viscusi & Zeckhauser 1977; Parsons & Monroe 1977). Note, though, that redistribution is only one element of gift giving. The more fortunate take care of the less fortunate.

The other element of the gift, undoubtedly the larger one, is the already noted fact that social security everywhere is an intergenerational transfer system of payments (Schulz and others 1976a). That fact makes the system operate just like a family in which the younger, the working, and the healthy look after the older and retired, the indigent, the sick, and the deviant. But the system represents a peculiar kind of family, one elevated to the national level, and bonded by the impersonal ties of bureaucracy. Borrowing a phrase from Nelson (1949) we can say, what was once the tribal brotherhood of the generations within the bonds of kinship social security laws has changed into a universal brotherhood of the generations within the modern nation. Nonetheless, relative diffuseness of the obligations and their perpetual character make the nation a true community as well.

Finally, and third, although social security rests on legally enforced obligations, the very nature of modern law makes taking care of older people more of a gift in the common-sense meaning of that term than in any preindustrial social order. This is explained by two characteristics of modern law both of which enhance the elements of freedom, voluntarism, and generosity in the gift and therefore also its elements of risk and uncertainty. One of these characteristics is that only political authority in modern society can create entirely new, legitimate, legal obligations, as a matter of course rather than in response to an emergency. Traditional political authorities always had to disguise new obligations as customs allegedly forgotten and needing resurrection (Weber 1922/1968: 215-30).

The other feature of modern law is that in democratic polities at least, legislating new obligations does require the political support of or voluntary consent from a sufficient number of the governed. This always is so in normative theory and frequently so in practice, even if often delayed. In the United States in the recent past, social security has been the most popular governmental program. This has been evident in at least two facts. As Myers (1975:105) showed, if we apply the automatic inflation correction to benefits legislated in 1972 retroactively to 1967, it turns out that the actual increases legislated over that period were more than double the rate required by the 1972 amendment. Also, from 1972 to 1975, Congress never permitted the automatic correction to take effect. Instead it legislated increases in order to take the credit for it. In short, generosity hitherto has yielded political payoffs.

Remembering that diachronic solidarity depends on creating an endless chain of intergenerational obligations, let us now illustrate how we might find evidence for it in each of our six areas of old age in industrial society. In the economics of old age we suggest that comparing the income inequality of the elderly with that of younger cohorts is an essential clue. Knowing that a large portion of retirement and old age income is social security income, similar levels of income inequality between the young and old indicate that a proper balance between the principles of equity (the tie of old age benefits to prior earnings) and welfare (redistribution from the economically strong to the weak) is maintained. That not only indicates a commitment to retirement as an institution in the life course of modern men and women but also generates among those who provide the gift of retirement expectations that they in turn are entitled to it.

In the chapter on retirement we also look for evidence on the degree of intergenerational consensus on a retirement phase in life as a social right. Again, the hypothesis is that if retirement is seen as a right rather than as a charity, those currently granting it by their payments will claim it for themselves in the future.

In the politics of old age we shall search for the degree of intergenerational political support for social security taxes. That is one indicator of political diachronic solidarity. The absence of partisan conflict over such taxes is another. In contrast, fighting about such taxes in the hope of catching votes along lines of intergenerational cleavage in the population and winning indicates a break in the chain of generations.

Turning now to the family, we should realize that modern societies have a far larger number of generations living at the same time, though not usually under the same roof, than ever was the case before in history. In eighteenth-century Austria, for example, having a grandparent alive was an experience confined to toddlers, perhaps to age three or so. The average life span was so short that there were usually only two generations living simultaneously. Most of the time a family was a nuclear one, just parents and children, and only for a few years was it a stem family with a grandparent present (Berkner 1972). Purely in terms of being alive and disregarding the question of who lives with whom under one roof, the situation is radically different in industrial society. The four-generation family, having great-grandparents alive, is no longer a rarity. One study found that about a third of the American elderly and just under a fifth of older people in the United Kingdom and Denmark are great-grandparents (Shanas and others 1968:143). In fact, if the average age of reproduction were to settle below age 25 and the average age of death above age 75, the four-generation family would become the rule. In a move towards zero-population growth, this would mean that during the last years of life every one of us would have very few siblings or any collateral kin of the same age, but three generations of younger people would be available. The structure of the family in modern times is long and thin, as it were. There are far more members of different generations alive at the same time and far fewer of the same age. Thus, whatever else we may be in the intricate web of our social identities, we are a part of a continuous stream of kinship that has become far more of a reality in industrial society than ever before.

The opportunity for intergenerational help also has increased. So here we shall be looking for norms and practices governing mutual assistance that generate perpetual obligations. Any flow of resources up or down the rank of age that implies an expectation to be taken care of in turn, if need be, indicates family diachronic solidarity. And what applies to helping in living also applies to helping in dying. The modern family has more generations potentially available to witness the dying of one of its members and to share that loss than ever before. Of course, the modern generations live in separate households, sometimes many miles from each other. But physically more of them are alive when the life of a family member ends. Can we detect, then, patterns of keeping company with the dying, of sharing the meaning of death, and of sharing the burden of loss organized in such a fashion that those whose turn comes next can reasonably expect a return of the loyalty that they gave to their forebears? If so, such patterns indicate diachronic solidarity; if not, the chain has been broken and the corresponding social identities are not handed down from generation to generation.

In conclusion, financing old age economic and social rights through social security is our main clue to a whole set of mechanisms by which modern societies may create a perpetual chain of obligations to care that join successive generations into a web of loyalty far outlasting the life span of any one person. To the best of our knowledge, no industrial society has yet made any really important retrenchment in social security rights. We attach great significance to this fact, particularly in countries that have had very violent and volatile political histories in the twentieth century. Two world wars and the history of countries on the European continent show that political regimes may come and go, but the gifts promised to the elderly were given, regardless of who was in power. In Germany, for example, the social security system has survived four changes in political regime since World War I. Among the older people living here today, one finds persons who were alive during the Hohenzollern monarchy, the Weimar Republic, Adolf Hitler's dictatorship, and either one or both of the two remaining republics in contemporary East or West Germany. Such persons could have sworn an oath of allegiance to four kinds of constitutions, if one counts the allegiance to Hitler as constitutional. They may have belonged to the political ingroup under one type of government and found themselves political outcasts under another. Yet, in old age they are the recipients of a social security gift never rescinded by any of the governments under which they lived.

It is indeed as if modern men and women use social security as a symbol of a common collective identity that lasts, no matter how drastic the other changes in their lives. This chain of perpetual intergenerational obligations is like a shout: "Let war and famine come and go, let the storms of history rage, caring for our elders is one part of ourselves that shall never vanish from this earth." Social security is not social insurance, like an annuity policy purchased from a private life insurance company.

But there may be one sense in which it is an insurance plan. In modern societies changes in scientific knowledge and technology have led to expectattions in which we regard social change as the rule and social stability as the exception. Perhaps social security insures us against the specter of total generation gaps, a Hobbesian nightmare pitting son against father, daughter against mother, and children against their elders. But with modern gifts being more voluntary than those of traditional social orders, that also is a subject for worry and nagging doubt. One reason for uncertainty is the numerical rise of the elderly and the rising cost of taking care of them.

THE AGE STRUCTURE
OF MODERN SOCIETY

People in industrial societies produce fewer children per family and also are more protected against the ravages of epidemic diseases than people were in the preindustrial era. Protection against epidemics means protection against a premature death and expectation of a longer life expectancy. When lowered fertility combines with a longer average life expectancy, the proportion of older people in society grows (Hauser 1976). This is sometimes referred to as the aging of the population in modern society. In the United States, for example, people aged sixty-five and over made up only 3 percent of the population in 1850, but the proportion grew to 9 percent by 1960 and is expected to reach 16 percent by the year 2030 (Sheldon 1960:32). Such growth in the proportion of the elderly is a universal characteristic of industrial societies (Cowgill & Holmes 1972:309).

A longer average life expectancy also means a demographic shift in dying. Blauner (1968:531-33) estimated that over half the deaths in hunting and gathering or simple agricultural societies were of children. But in industrial societies, death is normal only in old age. When death strikes earlier in the life course, we call it premature and regard it as tragic. Even when one qualifies Blauner's observations by noting that death in old age is normal only when industrial society is at peace, the study of old age still entails the study of dying, death, and bereavement. Yet being old is in part a social convention, and old age can last for decades before death comes. Let us see how.

As Rose (1965:12) explained it, for the United States, the Social Security Act of 1935 was the single most important factor in teaching Americans that old age begins in the sixty-fifth year of life. At sixty-five we become eligible for old age security benefits. That, we might say, makes us old. All persons of that age and above are the aged of society, a group created, certainly in part, by legislative fiat. In similar fashion, reaching age fifty-five makes a woman in Czechoslovakia old, at least officially. It does so for the simple reason of becoming entitled to a public old-age pension (Siklova 1974). The choice of the year in social security legislation defines old age as a social problem. It also generates statistics for our present situation and can tell us about the past.

Although the word retirement was not in usage in 1900, we now know that then only one third of all males aged sixty-five and over were no longer working, but two thirds were at work (Schulz and others 1976a:2) and, presumably, none was regarded as old simply on grounds of the magic number sixty-five. In 1975, four fifths of American men of that age group were retired, and only one fifth was still at work (U.S. Dept. HEW, DHEW Publication No. (OHD) 77-20006, 1976). All however, belong to the elderly in society. Still, it is by no means all a matter of social definition. Nature lets the human organism die in the seventh or eighth decade of life as it always did. Only by modernizing changes in public hygiene, medical knowledge, and nutrition has the number of people reaching a ripe old age increased. Drawing on the HEW publication just cited, we know that the average American male sixty-five years old in 1974 could expect to live another thirteen years, hence die at age 78. For a women the average expected age of death was eighty-three. Whatever the reasons, nature still lets us die within less than two decades after age sixty-five. But even so, we have today far more old people, both in absolute and relative terms, than at the turn of the century. We illustrate the fact in some detail for the United States because it makes up what is known as the demographic crunch in taking care of older people.

The Elderly in the United States

Figure 1.1 and Table 1.1 depict the growth of the elderly (aged sixty-five and over) in the United States. In 1900 there were just about three million of them, then making up about 4 percent of the total population. Since then, they have grown in numbers and in proportions, decade by decade. In 1910 there were just under four million, in 1920 just under five, and by 1970 we had over twenty million, then constituting over 10 percent of the total population. If one assumes an average of 2.1 children per female during her entire fertile existence, the latest projections are for 30.6 million older people by the year 2000, who will then comprise just under 12 percent of all of us (Table 1.1).

Table 1.1
Estimates and Projections of the Proportion of the United States Population Aged 65 Years and Over and 75 Years and Over: 1900-2000 (Percentages).

Year	65 Years and Over Total	Male	Female	75 Years and Over Total	Male	Female
1900	4.1	4.0	4.1	1.2	1.1	1.2
1930	5.4	5.4	5.5	1.6	1.5	1.7
1960	9.2	8.4	10.0	3.1	2.7	3.5
1990	11.8	9.7	13.8	4.6	3.3	5.9
2000	11.7	9.4	13.7	5.1	3.6	6.6

Sources: U.S. Bureau of the Census, Current Population Reports, Series P-23, No. 43, Washington, D.C. 1975:5 for 1900-1960; remainder calculated from U.S. Bureau of the Census, Current Population Reports, Series P-25, No. 601, Washington, D.C. 1975:82, 92.

The story for the really old (seventy-five years and over) is similar. In 1900 only 1 percent of the population was that old. Their proportions increased after the 1930s, growing to 3 percent by 1960 and to eight million, comprising about 4 percent by 1974 (see source in Table 1.1). By the year 2000, these really old will number 13.5 million, making up about 5 percent of the total population.

Up to the present and into the foreseeable future, the rise of the elderly also has meant the rise of the older woman. Table 1.1 shows quite clearly that there

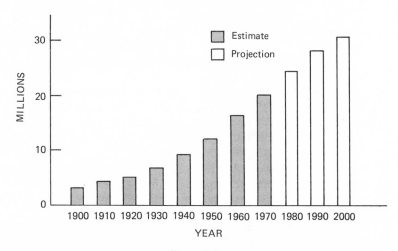

Figure 1.1

Sources: 1900-1970 U. S. Bureau of the Census, Current Population Reports, Series P-23, No. 43, Washington, D. C. 1973: 2; 1980-2000 calculated from U. S. Bureau of the Census, Current Population Reports, Series P-25, No. 601, Washington, D. C. 1975: 67, 72, 82, 92.

was no sex imbalance among older Americans (for both age cohorts) before 1930. It was only thereafter that women tended to outnumber men and at an accelerating rate. Modernization of society contributes to sexual inequality, favoring the female with a longer life. Just how much of a favor this is will be described in chapter 2.

A brief glance at the marital status and the living arrangements among older Americans also is instructive. Table 1.2 shows an impressive historical stability in marriage in old age. For the majority of women, growing to old age means living in widowhood, at the beginning of the century as well as in 1975. Just over a third of older women in 1900 were married; in 1975 that was true of 39 percent.

Despite changes in the sex balance among older people, over two thirds of older men in 1900 were married, a proportion that rose to over three quarters by 1975. Being old never did and does not now disqualify an older man from marrying as much as it does an older woman. In 1900, older men frequently were married to women younger than themselves, and this was true also in 1975 for over a third (see source, Table 1.2). Once we allow for the 5 percent of older people living in institutions in 1975, this difference in marital status is directly reflected in the prevailing living arrangements. Although the majority of older men lived with their wives, just one half the older women lived with

Table 1.2
Marital Status and Living Arrangements among Older Americans
(Percentages of All Aged 65 Years or Over).

Marital Status		Male 1900	Male 1975	Female 1900	Female 1975
	Married	67	79	34	39
	Widowed	26	14	59	52
Other:	Divorced	–	2	–	3
	Never Married	6	5	6	6
		99	100	99	100

Living Arrangements (1975)

Five percent of both sexes were institutionalized and of the remaining 95% one found:

	(Male)	(Female)
Living as Family Head	79	9
Living with Other Family Member	4	50
Living alone *or* with Non-relative	17	41
	100	100

Source: Facts about Older Americans, 1975, U.S. Department HEW, DHEW Publication No. (OHD) 77-20006, Washington, D.C. 1976.

spouses or other family members, and another 41 percent was either living alone or with nonrelatives.

Regardless of whether we use age sixty-five or age seventy-five as the year defining old age, American society has more older people now, both absolutely and proportionately, than ever before in its history. And the proportions will grow, at least within the short-term future into the early decades of the twenty-first century. To repeat, such growth of the elderly is not unique to American society but is a typical feature of all industrial countries. For modern people being old implies retirement from the work force. Indeed, for males the ability and the practice of retiring from work in later life has been the outstanding achievement of economic modernization to date. For some, of course, retirement has been an obligation. Subject to mandatory retirement rules, they were let go regardless of their own preferences. For whom the bell tolls in pleasure or in pain and how much retirement has become an institution, we shall see in the following chapters. At this point we highlight the economic significance of this demographic crunch with the help of two additional simple statistics.

One of these is called the old-age dependency ratio. It tells us how much older people in retirement depend on those still at work for transfer income, or how much of a burden the elderly are for the younger generations. The ratio results from dividing the population aged sixty-five and over into the population aged twenty to sixty-four, for example, to estimate how much of one retirement existence is based on one life at work. The trouble is that census statistics on age are far more reliable than are government statistics on labor force participation. One thus has to assume that all of the aged are out of work, and all of the nonaged used in the ratio are at work. Using that assumption, interpreting the ratio becomes a simple matter. In 1970 the corresponding U.S. old-age dependency ratio was .188 (Schulz and others 1976a:6). In other words, close to one fifth of the livelihood of one retired person depended on one other at work. Every one retired person was sustained by the labor of 5.3 persons. Assuming a move toward zero-population growth, Schulz and others also figured that this ratio will hardly change in the near future. It will go up a little by 1985 but will become the same again in 2000. But if we move towards a truly static population, in which all departing through death just are replaced, then there will be only 3.5 workers for every retiree.

This is only one part of the demographic crunch. Children do not work regularly, either, in modern society. Their schooling and their lives at home have to be sustained by people who work. Including the young with the elderly as the nonworking in society and dividing that number into those at work then yields what is known as the general-dependency ratio. Here we shall take leave of Schulz and colleagues and use the number of persons aged under fifteen to sixty-five and over to estimate the nonworking. This gives us a larger picture of several industrialized countries.

The number of people not working expressed as a percentage of those aged fifteen to sixty-four and assumed to be at work, yields a general-dependency ratio with a more dramatic interpretation. It tells us the proportion of the

Table 1.3
General Dependency Ratios in Ten Countries
(Percent of the Population not at Work*)

Country	Year	Dependency Ratio (%)	Country	Year	Dependency Ratio (%)
Austria	1959-61	61	Netherlands	1960-61	60
Germany	1964-65	55	Canada	1960-61	65
Ireland	1960-61	74	U.S.A.	1965	63
U.K.	1963-65	58	New Zealand	1960-62	69
Denmark	1963-64	54	Australia	1960-62	60

*Number of persons aged under 15 and 65 or over and for every 100 aged 15 to 64.
(Source: Kaim-Coudle 1973:19).

population typically not working in modern societies and dependent on those who work. Table 1.3 shows the story of the decade of the sixties for a number of countries. The figures can be read quite simply. Each country ratio shows the number of people not working for every one hundred in the labor force. In every country each worker is therefore bearing more than half the support of one nonworking person. For example, in the United States, 63 percent of a nonworker's expenses must be paid for by the labor of one worker! Some industrial societies are a little less burdened, some a little more, but the picture generally is quite similar. The majority is still at work in industrial societies, but the proportions of working and nonworking are growing rather close together. Clearly, that demands a highly productive economy. And one must raise the question of whether the expectation for supporting such a large proportion of nonworkers is realistic.

In concluding this discussion of the demographic crunch, let us make one cautionary note and add one other question. The above estimates actually are conservative. They do assume full employment among those aged fifteen to sixty-four. In reality the proportions of those not working, as shown in Table 1.3, are larger, particularly in the United States. Thus, we probably are even closer to the "one worker, one nonworker" ratio than it appears. In addition, if modern societies were to move toward zero-population growth as a steady state, there will be considerable savings from the reduced costs of child rearing and schooling, if we maintain such a pattern. But if Schulz and others (1976a:8) are to be believed, no one knows at this time whether that saving will offset the growing costs of maintaining the elderly.

From the point of view of social demography, then, the study of old age in industrial society is circumscribed by three facts. First, retirement from work is an invention of industrial society, and its rules define who is regarded as old. Second, the proportion of the elderly is growing. Third, in peacetime death is normal only in old age. These facts have influenced the most widely discussed *social* theories of old age in industrial society. And that influence permits us to relate these theories to our perspectives of abandonment, liberation, and diachronic solidarity as outlined above.

SOCIAL THEORIES OF OLD AGE

Most theories of contemporary social gerontology are also theoretical perspectives based on one or more sensitizing concepts rather than on internally integrated systems of concepts. In order to keep them distinct from the three perspectives of this book, we shall refer to them as social theories of aging. Depending on the number of distinctions one wants to make and on whether a theory applies especially to older people or to others as well, there are about eight that deserve mention here. These are: 1) disengagement theory (Cumming & Henry 1961); 2) the disprivileged minority theory (Barron 1961); 3) socialization to old age (Rosow 1974); 4) the application of modernization theory to old age (Cowgill & Holmes 1972); 5) subculture theory (Rose 1965); 6) activity theory (Maddox 1966, 1968); 7) age stratification and intergenerational linkage theory (Riley 1976; Bengtson & Cutler 1976); and 8) the application of exchange theory to the family life of older people (Sussman 1976). All of these eight can be related to one or another of the three perspectives in this book.

Disengagement Theory

Disengagement theory is exceptional in two respects. On the one hand, it focuses directly on the problem of death and long before that became a fashionable topic. On the other hand, it aspires to universality across cultures and across history, although it concentrates on the special problems of growing old in industrial society. But this exceptional status of disengagement theory is to be found primarily in its original formulation by Cumming and Henry (1961), rather than in much, if not indeed most, of its subsequent use by others. By and large, this theory does not have much empirical verification, but neither can one say that it has been falsified successfully (Hochschild 1975). What one can say is that the disengagement perspective has had an unfortunate history, one of misapplication. Most work on it has not stuck to the theme of dying and the problem of death. Instead, general patterns of disengagement among the aged were looked for, regardless of their closeness to death. Not surprisingly, not much disengagement was found. Let us illustrate the point from the area of politics. No society has disenfranchised its older people. An analogy to the mandatory retirement rule has never been found in the citizenship role. In the United States there often is sufficient interest in getting the vote out to make transportation to the polls available to those of the elderly who cannot manage on their own. As a result, voter participation is hardly affected at all by just chronological age after sixty-five. The degree of participation before that age tends to be maintained (Foner 1972). But this is not a failure of disengagement theory.

In the areas of dying, of death, and bereavement, that perspective works fairly well. This will become evident in chapters 6 and 7. Contrary to the original formulation, however, it is not a process of mutual disengagement between the dying and the surviving and between those in bereavement and others that actually is found, but rather more a pattern of one-sided abandonment of the dying and the bereaved. That is why disengagement theory belongs more to our abandonment perspective than to either of the other two. To clarify the difference we briefly summarize the original formulation and a few subsequent refinements by the inventors of this perspective.

Formulated to apply to the relatively healthy and economically secure among the old of all societies throughout history, disengagement theory makes three assertions. First, society and individuals prepare in advance for inevitable death by a gradual, mutually satisfying withdrawal from involvement with each other. Second, disengagement includes a decline in the overall scope of involvement of the old person with others in favor of more instant and restricted enjoyment and less serious commitments. This reduces patterns of dependency between the outgoing and the ongoing. Third, disengagement eventuates in a sense of psychological well-being for the old. The rate of disengagement varies with such factors as widowhood before the last child marries, continued working after the retirement age, and temporary increases in recreational activities. Factors other than preparation for death can lead to involuntary disengagement. These include rapid social change making the old obsolescent before their time, variety in socially valid life styles available for leisure hours, and culturally variant conceptions of a "good old age" (Cumming & Henry 1961; Cumming 1963; Henry 1963). Evidently, factors causing involuntary disengagement of older people link this perspective with ours on abandonment.

Disprivileged Minority Theory

In all but name, the original formulation of the abandonment perspective can be attributed to Burgess (1950). Not much interested in theory but a keen observer and assiduous collector of facts, this pioneer student of the aged in industrial society stressed that to be old now is to suffer from "role-lessness." Modern society simply provides no role or activity tailored for old age. In this view, there is no place for the elderly in modern life. They are left to float, unattached to others, slowly turning on some axis of purposelessness and therefore ending their existence in meaninglessness. Here Barron's (1961) perspective on the aged as a disprivileged minority group, one analogous to ethnic disprivilege, provides one theoretical thrust to abandonment. Misery in old age is not just a fact but an inevitable destiny for all who reach age sixty-five and beyond.

In Barron's view, old age has become an ascriptive basis for discrimination, just like race or gender. The term ascriptive designates a social characteristic ascribed to persons at birth and deemed immutable thereafter. If you were born black rather than white, female rather than male, you are not responsible for it;

but you are destined to live with the consequences for the rest of your life. Accordingly, old age in modern times emerges here as a matter of unrelieved gloom and doom. With the luck of peace and the aid of medical technology, growing to old age is a universal destiny. All, in the end, have to face many deprivations, with only the amount varying a little.

To illustrate this further, Palmore and Manton (1973) used a simple measure of equality or similarity between any two groups to assess "agism" relative to racism and sexism in the United States as of 1970. Agism is based on comparing the old (over sixty-five years) and the nonaged (twenty-five to sixty-five years); sexism compares men and women, racism one race against another. Comparing such groups on income, education, and jobs (for those who have them), they reported, for example, that age is associated more with income equality than sex but less than race. For most Americans, old age amounts to greater income deprivation than being black does. It also was found that agism, sexism, and racism tend to work together, leading to patterns of double or triple jeopardy. For example, one of the greatest income gaps separates the younger, white male from the older, black woman. The example shows how one answers questions about the abandonment perspective.

Socialization to Old Age

A more general theoretical formulation of the necessary abandonment of older people in industrial society is in Rosow's (1974) inquiry into socialization for old age. When we view this work in connection with that of Burgess's (1950) concept of "the role-less role of the aged," Rosow supplies the answer to why. By and large, his findings show that there is little if any socialization for old age. This means that there is no learning of roles and, therefore, one cannot play any roles. What was gained here in theoretical precision, however, came at some cost to empirical truth. People in retirement are not as helpless as one would expect from Rosow's point of view, a matter we shall discuss in chapter 4.

Application of Modernization Theory to Old Age

Perhaps the strongest case for the necessary abandonment of older people in modern society was made by Cowgill and Holmes (1972). Even theirs is not a very good case, theoretically. They apply tenets of exchange theory to inter-generational relations at the aggregate national level. Later, we shall comment briefly on exchange theory. At this point, let us note that the theory was designed explicitly for the family or some other small group, at least in its more recent and most prominent formulation by Homans (1961). When one applies it to groups of far greater size, serious problems arise, which Cowgill and Holmes ignored. Working from many qualitative and quantitative observations of the fate of older people in preindustrial and industrial societies, Cowgill and Holmes developed twenty-two general propositions. All of these show why modern societies necessarily have less use for their older people than did premodern societies and, why, therefore, becoming old in modern society must amount to suffering relative status deprivation. They held that the more modern a society is, the worse off relative to the nonaged its older people *must be.*

A few illustrations from their list of general propositions about the status of older people will give the essence of their position. For example, the status of the elderly is found to be inversely proportional to their supply in society; the larger the number of the elderly, the lower their status must be (and modern societies have more old people). Similarly, the status of the elderly is found to be inversely proportional: 1) to the rate of social change (and modern society has high rates); 2) to the rate of residential mobility (and people in modern society are more geographically mobile); 3) to the level of literacy in the country (and modern societies have high literacy rates); 4) to prevalence of children establishing their own households at marriage, separate from both parents (and modern societies have more of this neo-local residence pattern); and, finally, 5) to the prevalence of individualist values in society, of which, once again, modern societies have more (Cowgill & Holmes 1972:322-23).

Essentially, Cowgill and Holmes base their case on a few contrasting features in the organization of society in its preindustrial and industrial forms. First, the preindustrial social order had relatively few roles and few differences among them. For example, on a family farm the roles of parents and employers and those of children and employees were integrated with each other with little formal recognition of their differences. In modern society people play many roles in quite varied institutions with sharply contrasting and normatively contrary expectations. Second, in preindustrial life, change was thought to be the exception and continuity the rule. At least in expectations, if not in fact, society was thought to be fairly stable with each successive generation following many of the same customs of the previous one. But in modern society, change is expected. Third, most of the custom-regulating social life in the preindustrial order was based on oral traditions transmitted by memory, not machines, and by mouth, not print.

Simplicity of role structure means applicability of what one learned in one sphere of life to another. Stability of role structure means that one can learn by experience. Importance of an oral tradition means that one must rely for learning on those who have experience and wisdom, the elderly. Thus, pre-industrial social life generated considerable demand for older people because they had more of what every one needed. In the modern condition, lacking simplicity, stability, and the centrality of an oral tradition, there simply is no comparable demand for the elderly. That is why, said Cowgill and Holmes, modern societies abandon their older people, economically, socially, and cultur-ally more so than did preindustrial social orders.

What seems to be overlooked by advocates of the abandonment perspective is a simple fact of political life in modern societies, particularly in democratic ones. A minority whose political support is needed can, usually, accumulate a measure of political influence disproportionately larger than its size. When votes count, the one precondition for gaining influence is organization for joint action. In the United States, the elderly once appeared on the political scene as a formidable pressure group. That was the Townsend Movement of the early thirties advocating a federally financed scheme of caring for the elderly as one way to get the country out of the Great Depression. Though opposed by most economists at the time, the Townsendites were a force for elected officials to reckon with and the movement petered out only after the passage of the Social Security Act in 1935. Although contemporary opponents of the abandonment perspective make their case primarily in opposition to some of the social implications of disengagement theory, the very fact that the Townsend Movement once existed gives added impetus to these alternative theories, most of which are closer to our liberation perspective.

Subculture Theory

One of these is subculture theory. Rose (1968:187), for example, charged outright that disengagement theorists paint a far too biased portrait of the elderly in society, one derived from middle-age cultural ethnocentrism. In arguing for the development of a subculture of the aged, one with its own life style, organizations, and political objectives, Rose (1965:5-9) considered forces favoring as well as forces opposing such a development. Among the former, he listed the demographic changes of the age composition of the population, as outlined above, but also included growth in retirement communities, improved health among the elderly, more economic security in old age, and better welfare provisions for the needy. Among the opposing forces he considered mass media messages cross-cutting all social differences, attitudes resisting self-identification as an older person, continued part-time employment in old age, and welfare agents acting *for* the aged rather than patterns of organized self-help among the elderly. On balance, the forces for the emergence of an old age subculture seemed to him to have the edge over those against it.

Activity Theory

Activity theory, so labeled by Havighurst, Neugarten, and Tobin (1958:161), has a very different concept of being old in modern times than that of disengagement theory. Best exemplified by the work of Maddox (1966, 1968), activity theory is actually a kind of antiaging perspective. Its basic tenets can be stated in an assumption and a consequence drawn from that assumption. The assumption is that, excepting biological changes and health problems, the aged and the middle aged share identical psychological and social needs. As a consequence, "optimal aging" is described as staying active, resisting a shrinking social involvement, and finding substitutes for roles, activities, and others lost through retirement and death. Preparation for one's own death does not figure in this position at all.

As evident in the attention given to finding substitutes for roles, activities, or persons lost, or the development of retirement communities, these perspectives share implicitly an element that others make explicit. Both Havighurst and others (1969) and Streib and Schneider (1971) subscribe to a "differential disengagement-reengagement" theory. Oriented to the impact of retirement on such individual characteristics as life satisfaction and indicators of mental and physical health, they saw in retirement both a burden, a change *requiring* adjustment, and an opportunity. Loss of the work role may or may not be compensated. But that is not the whole story. One also may do more than just compensate. *Dis*engaging from the role of work and its demands may permit reengaging or newly engaging in roles and activities that earlier had to be sacrificed to the demands of work. All kinds of avocational pursuits, at home or in some social clubs, formal or informal, can be included.

Perhaps most clearly in Neugarten (1974), who gave us the liberation perspective in which there is new social engagement or reengagement, retirement holds out a promise. It may become a genuine stage in the life course of industrial people, a new institution in which men and women are liberated from the constraints of bureaucratized work and still lead a full life.

Age Stratification and Intergenerational Linkage Theory

Terms such as new engagement or reengagement in roles in old age direct one's attention to the relationship between the elderly and the rest of society. These relationships may be peaceful or conflicting. Attention to the potential for conflict is the virtue of the remaining social theories of aging in the modern world to be discussed here. The age stratification perspective (Riley 1976) for example, directs our attention to cohort effects. The basic idea is the recognition that successive generations experience similar dilemmas of specific life stages in different ways, simply because they live in different social environments.

For example, the way that grandmother raised her child in her day shows little resemblance to the grandchild, now in young adulthood grappling with child-rearing problems today. In grandmother's day there were no daycare centers for toddlers, but now that is a worry for many mothers eager to go to work. Similarly, when grandfather "retired," the idea of a retirement phase in later life had hardly taken root. Although grandfather quit work or found himself dismissed because of some infirmity of old age, grandson often does so because he feels entitled to the retirement years. The upshot of paying attention to the different social conditions in which cohorts exist is to question whether one can talk about universal problems of passing through some life stages that would present comparable dilemmas faced by each successive cohort as it ages, a matter presupposed in the developmental or genetic perspective on human personality (Erikson 1959).

To illustrate further, adolescence can be viewed as a period in life in which finding a secure gender or sex identity is the primary goal. Forty years ago, for a girl this may have entailed burying the idea of becoming an engineer; today it may have far more subtle parameters simply because recruitment into occupations no longer discriminates between men and women with as much legitimacy as it once did. When women have an official right to a career in the armed forces of a nation, as they do in the United States today, just what it means to be male and female no longer permits an easy solution, however burdensome that solution may have been for some.

To jump to the last stage in life, it may be very useful to consider the central dilemma of old age as the struggle for a sense of integrity, against the threat of a sense of despair and disgust with oneself and the life one has had simply because that life is ending and no longer permits any fundamental changes. But how much formal education a person has surely should influence how one copes with so intellectual an issue as assessing worth or meaning of a whole life. Since higher mass education appeared after World War II, most of our contemporary elderly are people with very modest education compared with the elderly of the future. These examples suggest that the experience of one cohort may be much different from that of another.

Focusing on the age stratification in society is one way of looking at the relations between generations *and* at the same time reveals the possibility that successive cohorts of older people, the middle-aged, and youth may be different social creatures by having been marked in their lives by very different experiences. One version of this approach to intergenerational relations is the social reconstruction perspective (Bengston & Cutler 1976). With attention to both differences and similarities in the formative experiences of given cohorts and an explicit concern with their relations to each other, this approach ranks among the most general in contemporary social gerontology. Depending on whether these relations form patterns of cooperation or conflict, issue by issue, and on the outcomes realized, this approach could indeed encompass abandonment, liberation, and the issue of the production of diachronic solidarity.

Exchange Theory

The social reconstruction perspective, however, is attuned mainly to the public sphere, and the private, small group sphere of the family is another matter. Intergenerational solidarity in the family has been studied from the perspective of exchange theory (Sussman 1976). Exchange theory analyzes interaction from the point of view of the search for reward, the avoidance of punishment, and how much of a stake individuals have in the group to which they belong. This theory emphasizes strategies of rational action seeking to maximize rewards and to minimize costs. As a matter of theoretical principle, the rational calculus always covers the option of leaving the group and seeking a better deal with another. It therefore is ironic to discover that precisely these more recent forms of the most rational family, when considered from the point of view of its members—communal or group marriage forms—also are the least helpful forms for older people. In essence, the most rational family forms are voluntary associations for mutual benefit, with limited liability. The person who cannot contribute according to expectations is dropped. As the body and the mind grows older, eventually the competitive edge goes to the younger members in such families. Consequently, it is the more "traditional" nuclear family, however extended now with more generations living at the same time, that provides comparatively unlimited acceptance of the elderly. With its marital vow of fidelity, "for better or worse until death do us part" at the core of its norms of loyalty, "the extended nuclear family is an all purpose care taking system" (Sussman 1976:221). That family home is still the place where they have to take you in.

Even very crude divorce statistics should suffice to indicate that most of our contemporary elderly entered marriage with the idea that it was to be a life-long bond. When they married, divorce and remarriage were far less prevalent than they are today. For example, the U.S. divorce rate (per one thousand of the population) stood at 0.9 in 1910. By 1950 that rate had risen to 2.6, only to climb to 3.5 by 1970. When one looks at the percentage of people eighteen years and older who are divorced, the 1950 rate corresponded to 1.8 percent divorced males and 2.3 percent females. These percentages had climbed to 4.0 and 5.7, respectively, by 1976 (*Statistical Abstract of the U.S.*, 1977:55, 74).

The same source also tells us that the marriage rate today is very high. In short, divorcing and remarrying is a recent idea, one conforming to the basic tenets of exchange theory. One, if not the core, notion of that theory can be described as the rational imperative: There is always a better deal to be had with someone else. That is why one may indeed speak of contemporary marriage among the younger people as a pattern of serial monogamy: marrying, divorcing, and remarrying. Glick and Norton (1973) estimated that between one fourth and one third of all women aged thirty will be divorced at least once in their lives. However statistical the expectation, if about one third of marriages can be expected to fail, that surely has some normative implications. Divorce has become more acceptable than it once was. Finally, fidelity is more brittle.

As for family relations between adults and their parents, then, one question raised by the emergence of serial monogamy is: Does this new normative orientation to the marital bond as a voluntary association that can be dissolved, for mutual benefit, and that has limited liability spill over into attachments to parents and children? If adult children were to treat their old parents, people completely beyond their choice, as if they could choose them after all, the chances of finding patterns of help producing diachronic solidarity because of their self-perpetuating character would be reduced significantly. It would not matter much just how equal or unequal they were and in what direction the patterns of mutual help in the family would point. They could be indicative of family abandonment or liberation or anything in between. Once the idea takes hold that parental obligation and filial duty is a matter of some child-rearing phase, however defined, but not a matter of life-long obligation, the family as a group that always has to take you in would vanish. Questions about the nature of linkages between the generations in whatever social context are vital to testing diachronic solidarity.

Summary of Social Theories

When one considers these social theories as a set, various characteristics stand out. One is that only disengagement theory has been specially designed for the study of older people. All others are applications of more general theoretical orientations in sociology or social psychology to the fate of being old. For example, the concept "subculture" has been used in the study of youth, ethnic groups, and social classes; Rose (1965) used it to investigate the lives of older people. Socialzation has been used most widely in studies of child rearing; Rosow (1974) applied it to the study of growing old. Modernization is a concept widely used in the study of social change pertaining to such institutions as the economy, the polity, and the education system of societies; Cowgill and Holmes (1972) applied it to the fate of older people in modern society. This difference between disengagement theory and the others may well be related to the fact that only disengagement focuses directly on the problems of dying and of death.

A second feature of these theories is that insofar as they focus on retirement in the broad sense of the term, they are relational in character, although more implicitly than explicitly. Speaking about abandoning older people is speaking about a relationship between groups, those who did it and those who suffer it. The same is true for Neugarten's (1974) liberation perspective. This, too, is an outcome of some relationships between groups, those granting privilege and those enjoying it. So it is also with Marcel Mauss's (1925) perspective on social security as a mechanism producing diachronic solidarity by creating self-perpetuating obligations that connect whole series of successive generations with each other. All the theories of aging mentioned above have this relational character. Such a character is implicit even in work most directly concerned with the determinants of life satisfaction of older individuals. It is this focus on the individual as the unit of analysis that frequently leaves the relational feature of these theories implicit. As Gubrium (1973:81) pointed out, most social theories of aging struggle for some congruence paradigm in which individual well-being is seen as harmony among a person's needs, behaviors, and resources, on the one hand, and the demands of his or her social milieu and the options in his or her retirement environment, on the other.

A third characteristic of these social theories of aging as a set is that only two are functional in attaching the significance of *old* age to both the elderly who have reached it and the younger people who will reach it. The question of whether old age serves a function or purpose, particularly for those not yet old, is one raised centrally only in Cumming's and Henry's disengagement perspective (1961) and in Neugarten's (1974) liberation view of retirement. In the former, mutually disengaging is a shared process of socialization for death, learning to exist without great dependency on others. In the latter, old age as a bundle of social rights is postulated as directly important to the younger still awaiting their destiny of growing to old age. As for the remainder, old age figures in one of two ways, but both lack the element of the tragic or any direct concern with the fact that human existence implies consciousness of death. Old age can be "old" as a matter of decrements, psychological, biological, and social. It becomes a social problem with abandonment as a threat and as something to be mastered somehow. Or, one studies old age as merely one element of age-strata relations, one variation on a much broader theme with little, if any attention to the ephemeral qualities of human existence, to lives ending, to the fact that, eventually, *old* age is life under the shadow of death. In the sixties, some observers claimed that Western civilization denies the reality of death (e.g., Feifel 1963; Fulton 1967). One is tempted to ask whether death still is denied by the social theorists of old age.

BEING OLD IN MODERN SOCIETY

Because there has been so little concern recently with the question of the place, the significance, and the role of being old in modern society, we end this chapter with more remarks about the two functions that old age may perform for younger people. One of these comes from Neugarten's (1974) liberation perspective on retirement. From the point of view of productivity or earning one's keep, the distinctive feature of the retiree is a right to be economically useless, yet to remain entitled to some decent standard of living. Perhaps then, the retired person serves to set boundaries to our pervasive tendencies to treat people as statistics, as we are encouraged to do at the work place. By such a "statistical orientation," we mean a way of treating others primarily on the grounds of what they can do for us. Due to the pervasiveness of the bureaucratic organization of work with its "objective and impersonal ethos," modern societies have a distinctively utilitarian moral flavor.

Social life in general tends to be seen as relationships of exchange. This orientation gives us the freedom to choose our associates. It also has determined the search for the distinctive features of modern societies from the birth of sociology with Hegel and Marx to the present, as evident, for example, in the work of Inkeles and Smith (1974) on individual modernity.

But that freedom also causes alienation, a feeling of seldom being treated as a full person, of being only a segment to others and so, eventually, disjointed segments to oneself. Further, finding acceptance for being useful and granting it to others on that condition also makes people feel at least a latent sense of insecurity. Who can really exclude the possibility of becoming relatively useless to someone about whom he or she cares at some future time? The retired person, that "useless" person from the point of view of economic productivity, may be quite useful, after all. He or she may show pragmatic, modern people that there are meanings to life not revealed by proving one's usefulness, that to ask about doing is not asking enough about human life.

As a legitimate stage in life, retirement may function to constrain the utilitarian perspective. Not contributing anymore to the nation's wealth but being entitled to the fruits of others' labor, the retiree reminds us all of some basic right to existence and to belonging. That right we grant to people *not* because of anything in particular that they do but only because they are human and are members of our society. This kind of constraining function on the work complex in modern society that retirement as an institution might play would be evident in two ways. If the retired as a group feel entitled to an adequate retirement income, acknowledging that it is paid for by the labor of others, a right to life so basic would be asserted as to exceed what a mere market mentality would grant. Similarly, if those still in the labor force agree to grant the elderly an income, one that the younger see as an inescapable obligation owed to the aged on grounds of age alone, that too asserts a basic social right to life. Whether or not retirement is seen in this light, as a gift to old age, will tell us about this function of the fate of being old in modern times.

But there is another need, one also distinctive of people in modern societies because it was not present in preindustrial social orders. It is that modern men and women expect social change. This produces a need for being assured of continuity of those basic social rights and obligations that confer civic identity, which stands above all other social role identities and outlasts them. Humans who expect change have extraordinary needs for reassurance of continuity of some identities. Let us illustrate.

Reassurance of Continuity

Through science and technology, change is virtually built into modern society. Only fifty years ago, practically all who arrived in a comatose state at a hospital died. Today we put many of them on machines that keep heart and lungs going, wondering sometimes whether we are dealing with the dead or the living. Only one hundred years ago, many sons followed in the occupational footsteps of their fathers. Today that is more the exception than the rule. *Then* father and son could see each other's likeness in the things that they did and in the life style that they shared; *now* they remain familiar to each other only in their family roles, often neither comprehending nor caring to understand the separateness of their work experiences.

Professor Marion Levy (1969) of Princeton University once exemplified this extraordinary consciousness about expected change today as the absurdity of modern parenthood. Parents, he argued, are expected to raise and prepare their children for life, and they feel obliged to do so. But they also realize that they must prepare their children for a society whose present form they do not understand and whose future shape they do not know.

Appreciation of one's ignorance of society's present form introduces a second source of uncertainty. People in modern society are aware of the complexity of the organization of social life. They know that what they see depends on where they sit. To a union member, the health of the economy or of the company are matters understood in terms of pay and job security. For a manager, it may be the price of money, overhead, cash-flow problems, investment climate, and the intricacies of consumer demand. Such recognized complexity means that the current organization of society with its abstract institutions has become a source of uncertainty. Two friendly people meeting in a bar can by their different viewpoints subject each other to radical uncertainty about some question of contemporary reality reported in the news. The same holds for the future, only more strongly so, if possible. Yet, however uncertain the future, we also think that we know that the future is not totally open. What we do today will affect what we can do tomorrow. Thus, we influence now, somehow, what can happen later.

In short, people in modern society are expected to assume responsib'lity for the future, even though they can have only limited knowledge of it. Governments, for example, set social security tax rates and pursue social policies, which not only take years to reach specified targets, but the latter also are based on anticipated characteristics of the economy, such as level of employment, the critical source for generating retirement income. This has a direct implication for moral responsibility. Put quite simply, persons who have paid social security throughout their lives have some right to expect that the next generation will pay in some commensurate way to maintain the system. Objectively speaking, they pay for those retiring ahead of them on the expectation that those coming from behind will pay for them. Such trust presupposes something about continuity of citizenship identities. For it is only a people who think they remain the same over time to whom we can appeal with reason that promises made be promises kept. Any public retirement income scheme based on transfer payments from the working to those no longer working requires solidarity between successive generations. It is the combination of the expected change, the impermanence of modern life, coupled with the need to assume long-range responsibility that poses a problem for modern society, one that preindustrial societies did not have to a similar extent.

The problem is: Modern society must produce diachronic solidarity, which is a sense of trust in the similarity of citizenship identities between successive generations, based on self-perpetuating obligations to care. Such a need for diachronic solidarity is by no means confined just to retirement income. Any formal organization in modern life, a church, a football club, a firm, a university, or the government, typically outlives any of its members. Realizing the objectives of such formal organizations often takes generations. Integration of blacks into American society is an example.

The need for diachronic solidarity is widespread. It is precisely because of the impressive growth of the proportion of the aged in modern societies and the way a significant portion of retirement income for them is being procured that we suggest: Contrary to Burgess's claim about the "role-less role" of the aged, modern societies do generate a demand for older people. The elderly, more so and better than any other group, symbolize a need for all. That need is our ability to trust that men and women will not change themselves to such an extent that they will renounce the promises made at one time when these no longer fit their pressing interests.

Importance of the Aged

In this respect, the aged are important for two reasons. They symbolize age more than other groups do, and age itself figures more prominently in the organization of industrial society than it did in many preindustrial societies. This already is evident in the number of life stages people commonly recognize.

During the Middle Ages in Europe, people recognized three stages in life: Infancy, adulthood, and old age (Aries 1962). A stage of adolescence or youth was unknown to them. But age and stages in life have mushroomed for us. Ours is a highly age-stratified society. We recognize infancy, the start in life with the total dependency of the infant on a mother figure. The "school age child" comes as the next stage, followed in turn by adolescence. Then comes a "studentry phase" (Parsons & Platt 1972), referring to the college crowd, people old enough to marry or to go to war but childlike yet in that they depend for their work, studying, on the income of others rather than being paid for it. We also recognize young adulthood when married people have entered the labor force but before the arrival of children. That stage comes next and is labeled "the procreative years." Once the children have left the home, we speak of the "empty-nest" family or the middle years with their "crises." Only then comes retirement or old age. In short, the agrarian social order of the European Middle Ages knew of only three stages in life; we commonly refer to eight. Furthermore, we use chronological age in building up career expectations, not only in formal organizations of the work place but also in family life. People who beget children after age forty appear to us a little odd.

This use of age to organize our lives has led to what some writers call "age-cohort homophily" and "age-cohort centrism." The first refers to patterns of social association that bind together those of like age and separate from each other people belonging to different generations. Age-cohort centrism refers to a tendency to look at the world exclusively from the perspective of a given age group and its experiences. Some suspect that forces like these create increasingly deep cleavages between the generations (Riley 1971:83). Certainly, such a mushrooming of age periods in the organization of social life has more potential for intergenerational conflict than before.

One also may suggest an alternative. Ours is that the aged, through the obligations owed to them and coupled with the recognition that old age is a universal destiny, may be able to mend these tears in the age-graded social fabric by reminding all that no one is an island unto himself or herself.

Although the problem of diachronic solidarity, producing a sense of shared identities that lasts from generation to generation, has not received much attention by sociologists, we can treat it as an extension of a similar problem which has been studied much more. That is, how any society, with some extensive division of labor, stays together at any given time. We can draw on this older tradition in sociological thought to determine the two services for society that the institution of retirement could provide in relation to each other.

The question of how a society is possible at all with the extensive division of labor, with many groups pursuing their special interests, gave rise to sociology as a discipline. It was the central concern of Hegel, Marx, Toennies, and Durkheim. One of the most prominent students who raised this question with respect to preindustrial societies is Eisenstadt (1971). Recognizing that human beings learn about obligations of solidarity in the family but do maintain in later life many relations with people with whom they do not share the bonds of kinship, his basic question was how a kinship type of solidarity is extended by people to their nonkin associates.

Solidarity in Society

We enter a family by birth, not by our choice but by our parents' choice. That is one reason why the basic right to belong is *ascribed* to children, as sociologists put it. Ascribing rights and obligations to people specifies mutuality in obligations of solidarity, free from a detailed accounting of performances. You belong there, even if you receive poor grades in school and are recalcitrant at home. According to prevailing norms, though not necessarily in practice, belonging in a family is not even dependent on reciprocity in attachments. Home is where they have to take you in.

Family ties also are typically diffuse. Members have fairly unlimited rights to each others' attention and care, and it is the person who does not want to answer a claim who has to make an excuse. Attention and care is an assumed right and denying the right requires justification. Such justification always comes by invoking some higher obligation. Thus, ascription of rights and diffuseness in the relations makes the solidarity of a family the paradigm of true human belonging. The question of how a society not primarily organized in terms of kinship loyalties stays together then becomes the question of how these basic loyalties of kinship are emancipated from the bond of kin and applied to nonkinship relationships without destroying their essence: ascribed rights and diffuse obligations. In Eisenstadt's view, a necessary precondition for such emancipation is belief in some supravening goal shared by members of society, regardless of the special groups to which they belong and the special purposes to which they devote themselves. If we name this problem, how special interests in society can get along with each at a given time, as the problem of synchronic solidarity, we then can quote Eisenstadt on the precondition of a commonly shared goal and can formulate a parallel proposition for the problem of diachronic solidarity. Altered somewhat for the modern industrial society, the first proposition is (Eisenstadt 1971:47):

> The solidarity of a modern society demands the effective symbolization of the supremacy of collective over individual goals even where, and especially when, purely individualist value patterns prevail. Any integrative mechanism must reflect such primacy.

The necessary complementary proposition which we offer is:

> The solidarity of a modern society demands also the effective symbolization of the supremacy of continuity over change in citizenship identities and their attendant rights and obligations even, and especially, under conditions of high rates of perceived social change. Any stabilizing mechanism must reflect such primacy.

One of the symbols of continuity to which we cling while otherwise believing that we live in a dynamic and constantly changing society is the social rights of old age. At the same time, what we owe to the old permits us to bestow on ourselves a sense of loyalty and belonging that resists all change. The question is how this might come about.

Distributive Justice

To find the answer we must go beyond the question of adequacy in old age income and address the question of justice in its distribution. All modern societies are stratified. Some more than others possess the scarce goods valued by society. One rather common pattern in Western industrial societies of legitimating this unequal distribution of rewards in life is the principle of differential rewards for differential contribution. This principle comes from the model of a free market in which people compete, ideally on an equal footing, but in which some manage to make themselves more useful in fulfilling demands than others do. Whatever the variations and details, in contemporary Western democracies the "market norm," the differential reward for differential ability to fill demand, is quite widely accepted (Parkin 1971). Even management in Eastern socialist "democracies," however conflicted their orientations in terms of the Communist credo dictating the abolition of all social inequality, constantly makes room for incentive pay in industry. One notion of just reward, then, recognizes the necessity of inequality.

The question is whether this "earned" inequality is preserved into the retirement stage. We have evidence about this on two points. One is that we preserve and apply the kind of social values by which we live throughout the active years in life also to its final stage when we are no longer economically productive. The other is that we then hand down these values from generation to generation because those who pay the aged so as to protect the differential income position they achieved during their working lives do so in the expectation of having the same protection when their turn comes.

Remember, old-age social security benefits are transfers going from the non-retired to the retired. To some extent this actually occurs. The majority of old age social security benefits in the Western world is tied to earnings before retirement. Those who made more or less before get more or less later on. Thus, in paying for older people all the younger ones who endure the taxes not only constantly reaffirm their commitment to the lasting validity of the moral rule, differential reward for differential contribution to society, but they also create obligations that perpetuate this stratification imperative. One element of this otherwise quite complex story of the rules of stratification and their associated notions of justice and fair play thus is upheld. Older people, therefore, and the way we have found to support them provide successive generations with a mechanism for continuity in one rule of justifying inequalities and so in ways of evaluating each other and some of the social morals by which people live.

How much a society uses the institution of retirement for this purpose is apparent in the inequality of old-age income relative to that prevailing among the same cohort of people before their retirement. If there is no change, we may conclude that ours is a way of providing unearned retirement income in old age that recognizes our fidelity to the rules of justice as something that governs our lives, the lives of our forebears, and those coming after us. This would be the outcome of our serious commitment to the idea that the fruits of labor of the active years should become the just deserts of old age. Obversely, if there is significant change, whatever else then needs saying, two things are clear. Justice in distributing the deserts of life is something that we deny each other at the last stage in life, and we do not care about continuity in these particular rules of the moral life.

As evident from the remarks just made, the available theoretical perspectives on old age in modern society remain rather desperately in need of integration. It is a safe guess that some aspects of older people's lives in modern times will fit the abandonment perspective, others that of liberation, and still others that of diachronic solidarity. Finding out which fits what and why may aid us in taking a first step toward a more integrated theory. That task will be faced after the story has been told.

2 economic security in old age

A specter haunts the halls of Congress, the corridors of the Social Security Administration, and the budget chambers of the executive branch. It is the prospect of conflict over social security taxes, of a new political cleavage that pits the younger against the elderly. The largest portion of social security revenues goes to retired people. Social security payments are only one portion of old-age income in the United States, but there are three reasons for concentrating on social security income. First, social security payments are a very important source of income for most retired Americans. Second, because private pension plans currently cover somewhat less than one half of the people in paid employment, social security will be important for years to come (Munnel 1977:6, 13, 143). Third, public pensions are similarly important in Western and Eastern European countries, thus enabling cross-national comparisons. Let us note also that there is a sense of crisis about social security not only in the United States but also in other industrialized countries. To illustrate, the *ABC Evening News* on May 17, 1978 stated that the House Ways and Means Committee voted for a "significant" rollback of the recently legislated increases in social security taxes, only to reverse its decision again the very next day. Elected officials are becoming concerned about a taxpayer revolt. Eight months later, President Jimmy Carter responded. Stepping gingerly so as to avoid as much as possible a reduction of the social rights of old age, he nevertheless proposed two cuts. One of these pertained to burial benefits, the other to the minimum retirement benefit for people who paid as little as $100 in social security taxes throughout their whole life (*Time*, January 22, 1979:52). A weekly news magazine in West Germany identified the problem with a headline best translated as "Old Age Security: Insecurity Has Arrived" (*Der Spiegel*, December 12, 1977:21). Providing for older people in industrial societies is becoming a public concern from Frankfurt to Tokyo (Takenaka 1974; Yoshida 1974). Finally, the crisis is not just media noise; scholars, too, find the term adequate to our contemporary reality (Boskin 1977).

Providing for the Elderly

In the United States, providing for the elderly is big business for the government. In 1975, $55 billion was paid out in retirement benefits under social security, and an additional $18.7 billion was disbursed to retired people under other government plans, such as the federal civil service, armed forces, and state and local governments (Munnel 1977:13). In contrast, in 1974, total payments to older people from private pension funds added up to barely $13 million (Munnel 1977:20). Once upon a time, and for a period lasting from 1935 to 1949, social security taxes were a modest 2 percent levy on the first $3,000 of earnings. But by 1977, 11.7 percent was levied on up to $16,500 of annual income, and social security had become the second largest item of the federal budget (Cowan 1977:2; Boskin 1977:xi). Yet, that proved insufficient, and there was another increase in social security taxes in 1978, raising the tax load to a level that put fear into the hearts of legislators as evident in the vacillation of the House Ways and Means Committee.

A glance at the source and destination of the federal budget dollar describes the crisis rather well. According to current estimates, every federal dollar collected in 1980 will come from the following sources: 43 cents from personal income tax, 30 cents from social security tax, 13 cents from corporate income tax, nine cents from "other," and five cents from borrowing. Of every federal dollar disbursed, 39 cents will go to the elderly receiving social security and other retirement benefits, 24 cents will go to defense, 16 cents to educational and medical aid, 12 cents to "other governmental expense," and nine cents to the interest on loans (*Time*, January 29, 1979:31).

Federal deficit budgeting and providing for the elderly seem to be connected. The largest portion of each federal dollar disbursed goes to the elderly. Can modern society afford to keep the promises made to the elderly, promises made before the reality of the demographic crunch dawned on policy maker and public alike? The reader should not expect us to answer that question. At the moment, it has no answer but remains a highly controversial issue among the relevant experts (Boskin 1977). We raise the question rhetorically only to alert the reader that the crisis is caused by two rather than just one structural feature of modern society.

The first one, now belonging to conventional wisdom in viewing the economics of old age, is the demographic crunch with the three salient facts mentioned previously. First, the right to retire was invented just before or concomittant with the rising number of elderly people in the population. Second, according to the general-dependency ratio, in modern society there is a slim majority of people working to sustain the population not working, the old and the very young. Third, although a further decline in fertility or a continuing trend toward fewer children per family should reduce the costs of child rearing and schooling, nobody knows whether such savings will significantly offset the increased costs of providing for the elderly.

The other feature is the modern or "postindustrial" structure of the economy in advanced societies. Though probably a controversial subject, it points to a trend toward declining labor productivity. This is important because the bulk of social security in all nations comes from a tax on wages. Even though the subject may be controversial, indications of lower labor productivity cannot be ignored. These pertain to a universal shift of employment into the service or "tertiary" sector of the economy in advanced societies.

Exactly one half of all Americans in the labor force in 1976 had white-collar jobs. Similarly, a majority of the nonagricultural labor force was employed in the service sector (U.S. Bureau of the Census, *Statistical Abstract of the United States*, 1977:400,406). Behind these statistics stands a three-step shift in types of occupations as the economy changes and modernizes. That three-step shift is universal, applying to all societies.

When industrialization began, employment in the "primary" or extractive sector of the economy shrank, and employment in the manufacturing or "secondary" sector expanded. People moved out of fishing, agriculture, forestry, and mining into the factories, producing mass consumption goods (e.g., textiles), and capital goods (e.g., machinery). According to the conventional account of modernization, this usually is called the industrial revolution. Eventually came the last step, the rise to prominence of the tertiary sector, the beginning of the postindustrial era. Patterns of employment shifted once again. This time employment in manufacturing mass consumption goods declined when automation took over, and people moved into the service sector, working there on symbols and/or processing other people. Banking, insurance, and research are examples of symbol-processing. Education, therapeutic industries of psychiatry and counseling, and medicine are people-processing.

We should add one warning to this simplified conventional account of modernizing change in economic structure (Rostow 1960; Heilbroner 1962; Bell 1973). The prominence of people-processing work is not as large as Bell (1973) believes. In the United Kingdom and probably elsewhere as well, one half the people employed in the service sector work in the goods-related area (Gershuny 1978:102). The goods-related area of the service sector refers to work in designing and in administering the production and distribution of consumer durables: washing machines, record players, cars, and the like. Rather than a service economy, ours is a self-service economy. Goods replace human services, turning us all into a "harried leisure class" (Linder 1970), because goods are cheaper than human services. But this does not reduce the concern with declining labor productivity.

Using long-term trend data covering several decades and a dozen countries, Kuznets (1966:88-93, 106-7) showed that the rate at which the service sector absorbed the labor force was much faster than its expanding contribution to the gross national product, the total worth of wealth produced in a country. That was true in the majority of cases studied. Thus labor in the service sector is less productive than that in other sectors. In contrast, the primary or agricultural sector had exactly the opposite characteristics. Over time, its rate of loss of the labor force (going to the factories) was much faster than the rate of decline in the agricultural sector's share of the gross national product. That means that modernizing the economy rested on the growth of labor productivity of agriculture.

Interestingly enough, the manufacturing sector displayed a mixed picture. Only in slightly over half of the countries studied was its growing share of national product larger than its rate of absorbing the labor force. Labor productivity in manufacturing has not been as efficient, historically, as this simplification of economic modernization implies. Still, long-term trend data show that labor in the service sector is definitely less productive than is employment in manufacturing and agriculture. There are similar findings from short-term studies of comparative productivity rates of the manufacturing and service sectors after World War II. From 1953 to 1967, for the United States and thirteen countries in Western Europe, Gershuny (1978:111) plotted the relationship between output growth (percentage per year) in manufacturing and in services. The results did not show a simple trade-off, in which increasing employment in services came at a cost to economic growth. In fact, there was a very weak but nonetheless positive relationship between output growth in services and output growth in manufacturing. As one expanded, so did the other. But among the fourteen countries, twelve showed a larger output growth in manufacturing than in services. Only the United States and the United Kingdom did not. In fact, in these two countries the output growth of the service sector was larger than that of manufacturing.

We have no assurance of continuing this pattern, however. Both in the long-term trend findings of Kuznets and in the short-term trend results of Gershuny, cross-national data show that usually a shift in employment to services is a shift to the less efficient use of labor. Other things being equal, and however debatable in other areas like capital efficient rates, this points to a decline in the rates of economic growth, if not to eventual stagnation. The prospect of zero-economic growth, of an economy in which small is beautiful and people live in harmony with nature (Gershuny 1978:37-45) may please the young environmentalists. For older people and those who care about them, it is a haunting possibility, inviting anxiety and unrest, not peace and quiet.

ECONOMIC FATE OF OLD AGE

Let us now turn to the economic fate of being old in America. We deal with this topic in four steps. The first compares the economic position of the American elderly to that of younger people. The second examines whether and how much caring for older people produces diachronic solidarity in commitments to society's norms of distributive justice. The third step discusses the cost of retirement in the United States and the issue of economic deprivation or privilege relative to preretirement earnings. Finally, we compare the economic position of the American retiree with that of retired people in other advanced societies.

The Income Position of Elderly Americans
Compared With Younger Americans

As described in the previous chapter, one way to ascertain the relative deprivation or privilege of old age is to compare older people with younger people. As a first step, we examine family income. Figure 2.1 depicts the mean annual family income by age and race in the United States for 1976, the latest year with available data. This graph shows the distribution of income cross-sectionally, by age of head of family. It compares the incomes received by people of different generations at one time. It does *not* tell us that being old (sixty-five years and over) in America today means ending up on the income level on which one began when young (fourteen to twenty-four years). What such data tell us instead is that the aggregate income of the elderly (65+) as a group is on the average almost as low as the mean income of that age group with the lowest income of all, the youngest (those aged fourteen to twenty-four). As can be seen, this holds for both races. This is not a characteristic of the particular year. Curves plotting the income distribution by age always have this inverted, U-shaped pattern. We must keep in mind that this is family income and therefore excludes the majority of older women and the one-fifth minority of older men classified as unrelated individuals because they were widowed, divorced, separated, or simply never married. The elderly covered here include the minority of older people still at work (about one fifth among men) with the majority in retirement.

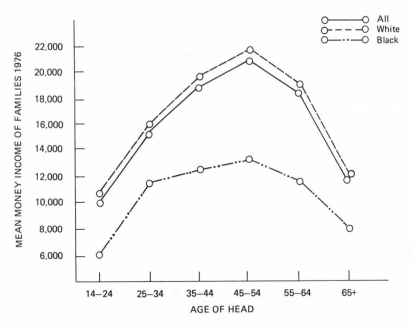

Figure 2.1
Mean Annual Family Income by Age and Race, U.S., 1976

Source: U. S. Bureau of the Census, Statistical Abstract of the United States, 1977:447.

This cross-sectional analysis of family income by age permits only three conclusions. First, at a given time, it is those in the middle years of life (45 to 54) who have the highest earnings. They make more than the generations still behind them in age, and they also make more now than the group a decade older as well as the elderly, most of whom are retired. Ten years hence in 1986, these peak earners of today will become the peak earners of yesterday, being replaced in the top earning position by the current thirty-five- to forty-four-year group.

Second, the difference in family income among age groups tends to be largest between the elderly (65+) and those in the last ten years of employment (55 to 64) as well as between the two youngest groups. Black family income does not drop as much between the last age group still in the labor force and the elderly as it increases between the very young (14 to 24) and the young adults (25 to 34). This suggests something about the redistributive effects of social security in old age. It appears that the poorer throughout their lives are not as often abandoned economically toward the end of life than are the national average of earners. We can confirm this impression by dividing the mean income of the elderly by that of the preceding age cohort (55 to 64) and by that of the peak earner cohort (45 to 54). Doing so separately for white and black families yields the following information: In 1976 the mean family income of elderly whites was 61 percent of that of white families in which the head was between fifty-five and sixty-four years old, and the white elderly made about one half (55 percent) of the earnings of the white families in the peak years of earning power (45 to 54). In contrast, the corresponding ratios for black families were 68 percent and 60 percent.

Third, the use of family income averages no longer permits us to describe the elderly in the aggregate as the poor in the nation. On the average, the youngest families (head aged fourteen to twenty-four), including teen-age mothers and children, have lower incomes than the elderly do.

On the average, then, being old (65+) in America means having an income amounting to about 60 percent of that enjoyed by people ten years younger and about one half that of those twenty years younger, who happen to be the peak earners in the nation. Compared to those in the middle and later middle years of life, older Americans suffer considerable income deprivation. On this score, American society abandons its older people. Being old means having to make do with significantly less income than that at the disposal of the middle aged.

Income by Families
and Unrelated Individuals

For a more detailed picture of the income position of the elderly American we must go back one year to 1975, the year with the latest available information. Table 2.1 shows the income distribution of Americans classified by age and family status. The latter distinguishes only the income of people living in families from that of people listed as unrelated individuals. Unrelated individuals are the widowed, the separated, divorced, or those who never married. We should note that the census classifies family income by age on the basis of the age of the family head and includes all income received by other family members regardless of their age. That is one reason why the income of unrelated individuals is far lower than that of families at all points in the age distribution (see the last row of median incomes). For example, median family income for all age groups was $13,719, but the corresponding median for unrelated individuals was a mere 35 percent of that ($4,882).

As for the income of elderly Americans, Table 2.1 permits the following conclusions. First, the median income of the elderly (65+), for both families and unrelated individuals is lower than the median income of any other age group, including the youngest (14 to 24). Second, 62 percent of the elderly unrelated individuals had incomes under $4,000, but for all other age brackets this was true for less than half. Third, the median family income of the elderly is only 46 percent of that of families in the forty-five to fifty-four-age bracket, the peak earners, and only 54 percent of the cohort ten years younger (55 to 64). Among unrelated individuals, the elderly have a median income only 48 percent of that of the corresponding age cohort twenty years younger (45 to 54), and elderly

Table 2.1
Money Income of Families (F.) & Unrelated Individuals (U.R.), United States, 1975

	All		14-24		25-34		35-44		45-54		55-64		65+	
	F.	U.R.	F.	U.R.	F.	U.R.	F.	U.R.	F.	U.R.	F.	U.R.	F.	U.R.
Number in Thousands	56,245	20,234	4,042	3,392	12,885	3,537	11,107	1,420	11,125	2,036	8,923	2,998	8,163	6,851
	100.0	100.0	100.0	100.0	100.0	100.0	100.0	100.0	100.0	100.0	100.0	100.0	100.0	100.0
Under $2,000	2.1	14.1	5.8	22.0	2.6	6.7	1.8	9.5	1.4	15.4	2.0	17.4	1.3	13.2
$ 2,000-$ 3,999	5.8	28.0	12.4	20.8	4.1	10.4	3.9	10.1	3.0	16.9	4.9	25.2	12.5	48.9
$ 4,000-$ 5,999	8.2	16.2	13.3	21.4	6.2	11.3	4.9	9.8	4.5	15.2	7.1	14.5	19.6	18.3
$ 6,000-$ 7,999	8.5	11.5	13.4	15.7	7.4	13.8	6.1	11.4	5.4	12.7	7.7	11.9	16.3	7.7
$ 8,000-$ 9,999	8.5	9.1	13.5	10.4	9.4	15.3	6.7	11.4	5.8	9.4	8.0	9.4	11.6	4.6
$10,000-$11,999	8.9	6.4	12.4	5.0	10.4	13.6	7.9	8.9	7.2	7.6	8.2	6.8	9.1	2.4
$12,000-$14,999	13.4	6.7	13.8	3.5	17.0	14.7	14.0	14.2	11.7	8.9	13.0	6.2	9.7	2.1
$15,000-$19,999	18.8	5.0	11.1	0.9	23.3	10.1	21.6	14.3	20.7	7.7	18.5	5.1	9.2	1.5
$20,000-$24,999	11.6	1.6	3.2	0.1	11.2	2.4	15.2	5.6	15.6	2.8	12.7	1.6	4.7	0.5
$25,000 and over	14.1	1.5	1.1	0.1	8.3	1.6	17.6	4.9	24.6	3.3	18.2	1.8	6.2	0.7
MEDIAN INCOME $	13,719	4,882	8,752	4,629	13,659	8,985	15,921	9,502	17,569	6,835	14,869	4,915	8,057	3,311

Age

Sources: U.S. Bureau of the Census, Current Population Reports, Series P-60, No. 105, Washington, D.C. 1977:35, 38-39; U.S. Bureau of the Census Statistical Abstract of the United States, Washington, D.C. 1976:404.

median income in this group is about a third lower than that of the cohort just before retirement age (55 to 64).

Thus, being old in America means suffering income deprivation relative to people in the middle years of life. And this is quite a significant level of relative income deprivation. For one half of the elderly in families it means having to cope with one half or less of the income at the disposal of families in the pre-retirement age bracket (55 to 64). For the unrelated individuals, poorer in general, it means having to make do with about two thirds of the income of those ten years younger. Stated another way: Being old in America amounts to a very definite underrepresentation among the higher income groups. Almost one half (49 percent) of the families whose head was aged fifty-five to sixty-four had incomes of $15,000 and higher, but only a fifth of the older families are in that range. In short, these data indicate more relative deprivation than relative privilege, and thus abandonment of the elderly rather than their liberation.

This table of income by age only hints at the impact of retirement. Old-age income so far has compared the income of people still in the labor force with that of people in retirement, which tends to raise old age income. Another point also should be kept in mind. This relative income deprivation in old age follows a work-life experience of steadily rising incomes. Kreps (1976:275-76) showed this to be so for two cohorts of men in the United States, one born during the period from 1895 to 1904, the other during the succeeding decade. In both cases, the income earned rose from age twenty-five to sixty-four, though the rate of increase declined after the mid-forties. Using data on the income of a given age cohort at different times in their lives as well as the cross-sectional data, Kreps found that the effects of economic growth are particularly important to understanding the rise of income even during the later stages of work life. She attributed income differences by age to job experience differences and to economic growth. More importantly for us, Kreps suggested that income differences caused by job experience tend to level off in the later years of life (although this varies by level of education, with the better educated less affected and experiencing the drop later). This means that rises in income during the last decade of employment are mainly due to economic growth. Unless we return to the higher economic growth rates prevailing throughout most of the last three decades, or experience not just a reduction of inflation to zero but in fact a general roll back in prices, the current crop of older workers (54 to 64) will not do as well as previous age cohorts did at that stage of life. The preretirement years, too, lean toward relative income deprivation.

Although relative income deprivation in old age points to abandonment, one must emphasize the term relative. For absolute levels of income, official poverty statistics tell a very different story. The nation's war against poverty has been waged with impressive success, one from which all the poor benefited but the

Table 2.2
Poverty and Age in the United States, Selected Years.

Age	A Percent of Persons Below the Poverty Threshold			
	1959	*1970*	*1975*	*Percent Change 1959-1975*
All	22.0	12.6	12.3	−44.1
Under 65	20.7	11.3	11.9	−42.5
65 and Over	35.2	24.6	15.3	−56.5

Age	B Percent of the Nation's Poor, By Age		
	1970	*1973*	*1975*
All	100.0	100.0	100.0
21 and Less	48.0	49.8	50.9
22-64	33.5	35.5	32.2
65 and Over	18.5	14.7	12.8

Sources: U.S. Bureau of the Census, Current Population Reports, Series P-60, No. 91, Washington, D.C. 1973:13; Series P-60, No. 81, Washington, D.C. 1971:3; Series P-60, No. 106, Washington, D.C. 1977:55; Schulz 1976b:Table 5.

elderly especially. As shown in Table 2.2, in 1959 just over one fifth of the nation was officially classified as poor, but by 1975 that proportion had dropped to 12 percent. The corresponding proportions of older people moved from about 35 percent to 15 percent, and those for people under sixty-five years of age from about 21 percent to 12 percent. Thus, although the proportion of the elderly officially designated as poor was still larger than that of the remainder of the population in 1975, the rate of decline among the elderly was larger (56 percent) than that among people under sixty-five years of age (42 percent). Poverty by the 1970s is in fact highest among the very young. In 1975, one half of the nation's poor were twenty-one years of age or younger, another third or so were in the twenty-two to sixty-four-age bracket, and only the remaining 13 percent were found among the elderly.

Poverty and Old Age

Although one could say that the war against poverty has been waged successfully up till now, it is a matter of battle victories. The war has not yet been won. Among the elderly (65+) the chances of becoming a poverty statistic increase with age, and they grow dramatically upon becoming an unrelated individual, for example entering widowhood (U.S. Bureau of the Census, Series P-60, No. 106, 1977:Table 15). In 1975, a third of the older elderly (seventy-two years and over) counted by the census as unrelated individuals were below the poverty threshold. Further, among unrelated elderly persons who have to rely exclusively on the government for their livelihood, there was a fairly good chance of being in poverty. Over one half of the unmarried older people (65+) with social security as their sole income were below the poverty threshold in 1975. The corresponding proportion of those whose social security payments had to be augmented with supplementary security income (SSI) was over two thirds. Finally, if those who could not collect social security had to rely on supplementary security income alone, the chances of escaping from poverty were slim indeed. More than 90 percent of elderly individuals in that situation were below the poverty threshold. That last group, just under 2 percent of our unmarried elderly, were the truly abandoned. The intention of the Supplementary Security Income Act is to prevent poverty (Schulz 1976b:566-68). Clearly, that objective has not been reached yet for the elderly.

Although old age in general does not mean being in absolute poverty, growing beyond age sixty-five increases the chance of becoming a poverty statistic. Information on the income of various age groups after reaching retirement age is very scarce. But all available studies show that the older one is, the more income declines (Thompson 1973; Schulz 1976a:17). In 1971, for example, just over one half of the nonmarried aged seventy-three and over were below the poverty threshold (Thompson 1973:4-5). Thus, growing old means continuous income deprivation relative to that of younger people. Such deprivation is more significant when one realizes that growing to old age also means failing health and rising medical expenditures.

Health Expenses

The elderly have more chronic illnesses, are hospitalized more and longer than younger people are (*Facts About Older Americans,* 1976, U.S. Dept. HEW 1977). For example, in 1974, 39 percent of older Americans had a chronic condition limiting some major activity (working or housekeeping), but the corresponding proportion among the nonaged was 7 percent. In the same year the chances of being hospitalized were one in six for older people as compared with one in ten for younger people. Also, once in the hospital, older people stayed about four days longer than the nonaged did. Older people had one third more visits to physicians than the nonaged did. Thus, growing to old age means having to cope with some health decrements. In 1975, a fifth of older Americans told the Louis Harris pollsters that poor health was a "very serious" problem for them (Louis Harris and Associates 1975:130). Poor health costs money, and this has to be considered when looking at income deprivation relative to that of younger people.

The 1975 per-capita, personal-health care expenditure among older Americans came to $1,336 (compared to $492 for the age group nineteen to sixty-four, and

$221 for those under nineteen). Among older people, $428 came out of their own pockets (Gibson and others 1977:5). That $428 made up 13 percent of the median annual income of the 6.8 million unmarried elderly Americans in 1975 and 5 percent of the median family income of the elderly (U.S. Bureau of the Census, Series P-60, No. 105, 1977:35, 38-39; *Statistical Abstract* 1976:404). Even though public funds provide for a far greater share of the health bill for older Americans than for people under sixty-five, the proportion of income spent on health by the younger out of their own pockets was certainly less than one half that paid by the elderly. Furthermore, growing to old age becomes ever more expensive in terms of health care. That expense has been rising recently, both for the older people and for the younger who share in the cost of medical care for the elderly. For example, national spending on health care increased at an annual rate of 12.7 percent from 1966 to 1976, and government spending on personal health care rose at an annual average rate of 19.9 percent. The expenditures for older people during this period grew at the corresponding rates of 15.5 percent and 25.3 percent, respectively (Gibson and others 1977:7).

All of these figures of *personal* health care measure only the costs of efforts to improve the health of persons. Research and training costs are *not* included here. By 1976, older Americans consumed a highly disporportionate share of the nation's health care bill. They, 10.5 percent of the total population, spent 28.9 percent of the nation's outlay (Table 2.3). Their proportionate share of the costs was almost three times their relative numbers, and almost a third of the costs they paid out of their own income. The per-capita *private* expenditure was $491, the *public* outlay (federal, state, and local) was $1,030 (Gibson and others 1977: 5). That $491 from their own pockets meant for many older Americans more than a whole month's income from social security, certainly for the nonmarried. A man who retired at sixty-five in 1976, after continuously earning since 1950 above maximum taxable levels for social security, received a monthly old-age benefit of only $353 (Myers 1975:49-54).

One reason for the high personal expenditure for health care among older people is that Medicare, the public health insurance program for the aged, "does not attempt to provide total coverage for the costs of medical care. . . . It is patterned after private health insurance coverage. . . . Thus, in 1976, Medicare benefits paid only 43 percent of all the health expenses of the aged" (Gibson and others 1977:10). But coverage under private health insurance among older people declined from 16 percent to 5 percent during 1966 to 1976 (Gibson and others 1977:9). Being old in America means not only less income relative to that of people in the middle years, it also means being deprived of a comparable level of health insurance. However, as the poverty data indicated, the economic position of the American elderly has improved in recent decades. Has there been a trend in the income deprivation of the elderly compared to that of middle aged since the post-World War II period?

Table 2.3
Personal Health Care Expenditures, by Age and Source of Funds, United States, 1976.

	Population		Personal Health Care Expenditure		% Distribution of Total		
	Number (in millions)	% Distribution	Amount (in billions)	% Distribution	Federal	State and Local	Private
All Ages	218.4	100.0	$120.4	100.0	100.0		
Under 19	71.8	32.9	$ 17.9	14.9	16.0	10.0	74.0
19-64	123.7	56.6	$ 67.7	56.2	17.0	12.0	70.0
65 and Over	22.9	10.5	$ 34.9	28.9	55.0	13.0	32.0

Source: Robert M. Gibson and others, "Age Differences in Health Care Spending, Fiscal Year 1976," Social Security Bulletin, 40, no. 8 (1977), 3-14.

In the aggregate picture of the elderly relative to that of other age groups, the focus at this point is on change. For this purpose, we can draw on family income in constant 1972 dollars, a measure that corrects for inflation. Table 2.4 shows the percentage distribution of family income by age of the family head in both 1952 and 1972. Using 1972 constant dollars, this indicates the changes in effective purchasing power at the disposal of the family. As evident in the last column, there has been an impressive improvement in the economic position of the elderly during these two decades. The proportion of older families with incomes under $4,000 declined from over one half (53.7 percent) to just over one quarter (27.9 percent). But there was growth in income during this period for all families of all ages. In terms of gross national product measured in constant dollars, the American economy registered an average annual growth rate of 3.5 percent between 1955 and 1972. This expansion, incidentally, was lower than that of France, West Germany, Italy, and Japan (U.S. Bureau of the Census, *Statistical Abstract of the United States,* Washington, D.C. 1976:394-95). The real growth in family income reflects the growth in the real wealth of the nation. But our question is whether the relatively deprived elderly participated in the economic growth as all others did less, or possibly more. In general, the answer to that question is a little less.

True, the proportionate exodus of the elderly from the lowest income class, a relative drop of 55 percent, was the largest among all age groups. But it was not much larger than the corresponding drop among the youngest families (52 percent) and those aged twenty-five to thirty-four, which also registered a decline of one half in the category of income under $4,000. Although all other age groups showed a net exodus from two or three of the lower income categories, it is only the elderly who registered a net decline in the lowest income class. Separating the income categories with an increase in percentages from those with a decrease shows this clearly: It was the middle aged who benefited the most from economic expansion. To the creators of wealth fell the spoils. The next group to profit were the youngest, and older people came last.

We recalculated the percentages in this table differently to obtain the relative representation of the young, the middle aged, and the elderly families in each income class over these years. According to these data, what appeared to be merely the low position of the elderly in the nation's real economic growth turns into *increasing* relative income deprivation over time as everyone else became richer. Sparing the reader another lengthy table, we will report only the main results of our homework. First, we found an increased representation of the elderly among those families with the lowest income over time. In 1952, older people made up just over one quarter (26.8 percent) of families with incomes under $4,000. But by 1972, they made up a third of these low earners. Elderly families also registered an increase among those receiving the second lowest income ($4,000 to $6,999) whereas their representation rose from a tenth in 1952 to over one quarter (28 percent) in 1972. Second, we also found increasing relative income deprivation among the youngest families (14 to 24). This is even more dramatic; their representation in the two lowest income categories almost doubled over this period. Third, the youngest families also registered increased representation in the three upper income categories, but the elderly registered declining representation among the two upper income classes over this period and showed stable representation in the categories of $10,000 to $15,000. Again then, the middle-aged groups reaped the largest benefits from economic growth. It also is interesting to note that the cohort one decade before retirement age (55 to 64) increased their representation only in the middle income categories, from $4,000 to $14,999, but their representation in the lowest *and the upper two* income groups declined. Thus, fewer of the benefits of economic growth also accrued to the older *in* the labor force.

We conclude that absolute improvements aside, elderly families did not participate in the economic growth of the nation from the fifties to the early seventies. Instead, relative to most families in mid-life, the elderly received increasingly less (relative) income. Lest one think that this story would have been quite different had the automatic price inflation adjustment for old age security benefits introduced in 1972 been in effect, let us recall that the period covered here saw several legislated increases in old age benefits. These legislated increases in benefits were larger than required by law since 1972 (Myers 1975: 105; Schulz 1974:8-9).

Consumer price adjustments in old-age pensions may not be enough to prevent leaving the elderly behind during periods of economic growth. Whether they are left behind depends on the relationship between changes in retail prices *and* wages. Whether or not retirement income is adjusted for postretirement growth in wages seems to be the decisive point. If such adjustments are made, the elderly are permitted to share in economic growth after their retirement; if no adjustments of this kind are made, the elderly are left behind. In West Germany, public pensions are adjusted in this manner; in the United States old age social security benefits are not linked to national wage changed after the person's retirement date (Schulz 1974:24-39). Whether we look at the income position of the American elderly in one year, 1975 or 1976, the last available with fairly complete information, or at trends in that position over two decades (1952 to 1972), these data point more to abandonment than to liberation.

Apart from income deprivation in old age relative to people in the middle years, there is the problem of justice in the distribution of income among various age groups in society. With census data that topic can be studied best by comparing the income of different generations living at the same time. Since a very important part of old age income is transfer income coming from the younger people in society, the distribution of income also tells us about diachronic solidarity in commitments to norms of distributive justice in America.

What are these norms of justice? How much have they been practiced in the recent past? What have been the trends of that practice? And what do the trends portend for the immediate future? These are the questions to be answered next.

INCOME INEQUALITY, AGE AND DIACHRONIC SOLIDARITY IN THE UNITED STATES

In chapter 1 we argued that any mechanism of intergenerational relations that creates obligations connecting successive generations through time indicates diachronic solidarity. Income inequality data for age groups at various stages in life in the United States permits us to study diachronic solidarity in American norms of distributive justice. Let us recall that the idea of diachronic solidarity came from the pay-as-you-go basis of financing social security in all industrial societies (Kaim-Caudle 1973). This mode of financing old-age income presupposes permanence of the system. By simply tolerating social security payroll taxes, those currently paying for the generation ahead of themselves generate expectations that younger generations will continue such obligations of care.

Table 2.4
Income of Families, by Age of Head, United States,
1952 and 1972 (Constant 1972 Dollars).

		Age of Head					
		14-24	*25-34*	*35-44*	*45-54*	*55-64*	*65+*
	1952	100.0	100.0	100.0	100.0	100.0	100.0
	1972	100.0	100.0	100.0	100.0	100.0	100.0
Under $4,000	1952	36.7	17.9	18.0	21.0	30.2	53.7
	1972	20.2	9.0	6.6	6.7	10.2	27.9
$4,000-$6,999	1952	35.8	31.6	25.6	23.4	22.8	20.1
	1972	25.7	13.5	10.2	8.9	13.1	30.4
$7,000-$9,999	1952	22.4	33.1	32.2	27.9	23.0	13.7
	1972	25.0	19.2	14.7	13.1	16.5	16.9
$10,000-$14,999	1952	2.6	8.0	9.4	9.3	6.5	3.6
	1972	22.0	33.1	28.8	26.2	26.7	12.4
$15,000-$24,999	1952	2.5	9.2	13.6	16.1	15.0	7.5
	1972	6.6	22.0	30.5	32.2	23.3	8.9
$25,000 and Over	1952	*	*	1.2	2.2	2.4	1.4
	1972	0.5	3.2	9.1	12.9	10.2	3.5

*Less than 0.5%

Source: U.S. Bureau of the Census, Current Population Reports, Series P-60, No. 90, Washington, D.C. 1973:42.

This implies nothing less than the recreation of the extended family, but in bureaucratized form. As Rosen (1977:95) commented: "Social security is an intergenerational family on a national basis, because, like a family, the nation shares resources across the generation gap." Let us see, then, whether the national family bonds in the United States have continuing commitments to norms of distributive justice.

Income Inequality

Our question is whether and how much Americans provide for the elderly so as to maintain commitment to the norms justifying inequality in rewards over time. In studies of stratification or social classes in society, such rewards usually are wealth, prestige, and power. We shall confine ourselves to inequality in wealth, using income as a measure. The norms justifying the unequal distribution of income in society, however, belong to more general, moral beliefs that sociologists call stratification codes (Eisenstadt 1971:87-98, 164, 234). Although we shall study only one of these, it is one of the most important sources of continuity in advanced societies.

Providing for the elderly so as to assure successive cohorts of continuity in stratification codes from generation to generation is one of the most powerful mechanisms of diachronic solidarity conceivable. The reason is quite simple. The rules justifying inequality in rewards belong to the most fundamental building blocks of the social order. They tell us who are the winners, who the losers, and why. Rules of distributive justice identify a society. They tell Americans who they are and Russians what it means to be a Soviet citizen. Let us see what one of these rules is in the United States and then use income inequality among age groups to discover whether the American way of taking care of the elderly upholds the rule from generation to generation.

As we know from public opinion survey data (Rainwater 1974:163-78), a great majority of Americans believe in the values of individual achievement, equal opportunity, effort, and merit. Their vision of a just society is a meritocracy, one that demands the unequal distribution of income. As Rainwater (1974:172) described the opinions of his respondents: "Obviously, equality of opportunity requires inequality of results, or else there is no point in the game." There is no doubt that Americans see equity in a system in which there is a quite marked dispersion of income. Despite some persisting doubts about the reality of equal opportunity for all, the actual income distribution among various occupational groups ranging from "top management" to "lower skill" jobs in 1970 was nearly identical to the range in annual income that appeared fair to most Americans (Rainwater 1974:166).

The doubts about justice and fairness in America focus on race prejudice and unequal opportunities for all. Otherwise, Americans deeply find their system to be one of equal opportunity with unequal rewards; that would be moral

(Rainwater 1974:174). Furthermore, the differential advantage or burden of birth is accepted "because after all, someone earned the wealth originally and it is all right for people to pass things on to their offspring" (Rainwater 1974:181). Americans, in short, still believe in the "spirit of capitalism" (Weber 1904-5/ 1958) in which work and differential success in the world of work has ethical significance for individuals as well as for society as a whole. The very idea of a classless society with a really equal distribution of resources is repugnant to them, like an old car without gas in its tank, sitting and rusting, going nowhere.

The prevailing norms of distributive justice in income are "capitalist" in tenor. That is why they can be expressed by a double imperative which tells Americans how and why income ought to be distributed. The guiding principles are: "differential reward for differential achievement in preparing for work *and* differential achievement in performance at work." Differential reward refers to money income, differential achievement to preparing for work by education; and differential achievement in performance at work refers to fruits of industry, initiative, and stamina on the job. People with more training and more difficult jobs *should* make more money, provided they have had equal opportunity in competing for both.

Such notions of distributive justice have direct implications for income distribution among various age groups in society. These norms assert the morality of the struggle for differential income advantage *and* that of the inheritance of differential advantage. They try to balance individual achievement *and* family inheritance. What father or mother attain in the world of work should benefit their children but only at the beginning of their careers. Such differences of birth should not be permitted to last too long into adulthood, for that would violate the values of individual achievement and equal opportunity. According to these norms, people also should have some fair chance in competing for scarce rewards.

Norms of distributive justice in this area imply a three-stage normative theory of income inequality, one pertaining to youth, the second to the middle years and the last to old age. The first maintains that income inequality early in life should be higher than that of early adulthood. Youth starting out in the occupational world should benefit from the differential achievements of their parents. But soon, say by age twenty-five or thirty, income inequality should drop, reflecting the loss of the advantage or the burden of birth. The second stage prescribes rising income inequalities for the move into mature and later adulthood. Such a rise would reflect the effects of competition, how people in an achievement society sort each other into relative winners and losers, into overachievers forging ahead and underachievers left behind. The third stage calls for the maintenance of a person's relative position in the income hierarchy achieved just before retirement into the last stage of life, until death. That means that the income inequality of the preretirement cohort should be identical with that after the cohort has retired. If the inequalities of late adulthood are the result of fair competition, hence reflecting the differential rewards obtained for differential achievement, then no one should be unfairly deprived in old age of the relative income position attained during a lifetime of work.

Norms of Distributive Justice

Let us note that these norms of distributive justice are built into social security systems in the United States and in Western Europe (Myers 1975; Kaim-Caudle 1973). These systems are based on two principles. One of these is equity (old age pensions tied to preretirement earnings), the other is welfare (redistributing income from the rich to the poor). The principle of equity directly reflects a commitment to the normative imperative "differential reward for differential achievement." But that imperative is too merciless and insensitive to reality, and that is why the welfare principle has been built into the system as a countervailing force. Capitalist norms of justice are harsh. They assume that everybody has a chance to work and tend to attribute unemployment to lack of individual effort in finding work. This often is quite unrealistic. Advanced societies produce both structural unemployment and structural underemployment. These terms describe two kinds of people in society. One is out of work because the skills he or she has to offer have become obsolete because of technological change, and there is no one willing to give a job to an "overtrained" person. The other, also having obsolete skills, does find employment but works at a skill and pay level far below that before his or her original skills became outmoded. The welfare principle in social security is a kind of adjustment ro reality. The redistributive features of social security, however, operate before as well as after retirement. That is why they do not affect our argument of the maintenance of the income inequality of late adulthood into retirement. In social security, unemployment compensation and welfare before retirement turn partly into compensatory pay in old-age benefits afterwards. That, at least, is the intention of the system.

Before turning to the data, let us emphasize one point. The whole argument of distributive justice in the income distribution of older people in society is that it is partly independent of change on the level of total old age income before and after retirement. The norms prescribe that the amount of income inequality should be stable as a cohort moves from work into retirement. That would maintain for each individual his or her proper place, which is the income position attained by competitive effort just before retirement. That would make retirement a just reward for a lifetime of work. Although there would be little justice also if retirement income were much less than what one had before, even if the amount of income loss were the same for all, we shall look at that part of the story below where we examine the income costs associated with retirement. At this stage, if we find that the income inequality of the preretirement period is preserved into old age, neither increasing nor decreasing, we will have evidence that the American way of caring for the elderly amounts to producing diachronic solidarity in commitment to the norms of distributive justice.

This commitment would be handed on from generation to generation for three reasons. First, as will be seen in a moment, a very important part of old age income is social security income; second, all social security income is transfer income; and third, the younger cohorts who support the elderly do so in the expectation of being supported similarly when their time comes. Each transfer between the generations at a given time obligates similar transfers into the indefinite future.

Before examining the facts, let us note a few of their features. Old-age income from social security in the United States is very important to all people in retirement. In 1968, 77 percent of all "aged units" (persons sixty-five and over and families with heads sixty-five and over) received social security income only; another 19 percent had a private or other public pension in addition to social security, and the remaining 4 percent relied entirely on another public pension (Munnel 1977:13). Although private pension plans have been growing in recent years, the importance of social security to the elderly persists into the present. In 1974, for example, only one third of all old-age social security beneficiaries had an additional private pension or annuity income, and in the mid-seventies such additional old-age income was very modest, amounting to $3,000 per year or less for 70 percent of that one third who had it (Munnel 1977:6, 21).

Social security is likely to remain an important source of old age income into the foreseeable future for three reasons. One, even in 1977 less than one half of the American labor force was covered by private pension plans; two, two private pension monthly benefits were exceedingly modest; and three, the benefit levels of most private plans currently in use are far more vulnerable to the eroding effects of inflation than are those of social security (Munnel 1977:143). Finally, although census statistics show that old-age income comes from varied sources, such data can be quite misleading.

For example, one half of older families (head over sixty-five) and about 18 percent of unrelated elderly individuals reported income from earnings in 1975, but social security income was reported by over 90 percent of both that year. Dividend, interest, and rent income also was reported (U.S. Bureau of the Census, *Statistical Abstract of the United States* 1976:394). If one were to interpret such data as indicating that most older people derive large portions of their regular income from earnings, one would be mistaken. The receipt of social security is subject to a retirement test prohibiting "substantial" employment. If we find, then, a combination of over 90 percent of the elderly reporting social security income and another half of older families also reporting income from earnings, the latter is likely to be wage income from occasional work, perhaps mail sorting in the postal service during the Christmas rush.

As one writer remarked: "For many older Americans social security (is) the major source of income in retirement" (Fox 1974:1). Keeping in mind that other government pensions also are transfer income from younger cohorts, we should ask whether and how much caring for the elderly in America produces diachronic solidarity in commitments to norms of distributive justice.

We answer that with the aid of the Gini Index of Inequality of the income of Americans at various stages in life. This index has a possible range of 1.0 to 0, with one indicating maximum inequality and zero indicating absolute equality. Our data cover two decades and the years 1952, 1962, and 1972. Access to income data in constant 1972 dollars to neutralize the effects of inflation was one consideration in the selection of years; an effort to control for the effects of the business cycle on income inequality in the nation was another. "Bad times" in the economy tend to increase income inequality, but the years selected here are similarly positioned in the ups and downs of the business cycle, thus neutralizing its effect (Weitzman 1974). The results of the effort are shown in Table 2.5. The upper portion presents the income inequality of different cohorts,

Table 2.5
Inequality in Family Income, by Age of Head,
United States, 1952, 1962, and 1972
(Gini Indices Based on Constant 1972 Dollars).

	1952	*1962*	*1972*	Percent Change *1952 to 1972*
Total				
All Ages	.368	.362	.360	− 2
14-24	.271	.312	.422	+ 56
25-34	.362	.301	.291	− 20
35-44	.349	.322	.287	− 18
45-54	.379	.345	.288	− 24
55-64	.422	.374	.329	− 22
65+	.462	.438	.414	− 10
Ratio $\frac{65+}{55-64}$	1.09	1.17	1.26	
Preretirement				.32
Postretirement				.34
Ratio: Postretirement over Preretirement			1.06	1.06

Sources: Calculated from U.S. Bureau of the Census, Current Population Reports, Series P-60, No. 90, Washington, D.C., 1973:42, 58 and the Pre- and Postretirement Gini Indices were calculated from Alan Fox, Work Status and Income Change, 1968-1972: Retirement History Study Preview. U.S. Department of Health, Education, and Welfare, Social Security Administration, Retirement History Study Report No. 10, 1976.

In calculating the Gini Indices for the population series it was assumed that the midpoint of the income category under $4,000 was $2,000, and that of the category $25,000 and over was set at $30,000. The formula for the Gini used is:

$$\text{Gini} = (X_i Y_i + 1) - (X_i + 1 Y_i)$$

in which: X_i = cumulative proportion of recipients in ith group
and: Y_i = cumulative proportion of income shares by the ith group

people born at different times and at different stages in life at the same time. The lower portion compares the income inequality of the same people before and after retirement.

The first point to note is the extraordinary stability in income inequality of the nation as a whole from 1952 to 1972 (first row, Table 2.5). There was a decline of only two-percentage points over this period. Second, this stability, however, effectively hides two contrary trends that emerge when age is taken into account. The youngest group (14 to 24) experienced an increase in income inequality by over one half. This is probably due to the rise in yough unemployment over this time. Third, in contrast all other age groups experienced declines in income inequality from 1952 to 1972. These declines varied in rate between about a quarter for those in the middle years (45 to 54) and a tenth for the elderly in society (65+). Note that these trends over time do not affect the argument of inequalities in the capitalist norms of justice. Only Gini values close to zero would mean the end of the capitalist ethos and, as the third column of figures for 1972 shows, American society has a long way to go.

Evidence of Diachronic Solidarity

Turning now to the evidence on diachronic solidarity in norms of distributive justice, income inequalities at the beginning of Americans' work life conform with norms. In two of the three years, there is a drop in inequality as one moves from the youngest group (14 to 24) to the next older cohort (25 to 34). This dip in inequality is confined to the cohort in early adulthood (25 to 34). Income inequality rises thereafter from cohort to cohort with each older one experiencing more inequality than the preceding one does. Up to age sixty-four, the period spanning the work life of Americans, these findings agree exactly with the norms of distributive justice as described above. But for the retirement years, we find less than perfect conformity with these norms. How much less will be an important consideration. Let us elaborate.

The fact that income inequality of youth is larger than that of early adulthood (25 to 34) reflects the differential advantage or burden of birth, which, according to norms, should not persist for long. The fact that income inequality rises after early adulthood agrees with norms that people should sort each other into winners and losers. The norms refer to people as they move through the life course. But our data reflect only the income distribution of different cohorts, not the same people. Only longitudinal data with many observations of the same cohort as it moves from youth to older adulthood would be able adequately to test to what extent morals are expressed through the unequal distribution of income. It is therefore important to note the striking consistency of these data with the implications of normative theory. Only the year 1952 was exceptional and only on one point. The Gini index of youth (14 to 24) is smaller rather than larger than that of early adulthood (25 to 34), and the expected dip in inequalities came a year later. In all other respects, the 1952 data are similar to those of the later years. Up to age sixty-four the data are consistent with the norms. Because of this consistency and the large age span covered by the data, we suggest that these findings are relevant. They show behavior in accordance with the norms of capitalist society.

The alternative interpretation is to attempt to attribute the pattern of income inequality by age to specific, historical cohort experiences. This would require nothing less than some fantastic conspiracy of cohort effects to bring about as consistent a pattern in income inequalities. Observe that the preretirement cohort (55 to 64) in 1952 was born before the turn of the century, between 1888 and 1897. But the youngest group in 1972 (those aged fourteen to twenty-four then) was a post-World War II generation born between 1948 and 1958. Two world wars and the Great Depression separate these people. Reliance on cohort effects as an explanation of so consistent a pattern does not seem promising. That is why we suggest that this pattern of income inequalities throughout life reveals that norms of distributive justice are implemented.

But when entering old age, the facts contradict the norms. Income inequality continues to rise instead of remaining constant with the preretirement cohort. That is true for all three years of observation. We then must estimate the effect of including among the elderly those still at work together with the majority in retirement; examine the trend in income inequalities, both as one moves from preretirement to elderly and as one moves from 1952 to 1972; and determine the size of the deviation of these findings from expected norms.

Data on old-age income that cover both people in retirement and people still at work tend to increase income inequality in the group as a whole. That is because those who continue work into old age still have rising incomes, but those who go into retirement have a drop in income (Fox 1976). This factor, which increases inequality among the elderly, should become less operative as one moves from 1952 to 1972, because the proportion of the elderly at work after age sixty-five steadily declined over this period. In 1950, 46 percent of older men (65+) were in the labor force; that percentage decreased to thirty two by 1960 and to twenty by 1975. The corresponding figures for women were 10 percent in the former two years and 8 percent in 1975 (Riley & Foner 1968: 42; U.S. Dept. HEW, HEW Publication 77-20006).

In contrast, the rate of increase in inequality between the younger cohorts and that of the elderly tended to grow from 1952 on. Only in 1952 can we observe a leveling off in the rate of increase in inequality from late childhood (45 to 54) over that of the preretirement cohort (55 to 64) to that of the elderly (65+). In that year, the rate of increase between the last two cohorts is smaller than that between the first and second. But the other two years show a continuous growth of inequality in these three age groups. What is more, although the income inequality of the elderly in 1952 was only 9 percent higher than that of the preretirement cohort, it grew to 17 percent in 1962 and to 26 percent in 1972 (see the ratios in the upper portion of Table 2.5). As the number of older people still working went down, income inequality among the retired grew as one moved forward in time. Finally, as shown in the lower portion of the table, a growth in income inequality also is directly associated with retirement from the labor force. These figures show income inequality before and after retirement for the entire national cohort entering retirement in 1972. Retirement brought about a 6 percent increase in income inequality.

An increase in income inequality upon leaving the labor force means that retirement cost the elderly their earned position in the income hierarchy of the nation. Accordance with the prevailing norms would show up in pre- over postretirement inequality ratios amounting to 1.00. Deviation from that 100 percent implementation of the norms of justice can measure the level of injustice or the extent to which caring for the elderly in America did not produce diachronic solidarity in commitments to the capitalist norms of distributive justice. The deviation measures the extent to which the differential rewards earned over a lifetime of work are withdrawn during the last stage in life. Because social security is transfer income, this deviation also measures the extent to which younger cohorts honor the elderly in society by maintaining them in their relative position of economic worth and so assure themselves of being so honored and maintained.

Let us remember that no society has ever been known for a 100 percent implementation of its values. From this point of view, the 6 percent deviation from the norms of distributive justice in America in the retirement sample of 1972 is almost unbelievably close to perfection. The amount of diachronic solidarity produced through caring for the elderly is impressive, and the level of permitted injustice is modest. Fox's (1976) retiree sample is the only one with adequate information to measure diachronic solidarity. It may well be misleading, and the cohort ratios (upper part of Table 2.5) with their mixed elderly, covering both the retired and those still at work, may be more realistic. If so, we would expect some reduction of the prevailing level of caring justly for the elderly and thus a decline in the amount of diachronic solidarity produced through caring for the elderly in the United States.

Contrasted with the quantity of justice just mentioned is its quality. One can imagine forms of injustice that truly add insult to the injury of mere quantity. The level of justice, after all, reflects only how well a society implements its norms. Qualitative injustice would require some abrupt change in the rules themselves. For income inequality in society, such a change in the rules of the game would entail change in the determinants of inequality as one moves from the world of work into the domain of retirement. Generally, the determinants of income inequality are the amount of formal education attained by an individual, the kind of occupation during most of his or her life, and the characteristics of his or her parents on these points.

The insult of qualitative injustice would be apparent, for example, if neither one's education nor one's occupation counted much in placing an individual into the income stratification of old age. On this score, Americans do exceedingly well. So far as is known, no qualitative injustice is even on the visible horizon. The determinants of income inequality in old age are basically the same as those for younger people. Here one can safely assume that these determinants have lasted through time. The same rules of the game now visible in their effects on income differences among older people operated when they were in the middle years of life (Henretta & Campbell 1976).

All this points to a rather impressive level of justice in the distribution of old age income in recent years. By and large, social security maintained commitment to norms of distributive justice from generation to generation. As indicated by the ratios between the cohorts (see last row, upper part of Table 2.5), that level of commitment to implement norms may be waning. This is a point on which the level of adequacy in old age income may shed some light. We are compelled to ask whether, if there is justice for the majority of the American elderly, does the fact that this is imperfect justice disproportionately affect some identifiable group among older people in the United States?

THE EFFECT OF RETIREMENT ON INCOME IN THE UNITED STATES: ABANDONMENT OR LIBERATION?

One measures the impact of retirement on income by comparing retirement income with preretirement earnings of the same people. Usually called the retirement replacement rate, or more simply the replacement rate, the measure expresses retirement income as a percentage of preretirement earnings. If one made $15,000 per year at work and had an annual retirement income of $9,000, the replacement rate would be 60 percent. But there are two complications. The first is the choice of time period for measuring preretirement earnings. The second is the choice of year or years for measuring income in retirement. By and large, both problems are solved by the scarcity of data. To date, very little about any replacement rate is known for very old people, over age seventy-five. All available information applies to early retirees in the first half of their first decade of retirement. The most interpretable replacement rate of retirement income from all sources uses selected years during the last decade of employment to measure preretirement earnings. The main advantage of the retirement replacement rate is that it permits adjusting retirement income for the kinds of expenditures, such as commuting, which are directly associated with work. With such an adjustment, one can ask whether retirement means liberation for some people, even though the income at their disposal may be less than what they had before retirement. The same holds for the concept of abandonment. Just losing money income when leaving the labor force does not measure it. But an adjusted retirement income significantly lower than preretirement earnings more realistically defines abandonment.

Further, if such terms as abandonment of the old or their liberation are to be anything more than vague impressions, we must have a numerical standard.

There are three difficulties in developing such a standard. One is that most people in the United States know less about their pretax, annual income than about their take-home pay. Though we know the size of our paycheck, our annual income becomes apparent only when we file our income tax statement. A second difficulty is that the tax load on citizens varies quite a bit, both before and after retirement. The third difficulty is that income *requirements* vary over the lifetime. In a family, for example, the costs of rearing children occur early in its history. Commuting to the place of work is a cost associated with working, one that the retired save. Facts such as these have given rise to the claim that older people need less income, one perhaps best treated with a certain amount of suspicion, particularly when made by persons not in retirement. To give an opposing example, let us simply recall that older people also need more medical care. With difficulties such as these, the best one can do is provide a rough standard of adequacy of retirement incomes.

In grappling with these problems, Schulz (1976a:72) found that an adequate retirement income would have to be between 60 percent and 65 percent of gross preretirement income, the latter referring to the average income of the five years prior to retirement. This level of replacement was based on considerations of reduced expenditures attributable to retirement, reduced taxes in old age, and less need to save. Such a Schulz-adequate retirement income, as one may label it, is one that permits continuity of life style. Persons or families who make between 60 percent and 65 percent in retirement of what they earned previously can carry on pretty much as before, inflation permitting *and* provided that they dare dip into savings for other than emergency requirements.

Taking the midpoint of the range in the replacement rates suggested by Schulz, we can use about 62 percent replacement as our adequacy standard. Significant departures from adequacy then are cut-off points to indicate abandonment on the one hand and liberation on the other. Admittedly somewhat arbitrary, let us decide that having to live on a fifth less than 62 percent of what one was used to would require a significant curtailment of expenditures and therefore would indicate abandonment. Similarly, having a retirement replacement rate one fifth above Schulz-adequacy would be better than one's work life and thus would indicate liberation. Accordingly, we label a 42 percent replacement rate, give or take a percentage point, as indicating abandonment. We also label an 82 percent replacement rate, give or take a percentage point, as indicating liberation. We shall not worry about a couple of percentage points because the numbers are more a matter of convenience than of absolute intrinsic meaning, and the available data do not fall exactly on our cut-off points. For similar reasons, we shall feel free to depart a little from the five-years average rule of preretirement earnings of the Schulz-adequacy standard. The main advantage of a numerical standard is hardly affected. Should the reader prefer other cut-off points, available data permit easy calculation of these alternative rates of abandonment, liberation, and adequacy. In any case, we now can answer a few basic questions. How many of the American elderly are abandoned, liberated, or adequately provided for? And, in broad terms, who are they, middle-class or working-class people?

Abandoned, Liberated, or Provided For?

As a first step in answering these questions, we rely on the latest available information of a nationwide sample of Americans who entered retirement in 1972 (Fox 1976:Table V and p. 18). For most of the respondents, the sample shows the first year's retirement income compared to that of the fourth year before retirement. In current dollar figures, the median retirement replacement rate for married men and their spouses was 70 percent. Thus, in 1972, one half of the married elderly were certainly adequately provided for. But in 1968 dollars, or constant purchasing power, the picture changes dramatically. In terms of real money, the median replacement rate was only 56 percent, below adequacy. Thus, in 1972, one half of the married and their spouses had lost almost one half the purchasing power available to them four years before they retired in 1968. The situation was more precarious among nonmarried men and women. Their median current dollar replacement rate was only 59 percent, already inadequate; their median constant dollar replacement rate was a mere 47 percent, rather close to our abandonment benchmark.

In addition, Fox's (1976) data reveal a pattern of downward mobility in income associated with retirement. Among married men and their spouses, 18 percent of the sample could be found in the lowest income category (under $5,000) in 1968, four years before retirement. But by 1972, already in the first year of retirement, their representation in the lowest income category had more than doubled, jumping to 37 percent. Practically all of this downward mobility originated from the two highest income classes. The pattern of mobility was similar though less dramatic among the nonmarried. Thus, the more affluent at work suffered more in income deprivation than the less affluent did. The finding points to the redistributive effects of social security.

The replacement rates based on one year of preretirement earnings can be misleading. The year may have been one of unusual earnings, good or bad, thus misrepresenting normal preretirement income. A safer procedure is to take the average of several years of preretirement earnings. The best available American data on this are based on the entire national cohort of people coming onto the old age social security benefit rolls in 1970 (Fox 1974). We present replacement rates of the first year's retirement income as a percentage of the average income of the three years with highest earnings during the decade preceding retirement. Choosing years of high earning before retirement of course lowers the replacement rate compared to using only one year of pre-retirement income. Still, because earnings from work rise with age, such a procedure seems the most realistic in terms of one's subjective experience of retirement costs. The procedure corrects for chance fluctuations in a given year while preserving the experience of rising incomes before retirement. The one disadvantage is reliance on current dollar estimates. Since these three years of highest earnings vary quite a bit among individuals, correcting for inflation is difficult.

Shown in Table 2.6*, these current dollar replacement rates yield a dismal picture of the retirement income for most older Americans. Among married men, retirement income from social security *and other* pensions showed a median replacement of 49 percent in current dollar terms! One half clearly had inadequate incomes. Twenty-six percent had retirement replacement rates of 40 percent or less. Just over one quarter of the married men were abandoned, even without any adjustment for inflation. Among married women, retirement income from social security also showed a median replacement rate of 49 percent. One half of the married women had inadequate incomes. One fifth of these married women had replacement rates of 40 percent or less, thus belonging to the abandoned. The median replacement rates of the nonmarried men and women were a little higher, 52 percent and 54 percent, respectively. But again, one half had inadequate incomes.

For those with social security *and other* pension income, we find one fifth of the nonmarried men and 14 percent of the nonmarried women in abandonment. That is, their replacement rates were less than 40 percent. Following the rule that 82 percent replacement or better signals liberation but letting it start at 81 percent, given Fox's data, we find that 6 percent of the married retirees (both men and women) belong to the liberated. The corresponding figure among the nonmarried is 7 percent, once again for men and women separately.

Turning now to those retirees who had to rely on social security income alone, let us note that they made up about one fourth of the married who retired in 1970 and about one half of the nonmarried (Fox 1974:1). Practically all of these people are classed as abandoned. Ninety-nine percent of the married men and 88 percent of the married women rank among the abandoned. The corresponding figures for the nonmarried are 99 percent and 91 percent. Clearly, relying only on social security, old age means economic misery. The young and working do not care enough for this minority of the elderly.

When we do not distinguish the source of retirement income, the following aggregate national picture emerges (see lower portion of Table 2.6). Fourteen percent of all Americans drawing retirement benefits in 1970 had a Schulz-

---

*Although the figures are based on those whose taxable earnings under social security were at the maximum or exceeding it, up to $15,600, they are, nevertheless, sufficiently representative of all. This is evident in Fox's (1974:5) estimate that coverage of all higher earners would have yielded replacement rates from social security alone of only 1 percent different among males; all other replacement rates were the same.

Table 2.6

Replacement Rates of the First Year's Retirement Income over Mean Estimated Total Income of the "Three Best Years" during the Last Ten before Retirement, by Level of Replacement, Marital Status, and Sex; United States, 1970.

Replacement Rate	Married Men		Nonmarried Men		Married Women		Nonmarried Women	
	Soc. Sec. Only	Soc. Sec. +	Soc. Sec. Only	Soc. Sec. +	Soc. Sec. Only	Soc. Sec. +	Soc. Sec. Only	Soc. Sec. +
	Percent Obtaining Replacement Rates on Left							
0-20	27	1	20	(*)	3	(*)	4	(*)
21-30	57	6	58	5	45	5	33	1
31-40	14	19	21	15	40	20	54	13
41-50	1	29	1	27	9	28	8	28
51-60	(*)	22	1	25	3	25	1	25
61-70	(*)	12	(*)	16	(*)	13	(*)	20
71-80	(*)	5	(*)	6	(*)	3	(*)	7
81-90	(*)	3	(*)	2	(*)	2	(*)	4
91-		3	(*)	5	(*)	4	(*)	3
Median	24	49	25	52	31	49	33	54

Replacement Rate	Total 100	Men 100	Women 100
Abandoned: 40% or Less	24%	26%	19%
41%-60%	51%	51%	53%
Adequate: 61%-70%	14%	13%	17%
71%-80%	5%	5%	5%
Liberated: 81% or More	6%	6%	6%

(*) Less than .05%; Soc. Sec. = Social Security; Soc. Sec. + = Social Security and other pensions

Source: Alan Fox, Earnings Replacement from Social Security and Private Pensions: Newly Entitled Beneficiaries, 1970. (Washington, D.C.: U.S. Department of Health, Education, and Welfare, Social Security Administration, Office of Research and Statistics, 1974), Report No. 13, Table 7.

adequate old-age income, with women slightly over- and men slightly underrepresented in this group. Fifty-one percent had inadequate retirement income but were not abandoned. American society abandons just under one quarter (24 percent) of its elderly in retirement, with more men (26 percent) than women (19 percent) among them. We also find that another 5 percent of all in retirement had a better than adequate income, but not sufficient for liberation. The liberated make up only 6 percent of all retirees. When it comes to enjoying a more than adequate retirement income or finding oneself in a state of liberation, there is no sex discrimination. If we say that Schulz-adequacy or better makes retirement the golden years, it is exactly one quarter of all who can really enjoy their retirement.

When we ask who are the liberated, the adequately provided for, and the abandoned, available information is so scarce as to permit only a very approximate answer. We really know only who is *not* abandoned. They are the retired federal civil servants. Not just in the United States but also generally in Western industrial societies, the retired bureaucrats from the national governments are the privileged retirement plutocrats among the elderly. Their pensions, in effect during the early 1970s, averaged about two thirds of the last annual salary received. Such a replacement rate over the last year's earnings occurs in an employment setting in which length of service itself directly increases income applied to all ranks. This high replacement rate was so exceptional and so cross-nationally uniform as to inspire Kaim-Caudle (1973:37) to use it as a standard against which to measure a nation's performance in caring for its elderly.

Any other details are hard to find. For example, we find surprisingly little variation in retirement replacement rates by occupation in the data just used (Fox 1974:Table 8). All one can say is that ex-clerks and salespersons seem to benefit more from somewhat higher median replacement rates than any other occupational group retiring in 1970.

Returning once again to Fox's (1976) study of the entire national cohort retiring in 1972 yields more information. Let us remember that the replacement rates are determined by comparing the income of the first year in retirement with that of the fourth year preceding retirement. When we calculate constant dollar replacement rates, and neutralize the effects of inflation over the period from 1968 to 1972, the following picture emerges (Fox 1976:Table 3). The minority of the American elderly for whom retirement *appears* as liberation came predominantly from the ranks of those who were poor while still at work. For them, retirement does *not* mean liberation from poverty to any important extent. If we consider the official poverty thresholds (Fox 1976:17, 20), two facts become apparent. Many, probably the majority, of those with work income in the lowest income bracket were in official poverty while working. Upon retirement, just over two thirds (67 percent) of the married of these "poor when at work before" had a nominal replacement rate of 100 percent, but they suffered a real income loss of 20 percent. Their liberation was only statistical.

They were in official poverty before, and retirement did not liberate them from poverty.

Escape from poverty was limited to a small minority, less than one fifth of these people. Among the nonmarried retirees who appear liberated the situation is quite similar. The great majority was poor before retirement and stayed poor in retirement. Again, less than one fifth escaped poverty through retirement. In short, there is very little real economic liberation associated with retirement in the United States. What little one does find tends to be limited to those retiring from the lower paid jobs.

In terms of constant dollar replacement, very few of the new retirees in 1972 fell into the Schulz-adequate bracket of retirement income even when the range was enlarged to 61 percent to 70 percent real replacement. The majority clustered in either the "more than adequate" range (71% to 80%) or the "less than adequate" range (41% to 60%). Regardless of marital status, those with more than adequate retirement income came disproportionately from the lower paying jobs in the economy. Again, we would attribute this to the redistributive effects of social security benefits. But there was no or little pattern in the level of pay from which people retired among those who had a less than adequate income in retirement. The married with less than adequate retirement income had retired from high, middle, and low paying jobs. The nonmarried came more often from middle to low paying jobs.

Finally, those for whom retirement meant abandonment are more clearly identifiable. Among the nonmarried, abandonment was the fate of those who had neither high nor low paying jobs but found themselves in the middle-income range before retirement. Among the married, abandonment was also the fate of those who retired from jobs in the middle-income range, but there is a definite pattern. The more one made at work, the greater the chance there was of finding oneself abandoned afterwards. No less than 43 percent of people retiring from the second highest income category in 1968 found themselves with a real replacement rate of under 40 percent in retirement four years later. If one were a professional or in the upper middle class before retirement, one's chances of becoming one of the abandoned in retirement were definitely higher than of those retiring from middle or lower middle class incomes. Interestingly enough, according to newspaper accounts, the contemporary "tax revolt" in the United States is said to be concentrated among the middle-income groups. They sense already, it seems, that they will not receive retirement benefits commensurate with the social security tax load placed on them. Tentative as they are, Fox's (1976) data support their suspicion.

Combining the information in Table 2.6 with that from Fox's (1976) retirement history sample prompts the following, tentative conclusions. American society abandons about a quarter of its older people. They tended to work in middle-paying jobs before retirement. About one half of the elderly in retirement have less than adequate but higher than abandonment income, and they used to work in the higher paying jobs before retirement. Just under one fifth of our retired have more than adequate income but cannot be called liberated. They retired from jobs in the middle and lower middle income range. Only 6 percent are statistically liberated, but many of these do not even escape official poverty upon retiring.

Finding that about one quarter of the American elderly are abandoned by younger people again raises the issue of justice. Clearly, abandonment implies injustice. Table 2.5 tells us that retirement income was 6 percent more unequal than preretirement income was and, therefore, more unequal than it should have been. Apparently, this increase in inequality means downward income mobility, down far enough to register as abandonment for about a quarter of the American elderly. The violation of the norms of distributive justice for the elderly as a group is modest. But for a minority of the elderly, the injustice is massive. Since most of the abandoned do not belong to the poor of the nation, either before or after retirement, further efforts to prevent poverty among the elderly are not likely to affect the prevailing abandonment rate. This fact, more than any other, raises the question of whether Americans do less than others in caring for their elderly.

CARING FOR THE ELDERLY: THE UNITED STATES IN CROSS-NATIONAL COMPARATIVE PERSPECTIVE

Income comparisons across national boundaries pose vexing problems. The hurdles of comparing varying currencies with varying purchasing powers must be overcome. Nonetheless, the fact that Americans provide *relatively* less well for their elderly than do other nations can be established with a satisfactory degree of certainty. But the word relatively should be emphasized. About a decade ago, Shanas and others (1968:369) found that the American elderly were absolutely better off than their counterparts in Great Britain and Denmark. Such findings came from very complicated constructions of equivalent purchasing power units across national currencies, income data, and retail price information. We cannot offer comparable data. We can only provide information about old age income relative to that of younger people in several societies and replacement rates of social security pensions over preretirement earnings. We can compare only roughly how well older people are taken care of by the nonaged in each country. Nonetheless, this can answer the question of interest here: Relative to that of younger people and relative to what one earned before retirement, how does the economic cost of retirement in the United States compare with that of other advanced societies?

We shall answer in three steps. The first compares the income of the elderly with that of younger people still at work. Our comparison uses old-age social security pensions as a percentage of the earnings of male workers in the manufacturing industry. This statistic is compared to a directly related item, namely, how much governments tax the younger still at work in order to provide for the elderly in retirement. That tax load can be roughly measured by a readily available statistic, which is the percentage of a nation's wealth (gross national product or GNP) allocated to expenditures for old-age social security. The second step compares actual retirement replacement rates from social security in the United States with hypothetical replacement rates derived from Western European social security policies. In each case, the replacement rate refers to retirement income as a percentage of the average of the last five years of earnings while at work. The hypothetical replacement rates are determined by applying the West German and Swedish social security provisions to American data. The comparison tells us what proportion of the American elderly *are* found among the abandoned, the more or less adequately provided for, and the liberated, and what percentages *would be* found in these categories if the United States had the social security system of the Germans or the Swedes. Finally, our third step compares whole ranges of replacement rates of retirement income over pre-retirement earnings, a procedure that works quite well in comparing the United States with countries in Eastern Europe. The results of the three comparisons are presented in Parts A, B, and C, respectively, of Table 2.7.

Our first comparison, old-age pensions as percent of male workers' earnings in the manufacturing industry, is now a decade old. It has to be treated cautiously. The United States then ranked sixth in a group of eight Western democracies in caring for the elderly (Part A, Table 2.7). Five Western European countries took better care of their aged and two, Canada and Great Britain, took worse care than the United States did. Although the relationship between the level of caring for the elderly and the proportion of national wealth allocated to that care is not as strong as one might have expected, it is still clear that the better economic care of the elderly in Western Europe also costs the Europeans more. Sweden and West Germany, for example, allocated on the average more than double the American portion to providing for their elderly. On this score then, the United States did less well than several countries in Western Europe. Part B of Table 2.7 also tells us that this finding is probably not outdated.

Before turning to the results of our second comparison among the United States, West Germany, and Sweden, we shall make two notes on the data. First, the projected replacement rates for 1980 were based on regulations in effect in 1973 (Schulz 1974:256). Several increases in social security benefits in the United States have been legislated since that time. But we should also remember that old age social security pensions in West Germany were not only periodically

Table 2.7
Old Age Income, the United States in International Comparison

A

Old Age Pensions in Relation to Income from Work and National
Expenditures for Older People

	Old Age Pensions as Percent of Earnings in Manufacturing Male Workers	National Expenditures on Old Age, Survivors, and Disability Insurance as Percent of GNP	
	1968	*1968*	*1971*
France	98	4.2	4.2
West Germany	56	8.0	7.6
Sweden	54	5.1	6.0
Belgium	45	4.7	5.0
Netherlands	43	6.9	6.3
United States	43	2.8	3.4
Canada	39	2.2	2.4
Great Britain	36	3.8	3.5

B

Projected (1980) U.S. Old Age Income Replacement from Social Security
According to 1973 Regulations: Actual and What It Would Be with a
German or Swedish Pension System. Replacement for Couples over the
Average of the Last Five Years of Earnings.

	Percent of Couples Receiving Replacement Rates on Left		
	Actual 1980	*With a German System 1980*	*With a Swedish System 1980*
Level of Replacement from OASDI	100*	100*	100*
Less than 40%	62	10	14
40% to 59%	25	28	43
60% to 79%	7	50	30
80% and Over	7	13	14

*Failure to add to 100 due to rounding

C

Retirement Income Replacement Over the Last Year's Preretirement Income[1]
in the United States and Eastern Europe (Current Dollar Replacements)

	Percent of Older People with Replacement				
Replaced	*U.S.*	*U.S.S.R.*	*Poland*	*Rumania*	*C.S.S.R.*
Below 50%	24	All	All	All	All
50% to 74%	37	55% to 100%	80% to 95%	60% to 85%	50% or More
75% or More	39				

[1]Replacement bases vary as follows: U.S., fourth year before retirement (data for couples and nonmarried women only); U.S.S.R., last preretirement year or average of five "best" prior to retirement; Poland, last year or average of "best two" during preceding twelve years; Rumania, last year; C.S.S.R. average of the last five or ten years of work.

Sources: Parts A and B: James Schulz and others, Providing Adequate Retirement Income (Hanover, N.H.: University of New England Press, 1974), p. 26 Figure IV, 256; Max Horlick, "National Expenditures on Social Security in Selected Countries, 1968 and 1971" (Washington, D.C.: U.S. Department of Health, Education, and Welfare, Social Security Administration, Office of Research and Statistics, Research Note No. 29, 1974).

Sources: Part C: U.S. calculated from Table 5 in Alan Fox, "Work Status and Income Change, 1968-1972: Retirement History Study Preview" (Washington, D.C.: U.S. Department of Health, Education, and Welfare, Social Security Administration, 1976); all other countries: U.S. Social Security Administration, "Social Security Programs Throughout the World" (Washington, D.C.: 1975).

adjusted for inflation in consumer prices but also for changes in national wage rates after retirement. This means that the aged in West Germany share in the economic growth of the country achieved by younger people at work long after the old have retired from the labor force. For this reason alone, it seems to us exceedingly unlikely that the data in Part B (Table 2.7) could distort the contemporary situation. Second, let us emphasize that these are replacement rates from social security only, but the replacement is calculated over the average of the last five years of earnings before retirement. That is why the proportion of the abandoned under the American plan is lower than the corresponding percentages in Table 2.5. The latter reflect replacement over the three years with highest earnings during the last ten years before retirement. Finally, let us note as well that replacement from social security only is a very good measure of three things. These are: 1) the national policy of a country pertaining to the care of the elderly; 2) the tax burden placed on younger people in the labor force by that policy; and 3) the tolerance or willingness of the younger to care for the elderly.

As evident in Part B of Table 2.7, there would be far fewer abandoned older people in the United States if Americans had either the West German or the Swedish social security system. Under the West German plan, only one tenth of the elderly would be abandoned instead of the 62 percent under the American social security system; under a Swedish plan, the proportion of the abandoned would shrink to a mere 14 percent. In the next range of inadequate retirement income (40 percent to 59 percent replacement from social security), it would make no notable difference if the United States had the West German system. Under a Swedish system, in contrast, there would be more elderly in the United States with inadequate income than there are in fact.

Other cross-national differences appear in a retirement income of Schulz-adequacy or better (60 percent or more replacement). Although the American social security system provides that level of retirement income for only 14 percent of the elderly, under a German plan, the United States would have 63 percent of its elderly in that range; under a Swedish plan, 44 percent of the American elderly would be above Schulz-adequacy. On that score too, then, the United States takes significantly less care of its older people than the West Germans and the Swedes do. Yet, even under a German or Swedish system, old age would amount to substantial economic privilege only for a small minority. If we take the over-eighty-percent replacement from social security as approximating the condition of liberation, the American system produces 7 percent, a fraction that would double under a German or Swedish plan. But even so, liberation would not be common in old age.

The United States and Eastern Europe

Finally, how does the United States compare with Eastern Europe? Evidently, also rather poorly (see Part C of Table 2.7). Once again, let us stress that these are comparative estimates of retirement income relative to preretirement earnings in each country. It is not that the elderly of Russia, Poland, Rumania, and Czechoslovakia are absolutely better off than the American elderly. Because the Eastern European countries are still less developed economically, probably the reverse is the case. But none of that affects the question of how America's care for the elderly compares to that of Eastern Europe, considering retirement income in relation to wages. In answering this, we assume that practically all retirement income worth considering in Eastern Europe comes from social security. That means one should compare it with American retirement income from all sources, not just social security. We draw once more on Fox's (1976) study of the American cohort entering retirement in 1972.

Unfortunately, his current dollar replacement rates covered only part of that cohort, married couples and nonmarried women. Since little if anything is known about inflation in Eastern Europe, we had to follow replacement rates in current dollars. Further, because older nonmarried women in the United States are poorer than their male counterparts, exclusion of the latter somwwhat lowered the replacement rates. Couples still provided the largest numbers in that 1972 retirement cohort. Accordingly, the distortion should be fairly small, enough not to misrepresent the dramatic cross-national differences.

Whereas almost a quarter of Americans had a replacement rate of under 50 percent, losing one half or more of their income upon retiring, that applied to no one in Eastern Europe (Part C, Table 2.7). All retirees there received one half or more of their preretirement incomes. In Poland, the lowest was a replacement rate of 80 percent; in Rumania the corresponding lowest was 60 percent. Poland provided for all of its older people in terms comparable to only 39 percent of older Americans. Only Czechoslovakia treated its older people as stingily as the United States does. True, none of the elderly in the Soviet Union had a replacement rate of under 35 percent, but we are not told how many of the elderly had pensions significantly above a 55-percent replacement. Presumably, all had to make do with inadequate retirement incomes. But in three out of four comparisons, the United States once again fared poorly.

Some readers may doubt that one can compare the United States with Eastern Europe at all in this respect. De Beauvoir (1972) for example, mentioned that pension replacement rates over prior earnings in the Soviet Union exaggerate the well-being of elderly Russians relative to their Western counterparts. She feels that so many nonmonetary forms of income are associated with work in Eastern European countries that purely monetary comparisons are not valid. Among such nonmonetary forms of income which come with work but are lost on retirement, one finds such items as paid vacations and housing advantages. Still, we disagree with such skepticism. We remind the reader that an elderly person in Eastern Europe has no medical care costs to pay out of his or her own pocket. All health care there is public, and insurance coverage is nearly universal. But as shown above, despite Medicare, the American elderly have to pay for much medical care themselves, and that should more than make up for the difference in the comparison.

THE ECONOMIC POSITION
OF OLDER AMERICANS SUMMED UP

There have been two improvements in the economic condition of older people in the United States since the close of World War II. One of these has been an impressive decline in official poverty among older people. The other has been greater coverage of the employed American labor force by private pension plans. That coverage grew from 22 percent in 1950 to 46 percent in 1975 (Yolahem 1977:22). Still, our estimates of the extent to which retirement income replaces income from work included people with such additional income, unless we specifically designated the statistic "replacement from social security only." Also, much of the effect of private pensions will emerge only in the future, under the threat of inflation to which private pensions remain more vulnerable than social security does.

Beyond these two developments, we noted that the American elderly suffer income deprivation relative to people in their middle years. Although that in itself is hardly surprising, more significant was the finding of a trend of old-age income deterioration over the two decades from 1952 to 1972. In real dollars, adjusted to inflation, older people in America are becoming progressively less well off compared to those in the middle years and at work. We suspect this is primarily because old-age social security benefits in the United States are adjusted for changes in consumer prices but not for changes in wages after people have retired. We hold that the greater abandonment of older people in America relative to both Western and Eastern Europe results from this difference in social security policies. Let us note that whoever may shape these policies, it is, finally, the public who either tolerates such policies or refuses to go along. That may be somewhat more true in Western pluralist democracies in which political leaders have to struggle openly for office, but the public's voice is, nonetheless, not absent in *any* advanced society. Polish workers, for example, have been known to strike over food prices. Thus, national social security policy reflects, ultimately, how much people care about the elderly.

In the United States where we had access to income data of persons at various stages in life, we could investigate the issue of the just and fair distribution of old age income. We used these data to measure how much diachronic solidarity in commitments to norms justifying income inequality is produced by younger age cohorts supporting the elderly. Generally, we found that the income inequality of people at various life stages in the United States conforms to prevailing norms of distributive justice.

There is somewhat less justice in the distribution of old age income, but in terms of retirement replacement rates that deviation is only 6 percent more inequality than required by norms. Since that is an almost unbelievable level of value implementation in society, we stressed that the deviation from norms is larger when comparing old-age income of both the retired and those still working relative to the ten-year younger cohort before retirement age. We found that those deviations also meant more income inequality among the elderly than required by norms of distributive justice. Instead of maintaining the income inequality attained just before retirement, the inequality in retirement income was 9 percent larger in 1952, a deviation from norms which rose to 26 percent more inequality than prescribed by 1972. Quantitatively, injustice seems on the rise, signaling a weakened commitment to norms of distributive justice in caring for older people. Qualitatively, we found no injustice whatever. There was no change in the determinants of income position as one moved from middle age to old age.

Although the majority of the American elderly has a fairly just old age income according to prevailing norms, the minority who are unjustly cared for experience severe deprivation. About one quarter of all the elderly in the United States find themselves abandoned to relative economic misery, and that much abandonment cannot be found either in Western or Eastern Europe.

Although the Eastern European countries on which we could find information do not abandon any of their people in retirement, it is a fairly safe bet that many of their older people are worse off than elderly Americans are. But that mostly reflects differences in the wealth of the nations compared and applies to people at all ages.

As for Western Europe, if the United States had a social security system like that in effect in West Germany or Sweden, the proportion of the elderly abandoned in America would be reduced by about six to four times, respectively. Although there would not be much change in the proportion of the American elderly with inadequate incomes, the fraction with a Schulz-adequate or higher retirement incomes would rise about four times under the West German system and about three times under the Swedish system. Thus, the income cost of retirement is higher in the United States than in West Germany and Sweden. It is apparently also higher than in France, Belgium, the Netherlands, and three out of four Eastern European countries. As far as can be ascertained here, Americans do care less about their elderly. These facts should suffice to place the onus of proof on those who may want to argue that Americans cannot afford to take better care of their elderly.

3 the politics of aging

INTRODUCTION

There is a direct link between how the elderly fare economically and the politics of aging in the types of societies with which we are concerned. In modern society people look much more to government as the most important agency for solving social problems and for regulating social life than they did in the past. An impressive increase in the scope of governmental tasks is one of the uncontroversial points of the history of modernization.

Deutsch (1970:67), for example, offered estimates showing that the Roman Empire around A.D. 100 used about 7 percent of its wealth for government expenditures. The Athenian Republic had more governmental services around 450 B.C., allotting about 15 percent of its gross national product to them. Just how big "big government" has become in modern times becomes apparent when we realize that in the middle sixties about 30 percent of our GNP was allocated to the public sector; in the United Kingdom the corresponding figure was about one third; and in France it was over 35 percent.

Although "power over nature is something men can share, power over men is something for which men must compete" (Deutsch 1970:25). In democratic politics, the choices about resource allocation that government makes are formally responsible to the preferences of a diverse electorate. Some responsiveness of government, at least to the active and organized parts of the public perceived to influence the outcomes of elections, is built into the political system. Formally, each citizen is entitled to one vote, cast in privacy. Voting behavior, however, is subject to a number of societal and organizational influences which do constrain purely individual choices.

One of these is the political party system. Clearly, a two-party system presents fewer opportunities to make choices than a four-party system does. Also, it is the party which selects candidates for office and designs platforms in a manner to appeal to targeted voter groups. Other social affiliations, such as membership in ethnic and religious groups, in unions or other occupational groupings, also influence the voter's choice, directly and indirectly. In the United States in particular, the political influence of lobbies or organized pressure groups has been prominent in political life. This is probably because of its highly diversified population and also because voter turn-out tends to be rather low when compared with other industrialized nations. Consequently, politicians seem to be more prepared here than elsewhere to listen to voices claiming to speak for special interests.

Various special interests are often all that is available to guide the politician. Situations in which one issue actually determines "the will of the people" are rare, and politics usually means dealing with many, often conflicting interests. In city politics, this diversity is shown in the form of bloc voting, usually organized according to ethnic bonds. But there are lobbies or organized pressures on all levels of government, often with their own buildings, budgets, and permanent staffs. They are related not only to elected officials but also to appointed governmental bureaucrats in a variety of ways. Campaign contributions, propaganda aid, promises to deliver blocs of votes, and, above all, information to articulate properly informed and dependable positions on various issues are the main chips offered in the poker of politics.

The Position of the Aged

Within this context the aged have become a potential political resource. After all, people over sixty-five now represent 15 percent of the voting population of the United States. As an aggregate, they could be seen as a constituency of the newly disadvantaged. As chapter 2 showed, in accordance with the decline in income associated with retirement, this view is legitimated in the sheer facts of economic life. Substandard housing, the burden of medical expenses in old age, and reduced prestige associated with negative images of being old also could contribute to the formation of the elderly as a political force. It is one that for its numbers alone politicians would be wise to watch.

This state of affairs led Rose (1965) to develop a theoretical perspective of the aged in modern society as a subculture. He thought that their growing numbers, as an increasing proportion of the population as a whole and of the voting population in particular, together with increased contact among the aged, would lead to group consciousness based on the common fate of relative disprivilege. Freed from work and child-rearing responsibilities, old people have more time for political activities than others do. Since many are active and have sufficient income to engage in political efforts, Rose thought that growing group identification would lead to political organization. After all, "the American way" of social justice usually entails conflicts and accommodations among competing interests. Rose therefore argued that older people and politicians seeking a new constituency would recognize the obvious and see the tremendous potential for a new political force in American life. Between them, they would eventually bring that force into being.

In contrast, more pessimistic and more impressed by the stigma of being old in a youth-oriented culture, Rosow (1967 1974) saw little if any prospect for building a viable political force on the basis of age alone. In his opinion, a general devaluation of old age would automatically quash any attempts at age-based politics. Efforts to mobilize the elderly as a separate political force would lead to little more than hostility by the general population. In such a contest between the generations, the elderly, as a minority, no matter how sizable, would be the losers. In Rosow's opinion, expectations of the elderly as a separate political force are far too simplistic, the elderly themselves too realistic to even try it, and a growing sense of apathy among them a significantly more likely development than the alternative position taken by Rose.

In short, in Rose we find shades of the "disengagement selective reengagement" perspective on old age. Released from the constraints of work and suffering a variety of relative deprivations, older people should be expected to become a new political force. In Rosow's view, disengagement might well extend to the political sector of life.

Our Three Perspectives and the Politics of Aging

The two quite different views prompt questions about the politics of aging that relate to our three perspectives. Rosow obviously speaks from the perspective of abandonment. If his view is essentially correct, we should expect to find old people being elbowed out of politics, directly or indirectly. If younger people rejected the older generation as obsolete and irrelevant, for example, we would not expect to find them in positions of political leadership. The most obvious rejection would be to take away from people sixty-five and over the right to vote. This has not happened nor is there any movement in this direction. It should, in fact, be pointed out that a citizen's participation does not depend on direct economic contribution. If it did, then full-time housewives, the unemployed, and other "nonworking" segments of the population would be excluded from voting. As it is, only the very young and noncitizen are excluded. In Rosow's depiction, there could be, however, psychological disenfranchisement. If older people saw themselves as unwanted political actors, the result would be to withdraw from political activities and interests as they advanced beyond the middle years.

The Rose perspective comes much closer to the liberation viewpoint. Freed from earlier obligations, older persons could enter or reenter political life with unusual vigor. They then would be found in exceptionally high proportions at the polls and in other types of political activities. The elderly also would lead the nation in keeping abreast of political events. But there is a twist in Rose's thinking which veers toward the abandonment perspective. Rose perceived high levels of political participation for older people as efforts in their own behalf to remedy their deprivations. Consequently, they would behave politically as an "aging bloc." The assumption of this view is that older people would have to raise their status by their own efforts because younger generations could not be expected to support their cause. The truly liberated old person, we submit, might well choose to put more time and energy into political affairs but not as an aging advocate. Rather, he or she would behave as a "citizen of the nation," demonstrating to younger generations the duty of citizens of democratic countries to participate actively to political life. On these grounds, the liberated person, freed from constraints of work and other duties of middle life, would be expected to be more active politically but to respond to political issues similarly to how younger segments of the population do.

What has just been said could be taken as one half of diachronic solidarity. Patterns of voting on issues consistent with those of younger generations would express a sense of identity by the older with the younger. But the diachronic solidarity perspective requires more. If the politics of aging is characterized by diachronic solidarity, then that social identity has to be shared by other age groups. Not only would we expect to find younger age groups highly supportive of legislation favoring the aged, but there also would have to be evidence that the younger groups expect continuity of the social rights granted that will be passed on from generation to generation.

We shall examine the evidence available in light of the kinds of "proof" cited above for one or another perspective. The United States will be scrutinized most closely, but there is considerable material from other countries as well. We shall discuss political orientations and attitudes, political behavior, and intergenerational conflict or cooperation.

POLITICAL ORIENTATIONS AND ATTITUDES

This section is on whether political orientations and attitudes vary between older people and other age groups, and, if so, whether the variations can be perceived as age linked.

One way in which older people consistently have been found to be different is in being politically more conservative than younger generations (Hudson & Binstock 1976; Binstock & Levin 1976). The relationship between conservatism and advanced age holds across class lines. But in order to interpret this statistic, it is necessary to define conservatism. The most widely used indicator of conservatism is party identification, which is not a very good basis for predicting political attitudes. Careful analysis shows that identification with the more conservative party is related to early affiliation with that party and not with "growing more conservative" as one ages. Proportionately more old people belong to the Republican party in the United States, it is argued, mainly because affiliation with that party was more widespread when they were younger. This is so for two reasons. Over time, there has been a sharp rise in the proportion of Americans who call themselves "Independents," that is, not identified with either party. At the same time, the Republican party lost more of its members. Republicans indeed have become a small minority in the voting population. It is an interesting sidelight on American politics that early affiliation tends to persist among all ages. It works in the following manner: A man in his thirties, for example, who first registered as an Independent, is likely to keep that label although in actual behavior he may find himself consistently voting for one or the other party. Similarly, older Americans, who registered as Republicans when Republicanism was more popular, remain loyal but do not necessarily follow the straight party ticket. If this pattern of loyalty to first party identification holds, then, we should expect successive cohorts of old people to reflect the party structure of their youth but at the same time we should be very cautious about attaching political significance to it. It is quite possible that this age-related difference is more apparent than real in its impact, a matter to be explored below.

It should be noted at this point that age is not related to value choices of what American society should be like. Across all age groups, Americans largely agree on abstract ideals. They believe in democracy and in accepting the will of the majority, while at the same time incorporating concern for minority rights. On the abstract level of what constitutes a desirable society, differences in party identification by age do not lead to age cleavages.

Within that consensus, however, there is a great deal of variation in the positions on issues related to "how to get there." In contrast to the rather high stability of party identification, Americans tend to be quite changeable and even contradictory in their positions on specific issues from the perspective of some right-left or conservative-liberal categorization. Persons of all ages in this country have been found to show more loosely structured attitudes toward specific issues than toward basic political attachments (Free & Cantril 1968; Glenn & Hefner 1972). Americans tend to slip around in terms of where they stand. They resist being pigeon-holed, frustrating those who would like to assign them to neat boxes on the basis of consistent preferences logically related to one another.

Older people show no more tendency to hold contradictory beliefs simultaneously than younger ones do, but they do appear to change their beliefs somewhat more gradually. This lower degree of plasticity coupled with some evidence that older people are generally less favorable to government intervention has been labeled conservative. Yet, a summary of research results compiled by Riley and Foner (1968:473-75) did not show the elderly to be consistently conservative on substantive issues. Compared with younger generations, they allied themselves sometimes more with the right and sometimes more with the left. Toward the pole perceived as conservative, people over sixty-five were less favorable—but among the middle class only—to government control in general, less tolerant of political and social nonconformity (even with education controlled for), less willing to support racial integration in the schools, and more opposed to a black or Catholic president of the United States. But the elderly were more liberal on other issues. People sixty-five and over were more likely to feel that the government should help those who want to work to find jobs, more favorable public housing, and more supportive of publicly owned utilities. On an apparently highly "age-conscious" issue, people over sixty-five were more likely to endorse government guarantees of low-cost medical care and the use of social security taxes to support old-age medical insurance. Declining health affects older people more than younger people, so here older people are presumably speaking in their own interests. Yet it is important to emphasize that the majority in younger age groups also supported the positions on medical care and medical insurance. The aged simply have been slightly ahead in a climate of general agreement. Indeed, most of the variations found by age tended to be small, and on a number of issues, there were no differences at all. At the time of the Riley and Foner review, for example, no differences were found in supporting government aid to schools or enforcing antidiscrimination policies in housing.

Subsequent studies in the United States generally confirmed these differences (Campbell 1971; Foner 1972; Clemente 1975) which show older people sometimes a little bit to the right and sometimes a little bit to the left of the rest of the adult population. One more recent variant is that older people have become comparatively less supportive of public expenditures for education which is also perceived as an age-related trend. They are, after all, not likely to have school-age children. At the same time, the later studies show few discernible differences by age on greater governmental responsibility for full employment a minimum wage. Slight shifts in time, then, have moved the oldest adult group slightly out of line with the general population on educational support, yet have aligned them with younger groups on full employment. Although other differences cited earlier remain, the gap seems to be narrowing in the issue of racial integration.

The differences then, are not particularly stable. It is not easy to attribute them simply to the process of "growing old." People move through life stages as though they were on a escalator, and new cohorts moving into the age bracket of sixty-five and over with different life experiences may easily shift attitudes. Across age groups as well, politically linked attitudes seem to reflect the general social climate at a given time. For example, although responses reflecting political alienation appear at first glance to be somewhat higher among the oldest and the youngest age groups in the population, an analysis of several time periods showed that "the times" affect relative alienation of all age groups far more than age itself does (Bengston 1976:41). All age groups were found to have higher levels of alienation in 1952 and in 1968 than any one age group had in 1960.

"Growing old" does seem to show a stable relationship to a higher endorsement of medical care issues regardless of cohort or time period. So far, however, this is the only area among those examined for historical experiences or pressures common to all age groups at different times, that reflects attitudinal changes caused by maturation. On the whole, based on what is now known, there is little evidence of an "aging vote" or any noticeable trend in that direction. In fact, as Campbell (1971:114) concluded: "Attitudinal differences within age groups are far more impressive than between."

This last point brings us to the phenomenon of old age identification and how it affects the attitudes of older people. In a national sample drawn in 1972 (Bengston & Cutler 1976:155), it was found that among persons over sixty, there were consistent differences in a series of eight issues among those who identified themselves as old and those who did not so identify themselves. Such findings suggest that development of aging consciousness could have a perceptible impact on solidarity, political action, and possibly political organization. It is again only relative variation in issues that range from inflation and military spending to self-ratings on political philosophy and economic situation. On every item all respondents sixty and over are on the same side of the fence, that is, either a minority or majority of the total group agreed on the response to every item. Furthermore, the discrepancies between proportions of old-identified and non-old-identified were small, about five to ten percentage points, with one notable exception. The exception was federal medical programs. On this issue the old-identified were much more supportive (71.7 percent) than those not so identified (51.9 percent). Perceiving oneself as old does have some impact, although usually a rather small one, on other issue responses. But it may not necessarily signify an age-consciousness leading to political mobilization. If the over-sixty group was divided on other dimensions besides old-identification, such as relative age or health status, there might be similar group divisions. If only those who are older and frailer supported health care, for example, the political implications would be minor. But it is very probable that such persons are those among the aged who are the least likely to make an active political effort. Another consideration around the meaning of age-identification comes into play when we note that the national survey also included "the young," arbitrarily conceived as the group between eighteen and thirty-five. This group was no more likely to identify themselves as young (38 percent) than those sixty and over were likely to identify themselves as old (38 percent). The concept of age-consciousness still has not been explored adequately in terms of interpretation and implications.

We can conclude that the differences found between older people and adults in earlier stages of the life cycle did not lead to very strong evidence of significant and durable political age cohesion. Older people are more likely to be attached to conservative parties, but that attachment is related to historical experience rather than to a shift toward growing conservatism with aging. On broad societal values, no differences in orientations were found among age groups. On more specific issues, people over sixty-five tended to be more conservative on some items and more liberal on others. The differences that were found tended to be small and subject to change as age cohorts change or in response to the social climate of the times.

In the Riley and Foner summary, those over sixty-five were more in favor of full employment; yet later studies showed an alignment on this issue including all age groups. On another issue, older people were aligned in the earlier period but moved toward a relatively more negative stance on public support for education. Given current grumblings about property taxes in particular, it may well be that the rest of the adult population also will move in that direction over the next few years.

The one issue in which simply growing older was consistently related to attitudes is medical care, and here, too, old-identification, whatever its underlying dimensions, also had a sizable impact. Yet at no time since this issue has been raised in American political life has less than a majority of younger adults taken a favorable stance on the same issue.

With some minor reservations, then, it seems reasonable to support the view of Binstock (1974) that a full life cycle of experiences and attachments, not only political but also educational, occupational, ethnic, and familial, is more influencial than age itself in explaining responses to the issues. These competing factors dilute the potential for mobilizing a cohesive voting bloc, even among the disadvantaged aging. There seems little reason now to believe that this picture is changing despite the growing segment of the population considered as old (Maddox 1970, 1974).

In Other Countries

The data from other countries support the findings in the United States mainly on two points. Compared to younger adults, people sixty-five and over in France, Germany, Great Britain, Italy, Japan, and Sweden are the most likely to be identified with the most conservative party on the particular national scene (Lipset 1959; Rose 1964; Watanuki 1967; McKenzie & Silver 1968; Butler & Stokes 1971). At the same time, Converse (1969) found another pattern similar to that of the United States in France, Germany, and Great Britain. Older people are still identifying with the party of their youth, but the proportions of Independent voters have increased among the younger generations. Again, it does not seem to be a matter of growing more conservative with age.

Unfortunately, political attitudes toward specific issues are not available by age group in the other industrialized societies. It would be a quantum leap to suggest that age cleavages are as small and unstable elsewhere as they are in the United States. Indeed, there is one study that argued that intergenerational conflict may be building up in five of six European countries surveyed (Inglehart 1971). The findings from this study will be considered more closely in a later section. It should be mentioned at this point that the research focused on a value cleavage rather than on political issues. The value also was not conceptions of a desirable society but rather priorities given to "acquisitiveness." It was argued that the young are turning away from "bourgeois" materialism but their elders, particularly those in their late fifties and above, are not. The conflict is seen as looming in the future. So far only a minority in any age group gives priority to nonbourgeois values. Generally speaking, it can be seen as relative consensus with some erosion at the lower points in the age profile. Nevertheless, given this study together with the absence of data on attitudes toward specific issues, we are not in a very strong position to compare other countries with the United States.

Among Americans there is clearly no support for a subculture of aging in politics. Despite the higher tendency to align with the Republican party, older people tend to think politically much the way that younger adults do. They do not vote on issues as an aging bloc, as one would expect if they felt abandoned by the rest of the nation. There is more a sense of intergenerational continuity which shifts slightly in response to cohort change and the general social climate.

Only on medical care are old people, especially those self-identified as old, consistently more favorable to government intervention. But they are not alone. A majority of younger adults has consistently supported them. This may suggest diachronic solidarity. Older people, through their political attitudes, are identified with the rest of the population in their solutions to political problems. In turn, a majority of the younger population supports legislation that will most benefit the oldest group. Solidarity is expressed when younger generations support what the oldest need most, even when it comes out of their own pockets. Whether or not the right to low-cost medical care is supported in the expectation of that right being applied to succeeding generations is, of course, not clear at this point.

The information from other modern nations is less certain. The interpretation of higher conservative party identification as a consequence of early identification rather than of growing conservatism with age seems to hold. But we have found no data on patterns of issue support. The Inglehart study warns of inter-generational value conflict brewing in five European countries, but there is no evidence on how the value priorities examined affect issue voting, if indeed they do. We might add that his data could be used to argue more for a subculture of the very young, and only the well-educated very young at that, rather than for a subculture of aging. It is the youngest group (16 to 24) that is the most out of line with the rest of the age profile on value priorities. We can, however, make no inferences at all about diachronic solidarity for other countries in relation to political orientations and attitudes.

POLITICAL BEHAVIOR

To be old does not seem in itself to have much influence on political attitudes. To express one's preferences to a public opinion pollster carries little political weight unless it is accompanied by action. We turn now to whether the elderly continue to be active in political life and, if so, how. We will look at several types of political activities, some presumed more consequential than others, and make interpretations in the light of the collective findings.

Political Interest
in the United States

To begin with the broadest and most general question, information available from the United States indicates that political interest not only does not dissipate with aging but increases throughout adult life (Hudson & Binstock 1976; Hendricks & Hendricks 1977:335). By political interest we mean simply self-reported level of interest in and voluntary exposure to political stimuli through the mass media and other channels. Data from a 1960 Gallup poll (Glenn & Grimes 1968) quite clearly demonstrate a linear relationship between age and political interest. As age increases, so does political interest. We have to remember that these are cohort data, meaning that we are looking at different people in several age strata at one time. Longitudinal data would allow us to follow the same people over the life course as they move from age stratum to age stratum. With such data, we would feel more confident in relating differences to the aging process, rather than possible variations by specific cohorts in how they behave politically. Unfortunately, most of the data on political behavior come from studies of cohorts so this is what we will have to use.

In the 1960 cohort data, the lowest level of political interest is among those aged twenty-one to thirty-nine, and the level increases steadily to its highest point among those sixty and older. The relationship between age and political interest holds even when age and sex are controlled for. Those with higher educational attainments usually are somewhat more likely within each age group to report higher political interest, as are males. The one exception to the findings on sex differences is among the oldest females with the most education who outdistance the males in the corresponding cell. This group displays the highest level of political interest of all the subgroups. Unfortunately, there are no refined age breakdowns within the group of sixty and over, so that it is almost impossible to tell from these data whether and at what point political interest might begin to decline again in very old age. Given the overall high level expressed by those sixty and over, a group that has many members who are very old indeed, it seems safe to attribute a sustained interest to the end of life to a sizable proportion.

Political Behavior
in the United States

In actual voting behavior, that is, going to the polls and casting a ballot, there is a somewhat different curve (Olsen 1972; Glenn 1974; Hudson & Binstock 1976: 375-77). Voting behavior does increase with age but tends to reach a peak in late middle age and decline after age sixty. The decline, however, is relatively mild and never descends to the low levels of those in their twenties and thirties. But why do older people express more interest in politics, yet turn up less frequently at the polls? Here we do have more refined data with which to work. Data available on national voting behavior in the United States in 1972 (Hendricks & Hendricks 1977:341) were broken down into fairly discrete age groups and also controlled by sex. From this analysis, it was discovered that the decline in voting could be explained partly by the disproportionately larger number of females in the oldest age groups. Politically interested or not, women received the franchise to vote much later than men did and have traditionally lagged behind men in participation after the franchise was granted. If males only are compared across age groups, there is a steady increase in voting participation by age which reaches its peak among men aged sixty-five to seventy-four. Only after age seventy-five is there a slight decline. Examining the trends among women in the 1972 data, it can be seen that, except in the very youngest age groups, they consistently participate at a lower rate than men do. Also, their participation at the polls peaks between ages forty-five and sixty-four and declines thereafter. Lower educational levels among the oldest age groups also are seen as contributing to voting decline. We suspect that there are other factors that make it quite possible to sustain high political interest and yet not be able to get to the polls. To be ill, to be poor, and especially to be both, may interfere with the opportunity to formally register a political preference.

All things considered, the voting behavior of older people does not support the notion that aging is related to political disengagement. Any decline in aggregate participation may be attributed to sex, education, and other barriers inherent in the aging process. The influence of sex may well change over time. Younger women are more likely to take the right to vote for granted, and their increased work role participation also may stimulate voting behavior. Already in the youngest age groups, the 1972 data showed women to be a bit more active than the men were in this respect. Educational levels also seem bound to increase among the cohorts moving into the old-age brackets. Nevertheless, declining health and other resources doubtlessly will inhibit political activity at least among the very old.

This contention is borne out by data that show that for the more active forms of political behavior, such as campaign involvement, the decline in participation is more noticeable with increasing age. Working in behalf of a candidate, being active in community organizations, and contacting public officials are on their highest levels among those in late middle age, but involvement in such activities drops markedly after age sixty. Again, this picture could change if women became more politically active and if the educational level of the oldest cohort rose. It seems reasonable, however, to argue that the decrements of age will continue to affect high-energy political involvements, as compared with the more passive and infrequent act of voting. Even here, however, old people are clearly more likely to be active than are the relatively apathetic young of this country.

Political Leadership
in the United States

In the most active political role of all, national leadership, the participation of the aging and the aged is striking. Older people are the best represented of all adult age groups among the elite who play strategic roles in the polity (North & Pool 1966; Riley & Foner 1968:495-97; Hudson & Binstock 1976:378). National political leaders are likely to be well into middle age when they attain their first position.

In the United States, the biggest age group in control of national political positions is that aged fifty to seventy. Until now, individuals are most likely to serve as presidents, cabinet ministers, or ambassadors between the ages of fifty and fifty-nine, although substantial proportions continue to serve well into their sixties. The evidence also points to rising age levels in those positions in more recent times. Supreme Court justices also are typically appointed between ages fifty-five and fifty-nine, but the majority continues to serve well beyond age sixty-five, and some have persevered beyond age ninety. Supreme Court justices are appointed for life and need not turn to the electorate for support, but the elective process in itself has not prevented sizable proportions of senators and representatives from holding office into advanced old age. In fact, the proportions of people sixty-five years of age or older among top public officials (elected or appointed) are far higher than those to be found in most other occupational sectors. This preference for selecting political leaders from the more "seasoned" age groups in the population seems most peculiar in a culture described as youth-oriented and ageist.

But why should the political arena be exempt from the exclusion of old people? It has been found that older incumbents of high political office do not appear to think much differently from their somewhat younger counterparts. They are neither more conservative on issues nor more likely to orient themselves to age-based interests and constituencies. Like other national leaders, they pay attention to national issues and the concerns of their constituencies in all age groups. In other words, old politicians cannot be distinguished in thought or deed from the rest of the leaders. This, however, need not be readily discernible to the population at large. In fact, ageism should be directed simply to chronological age. Negative stereotyping decrees that "old is old" with no respect for individual capacities. Yet there has been little complaint about aging politicians. The idea has been advanced that an aging elite symbolizes continuity and stability and appeals to the electorate on these grounds. If this is so, it rather fits our notions of functions that old people can provide for the nation.

In times of rapid change and uncertainty, old people leading the state signify that there is a continuity in national affairs. We certainly do seem to worry much more about whether someone is "too young" rather than "too old" to cope with the responsibiity of high office. To be sure, we are concerned about the relative health and vigor of our presidents especially. Death of the holder of that highest office is traumatic for the national psyche, as we have learned. Even so, no formal upper limit for incumbency in that office has been imposed to match the lower one. Those older people who have the capacity and the willingness to carry on in national office appear often able to do so well beyond the age defined as old.

We have seen that older citizens in this country have to be considered politically active as a group. Their interest is the highest of all age groups. Men, at least, also turn out at the polls well beyond retirement age, peaking in fact between ages sixty-five to seventy-four. That the overall curve after sixty-five declines is largely explained by the lower participation of women. In the more intensive political activities, the impact of age is more visible. It appears that we can most expect involvement of old people in those areas that do not require a sustained physical effort. Yet even here many more old people are engaged proportionately more than the presumably far more vigorous young. Any decline in activity can hardly be attributed to apathy as with younger people who are neither very active nor even very interested. It is quite apparent that the oldest people do feel a responsibility to keep up with political affairs, which outstrips that of all younger groups. In the most vital area of political life, national leadership, older people, including many who are very old, are well represented. For some, holding office late in life is a direct result of the "people's choice." For others, tenure in office may stem from presidential appointment. In either case, trust that our elders can carry the responsibilities of high office is surely indicated.

It is remarkable how faithfully this general pattern of political behavior among older people is reflected in the findings from other countries. Havighurst and others (1969) studied two occupational groups, belonging to the middle class and the working class, respectively, in Austria, Germany, Italy, the Netherlands, Poland, and the United States. In each country the samples, which were small but carefully selected, consisted of males in their seventies. The researchers measured the activity levels of the men sampled in twelve different social roles. In most areas, the cross-national differences in types and levels of participation in the social roles were impressive. But there was one exception. Levels of participation in the political role were strikingly similar in all countries. Since the data on the contents of this role were not presented in any detail, we have to assume that the similarity between the other countries and the United States reflects the patterns presented earlier in some detail. The men in their seventies then would be at the peak of political interest, still active in voting but less so in more intensive activities.

There were no direct comparisons in these countries with other age groups or with women. Nie, Verba, and Kim (1974) did supply this kind of information from a study of five nations. This group of nations can be considered more varied in contrast to the Western democracies surveyed by Havighurst and others. Asian and African nations were included in the study, and national sampling was carried out in Austria, India, Japan, Nigeria, and the United States. The heterogeneity of the sample of countries was deliberately planned. The authors wanted to include nations with very different patterns of historical experiences. They stated:

> If we find uniformity in relationship between political activities and age across these nations, it is unlikely that such uniformity was produced by uniform generational experiences. It is far more likely that such uniformity reflects the uniform impact of age (Nie, Verba, & Kim 1974:322).

Clearly, they hoped to be able to make a case for age as the explanatory variable for levels of political activity by comparing countries in which cohort experiences would have been quite different.

On the whole, the results supported the argument. The data were analyzed by dividing the national samples into five age strata: the twenties, thirties, forties, fifties, and sixties and over. With only very minor variations, parallel patterns by age were found in all countries. Participation was lowest in the twenties, rose through the early years, and peaked in the fifties. In the age group sixty and over, activity declined, although it remained higher than in the twenties and thirties. This pattern holds for both sexes, but women consistently participated less than men did. The greatest gap between the sexes occurred in India, followed closely by Japan and Austria. In Nigeria and especially in the United States the "sex gap" was much narrower. There was very good evidence overall for a uniform pattern by age regardless of country.

We should comment about the universal decline in activity after sixty. In this study, the major scale of political activity was based on campaign efforts, participation in community projects, and individually initiated contacts with public officials. Voting was not included. The rationale for excluding voting behavior was that it is the most passive and the least important of political activities. Also, including voting could discriminate against those in their twenties who would be more likely to have difficulties in meeting residence requirements. To dismiss voting in this summary fashion seems to neglect that voting is considered both a right and a duty of citizens in democratic countries. To express one's social membership in this way does not deserve to be denigrated. In their zeal to protect the young from discrimination, then, the authors may have artificially decreased the political role of the elderly, for many of whom the less energy-consuming task of casting a ballot may be the only feasible form of political action.

Another problem is that there was no breakdown by relative age within the group sixty and over. For this group, then, we are looking not at a decade of the life cycle but rather, a span of twenty or thirty years. There is no way of telling whether a rise still might have occurred among the less older men and then been offset by those of very advanced age. Voting behavior was measured separate from the major scale, and the authors did find that voting patterns declined less sharply among those over sixty. Also, when only males were considered and education was controlled for, even the more active political activities for the over-sixty group were on or above the mean level for all males.

There were at least some clues that some age range of older males actually increased their activity level compared to those in middle age, if voting were counted and if allowances were made for those with the least education. In this connection and in accounting for universal sex differences, we should question whether these patterns are determined only by age. If succeeding generations moving toward old age are better educated, as it appears they will be, and if women become more regular political actors, the profiles by age and activity level will probably change. Even more investment in political life by those who have been freed from mid-life obligations might well be the result.

The consistency of political behavior and aging participation in other modern nations also extends to national leadership. In other countries, too, national political leaders are likely to attain their first office after they are well into middle age. Except in times of revolutionary change, in most countries, disproportionate numbers of leaders who are in late middle age and early old age were found. Often the very top positions are held by very old persons, many years beyond the general age for retirement. This connection between aging and political power has been found not only in the West but also in the Soviet Union and China (Blackwell 1974; North & Pool 1966:383). Schlesinger (1969) found a roughly similar pattern when he compared legislative data for five European countries with that discussed earlier for the United States. It therefore holds that the political arena is one in all countries in which the aging and the aged occupy high leadership positions.

If the elderly are obsolete or unwanted, they do not seem to feel it, at least not in fullfilling their duties as citizens. Not only in the United States but in all countries for which data could be supplied, political activity is high. There is no evidence of subjective abandonment. Even in key national positions, since old people everywhere are highly visible, there is little to support the position of age discrimination in political life. On the contrary, whether they are elected or appointed, there is apparently social demand for old people which is more likely to be found here than in other spheres of life.

Compared to younger people of all ages, there is some evidence for reengagement in interest and in voting patterns, especially for older males below age seventy-five. We cannot consider this liberation, however, since it does not extend to the more intensive forms of political activity. Old people cannot be seen as using their new freedom to throw themselves into political life with exceptional vigor, compared with the still structurally restrained middle aged.

In the area of leadership some case can be made for diachronic solidarity. If the presence of "gray heads" among the national leaders does indeed reassure the public that the country will survive despite social change and other threats to national stability, then this is an expression of the need to preserve continuity. Younger people are saying to aging leaders, in effect: "We want to perpetuate our way of life." The aging leadership responds in kind by concern with the issues that affect all the generations, rather than only those affecting their own cohort.

INTERGENERATIONAL CONFLICT
OR COOPERATION

The concept of ageism cannot be easily dismissed. It may be operating, as some contend, to sanction the relative economic disprivilege of older people. As we saw in the last chapter, a sizable proportion of older people can be classified as abandoned because they have had to suffer more than acceptable erosion of the life style they enjoyed when younger, and because they do not share the rising standards for the rest of the population at a given time. This is particularly glaring in the United States, where the standard of living of the population is unusually high. Many other countries, by comparison, take better care of their old people. Perhaps this is why ageism has been studied far more in the United States. If younger people do in fact view those in late life as "social rejects," this may lead to an unwillingness to give up anything for their support. This is one form that intergenerational conflict could take, pitting the younger against the oldest groups in the scramble for a share of the nation's goods and services. We will begin our discussion of conflict and cooperation in this area, using the case of the United States only.

Ageist Attitudes

Much has been made of the negative social labeling of old people in our society (Martin 1973; Kuypers & Bengston 1973). In a review of findings of perceptions of the elderly, both social and individual, a rather staggering composite picture was drawn:

> [Old people] . . . are generally seen as ill, tired, not sexually interested, mentally slower, forgetful and less able to learn new things, grouchy, withdrawn, feeling sorry for themselves, less likely to participate in activities (except perhaps in religion), isolated, in the least happy or fortunate time of their life, unproductive, and defensive, in various combinations and with varying emphases (McTavish 1971:97).

After taking a closer look, however, one wonders how to interpret such a picture. First, most of the studies were made using relatively small groups from that much overworked population for research purposes, college students. Thus, what we have mostly came from the well-educated young, undergraduates in their late teens and early twenties. Secondly, there is an obvious admixture in the items in the surveys between what seem to be personal traits of older persons and items more accurately described as related to the social condition of that population group. It is a very different proposition to say that old people are disliked by the rest of us than to say that they are more likely to be found among the unfortunates of our society.

Some recent investigators have asserted that ageist attitudes vary by age group, contain mixtures of positive as well as negative attributions, and need to be sorted out as to whether they refer to traits or to life conditions (Bell & Stanfield 1973; Thorsen, Wheatley, & Hancock 1974; Brubaker & Powers 1976). In our opinion, it may make a huge difference in political implications to distinguish between traits and conditions. If older people are rejected because they are perceived as sharing certain devalued traits in our society, that is ageism. But if much of so-called ageism actually centers on deploring the conditions under which many old people live, this actually might mobilize the population to support an improvement in their life style, especially if younger adults expect to receive the same social rights in their turn.

The extensive national poll carried out by Louis Harris and his associates (1975) offers us some clues. This poll seems to be the most recent measure of ageism, and we can distinguish between personal dimensions and social conditions from the data offered. Negative personal attributes certainly were ascribed to older people by younger generations. Dividing the sampled populations into two age groups for general analysis purposes, it was found that the younger (18 to 64), were more likely than the older (sixty-five and over) to agree that "most people over 65" were unalert, closed minded, and unproductive. Finer breakdown showed that the youngest group in the sample was the most likely to endorse these negative stereotypes and that their responses were in sharpest contrast to what the oldest group said about "most people over 65." In other words, there was the most willingness to see old people in a negative light among very young adults, but this response tended to decrease among older age groups. Those over sixty-five were the least likely to agree.

When members of the oldest group were asked not about "most people over 65" but to describe themselves personally, the picture changed. Although they tended to agree that most of their agemates were not like this, they saw themselves as "bright and alert," "open-minded and adaptable," and "good at getting things done." There was, then, some agreement that old people are likely to possess certain negative traits, but the degree of agreement receded as age advanced. Those over sixty-five did not accept the negative stereotypes for themselves.

At the same time, there also were some positive stereotypes that were shared across the age spectrum. All age groups tended to agree that most people over sixty-five were "very wise from experience." Again, the very youngest group was the least sure, but even a large majority of them agreed, and the consensus built as age increased. Interestingly enough, all age groups except those who themselves were sixty-five and over, solidly agreed that most older people were "very warm and friendly." The oldest group was the least likely to see themselves in this apparently positive light. Overall, the picture was mixed and on balance more negative than positive.

All in all, it appears that most everybody agreed that most old people slow down and become more rigid but at the same time have accumulated wisdom and a certain empathy which allows them to be warm and friendly to others. The life-cycle consensus on these points is hardly complete but is more interesting for general agreement than for the variations in subscription. Old people themselves were the least likely to accept the stereotypes, either negative or positive, with the exception of "very wise from experience." Asked about their own attributes, they seemed to identify more with activist mainstream values, and perhaps this is also why they did not especially endorse "very warm and friendly" even for their agemates. Still, since most younger people tended to devalue old people along activist dimensions, one could infer that they saw most old people as rather useless and not entitled to political support.

Political Support

Before we can explore that possibility further, the Harris data can be broken down to show that younger people, far more than the elderly themselves, see old age as a time of social disadvantage. People of all ages thought that health was the worst problem, but the younger generations (18 to 65) believed that loneliness, financial deficiencies, lack of independence, and social rejection were far more prevalent in old age than the oldest group itself did. The aura of illness, poverty, and social deprivation was even more pronounced than the attributions of negative traits. It may even be that those younger than sixty-five think that the elderly "are the way they are" in personal traits because of the social deprivation they suffer. In all age groups almost everybody agreed that there are some advantages to being old, especially in terms of having increased leisure and freedom from the imposed obligations of mid-life. Presumably, however, even these advantages can be enjoyed only if social conditions permit.

However the connection is made in people's minds between character traits and social disadvantage, and between the latter and the ability to enjoy what privileges exist, the political consequences are most interesting, as illustrated by the Harris data. Although the authors of the report on the poll deplored the images of old age in the mass media as presenting a far too negative picture of old age, which results in the acceptance of negative stereotypes even by the elderly of their own agemates to some extent, the overt consequences appeared to be political support mobilization. Rather than generational conflict, the data from the poll showed younger generations as willing to cooperate in obtaining for the elderly better benefits and opportunities. For example, there was a strong public mandate to roll back guidelines forcing people to retire at a certain age. Eighty-six percent of the sample was opposed to forcing anyone to retire because of age. At the same time, a similar consensus upheld the right of those who choose to retire or are no longer able to work to turn to the government for financial support. Note that "choosing" to retire is supported, regardless of whether or not there is physical infirmity. Sixty-eight percent of the total sample agreed that the federal government should provide the necessary income through social security. It is possible that support of this item was artificially low simply because of the emphasis on social security as the only means of providing income.

The idea that government with its powers of taxation has both the responsibility and the means to support older people was endorsed by a much larger proportion of 81 percent of the total sample. Some of the people included here but not in the previous item may have seen alternative modes of taxation as the route to support for the retired. On all of the above items, the support given by those under sixty-five was as high or higher than that given by the sixty-five and older group. The public represented here by a "vote" of 76 percent in favor agreed that old people should receive enough money to live comfortably in old age regardless of their previous earnings. This agreement seems to signify that we care about the aged as members of our society regardless of achievement. Finally, an overwhelming 97 percent of the total sample supported cost-of-living escalator clauses in social security payments.

These statistics make it clear that the population as a whole supports improved conditions for old people, knowing quite well that the means for improvement will have to come out of their own tax dollars. The items in the poll referred to taxes much too regularly for those who answered them to be able to avoid this hard fact. Thus, although the elderly were seen as relatively useless, they also were seen as deprived. However these two concepts are related in the public mind, those polled of all ages were behind government intervention on the behalf of the aged. They thought that the elderly had a right to a better life, and the younger were willing to support that right. We have seen some evidence of ageism, but it does not lead in the direction of abandonment when political issues are involved. Just as in the stand taken on health care, younger people back those over sixty-five on retirement and financial benefits.

Politics of Age-Based Groups

In the United States.   We can see more evidence of intergenerational coop-eration in the politics of age-based organizations and interest groups, and here there are some findings from other nations. To turn to the United States first, the questions center on how much of a political force such organizations and groups have and whether they act as a cohesive bloc to influence legislation.

There have been scattered political movements based on age in our history, especially in the era preceding the passage of social security legislation (Riley & Foner 1968:478-79; Putnam 1970; Pratt 1976). These earlier movements focused on a single issue, old age pensions, and disintegrated when the relevant legislation was passed. The associated organizations were aligned with one another in creating political pressure toward a common goal. Although they certainly helped to shape political debate and had access to legislators who listened to their views, it seems apparent that the passage of social security legislation depended heavily on the support of other nonage interests. The success of the cause, then, was not due as much to an aged-based bloc of organizations acting in concert as it was to the more general mobilization of public support.

Pratt (1974) saw these earlier age-based organizations as only the beginning of a general "politization of aging" in the twentieth century. Although the variety of interests has increased in terms of groups to be found on the national scene today, all are a part of the same general movement with the common theme of aging. Changes in both the age structure and the social structure of modern societies have made the old more visible. In consequence, the nonaged as well as the aged have become involved. Some age-based organizations actually depend for their memberships on younger people who claim to be working in behalf of the elderly by providing services or carrying out gerontological research. The organizations, then, represent a variety of purposes and perspec-tives. Yet Pratt believes that all age-based organizations, each in its own way, contribute to the development of increasingly benign public views of old age.

Binstock (1972) had a somewhat different view of the scene. He found that the variety of groups operating today is more competitive than cooperative. Rather than working for one broad cause, he argued, the goal for each identifiable organization was to be the loudest voice in the aging field, thus forcing other age-based groups into the background. Common to both these views, however, is the acceptance of aging as a lively and many-faceted political arena today.

There also was agreement that none of the age-based political organizations actually could deliver large blocs of votes, even when their memberships were numerically very impressive. To cite only those which actually depend on old people themselves as members, millions of people belong to such groups as the National Council of Senior Citizens, the National Retired Teachers Association, and the American Association of Retired Persons. Such groups obviously represent an implicit force that any astute politician would hesitate to alienate. But organizations like these have not actually put that force to any kind of test at the polls. Citing membership statistics is more in the nature of a bluff that could be called. Extensive studies in this country have uncovered no evidence that potentially powerful, national age-based organizations have been able to mobilize the votes of their members to affect the fate of a particular proposition, candidate, or party. The patterns of voting behavior in any age group, as we have seen, are much too complex to anticipate that mere affiliation with one organization will be sufficient to ensure membership backing for the beliefs of that organization.

It is highly doubtful, then, that age-based organizations can really "deliver the vote" even of their own memberships. Nor do the organizations per se behave as a bloc. They seldom, in fact, seem to see eye to eye when promoting specific benefits, programs, or services. There is neither the internal cohesion nor the concerted action among organizations, except perhaps to keep the theme of aging prominent in national affairs, which would sufficiently explain the increasing benefits that have accrued to the elderly in recent years.

Rather, it is much more probable that historical, cultural, and ideological forces in the wake of social change have combined to bring about national agreement that "something must be done" in terms of social intervention for the elderly (Hudson & Binstock 1976:392). Many disparate groups in political life have joined forces to support this cause. Age-based organizations can be and are influential in keeping the cause alive, but they must have strong cooperation from other groups to bring about an effective federal response. Again, we have to conclude that what is happening is not a conflict between special old-age interests and other political pressure groups but rather general cooperation among diverse groups, backed up by the kind of public support demonstrated by the Harris data.

In other countries.   Available information shows the politics of aging to be much the same elsewhere. In Denmark, in Great Britain, in Sweden, and in the Netherlands, researchers have documented the growth of potentially powerful, age-based interest groups with huge memberships (Friis 1969; Finer 1958;

Havighurst 1960). As in the United States, concomitant with this development, the elderly have received increasing national attention and more and better benefits from the government. But Heclo (1974) found no evidence that these groups were directly influencing voting on issues or candidates, at least in Sweden and Great Britain. The results of his study supported the findings from the United States. Again, the membership of the age-based organizations did not act as a concerted body at the polls, nor did the several organizations with a specific base in aging always unite around the same or even simiar themes. Age-based organizations abroad as in this country have influence, but it takes the combined support of other pressure groups, backed up by general public approval, to explain the unusual beneficence toward the elderly of national legislators in recent times.

Cross-cultural information, then, leads us to believe that age-based pressure groups are only a part of a general societal movement to intervene in behalf of old people. Perhaps individual interest groups do compete among themselves even when they all are supposed to be working for the same cause. On a broader level, there is a real sense of cooperation. One can question whether that cooperation is firm enough to be sustained when national growth rates are stagnating and the proportion of elderly persons continues to rise.

Intergenerational Conflict

In the United States Hudson (1978) proposed that the consensus behind improving the social welfare of old people in this country is being destroyed. In his opinion, the widespread belief that old people are singularly disadvantaged by low income, poor health, and a particular vulnerability associated with their stage in the life cycle temporarily held that consensus together. But public policies aimed toward the elderly have improved their aggregate well-being. Consequently, their status has risen relative to younger disadvantaged groups, who now will begin to pressure for equity. If so, we are entering a phase in which intergenerational conflict will increase, especially if total resources come to be seen as more and more limited. We may have been documenting an era of support for the aging that already is passing into history.

But a skeptical note must be introduced for regarding the elderly as just one of a number of disadvantaged groups. The aged are a minority group statistically, but they are a minority group with a difference. That group is one that everyone who listens to statistics on longevity can fully expect to join one day. Since those who are now old in that sense represent everyone's fate or future, common cause for that particular group may have remarkable staying power.

From what has been happening until now, we can add one more item to this exploration of intergenerational conflict. It is possible that the positions that people take on issues and the operation of interest groups in political affairs mask generational differences that are more subtle and at the same time have greater importance. Differences in value orientations among age groups may not be immediately discernible in measurable political behavior, yet could eventually have an explosive impact on political life. Studies of value orientations are not easy to find, and what people choose to select as important values to probe vary from study to study. Not even those that do receive attention would be accepted by everyone as really central to a given society.

Recent studies in the United States have attempted to explore the relative distance between age groups on both general and specific levels by contrasting three groups representing three generations: youth, middle age, and old age. On the general level, the concept of the "generation gap" was the focus (Hitt and others 1970; Bengston 1971). Representatives of each of the generations were asked to estimate their closeness to the other two. Youth saw the least closeness or the widest gap between themselves and other age groups; those in old age perceived the narrowest intergenerational differences. All groups perceived considerable distance. It is difficult to gauge the significance of this evidence for the generation gap or in this case, more accurately, gaps. The perceived gaps become very much smaller when people are asked about the closeness among the three generations in their own families, rather than in the society at large. In the abstract, then, the gaps appear sizable to all three age groups, but they shrink when specific social relationships become the focus.

When selected value orientations rather than perceived closeness were measured, the generations did not really seem to be at odds. Elderly parents and their middle-aged children were in agreement in their views on fatalism, optimism, and individualism versus collectivism. These two generations differed significantly only on child-rearing principles and materialism versus humanism. When the youngest generation was added into the analysis, their value orientation emphases tended to cut across those of the two older generations. They shared some orientatic s with their grandparents only, some with their parents only, and some with both older generations. There is no value in which at least two generations were not aligned. At least two and often all three were in close agreement. Even the differences that did exist are a matter of degree rather than of sharp contrasts.

Bengston and Cutler (1976:148-50) concluded that the generation gap is more imaginary than real. The vague perceptions of gaps in the larger society, held especially by the youngest generation, are not reflected in their descriptions of their own families. For values, there was more consensus than conflict. Certainly there was nothing like perfect harmony, but even the widest age gap, that between old age and youth, was bridged by shared beliefs. Each generation has had its own historical experiences. This may be why there were some differences here and there. Probably any "time cut" would reveal some disagreements among the generations. But this does not mean that the value constellation as a whole was disturbed or that new cohorts coming along would not revise the picture. In this study it is clear that sometimes the wheel "comes full circle," for old age and youth agreed, although middle age was somewhat out of line with both. The social climate of a particular period also had an influence which may not necessarily last. We suggest, for example, that the dissent of the sixties in the United States was more a reflection of events that affected youth disproportionately in that decade. It was not, however, necessarily a sign that the young of this country were on a permanent collision course with the middle aged and the old.

In other countries.   The same argument can be made for the study of six European countries, mentioned before. Inglehart (1971) proposed that his results showed a value conflict to be developing between old and young in Belgium, France, Germany, Italy, and the Netherlands, although not in Great Britain. He measured just one value orientation which he called "acquisitiveness" or bourgeois materialism. His samples were given four items and were allowed to choose two of the four as value priorities. Two of the items stressed economic issues, the other two political rights and freedom. The findings showed increasingly stronger identification with the "nonbourgeois" priorities on rights and freedoms as age declined. The samples from the six countries were divided into six age groups. The increase was very small as one moved from age group to age group by decreasing age, and not always perfectly reflected, but there was a definite overall trend. Inglehart argued that the young have been socialized in a climate of sustained affluence and take economic security for granted. Their elders, however, grew up in less secure times and still are preoccupied with material matters. On this basis, even though only a minority even among the very young as yet give priority to nonbourgeois values, he felt that a serious clash was in the making. If the younger generations coming along are more and more unaffected by acquisitiveness, they eventually will engage in political combat with their elders to effect social change.

This prediction has some flaws. First, it assumes continued affluence so that future youth cohorts increasingly will eschew materialism. We need not belabor the dubiousness of this assumption. But even if it should prove correct, the gradual change, which has been graphed by Inglehart age category by age category indicates a possible value shift, very slowly realized, rather than any young-old confrontation. As the data stand, there is much more evidence of social consensus than of conflict. The majorities of all age groups agree with one another on priorities. A "social escalator" on which new age cohorts enter political life as old cohorts exit would dissipate any conflict even if nonbourgeois values do continue to increase among the young. On this one value dimension at least, it seems that in European countries also, the generation gap does not really exist. There seems to be no very solid reason to argue that either in the United States or elsewhere there is or will be age-based political warfare based on value conflict. On the contrary, intergenerational solidarity on basic themes seems to be holding well. All the generations belong to one and the same social identity prevalent in the nation.

We have found some reason to believe that ageism exists in the United States.

Many of the negative attributions, however, seem to be related to perceiving old people as socially disadvantaged rather than as personally unattractive. The impression of social disadvantage is translated into a willingness among the younger to help the older obtain from the government more adequate benefits and services, not the withdrawal of concern that ageist attitudes are expected to produce. The Harris poll consistently supports the contention that the younger are prepared to support a better life for their elders. The pattern of intergenerational cooperation in improved conditions for senior citizens also was reflected in the discussion of age-based organizations here and abroad. These organizations do have political influence but not the cohesive clout that would explain the ever increasing public resources given to the old over this century. Rather, the largesse of legislators must be attributed to the support of diverse pressure groups and to the consensus of the people generally that this is a priority social cause. That younger generations do identify with the older on social rights for the aged is an expression of diachronic solidarity. It seems to have survived from generation to generation over many years as the once young have grown old and new young have moved into place. Perhaps, however, this is not a social concensus that will continue given the economic crunch. If so, only a slice of "preserving social rights in perpetuity" has been uncovered but is not a truly lasting contract.

But the aged are a group with whom all can identify since they symbolize the future of us all. On this basis, popular support may resist erosion in this cause more than all others. Even "generation gap" studies do not reveal any likelihood of social identity being lost through age-linked conflicts. The data in this area come largely from studies of the turbulent sixties when the alienation of youth was seen as a national crisis in the United States and in other countries as well. Things seem calmer now. But even then, value consensus among the generations was evident, testifying to social continuity despite social change. The old are still with us in spirit. The young do not repudiate existing values. Support for the elders seems to rest on the firm ground of solidarity with no serious fissures in sight.

CITIZENSHIP AND SOCIAL IDENTITY

Citizenship is not granted because of what one does but because of who one is, an accepted member of a particular society. How the citizen's duties are carried out in late life show the limits of achievement in defining our social selves. We are not just what we contribute in the marketplace, not just cogs in a bureaucratic wheel which pulls us in and spins us out at will. We belong in a much more fundamental sense, and this is apparent in our continuous right to exercise political judgment, whether employed or not. Old people, most of whom are retired if indeed they ever worked formally at all, still are citizens, and they show that they understand this. They are active in the political life of all societies we have examined. The continuing involvement of old people amounts to a cultural universal in democratic industrial societies. They are very well represented in political participation of various types. The point of continuing social involvement beyond achievement is underscored because men, who are more likely to have received the coup de grace of formal retirement, are also the more engaged actors. There is no evidence that work withdrawal makes persons feel politically useless. There is no sign of abandonment in the sense of subjective disenfranchisement. If the old feel unwanted in political life, it is not reflected in their behavior. No one attempts to remove their political rights, and they do not relinquish them voluntarily.

Physical decline and other obstacles in old age eventually may force the reduction or perhaps even the cessation of activities. But this is a different matter. Social discrimination, it was said, could be manifested in two ways. Old people could feel rejected by younger generations and move out of the political arena. This does not happen. But they could also stay engaged as a defensive action. Knowing themselves to be devalued by a younger population which was indifferent to their concerns, old people might mobilize as a subgroup to protect their own interests. They would then think and act like societal "strangers" demonstrating deviant political attitudes.

At first glance, being identified as "more conservative" than the rest of the adult population looks like a move in that direction. But in the United States as well as in other countries, more conservative simply is defined as more likely to belong to the most conservative party available on the particular national scene, which seems to be more a result of historical accident than of a generalized stance on political issues. At least in the United States, detailed data show little impact of greater conservative affiliation on actual thinking about specific issues. People over sixty-five sometimes are a little to the right and sometimes a little to the left of younger adults. But the differences are generally small and not very stable over time. Age groups swing in and out of line with one another as cohorts and in response to the general social climate. On the whole, old people are very much in the mainstream in their political attitudes.

There is no identifiable aging subculture. Liberation is no more in evidence than abandonment is. If there were liberation, older people would be more fully engaged than those in earlier life stages because they now would have been released from earlier responsibilities. Although the elderly do exceed the young in their involvement, the highest peak of political activity occurs in late middle life. Only in political interest and, for young-old males, at the ballot box can any signs of a resurgence of political concern after age sixty-five be found. If entering a life stage in which the burdens of work and family are ended or greatly reduced provides a release of energy into more intensive concern with national affairs, it is not very evident. The realities of very old age probably in themselves work against the liberation perspective. There seldom were detailed enough age breakdowns to separate the young old from the old old. Nevertheless, from what is available, it is possible to say that those over sixty-five do not seem as a group to set "good examples" for the rest of the citizenry by reactivating their involvement in political life or by finding new ways to express their concerns.

SUMMARY

The aging and the aged are highly visible in national leadership everywhere. In this most focal of all political activities, discrimination against social elders can hardly be argued. Old politicians may actually symbolize to the citizenry that the identity of the nation continues in spite of social change. They reassure us that our way of life will be sustained in its essentials whatever upheavals may be produced through modernization and global contact. Their relevance to politics as symbols of continuity and stability seems to be supported by our findings on intergenerational conflict.

On value orientations, different generations generally agreed. This suggests that basic social identities persist over time. Although this material is rather sparse and at best suggestive, the operation of diachronic solidarity seems apparent in the support of younger generations for the social rights of the old. Wherever we looked, at public opinion polls or at social movements, the channeling of resources into a better life for the aged which has been gaining momentum over this century can be explained only by a consensus in this area. As the proportion of old people has grown, their benefits have expanded. This beneficence could only have been produced at increasing cost to the taxpayer. Yet the consensus apparently has grown over the last quarter of the century. Younger people agree with older people that social rights of retirement, finances, and health care must be extended to senior citizens. Increasingly, social rights include maintenance of a life style adequate by national standards. Perhaps the cooperation of younger generations can be explained by long-term self-interest.

In modern societies, all of us can expect to grow old and most of us will. Therefore, we extend guarantees to the now old to protect our own futures. We think that there is much more than self-interest involved. Because the aged have become such a visible population group in industrial societies it has made them the appropriate ones to affirm continuity of the collective identity over time. The changes they have witnessed over an extended past and yet been able to survive as part of our national membership today offer living proof that our society will persist. The social rights extended are the formal recognition of our need to believe that social identities transcend individual lives and persist from generation to generation. Some societies, those with the most turbulent and therefore the most insecure pasts, may have a greater need to reassure their members of continuity over time which promises the same for the future. The United States does not provide for its elderly as well as some other nations do, given the relative resources available. A relatively tranquil past, undisturbed by political revolutions or foreign invasions for more than two hundred years, may make this country more confident of the security of the American way of life. Yet even Americans recently have offered a substantially improved "benefit package" to the old. Continuous technological change and troubled world events both economic and geopolitical may increase the need to "hang on to the elderly" as symbols of a past which is also part of the present and which will endure into the future. In this climate we would expect, if our reasoning is correct, that any attempt to reduce benefits to old people would meet concerted resistance everywhere even though the costs are high and rising in all industrial societies.

4

retirement: an emerging social institution

INTRODUCTION

Retirement, as it is understood today, is a relatively new but rapidly spreading phenomenon. Retirement applies to increasingly more people, both in mature industrial societies and in societies still industrializing. A recent review listed 105 nations that have introduced plans for old age, disability, and survivors' benefits (Greenough & King 1976). Definitions of retirement vary, but in economic usage as well as in common parlance, it simply refers to withdrawal from paid employment. Many countries now offer economic assistance to persons who have never been in the paid labor force after they have reached a certain age, but this is not what we understand as retirement. Rather, the term is used to mean that the worker has a right to withdraw from the labor force under certain conditions and to receive a pension in exchange for his or her contributions to the material well-being of society:

> The most essential characteristic of retirement as a social institution is that the norms of society allow an individual by virtue of the work he performed on the job to establish a right to an income without holding a job, and this income in turn gives the individual the opportunity to play the role of the retired person (Atchley 1976:2).

It is this exchange of support for past rather than current work performance that is new. In this chapter the focus in on where, under what conditions, and with what effect, this young institution is operating. Being a new institution and one that affects so many and so much, retirement has been viewed from quite contrary perspectives with very mixed sentiments. There have been fear, pessimism, hope, and optimism. Both the novelty of the institution and the nature of the response to it make it necessary to examine the subject in historical perspective. Information about the work role of older people in preindustrial social orders is a first step for gaining any understanding of retirement in the modern world.

Viewed from the perspective of abandonment, making people retire from work just because of age is to label them obsolete. Only industrialized societies do this; only they have invented mandatory retirement rules on the basis of nothing but the attainment of a certain age. People also retire voluntarily. But the issue of mandatory *or* voluntary retirement has received so much debate recently as to deserve a separate section in this chapter.

According to the perspective of abandonment, retirement is a mechanism to remove those who have not kept up with rapid technological change and a burgeoning body of scientific knowledge. Old people are not released from work as an earned privilege; that is simply a euphemism to hide the real purpose of retirement. In actuality, they are being shoved out of the marketplace against their will to make way for younger, more up-to-date workers. If abandonment is operating, the retired in modern society are in a disprivileged status. Because they are old, they are useless. And because there are proportionately so many of them, some means had to be developed to ensure mass movement out of the labor market for those of advanced age.

By contrast, then, we would expect to find old people being treated with more respect in other types of societies. They would still be " in production" and entitled to the esteem of younger members of society. At the same time, industrialized societies would show a universal mandate to deprive old people of the right to work. In every modern nation, we would expect to find that the aged had vanished from the labor force. And this would really amount to banishment. Old people would be leaving against their will at the behest of an uncaring society. Retirement also would affect other social spheres. Officially labeled as useless, the retired would find doors everywhere closed to them. Ejected from work and socially discriminated against generally, old people would be deprived and isolated. We would expect aging persons to resist retirement and then to react to the inevitable with diminished self-esteem.

Opposing this dismal picture is the perspective of liberation. In this view, retirement is an earned privilege which permits freedom from work and associated routine obligations. The retired symbolize to those still at work that one day release will come. For although mid-life has its rewards, it also has its burdens. Through the institution of retirement, society recognizes long years of contribution to the resources of the nation. Old people move to a privileged status in that they can do things for which younger people never have the time. They are freer to be themselves, to make their own choices, to be in effect, "human again." Liberation, then, would be evident in active and varied participation in social and other leisure activities. This participation might take new forms or it might be expressed by reengagement in spheres of life which had to be neglected in busier middle years. Of course, liberation requires both social opportunities and financial ability to maintain a chosen life style. But when it does occur, we should find the retired expressing pleasure and relief over the release from bureaucratic, routinized, and often dehumanizing work. The effects of such release would then register as high morale and a positive sense of self-worth among the retired.

Besides abandonment and liberation, still a third alternative will be explored. Retirement as an institution can be a reminder to the younger and still working that human worth is not solely measured by contributions to economic productivity. Symbolized by the retired person, that reminder may appear in the form of a social right. By caring for the elderly in retirement, a chain of obligations is set in motion which perpetuates that social right to belong, regardless of economic usefulness. The question, then, is whether retirement operates so as to produce diachronic solidarity in the right to belong to society. If the aged are seen as belonging to society with full rights to financial, health, and social opportunity security, membership identity is divorced from the market mentality with its emphasis on earning one's keep. One kind of evidence for this would be intergenerational consensus on the idea that retirement is a legitimate life phase, with firm national pledges of adequate maintenance. Also, there must be a sense of shared trust, among old and young alike, that the social rights of retirement that are established exist in perpetuity. Those still working must support those in old age in the expectation that younger generations will care for them in turn. To the extent that there are such expectations, we have a measure of diachronic solidarity in commitments to retirement as an institution in society. A further indication would be protest against proposals to reduce rights to retire. Such protest again would have to be a cross-generational phenomenon, with young and old alike resisting efforts to curtail retirement as a right granted to the elderly. This is because such a right, in essence, proclaims two things: first, once a member, always a member; and second, no matter how much change there may be, our way of life will be preserved in its essentials.

Applying the diachronic solidarity perspective to retirement simply means inquiring whether the great increase of the elderly in modern society serves the purpose of assuring all about continuity of those values that men and women use to understand their national way of life. Clearly, the felt need for such assurances as well as using the elderly to satisfy them may vary from nation to nation depending on historical experiences. That is why we will test this perspective along with the other two insofar as available facts permit.

As mentioned above, looking at the facts of retirement from the perspective of abandonment requires a historical approach. The same is true for the family life of older people, a subject discussed in the next chapter. In both areas, the reason why a historical approach seems necessary is simple. The proponents of the abandonment perspective argue for the relative disprivilege of older people in modern society from the vantage point of history. They claim that older people in preindustrial societies were more needed and therefore more honored and better provided for. Examining this claim will be a first step. Having done so, we shall explore retirement rates and policies in industrialized nations. Then we shall present findings about retirees' reactions and adjustments to retirement. One part of such adjustment, and an important one for the three perspectives we use, is the question of whether or not a genuine retirement role has been found. Whether retirement is a social institution depends on whether being retired amounts to playing a social role, with its rights and obligations understood by the retiree and others. Only by answering this question will it be possible to weigh the evidence and to conclude whether and what in the retirement experience points to abandonment, to liberation, or to diachronic solidarity.

OLD PEOPLE AND WORK
IN PREINDUSTRIAL SOCIETIES

It often has been stated that there was no such thing as retirement in preindustrial societies. The implication was that older people were kept at work because they were held in high esteem by younger groups in the population (Cowgill & Holmes 1972). In fact, the story is far more complicated. By and large, the fate of being old in preindustrial societies depended on three things: 1) need or demand for older people, 2) economic surplus or means to support the old, and 3) power possessed by older people through their control of property.

The need or demand for older people was higher in preliterate societies than in those with a written culture. In the former, all knowledge ranging from religion to the provision of material sustenance, from child rearing to treating illness, from distributing goods to problems of authority and leadership rested on knowledge transmitted orally. The older people had absorbed more of this knowledge than the younger people had; that is why they were in demand. With the invention of writing and the keeping of written records, written knowledge could substitute for older people, and dependence on them declined accordingly.

At the same time, preliterate societies also were those with the least capability to produce economic surplus. Although they needed older people more, they also could least afford to keep them alive after age had turned the older person into an economically useless being. Generally, societies having a written culture also produced a greater economic surplus. They, in contrast, needed older people less but could better afford to support them. In addition, when older people kept control over property, a prominent feature only among elite strata, younger people were dependent on their elderly. Let us look at some details.

Preliterate societies usually are divided into two major types, depending on the way people made their living. There were the hunting and gathering societies and the subsistence agriculture societies. Hunters and gatherers relied for their existence on available game and provender such as roots and berries growing wild in their habitats. Subsistence agriculture societies differed mainly because members had learned to preserve seeds and to grow their own crops.

Within both these types there was much variation in the treatment of the aged. By all accounts, one common fact was that few members survived into old age. Life was very hard, and groups often were decimated by famine and disease. At the best of times, there was usually barely enough food for survival. The nomadic existence of the hunters and gatherers was especially precarious. Their livelihood depended on ceaseless migration in search of food. The journeys were likely to kill off the weak and the infirm or the injured. Subsistence agriculture made life a bit more stable and secure, as long as the climate cooperated. Living beyond full maturity was a little more common. But in either type, the chronological age at which physical signs of growing old began, such as gray hairs, wrinkles, and diminishing strength occurred would have been well before forty (Thomlinson 1965). All the information available suggests that people who grew "old" in these terms were not retired. They still were expected to produce a share of the scarce means for survival but were transferred into tasks more suitable to their life stage. This transfer has been considered a "second career" (Clark 1972; Cowgill & Holmes 1972), since it kept old people active.

The other side of the story is that there was no recognized responsibility to care for persons who were not able to continue working (Donahue, Orback, & Pollack 1965). Exactly how it was decided that a person was no longer useful or useful enough, we shall probably never know. Simmons (1945), however, concluded that in eighteen of the thirty-eight cultures he studied, nomadic and agricultural, all old people were neglected or abandoned. Death may have been slower among the nomads than among the agricultural and sedentary people, but the end result was the same.

The Fate of the Elderly in Preliterate Societies

De Beauvoir (1972:38-87) exhaustively worked through the data on preliterate societies in the Human Area Files, and the remaining remarks borrow heavily from her interpretation. Her findings show that there was a relationship, although an imperfect one, between the relative resources of the community and the fate of the older persons. If the ability of the total group to survive was always in question and group life was permanently precarious, older people had little chance of being kept alive. Some societies abandoned their elderly by just leaving them behind, isolating them without food either within or beyond the confines of the community, or putting them to death. In other communities, more or less elaborate ceremonies accompanied the same fate. One cannot conclude that these measures meant that the elderly were despised and that their deaths were caused without regret. What mattered was that the group should continue, and it could not afford to maintain its weakest members. Old people often consented to their own deaths. Sometimes, they even took the initiative in a manner that Emile Durkheim would have called altruistic suicide. For the good of the group, such persons would isolate themselves, refuse food, or commit suicide.

In preliterate cultures, a very common distinction seems to have been made between the young-old and the old-old, or the "gray heads" and the "nearly dead." In all but the most precarious economic situations, the gray heads were likely to be maintained as long as they could make some contribution to their upkeep. They might be expected to eat less or share their bowls with the youngest in the group, but they were not starved. When labor was no longer possible or became minimal, death was almost inevitable.

When the livelihood of the group became more secure and life more settled, and this was most likely to be in agricultural societies, the willingness of the community to support its weaker members increased. If a more settled life also led to richer cultural development, old persons were accorded social esteem. For example, if knowledge of magic and the spirit world, tribal genealogy, technology on crops and water sources and other related lore were valued, the gray heads often played very important roles. With no written accounts, all knowledge was stored in their heads, earning them respect and authority.

De Beauvoir saw such situations as a sort of "golden age" for the older persons. Waning physical strength was not important compared to the preservation of memory and mental acuity, and old people were used as advisors and supervisors. Under these conditions, in which the most respect was accorded, there occasionally was something like retirement. In such cases, even when these exceptional elders lost their powers, they had some chance of still being cared for. But even here, despite their magical and spiritual connections, the nearly dead were likely to be sacrificed once their abilities waned. Such a fate could be assigned to any incapacitated member of society, even an infant, but the very old were the most universally imperiled. Growing old was not a very common experience, but it was a recognized stage in life and did mean special treatment. Such treatment, however, varied greatly, according to commonly recognized bases of social esteem in which age competed with other considerations. Seldom was there anything like retirement, and when it developed, it remained a luxury, something affordable in good times only.

The Fate of the Elderly in Historical Societies

For literate societies with written records, most of the aviilable material comes from so-called historical societies. They had a considerable division of labor with sacred and secular elites, and urban as well as rural upper and lower classes. Here one finds the first beginnings of a "contract" guaranteeing support to the elderly in exchange for their past contributions to society. At this stage, people could rely on domesticated animals. The use of animal dung for fertilization and animal power for tillage increased crop yields sufficient to produce economic surplus. One also finds here the emergence of property rights to economic resources, which favored the elderly at the top of the social hierarchy. Conditions of life were less stringent, and more people lived to mature old age, particularly among the elite strata of society (Lacey 1968). Well-to-do persons with suitable heirs could bequeath ownership rights to lands and herds in return for support and care during their last years (Goody 1976). This is an example of Atchley's (1976:2) concept of the retirement role as a right to an income on the basis of work performed earlier. But that role, then, rested entirely on family agreements, and it was restricted to the few in society who held sufficient property. Most of the population owned no property, and on them fell the heaviest burden of toil, a way of life that permitted very few to survive into old age. Among the unlanded multitudes, the few who survived to old age had to continue working (Donahue, Orback, & Pollack 1960). When no longer able to work, the older person might be cast out to die of starvation. On the whole, poor families were quite unable to care for their older members, once they became too old to contribute to the family's material well-being.

De Beauvoir's (1972:88-215) analysis of historical societies concluded that nowhere in the Western world* did the condition of older people improve in comparison with the most favorable examples from preliterate cultures. De Beauvoir warned that what information has survived from historical societies in written form is limited. Only a small elite could read and write, and what was recorded was mostly about this elite. Still, she used many sources and pieced together the material to provide an extensive description. Although old people no longer could lay claim to be the primary "cultural storehouse" due to experience once written material was available, one still finds that the greater the relative security of people in general was, the better off the elderly were.

At the peak of the early urban civilizations of Greece and Rome, for example, there was a central role for elder statesmen. Again, this group contained a favored few who were honored because of economic prowess symbolized by the ownership of property. Philosophers argued over the merits of giving such power to the old, and myths about honoring age clashed with aversion and ambivalence in practice. Still, the privileged group of elders was not easy to unseat, and they often held on to office until natural death—or sometimes assassination—intervened. These civilizations declined, as the "barbarian hordes" reversed their history of conquest. There followed a period of savage conflict which made

---

*Several writers including De Beauvoir have found that the East was more respectful and considerate of old people in agricultural settings than the West was (Chandler 1959; Plath 1972). Although noting this as another variation in the experience of old people, we confine our remarks to Western historical societies simply because more information is accessible.

youth and strength supremely important to survival. There was no place for "useless mouths," and physical decline meant abandonment or being put to death.

The advent of Christianity, despite its professed concern for the poor and unfortunate, did not immediately improve life for older people. The infant church was preoccupied with gaining converts, sometimes at the cost of subverting its own principles. As it matured, however, the church offered alms to the orphaned, incapacitated, and aged. The concern of the church symbolized the inadequacy of the kinship system to care for all of its members.

Apart from the family, the charity of the church was the only recourse for those unable to care for themselves in old age. The early Middle Ages were turbulent, and the old were completely shut off from public life. Few public figures can be found who were not in early maturity. Indeed, feudal society was harsh even for the able-bodied. The young who managed to survive infancy were put to work early, and the few old people frequently had no alternative but to turn to begging.

In the sixteenth and seventeenth centuries, the life chances of the elderly improved somewhat. Changing social conditions extended the length of life, and during the Renaissance one finds more concern for older people. Some of the aged were better cared for, especially in the propertied classes. There also is evidence that poorer families tried to care for their elderly, but still a significant proportion of the older population often was without shelter and on the verge of starvation. The church increased its efforts and initiated institutional care in the form of almshouses.

The state also began to participate in caring for the elderly. The first legislation appeared in England with the introduction of the Elizabethan Poor Laws in 1603. These laws required caring for the indigent, and therefore many older persons, by assigning parishes the right to collect and distribute the poor-rates, equivalent to a community tax. Although neither church nor state efforts implied any reward for past performance in caring for the elderly, they at least recognized the nonperformers' right to existence.

Britain began its efforts in a time of relative peace and plenty. Here, the seventeenth century was a period of advancing trade and commerce and the growth of urban centers. Scientific knowledge grew rapidly. Medicine produced a population explosion with new methods of saving lives, curing illnesses, and repairing injuries. Technology substantially increased the yield of agriculture by producing tools close to machines in their output. For the first time and for more than a tiny minority, life became more than a hand-to-mouth existence. In this social climate, national concern for the care of the elderly took the shape of formal legislation.

There is no problem in agreeing that retirement, as we understand it, did not exist in preliterate and Western historical societies. But the emergence of retirement surely did not introduce the abandonment of old people. On the contrary, it is rare to find cases among preindustrialized societies in which a dignified old age was assured. Sometimes failing strength meant an immediate end to existence. More commonly, it appears that a "second career" was allowed but only as a concession to physical decline. The aging person was given lighter tasks, often in exchange for reduced consumption. Work of some kind seems to have been a law of life for all but the very youngest before the industrial revolution. The share of available goods was allocated in most cases according to the output of the workers so that old people received less or even nothing at all.

There were a few cultures in which the elderly received high respect and esteem. They were those whose cultural conditions accorded special value to experience, knowledge, or evidence of superior past performance. It was in just those societies or subgroups within them that there was at least a chance of being cared for after physical and mental powers had waned. But there, too, an economic surplus always was paramount to the ability to provide care for non-producing members of society. Economic surplus in itself still was no guarantee that care would be forthcoming. In short, contrary to a sentimental view of the past, there was a fairly high rate of abandonment of older people in those times.

THE RISE OF RETIREMENT

The industrial revolution brought us retirement as a societal institution. That revolution was an important change in human history because it brought the factory and the office as the main place of employment and with them the irreversible demise of the family as an important unit of economic production in society. As long as providing for the material basis of life was the business of families, taking care of the elderly was a question in which family obligation and loyalty was mixed with considerations of economic rationality. But the factory separated family and work life. Now men and women could be treated as economic objects, according to the laws of profit and loss. Modern organization, bureaucracy, and technology in the factory also brought with them the expansion of wealth and the production of economic surplus which had no historical precedent. That made retirement possible on a large scale. But it also poses the question of whether older people retire voluntarily or whether they are made to retire more or less against their own inclinations. Let us glance briefly at the history which produced the question, one that is now a social problem in contemporary societies.

The factory replaced both cottage industry and craftspeople. The rise of the factory was primarily because it was a far more efficient mode of production. In a factory with its bureaucratic organization, diversified machinery along with many workers could be housed, and more goods could be produced more rapidly and at less cost. Further, mass production and distribution could be accomplished efficiently with large-scale urbanization that concentrated the population into large cities. The burgeoning cities pulled the peasants from the land and turned them into new urban factory workers, with their economic lives administered according to the laws of supply and demand. For many, the new age of rising wealth was an age of rising insecurity. You had a job, indeed you could expect to have one, only if an employer could make your work profitable. If he failed, you were out of work, and, in old age, that was your fate as well if a more productive worker could be found to take your place.

The new market mentality and the urban migrations caused vast and largely unplanned population shifts. De Beauvoir noted some early responses to the human suffering that resulted from the upheaval. In Britain, where the chaos was especially marked, the Poor Laws were supplemented in 1782 to provide more resources for the parishes. In Britain and in other European countries as well, this period of history saw the emergence of grassroots community movements in the form of "friendly societies" to help those without visible means of support. Outside of Britain, however, friendly societies were discouraged and sometimes were forbidden because of a suspected association with the budding philosophy of Communism. Yet their existence and persistence undoubtedly helped to influence the states to intervene, especially in behalf of older people who were the most adversely affected by the urbanization trend and the new conditions of work.

Formal Retirement

In 1888, Germany passed the first legislation allowing persons to leave the labor force at age sixty-five with guaranteed economic support. Most of the industrial world followed suit during the next twenty-five years (Hudson & Binstock 1976). The United States was an exception and held out until the middle of the depression in the 1930s. It was reluctant to temper an unusually strong emphasis on individualism fostered by expanding geographical space and perceived unlimited opportunity (King 1971). None of the early pension plans was very impressive since, at their inception, relatively few persons could be expected to pass the age of sixty-five. As the proportion of the elderly in industrial populations increased dramatically over time, however, income maintenance policies have kept pace (Schulz and others 1974). Today virtually every member of the labor force in the fully industrialized countries is entitled to retire with a pension, and the benefits have become more substantial. Special tax advantages and service supplements for older people have been added to income programs. The public resources spent on older people have escalated along with their numbers, since most of those of pensionable age do retire.

Just to be capable of retiring large proportions of older persons requires industrial organization and technology. In an industrial plant, the use of complex machinery is highly efficient, and task specialization and synchronization further increases output. The output of any individual worker is multiplied. Fewer hands produce sufficient surplus to allow many social members to be excused from the labor force. Older persons are not by any means the only population group to be affected by the dominance of mass production. As this mode of labor organization spread and stabilized, women and children also left the factories (Kraus 1975).

One person, if properly paid for his or her productivity, could now support an entire family, and the mature male was accorded this role. Women, especially married women, and children had other social obligations to perform that indirectly contributed to the economy even though they were no longer "at work" (Parsons & Bales 1955). The rationale for choosing women to "retire" was based on the same reasoning that produced some kind of division of labor based on sex in every known society. Because women bear and suckle children, they have, by a variety of means, been assigned tasks that allowed them to stay closer to home. In land-based cultures, women certainly made important direct economic contributions but could integrate such work reasonably well with other activities. Once production moved into the factory and away from the dwelling place, the compatibility between work and other family roles was upset. The solution was to make the women responsible for home management. As a new specialist, she could attend not only to domestic tasks but also could be a source of emotional support and motivation to her husband and children. The husband would need a comfortable home and a reassuring presence to maintain his productivity in a demanding, impersonal work setting. In the early years, children would respond to their mother's affectionate guidance by learning the values and expectations of their society. As the children grew beyond infancy, they too had a special obligation in return for freedom from paid labor. Advanced technology required more formal education and training, and children entered the school system so that future labor needs would be met. What they did was not counted in the gross national product, but women and children were expected to use their time in ways that would produce valuable current and future inputs to economic productivity.

Like the support of other "dependents," income to the elderly also comes out of the pockets of those in the labor force. Much of this is done by transfer, however, and without conditions. Elderly people are not obligated to be useful as comforters, caretakers, and socializers (like women) or learners of future social roles (like children). The retired person receives societally distributed pensions in exchange for past performance only. From this point of view, it is possible to understand the claim for the "roleless role." According to this perspective, there is nothing more that society wants from the older person. In fact the system is actually mobilized to push out the aging worker by whatever means it can muster.

Even Atchley (1976:123), who by no means concurred with the abandonment perspective, stated that retirement at the societal level was primarily a mechanism for adjusting the supply of labor to demand. On this basis, he felt that increasing automation put a strong pressure on keeping older people out of the labor market. The abandonment argument goes much further, however, implying that in industrialized countries everywhere retirement would be mandated or at least accompanied by such carrot-and-stick measures as would ensure the disappearance of old people from the work force.

Finally, there is a "selective retention" hypothesis of obsolescence (Sheppard 1976). It proposed that the disappearance of older workers may not be complete. Most old people are forced out because they are superfluous and/or useless, but a few may be retained because they still are needed by society. The better educated and those in accelerating areas of the economy have some chance of avoiding retirement. People do not retire because they perceive retirement as a desirable social opportunity. Except for a fortunate few, according to the selective retention variant of those who argue abandonment, retirement is a response to social forces that leave the individual no choice in the matter.

Cross-cultural data make it possible to explore some of these propositions. First, we will consider the evidence for a decrease in labor demand over time which would put very strong pressure on older workers to retire. Next, we will examine public policies of retirement and consider their impact on retirement rates as these differ from country to country. Finally, we will test the hypothesis of differential retention by studying the characteristics of the retired and the nonretired of the same age, as well as the economic sectors in which people are more likely to be retained. This should help to answer the question of whether retirement is voluntary or whether older people are pushed into retirement. Only when we have that information at hand shall we let the retirees tell us their own views on that subject.

RETIREMENT IN CONTEMPORARY SOCIETIES: MANDATORY OR VOLUNTARY?

Two sets of facts are useful as a preface to this discussion. They are the trends and variations of retirement. There is no question of the growth and expansion of retirement in the contemporary world. Some form of retirement can be found in all societies today, even in those that are still basically agrarian. One explanation is that importing advanced medical knowledge and techniques led to demographic changes in agricultural and developing countries, increasing the proportion of the elderly in their populations. The result has been to recognize the need to support those in advanced age. The rule seems to be, however, that the more industrialized a country is, the larger its aged population is—and the more likely that its members will be retired.

Data from 1970 show that in contemporary agricultural societies about 4 percent of the population is aged sixty-five and over, in partly industrialized countries between 4 and 7 percent, and in fully industrialized countries more than 7 percent (United Nations 1971). Yet a comparison of seventy-two countries in these three stages of development in 1960-61 showed that less than two fifths of all males sixty-five and over were in the labor force in industrialized countries, as compared with sixty-one and seventy percent of the semiindustrialized and agricultural countries, respectively (United Nations 1962). Thus, although retirement is spreading to other types of societies, it definitely has peaked in the industrialized countries. This trend also can be verified by checking different periods in the same societies. Available data tell us that in industrialized countries, the percent of males sixty-five and over in the labor force declined sharply between 1950 and 1970. In contrast, the proportion of the elderly in the population grew at rates varying from 4 to 13.5 percent (Henricks & Hendricks 1977:51). These facts certainly point toward a diminishing labor demand for older people in modern societies.

A second set of facts makes the picture less clear: The level of labor force participation of older people varies considerably from country to country. A survey conducted in the early 1970s, covering most European countries plus Canada, the United States, Australia, and Japan of all workers sixty-five and over demonstrates this very well (see Table 4.1). Examining the labor force participation rates in descending order, one finds them varying from a high of over one third still participating in Japan all the way down to a tiny minority of only 2 percent in East Germany. Just about every other possibility is represented in between in these figures. It cannot be argued that this wide variation is simply a matter of relative degree of industrialization. Some of the countries with the highest participation rates, such as Japan, Yugoslavia, Portugal, and Norway, do have comparatively large labor segments in nonindustrialized sectors of the economy. But the same could be said for Spain, Australia, and Austria where participation rates for older people are much lower. The United States, which probably has the lowest proportion of workers in agriculture in the world, is only just below the midpoint in the percentage distribution of older people still working.

Retirement and Labor Demand

We now have a case for diminishing participation by older people in the labor force generally as a consequence of industrialization. But it does not apply to all countries equally. Modernization, through mechanization and automation, supposedly reduces labor demand. One way of avoiding high unemployment in modern nations is to remove whole segments of the population from the labor market. That leaves more room for aspiring job candidates. On these grounds, it makes sense for society to retire older workers. But does the demand for labor actually decrease when retirement rates curve upward? If so, we can accept the notion that there was pressure on older workers to move out, willing or not.

This question can be answered for six countries for which data are available at two points in time twenty years apart: circa 1950 and 1970 (Hendricks & Hendricks 1977:211). The countries are the United States, the United Kingdom, Japan, France, West Germany, and Sweden. This information is labor force statistics classified by age groups and sex. Considering females separately, we

Table 4.1
Labor Force

Participation of Older Workers by Country (n=18):
All Workers (Male and Female) 65 and over*

NAME OF COUNTRY	% WORKING
Japan	35
Yugoslavia	31
Portugal	29
Norway	21
Switzerland	19
Denmark	19
France	17
Canada	17
United States	16
Italy	13
West Germany	12
Australia	12
Spain	11
Sweden	7
Netherlands	7
Belgium	6
Austria	4
East Germany	2

Adapted from Schulz and others, 1976:51.

have summarized this information for males in Table 4.2. We decided to treat any change that was less than 3 percent as no change. Following that rule, the participation rates for males showed only declines (noted as "less" in 1970 and in 1950 in Table 4.2) and stability (noted as "same" for the two years in Table 4.2). It is apparent that the participation rate of the youngest age group (20 to 24) declined in all six countries.

In chapter 2 we noted that a shift in employment patterns in the service sector characterizes all advanced societies. Some productivity data also indicated that this signals a shift to the less efficient use of labor. Table 4.2 tells us that this also results in declining employment opportunities for the youngest males. For

Table 4.2
Stability and Decline in Labor Force Participation of
Males in Six Countries (1950 and 1970)

Age Groups	United States	Japan	France	West Germany	Sweden	United Kingdom
20 to 24	Less	Less	Less	Less	Less	Less
25 to 39	Same	Same	Same	Same	Less	Same
40 to 54	Same	Same	Same	Same	Less	Same
55 to 59	Same	Same	Same	Same	Less	Same
60 to 64	Less	Same	Less	Less	Less	Same
65+	Less	Same	Less	Less	Less	Less

a minority of these young men, this declining rate reflected attendance at the universities. For many, however, it meant being condemned to unemployment.

On the other hand, there was almost no change in the labor force participation rates of the next three age groups, those aged twenty-five to thirty-nine, forty to fifty-four, and fifty-five to fifty-nine. Their participation rates stayed the same in five of the six countries covered. The only exception was Sweden, showing a decline in participation rates in all age categories. Thus, most males spent the middle years of life at work, and a shift to the service sector did not affect these age groups.

In contrast, already the next older group of men, those aged sixty to sixty-four, showed more declines than stability in their participation rates. In four of the six countries that rate was lower in 1970 than twenty years before. A declining rate of labor force participation over this time period became even more dramatic in the case of the older worker (65+). With the single exception of Japan, their participation in the labor force dropped everywhere. The older a man was, then, the greater were his chances of being retired.

If a shift to the service sector means a shift to the less efficient use of labor, presumably employers respond by substituting machinery for workers wherever they can. As a consequence, the very young, so it seems, are not let in, and the old are pushed into retirement. Labor demand for middle-aged males is being maintained at the cost of these two other groups. Although that would seem to support the idea of abandoning the older worker into retirement, making him accept mandatory retirement rules because there is no demand for him, this changes when one looks at women.

Older Women in the Labor Force

During the same twenty years, women moved into the labor force in ever growing numbers. The stability of the patterns for men in their middle years therefore came at the same time that the economic systems accommodated a large influx of women workers. In recent decades women have been steadily reversing the pattern of withdrawal into home management and are entering the labor force in increasing proportions. The greatest increase is among married women, especially those whose children have begun school (Sheppard 1976). Earlier, women went outside the home to work before and immediately after marriage, but then "retired" when their children were born. Only if they remained single or if the husband's income was too low to provide an adequate family income, were they likely to stay in the labor force (Komarovsky 1964).

There are many reasons for the changing patterns and preferences of women (Troll 1975:126). Currently, women in advanced societies are having fewer children at younger ages than their own mothers did, while at the same time they face a longer expected life span. Taking some time out for child bearing and rearing is still customary, although by no means universal among today's women. But even when they do take time out, the prospect of the empty nest looms earlier in a much longer life cycle. Some women are simply turning to employment to fill their lives when the children are grown. Another possibility is that women may feel that many of their vital roles in the home have been taken away.

Many activities that used to be the province of wives and mothers now are carried out by professionals. Teachers provide formal education, physicians assume the responsibility for health care, and psychiatrists, psychologists, social workers, and even ministers give expert advice and counsel on child rearing and marital problems. To be "just a housewife" is devalued and begins to seem analogous to the "roleless role." This view is close to that of the women's liberation movement which regards women as deprived of the most valued roles and statuses in society unless they can leave the home. But whether this movement is the fuel for or the effect of other changes on the lives of women would be difficult to determine. What is clear is that there is a strong back-to-work movement which still seems to be growing.

Rates of women working have increased significantly in many countries, although they still are not as high as those for men. This trend is evident in all six countries just discussed, except in France where in 1950 the rates for women were already comparatively very high. In France a stable, high participation rate for women is balanced by the same pattern for men through the years twenty-five to fifty-nine. In old age (65+), however, one finds that both men and women participated less in 1970 than twenty years earlier. Japan showed a moderate increase in women working from twenty-five to twenty-nine only, matched by complete stability over time for males of all age groups from twenty-five upwards. West Germany had a similar pattern in the younger age groups, but both men and women withdrew more at the later time in the two oldest age groups. The United States, Sweden, and the United Kingdom showed the highest increases in women in the labor force, especially at ages forty through fifty-nine. In these three countries, there even are some very modest increases for women aged sixty-to sixty-four, and in the United States and the United Kingdom also for women sixty-five and over. In general, the rising labor force participation of women has at least matched if not exceeded the displacement of older male workers. We do not argue that modernization in the future will not create labor problems. We do suggest that an overall decrease in labor demand over this twenty-year span is not supported by the data available for four of the six countries. This argument therefore is weak as an explanation of the growth of retirement during the same time period.

Public Policy of Retirement

Still, something is operating to move older people out in increasing numbers in five of the six countries reviewed. The abandonment perspective would suggest the universal development of mechanisms to discard the obsolescent. We turn now to an examination of public policy of retirement and its apparent effect on labor force participation rates of the elderly in different countries. If societies wish to move people out of the labor force at a certain age, they can apply the stick or the carrot. The most obvious stick is mandatory retirement. At a certain age, employment simply ceases. Carrots can take the form of adequate pensions and health care provision. Whatever the policy may be, Atchley proposed that there are factors in a given culture that must be considered to explain participation rates. These include the level of health and the value placed on work (Atchley 1976:21). If this is so, then, sticks and carrots notwithstanding, we would expect to find more old people still at work in some places simply because the ability to work and the desire to continue are stronger. This possibility cannot be neglected in our discussion of national policies. Comparing social welfare and employment policies in different countries is difficult because of variations in terminology, the separation or inclusion of particular aspects in plans and programs, and accounting procedures (Jensen 1972; Schulz 1974). Still, useful examples and illustrations can be found and linked to the data discussed in the last few pages.

The rising levels of financial benefits and medical care in industrialized countries have been linked to an invitation to "step down." Kaim-Caudle (1973) found that nowhere in the developing or partially industrialized nations were there provisions for old age comparable to any in the mature industrial nations. And, as we have seen, retirement rates are higher in the latter. Kaim-Caudle, however, did find significant differences among the ten industrialized nations that he studied which can be linked to retirement statistics. Using carefully determined criteria, he ranked seven dimensions of social welfare and placed countries at the top, the bottom, or somewhere in the middle. For the two dimensions most relevant to this discussion, old age and health programs, Denmark and West Germany received top ranking for financial benefits, and Denmark also was at the top for health care. The United Kingdom was the only country besides Denmark to be placed at the top in health provisions. Australia was on the bottom on both dimensions, and the United States joined it in last place in health care. Recalling the figures for participation in eighteen countries in Table 4.1, Denmark, with the best overall provision, had 19 percent of persons over sixty-five in the labor force but Australia, rated the worst, had only 12 percent. The United States, with the relatively poorest health care, was in the middle with 16 percent.

If better benefits are intended to discourage work and are operating effectively, the picture should be very different. We would have expected the highest proportions of retirees to be in Denmark, followed by the United States, and then Australia. In fact, Denmark and Australia are in just the reverse order of what would be expected. Incentives, then, are not the only reason. Other forces must be operating to explain why more old people are at work in Denmark as compared with Australia.

Other policy provisions are not designed to entice older workers away but to make it costly or even impossible to remain in employment. One example is forcing people to stop work in order to be eligible for a pension. This forces retirement, whatever the personal preference, because the cost of remaining in the labor force becomes so high. But it is interesting to note in this connection that this type of policy is actually much more common in the developing or partially industrialized nations. Table 4.3 shows that the great majority of such countries do not grant benefits unless the individual has no paid work at all. By contrast, only a small minority of industrialized countries made such an "all or nothing" stipulation, and exactly half allowed persons who had reached the specified retirement age to collect full benefits with no limitation on other earnings. Again the facts contradict the assumptions of the abandonment-obsolescence view. On this criterion industrialized countries appear to be doing less "shoving" than those only partially developed.

Within industrialized nations, some examples can also be drawn from the six countries just discussed in connection with labor force statistics. The United States and the United Kingdom have earnings tests for benefits, but France, Sweden, and Germany do not. In addition, France, Sweden, and the United Kingdom actually provided incentives in 1970 to keep older people at work beyond retirement age. These countries offered increased benefits for each additional year spent in the labor force after retirement age (Hendricks & Hendricks 1977:238). Leaving the sixth country, Japan, aside for the moment, the United States seems to exert the most pressure to retire. It both reduces pensions if older persons continue to earn more than a small amount and offers no incentives for additional years of work. Sweden, by contrast, is the most encouraging. There are no earning strings attached to pensions; there are in fact increased benefits if work is continued beyond the age of pension eligibility. Yet, as we have seen, Sweden had the very lowest participation rates for any of the six countries, and the United States was in the middle with the other three.

Table 4.3
Relationship between Work Status and Pension Eligibility
in Developing versus Industrialized Countries*

	Work Prohibited	Partial Limitation	No Limitation
Developing (N=56)	65%	16%	20%
Industrialized (N=20)	10%	40%	50%

Adapted from Schulz and others 1976:50.

There were no Communist countries included in this analysis.

This country should really be in Sweden's place for it seems to be trying the hardest to ease out aging workers.

On the surface, the clearest signal that "no old people need apply" is mandatory retirement. At a certain age, the worker is dismissed, regardless of capabilities or preferences. Unless mandatory retirement is universal across all employment opportunities in a given society, however, work may still be a possibility. In the United States, for example, about half of all workers work where mandatory retirement rules are in effect, but the retired worker can seek employment elsewhere where the rules do not apply. Certainly, though, having such rules for a large proportion of the economy narrows the chances for older workers and makes it harder, if not impossible, to continue working if one wishes to do so.

Whether and to what extent do mandatory retirement rules force unwilling workers into withdrawal? In the United States, few former workers in a national survey gave compulsory rules as a reason for not working (United States Social Security Administration 1972). Also, Schulz (1974), studying a cohort of retired males, 54 percent of whom were from organizations with mandatory retirement policies, found that only 7 percent claimed to have given up work against their will. Mandatory retirement, coinciding as it has until recently with the age of eligibility for full benefits, may have simply reinforced the concept that sixty-five is the "normal age" to retire. This is quite different from seeing it as a mechanism that effectively pushes out unwilling older workers.

A most interesting case is presented by Japan, where all major industrial organizations had mandatory retirement policies set for age fifty-five. Japan is precisely where we found the highest rates of participation by older workers. The answer to this apparent paradox is that older Japanese workers often "retire," yet continue working. Jobs are available to them either in lower status positions in the same companies for which they were working before retirement, or in smaller firms and nonindustralized sectors of the economy. The majority of Japanese males does go on working even after age sixty-five. Clearly there must be opportunities, but is this continued work really what we would call voluntary? There are two different perspectives. One claims that continued work for the Japanese elder is an economic necessity because pensions are very small and in 1970 did not even start until age sixty, a delay of five years beyond the official retirement age (Fisher 1973; Tsukamoto 1973). That almost might be seen as a stick being used to keep the old at work, oddly coupled with widespread mandatory retirement at a relatively early age. But Palmore (1975:60) took quite a different view. His explanation referred to cultural forces. Palmore believes that there is an unusually strong work ethic or sense of duty to contribute to the collective well-being among the Japanese. Continued work then is not so much caused by economic forces but rather is a matter of self-respect for the Japanese.

Considering together public policies and relative labor demand over time, we can see that the relationship between increasing industrialization and retirement is an intricate one. To be sure, in most countries, retirement for older workers has become more widespread over time. But it should not be assumed that this response is involuntary. Over time, retirement with reasonable security has become more feasible, and people may be willingly taking advantage of it. Certainly, we found no reason to accept the argument of decreasing labor demand generally as creating strong pressures for older people to "move over and make room." Retirement policies are too varied among nations to identify any movement to divest the older worker of the right to work in modern societies.

The industrialized countries offer better provision to the aged than do other types of societies existing today (and certainly in the past). But at the same time they are much more likely to allow persons to continue earning while receiving full benefits, and some even offer incentives to keep the older worker in "harness" after retirement age. Even mandatory retirement, that bugaboo for those who argue that retirement is really deprivation, does not operate as it is expected to. Further, more recent changes in policy in several nations cannot be interpreted as either responses to labor demand or as accelerating the retirement movement, at least not consistently.

Sweden, where we did find some evidence for a general reduction in employment among the males of all ages, responded in a predictable direction. It now has changed policy to allow persons to retire at fifty-five with full benefits rather than at age sixty-seven as in the recent past. Sweden is concerned about unemployment among younger adults and has offered incentives for retirement at a younger age. This is still voluntary, but it is an attempt to reduce job competition by moving more old people out of the labor force.

The United States has similar unemployment problems, especially for the very young, but it has adopted a contrary approach. In this country, it has now been decreed that mandatory retirement age must be raised to age seventy. One can still receive a full pension at age sixty-five, to be sure, but this is a shift in the direction of keeping more old people in the labor force rather than moving them out.

In Japan, where the labor demand seems to be increasing over time and where the oldest groups were the most heavily involved of all nations for which we had statistics, there have been two changes that may be interpreted as incentives for older workers to retire, at least by age sixty-five. In 1974 the Japanese began a significant revision of retirement policies. First, private firms are now encouraged to revise the mandatory retirement age upwards to sixty. At the same time, benefits for the retiree, which begin at that age, have been upgraded. These changes would permit workers to work continuously in the same position until age sixty. This means that their earnings on the job will increase which, in turn, leads to a larger retirement bonus from the particular firm. Since pension eligibility now coincides with mandatory retirement age and since pensions are now at a more acceptable level, the expected net affect of the two changes would seem to be more retirement. There is no evidence as to whether, if at all, any of these new policy directions will affect retirement rates.

As we have seen, there does not seem to be a correlation between policy provisions and the proportion of old people working in the labor force. If this is abandonment, it is difficult to explain the anamolies. Some industrialized countries actually are encouraging older workers to continue working; others do a sort of balancing act, saying in effect that they will provide for the older workers if they leave, but they also will do that even if they stay; and still others seem more discouraging all around. Over relatively short time periods, also, policies shift between one position and another. These are hardly the consistent patterns of policy development we would expect from the abandonment perspective. Yet, liberation is not readily apparent either. If retirement is a welcome release, then we would expect those of pension age to be clearing out en masse, especially if benefits are sufficient for an acceptable life style. But even in the countries with the best benefits, some old people are still at work.

Selective Retention Hypothesis

The selective retention hypothesis attempts to explain this. It argues that the reason some old people are allowed to remain in the labor force is that they are "less obsolescent than others." Obsolescence as a concept does not work perfectly. If it did, none of the aged would be found at work anywhere. But obviously this is not what happens, so the concept has to be modified. The modification proposed is that the minorities still at work will be higher status, better educated workers. They have certain advantages that lead to a demand for their continued participation.

Recalling the great differences in participation, country by country, this proposition already looks a little shaky. It could, for example, hardly be claimed that the Japanese have more well-educated, high-status workers than the Swedes do. Yet Japanese elders are participating in the labor force at several times the rate of those in Sweden.

Still, in the United States at least, the proposition seems to work rather well. People from white-collar occupations, especially those in upper status positions and the self-employed, are the most likely to be found still at work after age sixty-five (Riley & Foner 1968:49-50; U.S. Census 1973, PC(2)-6A). Among blue-collar workers, by contrast, fewer continue working. Not surprisingly, the more years of schooling the individual has had, the more likely he or she will keep on working (Sheppard 1976:290; Hendricks & Hendricks 1977:34). In general, these statistics apply to both men and women.

Broken down by race, there are some complications. White males have higher participation rates than nonwhite males have, but the reverse is true for women when nonwhites are considered (Riley & Foner 1968:51; *Manpower Report* 1974). Since the men from racial minorities are disadvantaged in terms of education and occupational status on the whole, higher white-male participation rates are expected. But the rates for nonwhite women throw some doubt on the prevalence of "differential obsolescence" as a predictor of work involvement. The nonwhite females, in no better condition socioeconomically than their male counterparts are, when compared with white females, nevertheless more apt to work.

With very minor modifications the same pattern occurs when we look at those who are taking the option of early retirement, especially for men (Schwab 1974:24; Ireland & Bond 1974). Not only are those in the lowest status positions with the least education underrepresented after age sixty-five, they also are more likely to move out at an earlier age. Again, women, and this time all women, confuse the picture. They are not taking advantage of early retirement as men are, and there also seems to be a shift toward no educational differences between women who stay and women who withdraw (U.S. Census 1974, P-23, No. 48; Sheppard 1976). The percentage of women "in the eligible for early retirement" age group is smaller than that for men, as would be expected given their relatively lower occupational and educational attainments. Yet proportionately they all are still at work at the same rate when compared with the statistics for women of that age before early retirement was available. By contrast, white male rates declined 10 percent and nonwhite male rates 12 percent after early retirement became available. Just how well the women are educated does not seem to matter very much. Even in the United States, the notion that a few old people can stay in the labor force simply because society still has some use for them is rather imperfectly reflected in the statistics. Still, in the main, those with more occupational status and more education are overrepresented.

Data from a few other countries do not, however, support this pattern as a cultural universal. In Denmark, those who remained in the labor force were more likely to be white-collar workers as in the United States, but in Great Britain it was the blue-collar group that had higher participation rates after age sixty-five (Shanas and others, 1968). If it is assumed that white collar means higher occupational and educational status, then Denmark is more likely to hold on to these "less obsolescent" people, but Great Britain is more likely to let them go. In Japan, the situation is more compex. The older worker is most likely to be found in small business and agriculture, and generally in comparatively low status positions (Drucker 1971). But this has no great bearing on previous status, for the distribution is largely a consequence of downward mobility after age fifty-five. Thus, the selective retention hypothesis does not hold, once put into a cross-cultural matrix. Bengston (1969), after studying six industrialized countries, concluded that national differences were at least as important as occupational status in retirement behavior.

It could still be that older workers are retained only when they are economically useful on some other grounds. Perhaps they are pushed out or held simply because of the economic sector they happen to be in or because of general fluctuations in demand. That still would mean that society had all the leverage and that the individual was simply at the disposal of larger economic forces.

Obsolescence could still be operating on the grounds that the older worker would be the most affected, but the reason would not be his or her special qualifications relative to social needs. We can discuss this, at least in the United States.

Gordon (1963) and Kreps (1973) looked at the distribution of older workers in the labor force and found this distribution to be economically irrational from a societal point of view. Older workers tended to be concentrated in slow rather than in rapid growth sectors of the economy. To be sure, older workers who remain have comparatively more education, but they are not likely to be working in areas in which there are new opportunities because of technological advances (Steiner & Dorfman 1957; Palmore 1964; Goldstein 1966). Nor do fluctuations in general labor demand as the economy heats up or cools down appear to explain very much about the involvement of older workers (Jaffe 1972). Economic swings have had some impact, but they have been minimal compared with the general steady trend toward more and more retirement. Except for the unusual period of World War II, there has been a steady decrease in the proportion of those sixty-five and over at work in this country from 1920 to 1970, despite some fairly sharp fluctuations in demand in the marketplace.

In short, even when it is broadened a bit, the concept of differential retention is not very convincing. Butler (1972) even questioned the validity of the argument that higher status workers are the least likely to become obsolescent in societal terms. He wondered whether professionals such as physicians, judges, and politicians who are among the most likely to stay at work are not also the most vulnerable to obsolescence. If society is "pulling the strings," it should be the most concerned with getting rid of those in crucial positions in which new knowledge is accumulating at the fastest rates.

Butler's position does lead to another question about the distribution of work opportunities in the United States. Certain upper status workers, especially the self-employed, may have more control over whether or not they decide to retire. Age discrimination in the United States could be operating more effectively against lower status workers, partly because they are more likely to be subject to bureaucratic decisions. Many organizations are reluctant to hire older workers (U.S. Department of Labor 1965) either because of documentable increased pension costs or less validated, ageist orientations (Laufer & Fowler 1971; Schulz and others 1976:54; Bartley 1977). Biases against older workers also have been shown to be a problem in obtaining work for the hard-core unemployed (Wachtel 1966). For such disadvantaged persons, however, this has been a problem throughout life, which age only compounds (Sheppard 1977:290). For the more steadily employed, there are occurrences that may cut the work life short and that seem to affect the factory worker more frequently than his or her white-collar counterpart.

But organizational age discrimination explains only part of what happens. Older factory workers who lose their jobs through economic fluctuations or automation are less likely to be reemployed unless they are skilled workers. When there are economic shifts and blue-collar workers are laid off, they encounter age discrimination if they seek other jobs.

The problem is partly with the older worker, however, especially the factory worker. Compared with younger workers generally, older workers in this country have been found to be less willing to move to another community or region, that is, to "follow the market" or to change their line of work (Riley & Foner 1968; Dyer 1973). Among the older workers, the white-collar segment is more flexible at least in terms of seeking "alternate work," even if it means transferring into a lower paying job in a small business providing services or engaged in retail trade.

The older blue-collar workers are more subject to bureaucratic control in terms of hiring practices and organizational decisions on automation or closing plants. But at some point it also appears that work is no longer important enough to this segment of the work force to make sacrifices in other areas of life just to stay employed.

If older people generally had strong desires to continue to work, the apparently shrinking opportunities ought to lead to an upward curve in the unemployment statistics as age advances. And it ought to be steeper for the blue-collar worker than for the white-collar worker. But that is not what happens. Among males, at least, unemployment is highest among the very young (sixteen to seventeen years of age) and declines to a stable low of 3 percent by the middle years (35 to 55), remaining roughly on that level to the end of the life cycle (Schulz and others 1976b:50). There are no appreciable differences among the occupational categories in registered unemployment. Since white-collar workers are in fact more likely to be employed, that indicates that older blue-collar workers are the least interested in working. According to Schwab (1974: 50), the statistics accurately reflect the level of desire for employment. His findings imply that most older people leave the labor force simply because they no longer prefer employment. Not everyone agrees with that interpretation. Some argue that the statistics are deflated because older persons are often reacting to an unsuccessful search for work and just stop looking (Sabel 1966; Sheppard 1973). No doubt there is some truth in both viewpoints, for not all people feel the same about work and retirement. This issue will be clarified by examining subjective reactions to retirement.

At this point, we can argue safely that there are no cultural universals in retirement in industrial societies. Each country has its own rules and particular patterns. It cannot even be said that retirement is on the increase everywhere, although that is generally the most consistent pattern found. The level of retirement does not seem to be explained by societal factors such as economic demand or particular policies of retirement. It is obviously more complex than that. Something more than a process of modernization is operating here, although that process has worked to make retirement more feasible for more people over time. But whether better benefits are in reality a sugar coating for what is in practice a bitter pill has yet to be discovered. That probably depends very much on the special attributes of each cultural setting. So far, the three arguments for abandonment have not helped us to accept this perspective as agreeing with the available facts. There has been little to influence us toward adopting the liberation perspective, either. In fact, we have found no solution for the voluntary-involuntary dilemma. To pursue the problem further and to address diachronic solidarity, we need to move to the response of the public, both retired and nonretired.

REACTIONS TO RETIREMENT

Most older workers in industrial society do retire. The rates of working after age sixty-five have continued to decline in most countries as the century progresses. But not everybody retires everywhere, and in some countries more people work in late life than in others. This is a puzzle that refutes the hypothetical "law" that the aged must vanish from the marketplace in the modern societies. Looking at economic factors and comparative national policies did not lead to any conclusions about the implications of retirement. We therefore turn to the responses of affected people themselves and the general cultural climate in which retirement occurs.

If retirement cannot be explained simply as a response to societal pressures, other questions have to be raised. Perhaps retirement is becoming acceptable, at least in some countries and for some people. After all, it is a relatively "young" social institution which has been viewed with considerable ambivalence. But it may be gaining acceptance. If retirement is becoming acceptable, then several things should be happening. Public opinion among all age groups should favor retirement. It should be seen as an earned privilege and opportunity. And the retiring should exit willingly and adjust well to the experience. Retirement should be supported by adequate social rights that prevent it from being a "social dead end." People who retire should not only be entitled to an acceptable life style economically but also to social opportunities to use their new leisure as they see fit. Leaving work would not mean the loss of social membership in other life spheres.

Attitudes toward Retirement

But what is actually happening? Findings from several countries over time help to set the stage for a closer look at the American scene. The American data are the most detailed, but insights from other countries will be added wherever possible. Many investigators of retirement believe that the loss of the work role is a dramatic dysjunction in the life cycle for those accustomed to employment. Not only is "going to work" the means of life support in modern societies, but social worth is measured only in terms of economic contribution.

Productivity, as has been documented, certainly was very much valued in pre-industrial societies.

The role of the worker was not singled out in the same way. What is new in the industrial era is the organization of labor which makes paid work a separate sphere of activity, rather than an integral part of the general social life. To receive wages for a specific contribution to the marketplace is the prescribed way to claim income to support self and family. On the societal level, it also is the only one that is actually counted. Other kinds of social contributions are not even added to the gross national product. Consequently, society as a whole depends on the labor force to supply the goods and services necessary for its continued existence. It follows, then, that the work role is considered by many to be the major source of social status and self-esteem. Work may not be the "sacred calling" cited in the studies of modern society that argue that worldly achievement has replaced other aspirations, but it nevertheless is the only sphere of life on which society places a monetary value. It is the only means available to reckon one's contribution to the general welfare. Once one retires, one's contribution automatically is reduced to zero. Worse, the retired person is consuming resources from the national pool while no longer making any contribution. By this definition then, to be retired is to lose much more than just the satisfaction that may be derived from the work itself and the company of one's fellows in the workplace. It is to lose the foundation of social identity.

There have been at least some hints in the previous pages that the meaning of work and attitudes toward retirement vary from culture to culture, from subgroup to subgroup, and over time. Retirement today in most industrial societies affects a large majority of persons over sixty-five who ever have worked. But it was not long ago that relatively few people were affected. The expansion of both retirement possibilities and retired people can influence public opinion. The available literature suggests that favorable reactions have increased over time, at least in some countries. According to Burgess (1960:20), data from workers and other information available in six Western countries indicated that perspectives on retirement in the 1950s were largely negative. People felt that it was best to go on working as long as possible. They thought that giving up work would mean being deprived of vital activities for which there were no substitutes. These findings led Burgess to invent the term, the "roleless role." Loss of work leads to social isolation, lowered self-esteem, and general maladjustment. Although the data did not represent systematically sampled population groups, the trends everywhere suggested that retirement was involuntary and perceived as a social deprivation.

In the next decade, however, Shanas and others sampled older people in the United States, the United Kingdom, and Denmark, and came to more positive conclusions. Only part of that study, which was carried out in the mid-sixties, focused on retirement, but the results are most interesting in terms of reactions to retirement and the meaning of work. In all three countries, the majority of the people interviewed enjoyed retirement, and this finding held despite social class. As a group, Americans were the most satisfied with retirement, although they were also the least likely to say that they missed nothing from work (Shanas and others 1968:331). About half of the British and about half of the Danes reported missing nothing from work as compared with only about a third of the Americans. But what the Americans missed hardly corresponds to notions of the work ethic. They said that they missed money and, to a much lesser extent, people at work. Relatively few spoke of missing work itself or even missing "feeling useful" because one was no longer working. In fact, in none of the three countries were work ethic-related responses at all common. No more than a fifth in any of the samples gave answers that could be categorized this way. Americans and Danes were slightly more likely than the British to speak in such terms. The results of this study, then, showed that retirement was acceptable to those in that status in these three countries.

Burgess's predictions based on data from the fifties were essentially refuted a decade later. Losing work was seen as no deprivation at all by many people, and only a minority anywhere missed work for intrinsic reasons. These results were confirmed by another cross-national study carried out shortly afterwards (Havighurst and others 1969). Small samples of middle-class and working-class males in their seventies in Austria, Italy, Germany, the Netherlands, Poland, and the United States were interviewed, and the prevailing responses to retirement were positive. The numbers were too small to permit any firm conclusions, even about men in their seventies. But again Americans seemed to be relatively the most satisfied according to the discussion in the text. Although no questions were asked about what was missed from work, those who conducted this cross-national study agreed with Shanas and her colleagues that the concept of retirement as social deprivation needs to be revised. Retirement can be and indeed seems to be a satisfying experience for most people who have experienced it, at least when it occurs under certain social conditions.

In Western societies, more retirement with better social support generally seems to have made that status more acceptable in the sixties than it was in the fifties. But there are some anomalies in their general picture. For example, not all of the men interviewed by Havighurst and colleagues had completely given up work. In every country, small minorities were still working, although usually on a part-time basis. Only in one of the six countries, Poland, was there a relatively high interest in continuing work. And only in Poland was there more dissatisfaction found among those who actually were no longer working.

In all the other countries, to continue work was gratifying to some but to have stopped working was equally gratifying to others. Polish men put more stress on work. In this inclination, they reflected the attitudes of Japanese males, as reported by Palmore (1975). Palmore's data on Japan, in fact, agreed even more with Burgess's findings. Most Japanese men aged fifty and over expressed reluctance to give up work; they wanted to work as long as they possibly could (Palmore 1975:60). According to Palmore, interpreting the response of the

Japanese males, and Techniczek (1969), speaking for the Polish men, the higher work incentive was related to cultural themes. Both societies were said to be more collectively oriented, and continued work, accordingly, was more likely to be viewed as a social obligation to enhance the general welfare. People in more individualistically oriented societies can more easily relinquish the work role. Duty to the nation is less important to them.

But there is a complication in this explanation of how Polish and especially Japanese men feel about work. Both Palmore and Technizec rather strongly hinted that affluence depresses the work ethic. Japan and Poland belong to the relatively disadvantaged among industrialized nations. It is not cultural tradition alone, but also the national standard of living that maintains the commitment to work. In other countries, economic security has undermined that commitment. Being rich has made us fat and lazy in many Western nations. People can accept retirement not because it is a good thing in itself, but because work has less value. The implication is that work at one time occupied center stage everywhere in industrial societies. But where modernization produces more and more surplus, it no longer seems that important to "do one's part."

By this reasoning, the difference between Burgess's interpretation of the fifties and attitudes toward retirement is explained. We shall comment on that using data over time from the United States which do extend back to the early fifties. These studies did not show any diminution of the value placed on work. On the other hand, even though the United States often has been considered one of the most, if not the most, "achieving societies," there is little support for the notion that work is the core of life for most Americans. Some Americans have in the past and do still feel that way. But they are relatively few. A survey conducted in the early fifties showed that regardless of age, no more than 15 percent of all in the labor force in this country at that time identified work as the most important thing in life (Friedman & Havighurst 1954). A similar national study conducted more than a decade later produced almost precisely the same results (Williams & Worth 1965). Atchley (1971), reporting on a study of comparative samples of teachers and telephone workers, came up with the same number again. No more than 15 percent of either group had very positive orientations toward work as measured by indices of job satisfaction, work commitment, and work as a value for self.

These results do not support the idea that the work ethic is declining in recent times. They do discount the belief that placing primary value on work is prevalent in our society. Most Americans say they invest as much and usually more of themselves in other life spheres, especially that of the family. This does not sound as if giving up work would rob them of their social identity. Work does seem to be a respected necessity, all the same. A recent survey of white male workers showed that only tiny percentages of those under fifty would be willing to give up work immediately if they had sufficient financial resources (*National Survey*, University of Michigan 1969-70). The desire to leave work does rise among those fifty and over, especially blue-collar workers. But even in that group, most men are still not ready to leave. If money cannot entice male workers out of the labor force, then, work must have its own worth at least during some period in the life span. We suggest that work is no more and no less the center of social life today than it was in the fifties in America and that most men, in our country at least, believe that working is something they should do. But as the life span lengthens and longer terms in the labor force also become the rule, the idea at some point of having served long enough is gaining legitimacy. This concept is easier to accept simply because work has not been the beginning and ending of social existence and social worth for most of us.

Retirement certainly does seem to be becoming more respectable in the United States. The population at all ages supports retirement as a "good thing" for older people and as a stage of life with real advantages (Rose & Mogey 1972; Harris 1975). More and more, society at large perceives retirement as an earned privilege and an opportunity (Miller 1965; Ash 1966). No longer does public opinion view this option as a concession to failing capacities. Rather, general opinion stresses retirement as a right for people who have served in the labor force for many years to be supported by the rest in return for what they have given. That right is expected to be accompanied by intrinsic rewards. The younger tend to anticipate claiming this perceived freedom and leisure, not immediately of course, but in their own turn. It is this spirit building behind retirement as an institution that seems to be altering the experience.

But how do these visions of retirement actually work out? It needs more than visions to make the experience a good thing. More and more Americans have said that they retire voluntarily and also look forward to retirement (Katona and others 1969; Orbach 1969; Shanas 1972). To believe that retirement has been earned and that it does not lead to a social "dead end" undoubtedly makes it easier for people to feel comfortable with that status. Yet, everyone is not ready to quit, and some obviously distrust the promises. There is a mix of expectations. As the time to retire approaches, some resist leaving work, others are happy to go, and still others are ambivalent (Atchley 1976:78).

The resistors are likely to be found among those who place the highest value on work. Prominent government officials, executives, and professionals find it harder to retire because to leave work is also to leave a "calling." Many of them love their work and are deeply involved in it. They are skeptical of finding a new social identity when they have stopped. Other upper and middle status job holders do not share this commitment. They have nothing against work, but they feel they have served long enough. They are ready to enjoy retirement and feel secure about both financial matters and social opportunities. Among the working class, there is ambivalence. Most blue-collar workers are ready, often more than ready to retire, but they hesitate. Unlike the more affluent workers, they often find that work has become burdensome and even distasteful. The working class is obviously not deeply affected by the work ethic, nor do they seem to have any dreams about a golden leisure full of new opportunities. Their ambivalence is mainly in reference to money. The decision to retire is a balancing act between the wish to leave and the lack of freedom to do so with any sense of security. The specter of poverty intervenes. The United States does not offer sufficient financial "social rights" to allow secure passage from work for those who feel most that they need release from work.

The blue-collar workers' desire to retire on time or earlier is greater than that of white-collar workers and has been found in several other countries as well. The pattern has been described in France, in Germany, and in the United Kingdom (Shanas and others 1968:317; Schoeller 1971:88). French and British workers tend to hesitate for the same reasons that Americans do. But there is no ambivalence among the Germans. Those who are ready to retire also trust the "social contract." They know that their economic fate is secure.

Not everyone wants to retire, and some who want to are fearful of the consequences. It has been suggested that some who say they retire willingly are really only bowing reluctantly to the inevitable and making as graceful an exit as possible. They will be unhappy, and even those who think they will enjoy retirement may be wrong. They have an idealized portrait of leisure which will quickly turn into boredom. How does it all work out? The answer seems to be rather better than expected. The best evidence for the majority reaction to retirement comes from longitudinal studies that followed workers from the decision to retire into its aftermath. We can compare what people said just before retiring with what they said after they have retired.

Data from the United States demonstrate that most people are not despairing over an unwanted fate, nor do they feel disillusioned with the experience. On the contrary, retirees are much more likely to enjoy the experience than they themselves predicted that they would. Streib and Schneider (1971) followed a national sample from just before retirement through successive interviews extending from four to six years after the people had left work. They found only a small handful of "disappointees," less than 5 percent. A third of the retirees, by contrast, said that the experience was better than they had expected. Most people wanted to retire, and they felt even more positive in the first year after leaving work, and more so with each passing year.

One reason why leaving work turned out to be better than expected for so many was the ease of transition from the job. Few people felt they would miss the job, and even fewer did. Many more had expected to miss their colleagues, but, as it turned out, they usually got along without them quite easily. Similar results appear in other studies. Among retired telephone workers and teachers, over four fifths of a large sample enjoyed retirement (Cottrell & Atchley 1969). This was 20 percent more than those who had expected to enjoy retirement. Heidbreder (1974) also found the overwhelming majority of retirees quite satisfied with their lot.

From all the data, some adjustment problems can be found. Working-class retirees were a bit more likely to speak of problems than middle-class ones were. But in neither group were these problems likely to be tied in any way to missing work. Unexpectedly, proportionately more women than men spoke of missing work. We say "unexpectedly," because women are supposed to have the housewife role to fall back on. This is an alternate role to cushion the blow of work loss. The dissatisfied women told interviewers that family pressures pulled them from the labor force before they themselves were ready to leave. But in all groups, missing work was a problem only for a small minority, hovering around 7 percent. Not all of this loss was felt very strongly or accompanied by a real desire to return to work.

We might ask: What then happened to the people committed to work? Why are they not protesting the forces that call them obsolete before they are ready to give up their involvement? The answer is that many of them successfully resist retirement (Eisendorf 1972). Precisely those occupational groups who are most imbued with the work ethic are the most likely to be found still at work. Because they are able to remain, the ranks of dissatisfied retirees are thinned (Streib & Schneider 1971:160). But there is another aspect that needs to be explored. Why do so many people find retirement better than expected? There must be something in the aftermath that helps to explain that.

The Retirement Role

That brings us to the retirement role. Here we do have data from some other countries as well as from the United States. Everywhere we look "rolelessness" is hardly the way to describe what happens in retirement for most people. Americans, relatively deprived financially, seem to be the most blessed with satisfying social opportunities. They are, so to speak, making the most of the retirement role. We mentioned before that Americans as a group were enjoying retirement more than either the British or the Danes were. The same study (Shanas and others 1968:331) showed that what they liked most was the free time they could use as they wished and the opportunity to engage in interests and hobbies. In the other two countries, many more retirees liked retirement mainly for the opportunity to rest. Nowhere was "rest" the most frequent group response, but Americans were clearly more likely to be using their time in activities that they found rewarding. Since they also had the highest satisfaction scores, it seems that more opportunities were available to them.

Nowhere were most retirees just resting, which could be construed as a "role-less role." Everywhere, the working class gave this type of response more frequently, but even among them it was not the most frequent answer.

Bengston (1969), drawing on the Havighurst and others data, told us more about what people, in this case men in their seventies, were doing in retirement. Since this was an exploratory study, we will not go into great detail. But the flavoring and especially the variety from country to country is worth a few lines. In Austria, Germany, the Netherlands, Italy, Poland, and the United

States, the men were asked to rate their level of engagement in twelve social roles. The twelve roles were divided into three clusters: family roles (spouse, parent, grandparent, extended kin), formal roles (worker, church member, political-civic actor, club member), and information roles (friend, neighbor, acquaintance, leisure-time consumer). Everywhere these men in their seventies were quite busy when their activities across the three clusters of twelve roles were added up, but how much they did and especially what they did varied markedly from country to country. Summing all roles, the Austrians were the least active and the Americans the most. In Austria, family roles received by far the most attention and the other role clusters, relatively little. In the United States, by contrast, men were almost as active in informal roles as they were in family roles, but formal roles occupied less time. In fact, if only family and formal roles were counted, the Netherlands would be the "activity leader." Dutch men were more active in formal roles than were men in any other country. This seems to be mainly because they were unusually energetic church and club members.

Each country, then, had its own configuration. Again, working-class men tended to be less active than middle-class men were. This was true in every country except Italy, although in Austria and Poland the differences by class were very minor. The explanation of lower levels of activity among the working class is that they tended as a group to be in poorer health and also to have had less role engagement before retirement. The double constraints of failing health and prior patterns of restricted activities accounted for less activity when the work life was over. Indeed it does seem that, health aside, there was some continuity between what workers did during the working life and what they did in the aftermath. We are told that retirement generally involved some reduction of activity but that it was not very dramatic. Once work is over, the retired men turn to other spheres of life. The spheres are usually those in which they already were active. But now they reengaged and spent much of the time there that work had occupied. Everywhere most found life satisfying. Again, however, the Americans, who were the most active, also were the most likely to be enjoying retirement.

Yes, there is a retirement role, at least in most Western countries. Exclusion from the work role does not lead to dropping out of social life generally. What is remarkable, though, is the continuity between retirement activities and earlier phases of the life cycle. We could argue that, contrary to Rosow, people actually are socialized for old age. Atchley (1976:98-104) made this point in summarizing some of his own work and that of others. Minimally, the retirement role consists of two sets of social expectations held by both retirees and the rest of society. Older people should continue to assume the obligations of citizens and managers of their own affairs. Earlier experiences prepare for this.

Otherwise, the content of the retirement role is not specified. It varies according to the person and the cultural context. Generally, however, people do many of the same things in retirement that they did before. Because the role of work either ceases or is greatly diminished, they tend to do less. But this "less" is sometimes seen as "better," because there are fewer constraints. Many retirees actually do more of some things they have enjoyed because they have time to pursue their own desires. But the emphasis is on continuity and the receptivity of the social environment. Social barriers at least do not prevent most Americans from enjoying retirement. And older people rely on earlier experiences to pave the way into the retirement role.

Atchley also saw the retirement role as threatened by three villains: poverty, bereavement, and failing health. Missing work was not much of a problem, but enjoying retirement depended on continued activity and independence. We will treat bereavement in a later chapter, but we will discuss subjective responses to income and especially health now.

Poverty

In an earlier chapter, we saw that about one quarter of elderly Americans are economically abandoned. Another one half had inadequate retirement incomes. Income loss is so steep that even an acceptable standard of living is wiped away by retirement. What we want to know now, however, is how people actually react to income loss and income deprivation. Interestingly enough, the financial realities of retirement do not hit as hard as might be expected. Nor do they hit hardest exactly where we might have thought. Rather astonishingly, Streib and Schneider found that two thirds of all retirees said that they had sufficient income for their needs, even though income averaged only half of what they had when employed. Perhaps the key word here is "sufficient," for almost everyone agreed that more money would be useful.

A more interesting sidelight is that many retirees told interviewers that income should decline after retirement. One can only guess that some people really do feel less useful socially when they are no longer working. From that point of view, it is quite understandable that they have less at that time of life. This kind of response had undertones of abandonment. But a direct abandonment response would be to say that insufficient income is a problem, and some might expect the working class to complain more than the middle class did. But there is no difference between the two groups. Again, there are subjective factors.

The middle class, as a group, looked forward to retirement more and saw many uses for increased leisure. But some may have overestimated the resources that they would have to pursue their retirement dreams. Caught in the pinch of inflation which ate into savings and private pensions in which they were likely to have invested, middle-income groups reacted more bitterly than either the poor or the affluent, as was found in the Boston study of retirement (McEwan & Sheldon 1968). The really affluent is relatively unaffected by unexpected financial drains and inflation. But the middle class, by any standards better off than the working class, suffers more from relative deprivation. Compared with what they were used to and perhaps with what they expected, they feel "newly poor." That the working class complained so little, relatively speaking, may be related to the fact that what they have often was what they were used to. In the lowest income groups, social security alone accounts for financial support, and although that left many close to real poverty, they already were poor before retirement.

Most blue-collar workers, then, were less subject to steep income declines. Let us remember, too, that the working class did not seem to have any great expectations of retirement. They would not be as likely to be disappointed by foiled leisure plans. Also, some studies found that working-class retirees have a certain pride in managing on marginal incomes and "making do" (Kerckhoff 1976). Many saved money by spending increased free time working around the garden and the home. Even the poverty-level groups contained few complainers. One reason may be that their "abandonment" occurred usually much earlier in the life cycle. Old age and retirement had little effect. That they accepted their hard lot despite being fairly poor seemed related to never having shared in that affluence that creates the expectation that one should not have to "count every penny."

In short, the income loss which accompanies retirement created less of an outcry than might have been expected. Most older Americans seem to be getting along with less without complaining. Those who did complain were about equally divided between the middle and the working class. The middle class felt abandoned, not because of actual poverty but because of relative loss. Their life styles were eroded. Some of the working class also felt abandoned. Poverty ruined the retirement role for some, but not as much as we would expect and not always in the places that we would expect. The middle class usually seemed to manage a satisfying life anyway, and the working class again took up activities that produced savings to make life tolerable.

Loss of Health

Still, as Atchley warned, the retirement role faded into a sick role at some point when health failed. We could see this great shadow falling across many retirees even though most studies followed them only into a few years of retirement. Even the most optimistic outlook on the prospects for improved health and a longer life span with higher activity potential admitted that some health decrements have to be expected with age (Bortz 1972). Chronological age is only imperfectly related to keeping or losing one's health. Good health may last well beyond retirement age for some; for others, ill health may occur before that way station is reached. Many people, as we shall see, give health as a reason for retirement.

There are two arguments for the relationship between health and retirement. One is that retirement for health reasons is really involuntary. The assumption is that these people would really like to continue working if they could (Sheppard 1976:304). Since those who consider themselves in good health are more likely to go on working, it is possible that this argument is correct, at least in some cases. A more insidious assumption, however, is that claiming ill health is really an excuse. People who use it feel that this is a respectable reason to retire, but to retire out of mere preference is not. The second argument is a kind of "chicken-egg" dilemma. It states that because more retirees are in ill health compared with those of the same age who are still working, retirement actually causes ill health. This is another version of the abandonment argument. Because older workers are forced into retirement, they withdraw into physical and mental illness. Accordingly, people do not go into retirement because they are sick; they get sick because they are in retirement. We will do our best to untangle these two themes, although they are obviously not entirely separable from one another.

Ill health is a frequent reason given for retirement. In the Social Security Retirement History study, two thirds of the men and two fifths of the nonmarried women (married women were not included in this study) reported that health concerns were the main cause of their decisions to retire. Manual workers and blacks of both sexes were the most likely to give this response.

Many different kinds of answers were grouped under the general category of health. Sometimes people were speaking of a current state. They felt too sick, too tired, too worn out to continue working. Others spoke of a future state. They said that they had worked long enough and that they wanted to avoid the threats to health that more years of work might bring. Either way, there is no doubt that health was an impetus to stop working. Just how many would really like to go on working if they felt better is at least doubtful. The prevalence of leaving for health reasons was greatest among the least work-committed, blue-collar group, not only in the United States, but also in the United Kingdom and France (Shanas and others 1968:317; Laroque 1975). But the more important point is that so many people did feel that they could not or should not continue, whether or not they were being moved out prematurely. Was this often just an excuse because sickness made leaving work acceptable, and even if it were, would retirement only make matters worse? It seems simpler to start with the second part of the question because it provides a framework within which to answer the first.

It has been argued that retirement is the wrong medicine if workers are really concerned about their health. Retirement, with its consequent marginality, inadequacy, and rolelessness just exacerbates health problems (Palmore 1972; Blau 1973). There is some support for that view in studies that compared physical and mental health adjustment among the aged, and found that the employed had fewer problems (Thompkin and others 1960; Lowenthal & Berkman 1970). But the researchers themselves raised the issue of whether cause was being confused with effect. It might be that the more frequent problems found among the retired preceded retirement. If so, then illness produced retirement and not the other way around. Another survey found morale to be somewhat lower among the retired than among others of the same age who were still working (Simpson, Back, & McKinney 1960). But here too it was suggested that the difference was caused at least as much by other factors as by work loss—primarily health factors.

The only way to understand the problem is to study people as they transfer from work to retirement status. Longitudinal studies that followed people in this way demonstrated quite conclusively that health does not decline after leaving work, at least during the first few years of retirement (Streib & Schneider 1971; Atchley 1976). The retired reported being in just as good health as they were before leaving work, and there was even a slight improvement among blue-collar workers. This was true not only for physical health, but also for mental health and related psychological factors such as life satisfaction and self-esteem (Cottrell & Atchley 1969; Nadelson 1970).

Among the mental health indices reported by Streib and Schneider, there was only one negative change. The percentages of persons who said that they sometimes or often felt useless moved upward from 12 percent before to 27 percent after retirement. This certainly could be caused by work loss, since it fit in with the acceptance of reduced income. But generally retirement was not doing any damage. If people felt well before leaving work, they stayed that way. If they were ill, this state also was maintained. We already have answered both questions to some extent. Retirement is not bad medicine, nor does giving ill health as a reason to retire seem much like an excuse. If it were an excuse, then, we could expect that good health would return once the need for the excuse had passed. But ill health seems to persist even for several years.

Those who had health-related adjustment problems were found mainly in the same groups who were most likely to say that they were sick or likely to become so: the blue-collar workers, especially those from minority groups.

Ill-health, which comes to some even before retirement age, is real and real in its consequences. The relationship between health and retirement is consistent with a number of facts. When retirement and poor health coincide, it is most likely to be among those who most often accept on-time and early retirement even though they also are the ones who worry most about finances. It is also from the members of these groups that we get the most evidence of poor health after retirement. Far from being pushed out prematurely, we believe that many such workers are kept too long. Many years of hard physical labor and/or boring, repetitive jobs makes retirement a welcome relief even for those who are physically strong. For some of these workers, the physical and mental strain moves them into "old-old" age even before the sixty-fifth year is in sight. Release from labor obligations does not come too soon.

Retirement and Suicide

We reviewed facts that revealed that work loss does not seem to be damaging to health. For some, working too long may be a greater hazard. But perhaps the case has been overstated. After all, there have been few studies, and they do not probe very deeply into the retirement experience. We might look at one other, general social indicator and seek its implications for work loss. The higher incidence of suicide among older persons in industrialized countries compared with that of younger age groups, especially among white males in the United States, sometimes has been linked to work loss. White males are comparatively more likely to be in higher status occupational positions and therefore in the middle if not the upper middle class. They are less likely to complain about health problems and somewhat more likely to remain at work. But not all who would like to can continue. If the incidence of suicide can be taken as a valid index of social despair, it does rise with age but not as would be expected, given the known facts about retirement. Several illustrations will support that statement.

A good beginning is to compare the rates of suicide of older men in the United States and Japan. The table below is confined to retirement-related age phases. It is easy to see that the rates for men in the United States actually declined slightly for ages sixty-five to seventy-four, on which retirement has its most widespread impact. Suicide climbs only among the seventy-five and over groups, most of whom have been retired for a long time. Whenever suicide does occur, it is mostly among white males; blacks, the largest minority, have a very different pattern, as we shall see.

Turning to the Japanese men, the association between suicide rates and work loss is even more tenuous. The rates climb quite steeply between ages fifty-five to sixty-four and ages sixty-five to seventy-four. Yet the majority of Japanese men are still working after age sixty-five. In both countries, suicide is at its height from age seventy-five on. But the Japanese far outstrip the American males. It cannot be just the effect of incremental losses, beginning with the work role but then extending to other areas of life, that explains the delayed reaction. Japanese men should experience this later and never to any greater degree than

Table 4.4
Suicide Rates per 100,000 in the United States and Japan*

| | United States | | Japan | |
	Males	Females	Males	Females
55-64	34.4	11.5	33.0	19.1
65-74	32.9	9.4	50.7	36.1
75+	42.8	6.4	77.6	65.5

*Adapted from statistics compiled by the Japanese government, Office of the Prime Minister, Tokyo 1973.

American men do. Also, the suicide profile for women in the two countries differs dramatically.

For women in the United States, suicide actually declined steadily in the two oldest age groups depicted. But in Japan, the rates of suicide for women increased sharply over the years. In fact, Japanese women have the highest recorded rate of suicide for women in any society in the world. Since in neither society can women be seen as playing as large a part in the world of work as men do, the discrepancy must be related to something in the culture. Perhaps the high rates for both sexes in Japan can be related to the disruptive effects of cultural transition or to the traditionally greater acceptance of taking one's own life under certain conditions in the Orient.

The latter interpretation seems to be supported by comparative figures on suicide rates for ethnic subgroups in our own country, available from the Minority Health Book (U.S. Dept. of HEW 1975). Only a few ethnic groups are included, and the rates are not divided by sex. Still, using whites as a base line, the Chinese and Japanese populations in the United States show dramatically sharper increases by age with the highest rates per 100,000 occurring in the last two age groups charted, fifty-five to sixty-four and sixty-five and over. By contrast, blacks have the lowest suicide rates of all ages, and the rate per 100,000 actually declined during the last two stages recorded. For American Indians, the fourth subgroup, suicide rates vary even more. The peak came during ages twenty-five to thirty-four, and gradually subsided thereafter.

We have to conclude that suicide rates have litle ostensible connection with work loss either directly or cumulatively. Suicide rates are a "crazy quilt" when looked at from the point of view of work loss. They probably are better understood in relation to cultural norms, not to mention cultural norms related to sex roles. This bit of information just adds to the sense that loss of work is not a major theme in understanding reactions to retirement.

Retirement and Diachronic Solidarity

Considering the reactions to retirement, some themes lead us in the direction of diachronic solidarity. Portents of acceptance of retirement seemed to have become stronger over time. Both older and younger generations increasingly agree that retirement is not only acceptable but a good thing, under certain conditions. This movement does not reflect a declining value placed on work but rather, that the concept of "enough service in the labor force" is taking root. In America, at least, long before one had to make the decision oneself, one felt that retirement ought to be viewed as an earned privilege and a privilege to be anticipated.

In other countries, too, retirees seemed to be bolstered by this general climate, although we have only the indirect responses of retirees to determine this. We did note, though, that this is not a universal trend in industrial societies. Japanese elders do not favor retirement, and Polish men are unhappy if they cannot find at least part-time work after sixty-five. In both cases, the norm of "having worked enough" has not taken root. In other places, most people seemed to accept retirement and to take up social roles. These roles reflected more continuity than discontinuity in old age. As work phases out, people tend to maintain and even to expand the other activities of preretirement life. Society does not exclude old people on the grounds of uselessness.

But retirement is not satisfying to everyone, even in the United States where it is enjoyed the most. Some of the discontent is caused by missing work. But much more seems to be caused by lack of resources to play the retirement role. One resource decidedly lacking for many Americans is money. But most Americans accept this with surprisingly little complaint. The acceptance of retirement is not complete, since the basis of acceptance of income loss seems to be that people "no longer at work" should make do with less. But lack of income does interfere to some extent by causing some middle-class people to revise their retirement plans. The working-class retirees do not complain any more than retired middle-class people do. But everywhere, not just in the United States, the working class was least likely to be active in retirement. They were resting, it seems, given the data from the United States, at least partly because ill health had overtaken them even before they were released from work.

If the social contract of retirement is intended to offer adequate resources to make it an "earned privilege and opportunity," it is not being fulfilled. This does not seem to be because retired people are not accepted socially, but because the resources that allow people to retire with a secure economic future and soon enough to reap the supposed benefits, are withheld. There is too little liberation and too much relative abandonment so far to believe that retirement is a firmly established social institution, despite movement in that direction in many countries in the West.

BEYOND PERFORMANCE: RETIREMENT AS AN EMERGING SOCIAL INSTITUTION

Modernization created retirement. It did not, however, invent abandonment. We feel secure in stating that in most preindustrial societies, lack of more than just the bare means of survival led to the deprivation and even to the sacrifice of old people. There is surely no basis for any reasonable claim that keeping old people in the labor force indicated their higher status, associated with their small numbers. There are some exceptions, but in most cases the opposite seems to be true. Old people usually continued at work, if they were allowed to live at all, but their reduced contribution actually led to a more marginal existence.

Beyond the physical and mental ability to work, continuing support and social care was most unlikely. Anything like retirement in our sense seems to have occurred only among the most economically secure and culturally developed groups. The same practice appears not only in the survival cultures of hunters and gatherers and subsistence farmers, but in Western historical societies as well. Except for the favored few and in the best of times, aging meant abandonment. The kinship system could not or would not take care of its own, despite what those who argue for the "good old days" would like to think. On the contrary, very early in recorded history, the church moved in to care for the infirm and the indigent. As the centuries rolled on, community groups and eventually the modern state took a hand. In preindustrial societies, the basic necessities were all that "nonperformers" could expect to receive.

Only in mature industrial societies can many members be supported who make no contribution of their own. The group most affected nowadays are the aged for whom retirement rates have expanded dramatically over this century. Contemporary societies that are agricultural or partially developed also have retirement plans. These plans are an obvious recognition that some older people simply can no longer work. There are now too many persons everywhere passing the age sixty-five to ignore the infirmities that old age eventually brings. But the industrial societies go one step farther. Many retirees are by no means infirm. Are they being phased out before they are ready or is this a welcome release from many years of service? We have some answers. Societal forces, whether of labor demand or of social policy, did not really work the way we would expect if the obsolescence perspective were correct. Although older people were moving out more and more in most of the countries studied, this was not true everywhere. And it usually did not seem that more unemployment among younger workers was creating demand that the older move out. In fact, employment rates were quite stable among mature adult men, and in many places many more women were moving in during this twenty-year period.

National policies varied in how they handled retirement. There was no universal incentive for older people to retire. Some policies seemed designed to encourage workers to stay on after retirement age, others to encourage them to leave. We found little relationship between the provisions of the policies and the rates of older workers in the labor force in different countries. Not even the selective retention or "differential obsolescence" hypothesis was tenable. In the United States, more higher status older workers did remain after age sixty-five, but in other societies it was just the reverse.

The reactions of individuals within particular cultures offered more information on retirement. We found that retirement was becoming more acceptable in many Western countries, although not everywhere. Burgess's prediction that retirement would be resisted because it led to social isolation, rolelessness, and diminished self-esteem was not borne out by later studies. Only in Japan were the men likely to want to stay at work as long as possible. Retirement still seemed to be unacceptable in that country. In Poland, too, retired men in their seventies still wanted to keep at least a part-time job and were unhappy if they would not do so. Their reactions were not as strong as those of the Japanese, but continuing work did seem to be important as a social duty and to self-esteem. But in the other countries in the two major cross-national studies we examined, most people accepted retirement and were satisfied with their lives. Also, they usually were not relegated to anything like a "roleless" role. People used retirement time to engage in more of the familiar activities that they had been able to do while working. What people did varied very greatly from country to country, so there is no uniform retirement role. Its content varied by cultural climate. But those no longer working were not discriminated against in other areas of life. They continued to be members of society in good standing.

The case of the United States is especially interesting since both studies showed Americans to be more active and more satisfied than those in the other countries. As in most other countries, this was more true for the middle than for the working class. But the working class, we found, was not less satisfied because they missed work. Rather, they were more ready to leave work and hesitated only for financial reasons. But it was not so much money that hurt them in old age. Rather, members of the working class were much more likely to complain of ill health even before retirement age. That the health damage is real was reflected by continuing complaints about ill health in the years after retirement. Most American retirees seemed to accept income loss rather philo-sophically. But those who did complain were just as likely to be in the middle as in the working class. For the middle class, there was more relative deprivation than actual poverty. Objectively, members of the middle class were usually more affluent, but loss of income sometimes prevented them from retiring as they had planned. Working-class retirees had fewer plans for retirement, and they seemed to be able to manage well as long as they were healthy. But illness was a factor, and some were able to do little more than rest, even in the very first years of retirement.

Abandonment

Abandonment does not explain what is happening. Old people were not better taken care of or more respected in preindustrial societies. Quite the contrary seems to be the case. So, historically there is no "relative abandonment." Nor can we find societal mechanisms forcing older people out everywhere. Modern societies are not behaving very consistently or very effectively if there is a universal impetus to get rid of older workers. People themselves do not seem to feel abandoned either. Many, if not most, rather welcome retirement and even more find life after retirement better than expected. Retirees do not withdraw from social contact. They continue to do the things they did before retiring, and the social opportunities are there. Longitudinal studies also do not support the notion that retirement leads to diminished social worth or an increase in anomie. Old age provides too much social role continuity for that. Yet some people are abandoned. There are at least some faint overtones of the abandonment theme in the acceptance of reduced income among retirees and in the slight increase in responses of "feeling useless" after retirement. Still, this latter response applies to no more than a quarter of all retirees. To leave work generally does not lead to either physical or mental decline. There are problems for about a third of all retirees, but these center on income and health, not work loss. For some, income deprivation is a real problem after leaving work; for others poverty was a fact of life even earlier. Ill health, however, seems to be related to retiring too late, especially for those in physically taxing jobs. If abandonment is to be avoided for everybody, we still have a long way to go in the United States. Not only do we need a more adequate "social contract" financially, but we also need some mechanism to allow early retirement without penalty for those in failing health.

Liberation

Liberation is harder to pinpoint. People often do welcome retirement, but they usually are at least slightly less active in that life phase. And they do not seem to turn into "leisure leaders," as a group. Rather, retirees continue to do much what they were doing before leaving work, although some certainly seem to reengage. That is, they spend more time in roles they played before retirement and apparently find satisfaction in them. Americans, especially, do not look at this time of life as one for rest. Probably only a very few engage in leisure activities in perfect freedom. Most retirees do not seem to feel completely liberated from earlier life obligations. Their time, then, is not entirely their own. Many retirees are also restrained by income and ill health from doing what they might like. Poverty and ill health, especially the latter, deprive too many people even just after retirement of the ability to be socially active. Sickness, in fact, is probably the main cause of growing social isolation. As we shall see in later chapters, sickness among the old is hard to cope with in other institutions. Liberation, we think, occurs for the fortunate few but is hardly the general effect of retirement. This conclusion is borne out by the findings on before-after measures of life satisfaction and morale. People neither get lower scores as one would expect for abandonment, nor do they get higher scores as one would expect for liberation.

Diachronic Solidarity

When the aged were relatively few, their social status was more marginal. Now, however, all citizens can see their own future in the retirement role and support social continuity by favorable attitudes and economic transfers. The emerging institution now seems entrenched and represents solidarity between the generations. It explicitly recognizes that our older people belong to us on grounds other than their contribution to economic welfare. In less affluent societies, group continuity depended on favoring the working over the nonworking member. Affluence alone, however, does not account for the evident societal need to maintain the oldest generation regardless of health or economic status. If it is not in the interests of society to support old people because they are infirm or because there is too little labor space, then it must be symbolic of reward for the past and respect in the present. We suggest that industrial societies need to do this to connect the past with the future in the face of rapid technological change and constant exposure to other life styles and values. Retirement can contain an important social message: Although individuals and even governments may come and go, the older generation was like us in earlier years, and we shall be like them in old age. Caring for the older generation ensures that our way of life will continue over time. The clearer the message is, the more older people can make the retirement decision without apology or guilt, knowing that they still have a significant social place.

Not all modern nations have an equal need to use older people for, in our terms, diachronic solidarity. The United States has been relatively undisturbed by war and political upheaval, and its collective identity may seem more secure. For this reason, perhaps, it has been slower and less generous in expending resources on the older generation in comparison with many other countries. And retirees do accept some cost in income and in the obligation to pursue an active life in exchange for relinquishing their jobs. Yet in this country, there still is a general consensus that significant societal resources must be spent to ensure adequate life support "beyond performance." As shown in chapter 3, individual and immediate familial income is sacrificed in favor of the older generation as a group hitherto without much discord or dissent. Despite all our differences and disagreements, the fact that older people do receive extensive common support indicates a general societal need to preserve the elderly regardless of their particular characteristics.

A cautionary note should be made as to whether being retired is synonymous with being old. Most retired persons are reasonably independent, given pensions and other social rights. Retirement may be favorably viewed because its immediate recruits are visibly functioning human beings. Other facets of old age, which now come for most people rather later in life, may be less acceptable in terms of being able to see old persons as "belonging to us." We certainly cannot generalize from the retirement experience and the favorable climate surrounding it to aging itself.

Another issue is that everything that has been said about retirement relates only to the emergence and current stage of that institution. The apparently solid evidence that it is permanent, for good societal reasons, does not necessarily guarantee its future. Inflation in this country could turn the general population away from underwriting life support for older people because of the economic pressures on themselves and their families. Older people may become less sure of their right to retire regardless of health and economic status, if the younger age groups become more reluctant to offer support.

To achieve an intergenerational balance making the retirement status comfortable has not been easy in this country, and severe economic changes could upset that balance. Even raising the mandatory retirement age from sixty-five to seventy, although pension rights are preserved at the younger age, could create uncertainty as to whether one really has worked "long enough" by age sixty-five. As in other countries, the retirement policies and pension plans are being reviewed in relation to slower economic growth and concern about stagflation. It seems to us, however, that retirement has become too firmly established and legitimated in social life to be seriously eroded, although modest tinkering will surely occur.

5

older people in family life

INTRODUCTION

The place of the family in the lives of older people in industrial societies is also a subject of controversy. Unlike retirement, however, the family is hardly a modern invention. It has existed in some form in every society. But the fact that the family can and has taken different forms is what lies at the heart of the controversy. The modern family is viewed by some social gerontologists as having evolved in a direction highly disadvantageous to older people. The family supposedly is shrinking and may be in danger of disappearing altogether. In nonindustrial societies the family included various relatives, and several generations lived together in the same household. Today, the only family members who "count" are the marital couple and their immature children. Once the children are grown, they leave the nest to found their own families. All that is left of the original family is the aging couple. And if one spouse dies, that family is dead as well. This leads to a severe deficit in kin in old age.

Today the family is not only small but comparatively weak. It is no longer equipped to perform many functions. Once upon a time, so the story goes, the family provided for all the needs of its members. In fact, it dominated the social structure and had economic, political, religious, and other social functions. But in modern societies "organizations in Western countries are taking the primary place which the family held from the beginning of human history" (Burgess 1960:17). The burden of this change also falls most heavily on older people. They no longer can rely on kin for protection and security when failing capacities require such needs.

The belief that the family in industrial societies cannot care for the elderly has been vigorously disputed (Sussman 1976; Monroney 1977). There has been much information in recent years to demonstrate that the family in modern times does a great many things with and for its older members. Yet, there also is no doubt that the state increasingly intervenes in behalf of old people. Whether that intervention is a necessity substituting for family neglect or a beneficent increment to continued extended family ties is a question to be pursued.

Perspectives on Older People in Family Life

Again, we revive our three perspectives to help us determine the place of older people in family life. Abandonment necessitates comparing modern societies with preindustrial ones. As with retirement, the argument states that older people were better off before modernization. The major theme is that modernity wiped out the extended family, prompting the younger generations to desert the older. In other cultures, old people lived in the homes of their children and were cared for until their deaths. But nowadays the old are left to fend for themselves. We have some data on this, but it is sketchy. But if abandonment holds, we would expect to find its imprint on contemporary data. Aging parents would be suffering from relative deprivation compared with their earlier status in the family. They would be living alone, not through choice, and they would be neglected by their offspring. Adult children would feel no special obligations to their elders and in fact would put them into institutions if parents could no longer care for themselves. Even if the aging parents were well and active, their children would regard them as excess baggage. The response of older people would be subjective withdrawal. Knowing they were unwanted, aging parents would hesitate to bother their children and certainly would not take any initiative in keeping in touch with the "lost family." The spouse, if indeed there still was one, would be the only family the old person would have left.

The abandonment perspective has centered on relations between the generations or "bloodlines." For this reason, perhaps, most of the research has focused on this as well. We will broaden our search to include other relatives when possible, but relations between the generations will be the concentration of this chapter.

For the liberation perspective, a very different picture should emerge. We would expect to find that old people are very active in the family in modern times. They could even assume a status of relative privilege, using their increased leisure to find new and satisfying ways to build relationships now that the days of rearing their children are past. The most obvious new activity is being a grand-parent. Aging parents could be very useful to their own children, while at the same time finding pleasure in a new and very special relationship. There are other liberated roles that old people could play in family life. They could become the family integrators and chroniclers. In this role, old people would assume primary responsibility for bringing family members together and for gathering and passing on news about the family to other members. This, of course, is the very opposite of abandonment, in which the aged would be expected to withdraw and to "wait to be called," probably in vain. Another thing liberated old people could do is become the family's "leisure leaders," arranging special treats and new experiences for the younger generations.

Finally, our third perspective introduces something rather different. Libera-tion assumes that old people can perform family functions. But it does not define the role of the younger generations with respect to the older. If there is diachronic solidarity, both younger and older generations must have assumed specific obligations and relationships to one another. There will be shared normative expectations which will be followed with mutually gratifying results. The younger must consider loyalties and duties to old people as bonds that will endure over time as present generations pass away and new ones take their place. Only then could we make a case for the family as an institution operating to ensure that social bonds can survive in a changing world.

To understand the family in reference to the elderly in industrial society, we will begin by exploring the concept of family and then will consider how the forms it has taken affect size and function. For the latter, two polar types will help to explain the controversy over the family, especially when we relate myth to reality. Within that context, we then will look at the family today, how it operates, and where old people fit in, if indeed they do at all. There are some recent cross-cultural data that will highlight both similarities and contrasts among industrial societies. Building on that, the United States case can be examined in more detail. Finally, we will analyze relations between older people and the state, and how they affect the extent and nature of interaction between generations in the family.

THE CONCEPT OF FAMILY
AND TRADITIONAL AND MODERN
POLAR TYPES

Family, more broadly defined as kinship systems, whatever else they may do, provide the individual with a number of persons to whom he or she belongs in the special sense of having been born into, or acquired through marriage, a net-work of relatives:

Every kinship system provides each person in a society with a set of dyadic (i.e., paired person-to-person) relationships so that he stands, as it were, in a narrower or wider circle of relatives. During his life, the body of his relatives is constantly changing by deaths and births and by marriages, his own marriage and the marriages of his relatives (Radcliffe-Brown 1965:39).

Whatever other social ties an individual acquires, he or she is endowed with or contracts for a particular set of rights and obligations appropriate to the family and to no other social system. There are two ways of determining who is a relative: One is through blood descent which passes from parent to child through the generations and the other is bonds acquired in marriage or its equivalent.

Marriage

We can begin our examination of the family with marriage or the conjugal bond. Although there certainly are gaps in our knowledge of family life in preindustrial societies, anthropologists, ethnographers, and family historians provide much insight. In the next few pages, we shall depend on several sources for our discussion (Murdoch 1949, 1957; Goode 1964; Lee 1977).

For those who search diligently enough, some possible exceptions can be unearthed, but every known society seems to have some institution that could be called marriage. Marriage forms the basis for all "in-law" relationships, but it focuses on only two social positions: husband and wife. Minimally, marriage is entering an agreement granting sexual privileges as well as obligations to any offspring of the union. The spouses and their young children form the core or nucleus of the family. That is why we often refer to the modern family as a "nuclear" one. Supposedly, it includes that core and no other kin. But the nuclear family, as the term is understood today, usually refers to the monogamous marriage: There is only one husband and only one wife. To be sure, marriage is not always a "contract for life," as the divorce rates prove. But that is not a modern invention. Other societies, too, had serial monogamy, that is, a socially acceptable mechanism for dissolving the marriage contract and entering into another one at some later date. But one at a time is the rule in monogamy.

In some societies, both past and present, it is permissible to have more than one person in either or even both the husband and wife positions. Polyandry is a marriage in which there are several husbands for each wife. In polygyny, there are several wives for each husband. And in group marriage, several persons from each sex join together in a common union. Polyandry and group marriages seem to have been rather rare phenomena. Polygyny has been more common. This is the most "expansive" form of marriage, since it is the most likely to produce large numbers of offspring. Polyandry, by contrast, is like a birth-control measure. One women is a sexual partner for several men, but she can bear only one child at a time. Group marriage permits several persons in each spouse role, but the women can bear no more children than if they were living in a monogamous household. If numerous offspring are a safeguard for a comfortable old age, then polygyny is obviously the marriage form of choice. Indeed, it does seem to have been popular in many preindustrial societies, with both men and women. Still, even when polygyny was preferred, monogamy was a much more common practice. Rather equal sex ratios in most societies have worked against one man being allowed to monopolize several women. Also, to be able to support several wives and many children requires great personal wealth. The answer to whether the family is shrinking through the modern marriage form is, then, a qualified no. There have been larger families through marriage by one mechanism or another, but the most common is our own, sanctioned, monogamous type.

Social gerontologists in any case have not been particularly interested in changing the rules of marriage. They have been much more concerned with lineage, and whether and to what extent modern society has whittled away at the so-called extended family. Families that emphasize lineage are referred to as "extended" since they pass on family ties from parent to child from generation to generation. Unlike marriage, lineage ensures social continuity of the family because the object is to preserve the kinship line over time. Ancestry or "bloodline" is the most important criterion for membership. Marriage is considered essential, of course, for it guarantees proper descendants. Marriage is almost always exogamous; that is, members of one extended family "marry out" into another lineage, for every society has taboos against marriage with identified close blood relatives. But the marital unit is absorbed into the kinship network belonging to one or other spouse, rather than forming a new line of its own.

Extended families, like marriages, come in several varieties. One is the stem family. In this, the lineage is passed on by one child from each generation, almost always the first-born son. This child lives in the parental household, even when fully mature. Wife and children move in with him and thereafter owe primary allegiance to his lineage. In turn, his first-born son will remain in that same residence throughout his lifetime and so on into infinity. To the first born goes the family inheritance. This inheritance may be land or other property, or it may be an assumption of certain rights to use a particular area of land or to take up a specific trade. Whatever it is, and the basis of the stem family is some form of inheritance, it belongs to the one designated child when the parents die. Any other offspring are expected to leave the household and to make their own way after maturation. An affluent family can sometimes help the younger children by giving doweries to daughters so that they can marry well, or special gifts and other favors to the younger sons, but such arrangements are not obligatory.

A lineal-extended family uses the same principles but with more generous specifications in terms of descent lines. This kinship system specifies that all children of one sex will remain part of the parental household and inheritance. Sometimes the descent line is matrilineal; that is, it extends through the female line. But much more often, as with the stem family, it is through the male or patrilineal. All the sons will remain, if not under the same roof at least in the same residential compound. When they marry, their wives will join them not only in residence but as members of the husband's lineage. The daughters, by contrast, will move out into some other kinship group when they grow up and marry. Both the stem and the lineal families, through the emphasis on residence and inheritance, do provide a means of keeping aging parents and at least some of their adult children together. The lineal family is, however, clearly superior in the extent to which it provides "old age insurance." This possibility is realized best in the "fully extended" family, which is the term for a lineal kinship system with three generations coexisting as adults at the same time. In this complex, all surviving mature males from three generations live in the same locality, together with their wives and all immature children from the youngest group.

It is this last, and obviously most formidable, kinship system that is often envisioned when speaking of the traditional family. This family is not notable just for its size but also for the functions it can perform. This fully extended family is seen as a society in itself. It preserves its integrity by retaining all lineal descendants of one sex from several generations in the same place. Operating always from a land base and usually through the male line, kinship identification determines one's place in society, network of affiliations, and life chances (Winch 1971:30-41). All the social positions an individual will occupy throughout an entire lifetime are determined by family structure. Members' economic needs are served by using all of the able-bodied in some part of agricultural production. The proceeds of the cooperative labor go into a common pool of wealth to be distributed by the family head, usually the oldest male. The family head acts as the responsible executive in all matters pertaining to the welfare of the group. Large united families are useful for more than economic purposes. They also can protect and defend family territorial rights. Possessing both economic and political power, the kinship system also earns the right to control sexual access and reproduction. Marriages are made by family arrangements and not by individual choice. The traditional family also can teach the children or any "new members" all they need to know to assume expected social behavior, and kin guidance is present and sufficient for learning throughout life. Each succeeding generation inherits from its forebears the traditions of the group, including kin obligations and religious beliefs and practices. Since members are highly dependent on the family for all their social needs, there can be effective social control so that family welfare always comes before individual demands. Since the family group is large and joined in common cause, help is available for every member in times of illness or crisis. Old people are respected as creators and carriers of the family heritage; they receive considerate care in infirmity.

Indeed, no member need suffer from neglect despite his or her age. In short, the fully extended family is an institution that secures the needs of its members from the cradle to the grave.

At the other extreme is the nuclear family of industrial society, looking very puny by comparison. Instead of being a large and powerful network dominating the social structure, the modern family is seen as a small unit occupying a tiny niche among other, towering social institutions (Parsons & Bales 1955:10-15). Each family is composed of only the marital couple and their offspring. As these children reach maturity, they all "break off" from the family stem and set up their own, independent, living arrangements. Each marriage initiates a new nuclear family that terminates with the death of either spouse. Every person is still born into a family, but this ascriptive fact is relatively unimportant in satisfying social needs after childhood. Economic, political, formal educational, and religious functions are largely the properties of other institutions. The family therefore can perform only limited services for its members and is quite restricted in its authority.

Soon after infancy, the child enters school. It is in formal educational arrangements, and not in the family, that persons acquire the knowledge and skills to maintain themselves as adults. The family cannot guarantee its members a job, nor can it choose its members' associates. It usually is on the basis of individual performance and not family influence that social roles are allocated in industrial society.

But the modern family is not completely without purpose. It continues to perform a specialized but vital function without which the personality needs of individuals could not be met (Parsons 1954). At work and in other social spheres of life that are bureaucratically guided, the human being is expected to respond to specific demands. Only in the family, or perhaps in close friendships, can the individual as a personality gratify his or her expressive needs and seek emotional support. The family is the bastion of private as opposed to public space. Family love prepares and supports the child as he or she moves into more formal involvements and responsibilities. Caring for the child is virtually the exclusive province of parents. The human infant, totally dependent for years, is helpless without parental nurturance. Because there are so few caregivers, infants soon are motivated to mold themselves according to the parents' desires. They learn to want to do what they are expected to do so that they may keep their parents' love. By this process children become trained to do what society requires from its members to fulfill general value priorities. Through love and support of the young children on which they depend for their very existence, the nuclear family serves the larger society in a vital way. The family socializes children into deeply held commitments to membership. The value commitments they accept become inner directives to guide them in more specific choices and decisions that they must make as adult individuals.

People in industrial society have no kinship available for life-long, day-to-day instruction in the "right" behavior. Complex societies therefore depend on intense early socialization to equip individuals to do that for themsevles over a wide spectrum of social situations. More detailed knowledge and skills will have to be acquired elsewhere, but their uses will be guided by the early training received in the family.

This function is accompanied by another principle. The parents must prepare children to emancipate themselves from the "family of origin." In industrial societies, other spheres of life are separated from family control. Adults will be expected to use opportunities without regard to their effect on the larger family circle. Relatives usually cannot be of much assistance in helping individuals to establish their own social place in the larger society. Parents must "let go" and make it seem right to let go so that the mature offspring can act in their own interests in making their own way. Basic personality needs will still require family love, but these now will be transferred to the marriage.

The marital partner, then, takes over from the parents and provides these services until death or divorce parts the couple. The emphasis on achievement in modern societies fosters the continual splitting off of adult children from parents and siblings to establish their own lives. This may well lead to geographical and social separation of parents from adult children. This is the cost, but it must be borne. The parents, now aging, will be left alone. Yet it represents a failure in parenting if children refuse to "leave the nest."

Comparing Traditional and Modern Families

The contrast between the two types of families, the traditional and the modern, could not be greater. In one we find a large supportive network surrounding the person from birth to death and always providing replacements to keep the family line alive. In the other, small units with little protective power for the family member, are continually breaking off from one another and ending up in dissolution. But both become blurred when compared with empirical reality. The truth seems to be that traditional and modern family forms do not differ as dramatically as may be thought.

We will not be able to find the fully extended family in our own historical past. This particular family form seems to have been quite rare and may not ever have existed in most agricultural societies (Goode 1964). The main evidence for the existence of such a kinship system comes from certain parts of peasant China (Winch 1971). In Europe and also in Japan, the stem variety has been much more common. This, of course, is the most limited form of extended family, retaining only one child from each generation in the lineage. Working with historical data, Furstenburg (1966) and Laslett (1973) questioned whether even this more limited form of extended family was very prevalent in the West prior to industrialization. In Britain before 1800, Laslett (1978) found in the data he could amass from that period, only about 10 percent of all households in which at least one adult child remained under the parental roof. This seems to be a minimum requirement for an extended family. In the United States, in the early nineteenth century, extended families by this definition also were seldom found. It may be that the stem tradition was operating mainly among the privileged few. The extended family, after all, rests on inheritance, and the poor in society have nothing to hand down. This may explain some of the findings. But many stem families also may have simply been truncated through death. Given the brevity of the life span, there may have been families, ostensibly nuclear, that had quite simply "lost" the oldest generation. It is estimated, for example, that in nineteenth-century Europe, including Great Britain, France, the Netherlands, and Italy, no more than 30 percent of all families could possibly have contained three living generations (Levy 1965).

For the agricultural West at least, the image of the traditional family needs to be revised. Because of the brevity of the life span, having grandparents, parents, and grandchildren all living at the same time was rather uncommon. The poorer families, having no inheritance to pass on, could not form extended families. Even for those to whom an unbroken stem was available, this variety of the extended family was the smallest and the weakest. It did provide a mechanism to keep one, but only one, adult child in the home, which was old-age insurance for those who lived long enough. But the most common form of property inherited in the West was the family farm, and most farms were small. To keep the property intact from generation to generation, only one child, the oldest son, was entitled to inherit. Any other children had to seek their own means of livelihood. They were obliged to hire out to work on other farms, to become servants, or to become apprentices in craft or trade. The stem family could not even provide for its own children beyond the first born.

Still, insofar as it was available, the stem family did offer something to old people. It gave them a sense of continuity beyond their own lifetimes. It provided for care in decline and infirmity. Land-based societies, also, whatever the family forms included, offered more stability in family relations, at least in praceful times. People were more likely to remain in the same geographical area all of their lives and to have roots in the same community for generations. Family members, even when they did not actually live together, would in all probability remain in close proximity and also would have shared life styles. Farming communities were cohesive, with residents knowing each other well whether or not they were kin, and not comparative strangers as in urban settings. More support and care for those who did grow old, both by relatives and other members of the community, could be expected. The kind of distancing strains recognizable in the independence demands associated with social and geographical mobility were muted in the farming village.

Nevertheless, when compared to the stem family rather than to the more idealized portrait of the traditional kinship network, the nuclear family looks less like a midget next to a giant. And the modern family is not really nuclear after all. Once again the image needs revision. Most students of the family would agree that lineage as the basic organizing principle for kinship is not stressed in industrial societies (Blood 1967). Even tradition-oriented Japan may be moving away from this principle, although very slowly (Vogel 1965). In North America, it may never have been very important. Heavy immigration from other countries and younger people moving West to open up the frontiers pulled families apart even when agriculture predominated.

Still, the nuclear family does not adequately describe the family form most likely to be found in industrial societies. More typical is a kinship network referred to as "conjugal" or "modified extended" (Goode 1963). It differs from what usually is considered an extended family in two respects. There is more emphasis on the marriage bond than on lineage. The person in our society marries by choice because emotional support is needed from family ties. Marriage is not entered into to serve the requirements of the kinship line because that line cannot provide for any descendants in the modern world. The individual needs affective support in marriage so that he or she can survive alone in a bureaucratic environment. Accordingly, it is also the preferred pattern for the newly married pair to set up their own residences. Adult couples form independent households rather than living with their parents. Thus, the continuity of the lineage emphasis is weakened, and there is no built-in protection for old age as in shared households.

When a new family is formed, the couple does not actually foresake all the others. Other relatives still are potentially a part of the family. The modern family actually enlarges the kin pool by using bilateral descent. Not just one lineage as in the extended forms, but both sets of relatives from the husband's side and from the wife's side are counted as family. Yet, it has to be remembered that the major allegiance does belong to the marriage bond and that all other kin ties become secondary. Relations with parents and siblings, especially, must find a new footing when the parental household breaks up into new units as the children mature. How do the aging parents fare in this family constellation? How do their children behave toward them? These are the questions we will pursue in the next section.

Family Forms and Functions

From our discussion of family forms and functions, we find, first, that the extended family is in principle a perfect example of diachronic solidarity. It provides an unbroken chain of obligations between the generations extending through all time. Each generation can expect to receive from its elders that which they will, in turn, pass on to their children. But the extended family as envisioned was not generally realized. People did not live long enough to see more than two generations in the chain. Since even the smallest and most common, the stem family, was dependent on having an inheritance to pass on, poorer people could not use this symbol of continuity. The fully extended family is little more than a myth in Western history. Yet it is often this image that we have in mind when we talk about what Laslett (1976:80) called "the before" of industrial society. "The before" is a sort of never-never land where the elderly always had a right to live in their offsprings' households and depended on them for care in old age, and where no aging relative, certainly no parent, would ever be neglected or abandoned to an institution. This image ignores the more limited size and uses of the far more common stem family. It also neglects the reliance on inheritance, for those who had nothing to pass on to children might well be alone and destitute if they lived to be old. As noted in the last chapter, the long history of care of old people by nonkinship institutions shows that the family was not always able to provide for its own in preindustrial societies. The form but not much of the substance of diachronic solidarity is apparent.

It also should be understood that it was not, as often assumed, common for parents to live with their grown children. This just was not possible given the normal life spans in other types of societies. In hunting and gathering and in subsistence agriculture, people generally did not live much beyond their twenties. Even in more advanced agriculture, although life expectancies varied from place to place and time to time, they usually were not long enough to encompass three generations (Laslett 1978:97). In the sixteenth, seventeenth, and eighteenth centuries, historical records from France, Switzerland, Spain, Germany, Japan, and Italy show that living to have grandchildren was seldom possible. Only a small minority could expect to live long enough to see their first grandchild, and fewer still could hope to know them for more than a few years. This picture of life expectancy begins to change radically only after the first decade or so of the twentieth century. Thus, the idea that it was normal in the "before" for parents and adult children to live together is a statistical impossibility.

But now that we do have longer life spans, the organization of industrial society introduces a complex division of labor which makes a tightly cohesive extended network of kin difficult to manage. Bilateral descent combined with more generations alive at the same time does not in itself ensure family solidarity. In modern life, the family, whatever its size and emotional loyalties, is simply not intended to serve all possible needs. It must give up its members to the demands of formal institutions. Making one's way as an individual in an achieving society also may mean geographical and social separation from the original family circle. For all these reasons, we have to guard against measuring the family performance of today against some hypothetical family of the past. We now are in a social context in which all people expect, with good reason, to grow old. The cause of that expectation is directly related to the emergence of industrial society. Modern society is unique in its capacity to produce old people, and its performance has to be judged in that context. What has happened to the family in the process and how that affects the lives of older people is something which largely has to be inferred. We would do better to assess the facts of contemporary family life apart from an idealized, and quite false, measuring stick from the presumed past.

OLD PEOPLE AND THE FAMILY IN CONTEMPORARY INDUSTRIAL SOCIETIES

We do have many, many more facts about the "after" than about the "before." Before assimilating them in terms of family life in modern societies, we shall make a few preliminary remarks. The magnitude of the changes in family networks created by longevity is difficult to assimilate. Unlike agricultural societies in which relatively few people lived to witness the birth of their first grandchild, it is now very common in fully industrialized societies to have parents, children, grandchildren, and for a sizable minority even great-grandchildren, all living at the same time. It is true that this modern family is growing thinner as it grows longer. In other eras couples had more children, although they were less likely to live to maturity than they are in modern societies. But suppose we take just a bare replacement rate of two children per couple. A couple, now in their late fifties or sixties, who had two children, who each in turn had two children, would have four grandchildren. If that couple lived into their eighties, and the same replacement reproduction rate continued, eight great-grandchildren would be added. We quickly arrive at a large pool of descendants without even adding in-laws who can be counted in bilateral descent. Suppose that each of the original parents also had just one brother or sister. Parallel procreation by both sides of the family would multiply the network of living relatives several times. It is not necessary to go into more distant relationship possibilities to make the point. Longevity combined with bilateral descent can create a very large poll of possible family even when the line is thin. Not every older person, of course, will have all those descendants behind him or her. Still, nine out of ten older persons in industrialized societies today have been married at least once, and almost all those who have married have surviving children and grandchildren (Troll 1970). Those who have not married, like those who have, also have potential family resources in siblings and their children.

Recent data show that elderly members remain connected to their families despite industrialization and modernization (Paillat 1976; Pietrowski 1976). The degree of their connection and its uses are still being explored. It is not so much that we have turned away from marriage, but rather that marriage has become more voluntary. If you are not satisfied with your partner, you need not endure the partnership. You can dissolve the marriage and seek a better arrangement. Does this apply to "bloodlines" as well? Can one disown one's parents as too much trouble or as too different from oneself for a rewarding exchange? These themes will be pursued using comparative data when possible and providing a depth analysis of the case of the United States.

Living Arrangements among Generations

We shall begin with the living arrangements among the generations. Industrialized countries need not be all alike in how they develop family models. Variations in historical circumstances and traditions can lead to cultural variation in the treatment of older people despite similarities in economic organization. We turn again to the study by Shanas and others and that of Palmore to explore this possibility by comparing the United States, the United Kingdom, Denmark, and Japan. It is fascinating to observe that, in each of the countries except Japan, there seems to be a virtual taboo on married older couples living with their married children. The stress on independent households for conjugal pairs that we anticipated holds true for three cases, but not at all for the fourth. In the West, older couples are more likely to live with unmarried adult children and widowed (but to a far lesser extent divorced), aging parents to live with married children. Two mature couples occupying the same household is very rare. Palmore does not give us equivalent data for Japan for those sixty-five and older, so two boxes in Table 5.1 have to be left blank.

There is a slight trend even in Japan for married aging parents to live separately, but the overwhelming majority of all parents do live with adult children. In the other countries, as one can see, the marital status of the aging parent has some influence on living arrangements, as well as on the marital status of their adult children. The distributions for the three countries of the West show almost no households in which couples of two generations live together. But when the aging parent is widowed or divorced, there is more doubling up. The gap in the table between all married parents living with married children and all widowed or divorced parents living with married children *and* the total sum of all parents

Table 5.1
Frequencies of Types of Joint Households
in Four Countries (%)*

	United States	United Kingdom	Denmark	Japan
Married Parents Living with Married Children	02	05	01	—
Widowed or Divorced Parents Living with Married Children	16	23	08	—
All Parents Living with Adult Children	28	42	20	80

*Adapted from Shanas and others 1968:151-52; Palmore 1975:39.

living with adult children is explained by the fact that some adult children remain in the parental home because they do not marry. The statistics reveal that many joint living arrangements in the West can be attributed to the fact that adult children do not marry or leave home for any other reason. They just stay with their parents. There is some variation in the West with the British being the most and the Danes the least inclined to joint households.

But what is more interesting is that in these cultures, and in comparison to the United States, the patterns are rather similar. The most interesting observation is the use of the joint household to accommodate a single person of either generation and not two "intact" married couples. In any of the three Western countries if parents stay with adult children or adult children stay with parents it is usually because there is a missing spouse in one generation or the other. As long as both spouses are together in both generations, the couples almost always live apart. The situation is quite different in Japan. Again, there is a slight tendency to keep intact couples of two generations apart. But by and large the great majority of older parents live with their children, and it makes little difference whether the parent is part of a couple or widowed, divorced, or separated (Palmore 1975:39). The Japanese obviously favor the extended household despite their industrialized status.

Another interesting difference between the West and Japan is that in the latter aging parents are far more likely to live in the household of a son, but in all the Western countries they are more likely to live with a daughter. In fact, in Japan the aging parents usually do not move in at all; the son instead brings his bride to the ancestral household. In the West the extended household is uncommon, and when it is found, it does not follow the prescribed pattern. Rather than sons staying in the home of their parents, aging parents at some point take up lodgings in the households of their daughters.

Does this mean that in the West parents are much more likely to be estranged from their adult children? In all four countries, despite the differences in residence patterns, there is apparently plenty of opportunity for the generations to be in touch with one another. The Japanese obviously live closer to their children physically, and only 7 percent of older Japanese parents report having the nearest child more than thirty minutes away from their own dwelling place. The proportions of old people in this situation are 23 percent, 18 percent, and 25 percent in the United States, the United Kingdom, and Denmark, respectively. The custom of sharing a household obviously does help to keep the generations closer together. But at the same time, the great majority of aging parents in the West also have at least one child less than a half hour away. In fact, the frequency of contact is high everywhere. In Japan, 85 percent of aging parents report seeing at least one child every day or every other day. The Westerners do not do quite so well, but over 60 percent of older people with children in the United States and Denmark and close to 70 percent in Britain claim a similar frequency of contact. Perhaps because of its vast size, the United States is the only country of the four in which 10 percent of aging parents see a child only once a month. This still is a small percentage, but it is double the rate to be found in any of the other three countries.

We know more about frequency of contact than about the meaning and quality of relationships between the generations. According to Palmore (1977: 40), Japanese elders prefer living with their children and find this quite natural. The most frequent reason given for wanting shared residence is "to get care from children" (38 percent), followed by "companionship with children" (30 percent). Most older Japanese who live with their children also feel that they are useful to the household. What they say that they do varies from giving advice and watching the house while others are absent to caring for grandchildren and helping with household and gardening chores. But the point is that they seem satisfied that they are making a contribution. Even in Japan, however, there usually is some attempt in the joint household to separate the generations. Older people occupy separate quarters if the home is spacious enough and often take their meals separately from the younger generation and their youngsters. They definitely do not dominate the household. Yet they say overwhelmingly that they prefer the joint arrangement and feel useful and respected as partners in its management. Reciprocity seems to take the form of receiving care and companionship from children in return for advice and services.

Oddly enough, although Westerners much prefer independent households, the content of intergenerational exchange does not seem very different. Aging parents in Western countries also speak of helping their children with advice, gifts, and services of various kinds and of receiving affection from the younger as well as support in times of crisis, such as illness. However, the flow of "mutual aid" seems to be less continuous and less substantial in the West than in Japan. Denmark represents the extreme case in this respect because, although visiting is frequent between the generations, very little service exchange is reported. In the United States and in the United Kingdom, the generations are prepared to do things for one another when and as needed, although not usually on the basis of routinized, regular responsibilities (Shanas and others 1968:151). The older the parent becomes, however, the more likely the children are perceived to be providing necessary care. Until aging begins to take its toll in earnest, however, the patterns between generations in the Western countries are on the basis of frequent contacts of a more social than utilitarian nature, combined with rather inconsequential exchanges of gifts and services.

In all four countries, there are some class differences. In the three countries of the West, the middle-class older people are less likely than the working class to share a household with children, to live in very close proximity if a household is not shared, and to see at least one child every day or every other day (Shanas and others 1968:431-32). Independent living, then, is stressed somewhat more by the middle class. In Japan there is a similar class difference, since preferences for parents living with adult children decrease as the educational level increases (Palmore 1975:41). In no country, however, are class differences large enough to override the general patterns of relationships between the generations.

Palmore does not report on sibling ties in Japan. Probably the brothers and sisters of the older generation are not seen as very important to their well-being since the parent-child relationship is so close. The data from the other three countries also show that when there are children greater contact and mutual aid flow between the generations, and brothers and sisters of the same generation are much less close. For older people who have remained single, however, siblings are very important. In fact, the percentage of single old people who live with brothers and sisters is more than double that of widowed living with married children and many times as high as that of widowed living with siblings, as the table below shows. Although the proportions of older people who never married are small in all three countries, the data demonstrate how effectively getting married and establishing a family of one's own weakens the bonds between sisters and brothers.

These cross-cultural data show that most persons over sixty-five will be living alone or with their spouses in the three Western countries, but in Japan, in the homes of their children. Different living arrangements may have an effect on certain emotions such as loneliness. Table 5.3 shows that most older people everywhere say they rarely or never feel lonely and only very small proportions are often lonely. In terms of self-perceptions of loneliness, the Japanese and the Danes are relatively the most fortunate; yet their living partners are quite different. Older Japanese almost always live with children, especially in widowhood. The Danes have a more equal sex ratio in later life, which makes it more common in that country for older people still to be married. This fact may alleviate loneliness. Still, old age brings loss of spouse to many old people, especially women, in Denmark as in the other countries. And in Denmark, three fifths of all elderly persons who are widowed, divorced, or single live alone, a proportion significantly higher than in either Britain or the United States. Yet, in those two countries there is more loneliness, with the Americans being slightly less fortunate. In Britain, there is more evidence of an extended family pattern, and old people are less likely to be living alone than in either of the other two Western countries. Still, the British "loneliness quotient" is almost as high as

Table 5.2
Joint-Household Frequencies for Widowed and
Single Old People in Three Countries (%)*

	United States	United Kingdom	Denmark
Widowed or Divorced Parents Living with Married Children	16	23	8
Widowed or Divorced Living with Siblings	4	4	1•
Single Living with Siblings	38	47	22

*Adapted from Shanas and others 1968:151-52.

Table 5.3
Frequencies of Loneliness for Persons sixty-five
and over in Four Countries (%)*

	Japan	United States	United Kingdom	Denmark
Often Lonely	.04	.09	.07	.04
Rarely or Never Lonely	86	70	72	83

Adapted from Palmore 1975:50.

that of the United States and quite a bit higher than that of Denmark. Overall, cultural patterns of appropriateness seem to influence loneliness, especially since the Japanese who are embedded in an extended family are no different from the Danes who follow the nuclear household pattern most closely.

Extended Families and Industrialization

The preservation of the extended family residence in Japan into full industrial development has attracted much attention (Plath 1972). The whole approach to industrialization in Japan has been different from that in the West and probably has reinforced traditional family arrangements. The major Japanese firms today can be seen as "pseudo" kin institutions. Unlike the westerner, the Japanese worker will enter a firm at maturity and remain with that firm until retirement. The employee is expected to achieve, but within one company that will recognize efforts through pay increases and promotions. The company also is much more than a place of work. Not only does it offer security of location and retraining for new tasks and positions as the worker grows older, the firm also organizes much of the workers' social and recreational life.

This stability and security, considered in the West to violate the rules of competition and therefore to be economically inefficient, supports the extended family in two ways. Most obvious is the fact that the Japanese will not be moving around geographically during his or her working life. Parents and children can more easily remain together. They need not live together, but it seems quite possible that Japanese economic arrangements also reduce the demand for the independence of the individual. Company loyalty and kin loyalty move hand in hand to foster allegiance to the group. Unlike westerners, Japanese are not expected to leave the firm in search of new and better opportunities. Japanese parents, then, do not need to emphasize social self-reliance as much as Western parents do in bringing up their children. Consequently, there may be less psychological strain in maintaining joint households. The stem family was traditionally more common in Japan and emphasized more the authority of the oldest generation than in Western Europe, according to historical research (Laslett 1978:115). Religious beliefs centered on ancestor worship and stressed filial piety. This heritage from the past continues to affect family arrangements in contemporary times, though the stem has been modified.

Since World War II, not just the first-born son but all children inherit from parents, and in turn are obligated to provide them with support and care as necessary. Yet Japanese parents usually continue to reside in the home of a son, with other chilren playing a more modest role in later life contingencies. Depending on available space, the preferred arrangement seems to be for parents to live a little apart from the central living units of the adult children and their young. Yet the older parents claim to be consulted on household matters, and they much prefer living with their children to having separate homes of their own. Industrial growth has been accomplished in Japan so as to accommodate this kind of arrangement.

In the West, especially in the Protestant countries, a religiously grounded emphasis on individualism preceded industrialism. The latter reinforced individualist values including the right, if not the duty, of each person to seek the best economic opportunities wherever they can be found, and the right, if not the obligation, of the employer to hire and fire on the basis of profitability. At least since the Reformation, identification with a collective family unit has been weaker in the West than in Japan. Industrial society seems to have cut off what little practice there was of younger and older adult generations of the same descent line living together, at least for intact marital couples. In this respect, the United States, the United Kingdom, and Denmark are much alike in emphasizing the integrity of the marriage bond and the right to private, autonomous living. Old couples live alone together in almost all cases as long as both survive. The extended family does not dissolve, but it is maintained between separate households in the form of frequent contact and limited mutual aid. As people become widowed or move into higher age brackets, the children are likely to become closer, with increased contact and offering of services. Coresidence occurs usually only for the widowed, and only for a minority of widowed old persons at that. Single old people often live with brothers and sisters, but the survivor of a marriage, especially if that marriage ended through divorce rather than through death, is likely to live alone.

To some extent, these boundaries do fade with increasing age and with bereavement, but increased interaction usually stops short of the joint household. These patterns are modified by class and by country. In every country the working class seems slightly more amenable to joint households, and the British as a group are more likely to double up than either the Americans or the Danes are. The Danes, in fact, seem to be the most rigidly nuclear, having neither joint households nor service exchange between the generations. Still, in the West as represented here, we are looking only at variations of a common theme: Children do not live with their parents once they are married, and even when one of the aged parents is left alone, joint households are not the common residential solution. The three countries together contrast sharply with Japan in the management of family life in old age. The United States stands between the United Kingdom and Denmark in the degree to which joint households are formed. It differs from both the other countries in one major respect which may contribute to the more frequent feelings of loneliness: A larger minority of aging parents have contact with their children less than once a month.

AGING AND THE FAMILY
IN THE UNITED STATES

After the Children Have Left

Remembering that there is some variation in family life from country to country, we now can turn to a more detailed picture of aging and the family in the United States. In this country, most persons sixty-five and older are the heads of households or the wives of heads of households (U.S. Census 1965). Autonomous living arrangements for the elderly are customary in this society, and the number of "older people only households" has been increasing since larger proportions are married (U.S. Census 1960), and fewer live with relatives other than spouses (Murray 1967).

Much of the research on older people has concentrated on relations with children and other kin; so, strangely enough, we know rather little about how the aging husband and wife get along on their own after the children have grown. What is known seems to indicate that they enjoy life as a couple alone again. There were crises of adjustment to the empty nest and also to retirement, the most troublesome of which were differences in life goals and interests (Stinnett, Carter, & Mongomery 1972). But most marriages seem to improve as the couples get to know one another more intimately again (Blood & Wolfe 1960; Rollins & Feldman 1970). There is much positive emphasis on "new freedom" as middle-age roles are relinquished. The responsibilities of work that sometimes alienated husband and wife are in the past for most older couples, and their interests and activities are reorganized around similar themes. Marriages that for a long time had been subordinated to the demands of dependent children strengthen as such demands diminish or disappear. In fact, maladjustment is more likely to occur among couples whose grown children remain dependent on their parents (Lowenthal 1976:450). Older parents stress a preference for living independently (Somerville 1972).

Reliance on the marital dyad for the family resource of emotional support is, of course, not equally available to all aging persons, nor are the intact marriages all satisfying. Divorce rates are on the increase even among the once maritally stable middle class in this country (Glick 1975). Widowhood is common, especially for women. But older people seeking intimacy tend to remarry if possible to find a close relationship with another person or persons of the same generation. Divorced and widowed older men are very likely to remarry. In the postretirement phase, many men relinquish more formal network obligations with relief and seek more emotionally satisfying relationships that they find only in marriage (Lowenthal and others 1967). Women after divorce or bereavement in later life have fewer opportunities to remarry because there are more women than men of their age. Unlike men, women seem to have better capacities for close ties with persons other than a spouse and often compensate for loss of spouse by intimacy with others of the same sex (Blau 1961). Another solution is the commune or the "group marriage" in which a small number of elderly people, not necessarily of different sexes, live together in a common household for both expressive and economic purposes. A trend in this direction has been observed among older people (Ramey 1975; Conover 1975).

Rosow (1967) believes that older people, freed from the role responsibilities of middle life, are most concerned with closeness and empathy. To the extent that this is so, marriage seems to be the most appropriate setting for its expression for older people. They generally are satisfied with their marriages, more so than when the children were growing up and more so than if an adult child remains dependent. Older couples want to be alone with each other. If the marriage ends through divorce or death, a new marriage often will be sought. If this fails, compensatory ties may be formed with members of the same generation in other contexts.

This preference of the old for the old is manageable, however, only to the extent that health and income permit a reasonable degree of independence. When older people cannot support themselves as a couple or even as a group enterprise, their independence is threatened. Many older people seem ready to subsist very marginally in this country rather than to seek the help of other family members. More than income, however, ill health undermines the capacity of older persons to care for one another indefinitely, exposing the potential frailty of exclusive same-generation bonding for family needs in old age.

The Relationship Between Aging Parents and Children

The relationship between parents and their children after maturity in this society has been aptly termed "intimacy at a distance" (Rosenmayer & Kockeis 1965). The elderly want to live close to their children but not with them. The separate households remain connected to some extent, but societal complexity may automatically reduce linkages. Each household is not just residentially divided, but there is also an agreement that each pursues its own interests and goals and is responsible for its own maintenance. Adult children may go into quite different occupations from those of their parents; they may have quite different life styles and social networks; the generations may grow apart because there is little that can be shared. Such a process may occur even when families remain in close physical proximity to one another. Another factor that separates the generations is geographical mobility, and this type of distancing is more common in the United States than in the other countries studied previously.

Even when parents and children remain close in life style and geographical space, there seem to be some contraints on what they do for one another or at least on what they feel they should do for one another given the value placed on separate maintenance of households. Accordingly, the intergenerational exchange seems to be most comfortable when it is based more on emotion than on goods and services, and when the balance of giving and receiving is about equal between the generations. This balance does not happen automatically. It has to be achieved, and, if established at all, it may not endure until the end of life.

Studies show that grown children are not abruptly weaned from parental sheltering (Adams 1970; Feldman 1964). There is a flow of mutual aid, but the older couples do substantially more of the giving and the younger more of the receiving. After the first few years of marriage, the younger generation achieves more complete economic and psychological independence, and there is an attenuation in the flow of goods and services with neither requiring much of the other. There continue to be high levels of intergenerational activities (Shanas 1967; Sussman 1960; Youmans 1963), but the relationship is more affectional and egalitarian. The great majority of older people seems quite satisfied with this state of affairs, saying that they see their children and grandchildren as much as they want (Riley & Foner 1968:547). The adult children usually take more initiative and emphasize services more because of an association between life after age sixty-five and failing vigor and health. As long as the older parents are still fairly healthy, however, exchanges are mostly social occasions in which affection and respect are demonstrated, and there are only token gifts and services—small presents or amounts of money, advice, information, occasional help with a chore. Regular, consistent sharing of mutual responsibilities is left to the nuclear households.

This balanced "intimacy at a distance" seems to be a satisfactory arrangement for both generations (Cumming & Henry 1961; Kerckhoff 1966; Clark & Anderson 1967). Some older persons are dissatisfied, to be sure, and feel neglected by their children, although dissatisfied older parents seem to be relatively few (Brown 1970). Such parents actually may be neglected in that their children through indifference or hostility simply pay no attention to them. Or they may feel neglected because they want more from their children than is appropriate in the delicate balance of relationships between the generations in this society. In either case, those who feel neglected are outside the pattern in which warm and continuous interaction is mingled with a respectful detachment from the "other family's" affairs.

This friendly detachment seems to extend to the relationship between grandparents and grandchildren (Lowenthal 1978:438). Although in Japan and in some other countries such as Russia (McKain 1972), grandfathering and especially grandmothering may be fairly important in old age, it does not seem to be so in the United States. Although grandparenthood is perceived as fulfilling or at least pleasant in this country, only seldom do grandparents assume any primary responsibility in socializing their grandchildren (Hendricks & Hendricks 1977:275). According to Neugarten & Weinstein (1964), there are several distinctive styles of grandparenting which range from the playful to the formal, but the common outcome seems to be that seldom is there any regular responsibility in caring for the child.

Grandchildren have the most appeal when they are babies, and relations between grandparents and grandchildren tend to become more distant as the children mature. Older people are fond of their grandchildren, but they generally do not seem to wish to change the nature of their relations with them. Again, being an active grandparent might be seen as interfering with the responsibilities of the "other family," or older people may want to protect the freedom they have earned now that their own child-rearing duties are completed.

So far we have presented a rather smooth picture of family life between the generations. After an initially sticky period during which the adult child becomes fully independent, most older parents and their adult children occupy separate households, each of which is essentially responsible for its own maintenance. Yet between the households a steady flow of contact and sentiment is maintained. Although goods and services exchanged have only symbolic value, they indicate that the other generation is there and ready to help if necessary. Yet sensitivity forbids encroaching too far on the other household, and both generations are satisfied to maintain a certain distance. But relations with children have been found to have an equivocal effect on the morale of older persons (Rosenberg 1973). In other words, the older person who sees more of his or her children may not be any happier than the one who sees less. This seems to be related to a tipover point in the satisfactory management of parent-adult child relations at which the child begins to give more and the parent begins to receive more.

Up to the point of failing health in old age, the parent has gone through stages in which the child moved from the complete dependency of infancy to the rather complete independence from parental support of any kind. Then, however, the tide begins to turn in the other direction, and the younger generation may take on more and more responsibility for the care of the aging parent. This process is often referred to as role reversal. As ill health becomes evident, the family circle becomes closer either through pull (affection and esteem for the older person) or through push (a sense that the older person has few options and that kin must help). Children increase contacts, even making residential changes if necessary. Those who are nearest to the ailing parent take on supportive and caretaking roles, and even those who are far away will contribute what they can (Sussman 1976). Children seem to accept filial responsibility for ailing parents verbally and also actually (Litman 1971).

According to Blenkner (1965), filial maturity necessitates negotiating the assurance that children can be counted on when needed without giving the parents the pervasive pathological concern with being a burden. This may work when there is a temporary crisis or a short-term illness. But often it is a long process of going gradually but inevitably downhill. In such cases, it is usually true that the older person is a burden, and there is nothing pathological about this interpretation. One reason for this is the role reversal and the psychological strains placed on the aging parent. The reciprocal relationship becomes one of unequal exchange with the aging parent on the receiving end (Slater, Sussman, & Stroud 1970; Sussman 1976:219). Furthermore, the older person cannot draw on an anticipated ability to resume a more active part in his own behalf and thus is permanently assigned to a dependent status. All he or she has to offer any more is compliance, as options and resources shrink. Since finances are likely to be constrained even when the older person is well, ill health completely distroys any notions of independence. The aged person is seldom in a position to hire help (who would at least be subject to his or her economic authority) or even, for that matter, pay for his or her own medicine. But when the children come to the rescue, the response often is not gratitude (Blau 1963; Maas & Kuypers 1974; Sussman 1976:228). Sick older men and women tend to express dissatisfaction with their children, despite their efforts. The older person suspects a lack of acceptance on their part.

To feel deviant, or socially unacceptable, may be the fate of all individuals who undergo long, debilitating, and irreversible illnesses in an active society, but when the caretakers are one's own children, such an experience is especially poignant. The very persons for whom the parent modeled independence and to whom they taught the value of standing on one's own feet in life, now directly witness the failure of the parents themselves in this regard. Disabled older parents find it very difficult to be dependent on children for care. Their lack of gratitude—expressed in complaints and unpleasant behavior—leads to the frequent outcome of family members becoming disaffected with one another. Exactly what the older person expected, loss of respect and trust, actually comes to pass.

The role reversal and its psychological strains on the family are only one part of the burden. Children have demonstrated their willingness to care for family members, but there is some understandable anxiety about competence. The family as constituted in our society does not have the structural, organizational, and economic resources to care for an ill person over a long period of time (Parsons & Fox 1952). The family might manage to cope with the sickness of a young child in which the psychological costs of inappropriateness are reduced, and the parents themselves are still vigorous. But if care of an older person is undertaken, it is likely to fall most heavily on one or at most two children who themselves are in late maturity and simultaneously attempting to manage the final emancipation or early marital crises of their own children (Shanas 1962). Family units are much too small to permit drawing on auxiliary personnel to share in meeting the needs of the elderly unless there is ample money available. Sons and daughters must direct energies away from their other responsibilities, sometimes at the cost of personal feelings of inadequacy and marital conflict (Adams 1970; Sweetser 1963). And the image of older persons who have emptied their own nests and are approaching retirement undertaking care of octogenarian parents is not farfetched; it does occur. The exigencies of heavy care for the disabled may adversely affect the "younger" old people, creating an entire structure of frailty.

In short, managing a viable, extended-kin network and successful intergenerational relations is a problem in this society. The younger and older generations have worked out a mutually satisfactory adjustment of "intimacy at a distance." But the degree of independence of households makes the network connections rather loose and much too weak to manage long-term illness in the aged. Sussman (1976:232-33) suggested that elderly persons could alleviate some of the burden of the role reversal and reward caring children as well, through inheritance. Unfortunately, most old people have little to leave behind, and a long illness is likely to leave them penniless if not actually in debt, at least to their families. In the end, although family responsibility persists in the younger generation, the relationship between aging parents and children is likely to sour if life terminates in a lengthy illness. Although most children seem to do their best even to the point of considerably disturbing their own lives, eventually hospitals and other health systems take on the responsibility for care.

Other Relatives

Spouses and children seem to be in the foreground of the family network, but other relatives have some part in old age. In line with previous comments about "old preferring old" for intimacy, there is some evidence that involvement with relatives of one's own generation is strengthened in old age (Cumming & Schneider 1961). But the breakdown into separate units with separate destinies which occurred at marriage is not really united again. Depending partially on proximity, contacts increase but never reach the frequency and regularity of those with children. It is only among those who never married that the sibling tie seems to persist unbroken, so that living together or at least keeping in regular touch and exchanging services is common. Single siblings can and sometimes do provide services to one another in a manner somewhat comparable to that of married couples. Unfortunately, brothers and sisters as family-intimacy options do not seem to be easily available to those who have married, even when the marriage has subsequently been dissolved. There also is the possibility as in other same-generation pairing patterns of losing even close sibling ties through death.

Variations in Subgroups

In completing the discussion of family ties in old age, we shall study variations in subgroups in the United States. Probably the most obvious issue is that of the sexes, since women have significantly longer life expectancies than men do.

Because there is a smaller pool of males and because men more often have younger spouses, it is not surprising that women are much less likely to have a living spouse after age sixty-five. As Table 5.4 shows, most men were married even in very old age, but relatively few women had spouses, especially after age seventy-five. Although the average older couple can expect to have sixteen years together after the "empty nest," two thirds of all married women are likely to spend the last eighteen years of their lives as widows (Glick & Parke 1965). Data on 1970 show that only 59 percent of all older women, as opposed to 79 percent of men, lived with other relatives, usually as head of household or spouse of head of household in a couple arrangement. But twice as many of these women (16 percent) as men (8 percent) lived in an arrangement in which some relative other than self or spouse, usually a child, was the head of the household (Sussman 1978:221). Overall, women over sixty-five were much more likely to live alone (35 percent) than men (17 percent) were. Despite this apparent isolation, however, the great majority of all widowed older persons, four fifths of whom were women, expressed the desire to live alone and usually did so. There is some compensation in that women seemed closer to their children than men did. More of them (although still only a minority) moved in with their children, but beyond this, widowed women seemed to have closer ties to their children after bereavement than before. Women did seem to have more skill in managing expressive ties than men did with persons who were not spouses, and this alleviated potential loneliness in old age (Hendricks & Hendricks 1977: 263). This capacity extended across the generations, and more middle-age daughters cared for aging parents of either sex than sons did. How women were socialized apparently reduced independence demands, allowing more intergenerational continuity over time; yet there obviously still was a high value on autonomous living. As more women find jobs as a part of their life style, there may be changes in their orientations to family roles.

We noted that in comparing four countries, social class did influence exchanges between old people and their relatives. An additional comment for the United States can be made: adult middle-class children were likely to live farther away from parents and see them less frequently than working-class children did. Also,

Table 5.4
Proportion of Married Persons over Age 65
by Sex in the United States (%)*

Men		Women	
65 to 74	75+	65 to 74	75+
81.8	68.3	47.3	22.3

Adapted from Hendricks & Hendricks 1977:267 (data from 1975).

middle-class parents were somewhat less likely to live with their children than working-class parents were. Exchanges between parents and adult children were likely to center on money in the middle class and on services (housework, other chores, baby sitting) in the working class. These differences, however, were more of degree and kind; the patterning of relationships seemed rather similar. Middle-class families compensated for more geographical distance by longer visits between parents and adult children. For either social class, the "utilitarian exchanges" of money and services tended to be less important than expressions of affection between the generations.

"Social class" applies to a number of different situations, and it appears that the closest extended family ties were in the lowest socioeconomic groups (Sussman 1976:436). Here, parents and children and often other relatives were more likely to live together or at least to remain in very close proximity. Poorer families apparently depended much more on one another for both economic and social support, and were reluctant to leave the common neighborhood.

In this country, there are many racial minorities and white ethnic groups, but knowledge of their family patterns is so far very limited (Kalish & Moriwaki 1973). Some recent work has been done on the largest racial minority, the blacks, and we shall confine our remarks about subcultural variation to them. Statistics show that elderly black households were much less likely (67 percent) than elderly white households (83 percent) to contain only two persons. Four times as many elderly black families as white (20 percent versus 5 percent) had a child of eighteen or younger in the home (Hendricks & Hendricks 1977: 268). Thus, older blacks were less likely to be living as a couple alone, and their households were much more likely to encompass a broad age span.

Studies show more reliance on an extended kin system of a type somewhat different than that found for whites (Hirsh and others 1972; Jackson 1972, 1973; Shimkin & Shimkin 1975). The black family recognizes bilateral descent with more loosely related spouses and is centered on representatives of the oldest living generation. Affective ties are, however, concentrated on the matrilineal base so that younger descendants live either with or near the wife's mother. The emphasis on the female line is probably partly because black women are even more likely than white women to live longer than men, and partly because the greater economic participation of black women compared with white females during adult life has persisted for many more years. A relatively high degree of family connectedness of the black aged has been found on all socioeconomic levels, and the model of relations between older parents and children is one of parity or equality. Despite the greater emphasis on linearity, however, black elderly also expressed preference for intimacy at a distance, and family cohesion seemed to diminish among the economically more affluent. Thus, women, working-class persons, and blacks place less stress on independent living, but the overriding theme continues to be fairly consistent.

Summary

Briefly summarizing the family life of older people in industrialized societies, cultural variation seemed to emphasize the differences between East and West. Japanese traditions, adapted to industrial relations, accommodate a continuance of residential sharing and mutual aid reciprocity among the generations. Three Western countries, however—the United States, the United Kingdom, and Denmark—are more remarkable for their similarities than for their differences. The United States stands between the other two in the extent to which extended family ties are used both with respect to coresidence and to the flow of mutual aid. But the predominant patterns are the same in all three countries; in old age the marital bond is the most exclusive, and even when it has ceased to exist, reservations and boundaries are placed on relationships with other relatives. Beyond the marital tie, the use of social space in the kinship system seems to be limited for older people. If there are living children, contact will be mainly with them, although there is some regeneration of sibling ties in old age. But only single older people seem to capitalize on the sibling as a really close connection in old age. A more in-depth examination of the United States served to confirm the pattern, and highlight its significance. Adult children leave parents and siblings to establish independent households for which they take the responsibility. The tie to parents is less likely to be severed than that for siblings when there is marriage and a family, but it takes on a different aspect. Both parents and children recognize a certain priority of obligations to their own households in which boundaries will be crossed only at the peril of unbalancing mutual affection and respect. Family space is used selectively depending on whether or not one has children and whether or not one has a spouse in old age, but unless the marriage tie perseveres, the uses of kin are rather severely limited. Even emotional support by relatives other than spouse is special and rather reserved and can weaken if long-term illness incapacitates the older members.

THE FAMILY AND THE STATE

Older people in industrial societies gain a certain degree of independence through the state's guarantee of social rights. Economic, health, and other benefits are channeled directly to older persons rather than through any intermediate group such as the family. Yet, as we have seen, families still do a great many things with and for older people. But there are questions as to whether the efforts of the state and the family are complementary or are working at cross-purposes.

Generally, the obligations of children and other relatives are not specified by law. Family assistance to older people is voluntary. It is offered out of affection, respect, or a sense of duty. By not insisting on specific family obligations, it may be that the state encourages a certain distance between older people and their kin. To the extent that this is true, the government does foster the sense that older people are in its care and that family members can neglect them with impunity. If this were so, we would expect that kin ties would be weaker in countries that do not legally obligate the family to support older members, and we also would expect that health and social services would be provided equally to older persons whether or not they had close living kin.

Caring for the Elderly and the Law

Are relationships between older people and their kin qualitatively different in societies in which children are legally responsible for serving the needs of their parents as opposed to those in which they are not? To test the notion that the family withdraws once the state steps in, some tentative answers can be found by looking at historical and contemporary data that compare the two different situations.

The best "before-after" case comes from historical research in Great Britain where it is possible to trace the impact of legislation for family responsibility over several centuries (Anderson 1977:36-59). In the chapter on retirement, it was mentioned that England legislated the Elizabethan Poor Law in the early seventeenth century. The Law was instituted to give relief to the needy, although the right to relief was based on destitution, not just on poverty, and provided only the minimum to prevent death from starvation or exposure. The Law was revised in 1834, still stipulating pauperism as the criterion for eligibility, and designated not only the resources of the individual but also those of family members in the direct descent line as part of the accounting process. Children who were not themselves destitute were legally bound to support aging parents. The provision was intended to encourage "family affections" by by-passing any possible conflict about responsibilities between the family and the state. In effect, however, the legal obligations placed on the family seemed to have promoted a high degree of division within the family itself. Following passage of the 1834 amendments, statistics show that 30 percent of persons over seventy were on relief and that annually increasing numbers of old people went to live in "workhouses."

In investigating these trends, a Royal Commission attacked what it called the myth that the role and status of older people as dependents on the family was positive. The Commission found that older people who could not meet Poor-Law eligibility were unwanted drudges in the houses of their children, sometimes expressing the belief that death would be preferable to the obvious burden of their support. Old people often preferred the pittance available from their parishes to compulsory aid from their children.

The Law was difficult to enforce since neither parents nor children were willing to comply with its demands. Other negative repercussions on the family included conflict among the children as to which of them should be obligated to give aid to their parents. In short, the family situation was described as "very bitter." Even investigating authorities sent to determine eligibility for poor relief agreed that the legal requirements were alienating rather than cementing kin relations. In 1908, a noncontributory old-age pension was granted to all British nationals over seventy. Within four years, Poor-Law outrelief (community living assistance) recipients decreased by 95 percent, and, especially among poorer families, older people who now had something of their own to contribute became more welcome in the households of relatives. Incarceration in the workhouse was substantially decreased. Relatively few of the remaining inhabitants (16 percent) had any family at all. Anderson concluded that the beginning of the welfare state had a positive effect on family life by removing economic tensions and allowing that institution to concentrate on affection as the basis of support.

Studying one country in the process of transition from agriculture to industry provides limited insight. It may be that reactions were peculiar to that place in that phase of development. We do have information available on a number of industrial societies today which show some variation in law on family obligations. Unfortunately, however, the countries included have rather different histories and traditions, which make comparisons of limited value. Some never legally imposed responsibilities on relatives for the care of older people. Others did so for a brief period in history and then abandoned this approach. Still others, though few, have such laws on their books today.

Of six countries included in a recent cross-national effort (Shanas & Sussman 1977), only two, Yugoslavia and Israel, require adult children to support their aging parents. The other four, Austria, France, the Netherlands, and Poland, have no such laws. In all six, however, the general conclusions are much in line with those of Shanas and others. They agree that the state's providing assistance improved family relationships between the generations, whereas "dependency begets avoidance" (Streib 1977). Attempting to create a mutual responsibility by the state offering transfers but also obligating children to support did not improve relationships. Enforcing laws of family support was very difficult since both older people and their offspring resisted. Also, families in all countries were in close contact, although generally through "intimacy at a distance." Most aging parents lived separately from their children and preferred it that way. Contact, however, was frequent and mutually rewarding. State aid, making independent living possible, seemed to have been welcome and beneficial in maintaining intergenerational ties.

Living arrangements and degree of intimacy were somewhat variable. The two extreme cases, Yugoslavia and the Netherlands, deserve special comment. Yugoslavia is reminiscent of Japan in that nearly 70 percent of older persons who have children live in the same household with one of them (Smolic-Krkovic 1977). In both countries children are required by law to care for parents if they are in a position to do so. Yugoslavians also seem to agree that it is right for aging parents to live with children. Yet, as Yugoslavia becomes more industrialized, the number of joint households is growing smaller. Also, unlike Japan, there is a fair amount of geographical mobility in connection with work which tends to separate families. Since both men and women of the "middle generation" work, there is some evidence that old people are being neglected by their families, especially as they become less productive in the household. Despite closer residential ties and laws obligating support from children, inter-generational relations showed considerable strain.

A very different situation can be found in the Netherlands (Munnichs 1977) where families have the highest degree of both emotional and geographical distance. Compared to all other countries for which there are data, older people live at greater distances from their children and see them less frequently. The generations do not break off relationships, but the degree of intimacy seems to be even lower than in Denmark. Munnichs suggested that instituting legal responsibility might tighten family bonds. Given the experiences of other countries, however, it seems more likely that the quality of the parent-child relationship is responsible for the rather cold atmosphere, and introducing legal responsibilities would hardly improve the situation.

Overall, there does seem to be a kind of cooperative acceptance of responsibility between state and family when the state provides a minimum for independent living and allows the family to contribute voluntarily. Cultural circumstances do vary family arrangements, but it would be difficult to conclude that state intervention leads to poorer quality. Attempting to enforce children's obligations to parents only kindles resistance on both sides. As Kreps (1977) pointed out, relying on family support generates conflicts over what is right and/or feasible and induces guilt and strain. Assured that the older person will receive a certain income from the state, the family is freed from such problems, and ties between members can be more rewarding.

Distribution of Health
and Other Social Services

In some ways, however, governments seem to behave as if children and other relatives are responsible for older people whether or not there are legal sanctions. This becomes apparent when we examine the second question, pertaining to the distribution of health and other social services. An indirect measure of reliance on family care can be found in statistics on institutionalization for older populations. In all of the ten countries we have discussed in this chapter—Austria, Denmark, France, Israel, Japan, the Netherlands, Poland, the United Kingdom, and the United States—the evidence is that older people with families are far more likely to be kept in the community. People over sixty-five in nursing homes, mental hospitals, old people's homes and other "total care" facilities are mostly the never married, the childless and the widowed. Health and social services for community residents tend to be very sparse everywhere and again mostly for those without families. Even in the Netherlands, where the rate of institutionalization for people over sixty-five is more than double the average in other countries, it is disproportionately those without families who receive either total care or community services. Our depth data from the United States and that supplied by Monroney (1977) from the United Kingdom suggest that families provide very extensive aid in crises and even for long-term disability. Children respond to filial duty to an extent sometimes damaging to other obligations, since their efforts drain the limited resources of a relatively small social structure. The state, however, only helps those without families. Again, some kind of complementarity is achieved in an "unspoken" agreement, but in this instance government services are far less supportive of family cohesion.

It may be that governments and their approved agencies are uneasy about performing functions that they believe are better served by the family. Just as the family is not made responsible for economic support to the elderly, however, other specialized institutions are needed to supply the personnel, resources, and expertise in long-term illness. Bureaucratic institutions are probably the least capable of meeting the very personal needs of human beings, but this the family does well, according to the reports of most older people. The family can and does respond to short-term crises, as well as to day-to-day needs for emotional gratification. But it can continue doing what it does best under long-term exigencies without self-damage only with external assistance. We agree with those who feel that the unequal distribution of services favoring those without families represents, in the area of health and social services, more of an attempt to replace the family than to supplement it (Sussman 1977; Litvak 1970; Kreps 1977:32-33).

Families seem to need no public pressure to continue responsibilities for older members. They cannot, however, be expected to perform feats beyond their means. A more satisfactory division of labor, such as that which has evolved in the economic sphere, could alleviate the obvious stress which is harmful to both older people and the family generally. Over the long run, there will be problems. Bureaucracy was not meant for coping with persons as persons; that is for the family and other primary groups, such as close friends. Perhaps that is why one sees a logical division of responsibility between state and family in caring for older persons (Litvak 1970; Sussman 1977: Kreps 1977:32-33).

Health and social services are offered gingerly by governments and mainly to those with no visible close family. Thus, we agree that social services that attempt to support the family receive lower priority than those which attempt to replace it (Sussman 1977; Monroney 1977). By offering resources directly to individuals and by awarding scarce special services mainly to those without family, the extended family network is left with insufficient resources to pull itself together in behalf of older persons.

That there is a gap between what the state is willing to do and what the family is able to do appears certain. The proposed solution of giving societal resources directly to the family (usually the children) to rebuild a family network that probably never existed overlooks very serious problems. Cooperation must be within a viable framework that respects the family solution of intimacy at a distance and the very real exigencies of family life in contemporary society. With the majority of adult women working full time, there are no full-time caretakers at home for anybody. The retired couple devoting full time to each other is the nearest approximation, although that is a precarious solution. The interdependence of individuals as citizens and the state will have to continue, and relief, not further burdens, must be offered to the family.

THE FAMILY:
MORE THAN INTIMACY AT A DISTANCE

Much of the work on the family has compared the modern family to an ideal in preindustrial societies. This comparative view neglects the fact that in most known societies, certainly in the West, the family was responsible only for some of the life needs of its members. Generalizations about better integration and care for older people in agricultural communities overlook the evidence that there were relatively few older people and that extra-kin institutions had to intervene in their behalf even when the elderly were a very small proportion of the total population. Comparisons with preindustrial cultures have limited value for understanding relations in family life in industrial society, because of major changes in age structure and social structure. The family was never sufficient by itself, but a land-based economy did allow for more geographic and social stability and the fusion of social institutions. Industrialization more distinctly places the family as one specialized institution among many, with only limited tasks to perform. These are to provide early socialization for children and to meet the socioemotional needs of its members of all ages. Other institutions are charged with the responsibilities for other spheres of life.

Within this context, the information gathered supports the expectation that members will emancipate themselves from parental ties in adulthood so that they can deal with economic and other societal institutions on an individual basis. The emphasis on independence for nuclear family units, composed of spouses and immature children, seems to dominate despite minor variations. This applies to the older as well as to younger generations and is expressed as a preference.

This does not mean that family ties are cut in the extended network, but it has apparently led to the development of some normative limitations. For older people, potential family space is used very selectively depending on whether or not one has children and whether or not one has a spouse in old age. Parents remain in close contact with children, but the marital bond is paramount. Children move closer in bereavement but not usually to the extent of joint households. Only among older single persons are ties to siblings strong. Yet most older people do not feel neglected by their families in old age.

The continuing bond between adult children and their parents is the most widespread extended-kin phenomenon. It has been aptly characterized as "intimacy at a distance," because it indicates separate households yet a continuous flow of contact and at least token exchanges of mutual aid. This balanced state of egalitarian relationships, achieved after adult children are fully established in their own households, is mutually satisfying to all concerned. In the extremity of declining capacities in old age, however, children often find themselves giving more than is required by intimacy at a distance. Here children show a high level of responsiveness, but the balance is tipped toward dependence by the older generation. In the United States, at least, this imbalance has been shown to have unfortunate repercussions for both older people and their families.

The role of the state in bolstering or undermining family bonds in its activities on behalf of older people is somewhat ambiguous. Certainly providing the elderly with an income as a right as citizens appears to have strengthened rather than weakened family ties. Families do not shirk their responsibilities to older members because the state has taken a hand. On the other hand, government agencies do not allocate resources to families caring for the aged in their midst who develop chronic, irreversible illnesses and disabilities. Whether it is a deliberate decision not to interfere in family affairs or an unwarranted assumption that families should be able to care for seriously disabled older persons over an extended period, the position of the state in such instances contributes to making this the point at which usually strong and satisfying family relationships break down.

All the evidence suggests that the family in industrial societies definitely does not abandon its older members. There is a certain distancing among adult children and both parents and siblings which originates with the establishment of separate households. This distancing conforms to social expectations and is viewed positively by members of both the older and the younger generations.

The demand for independence may be modified by certain cultural traditions and arrangements as in the case of Japan. In Western societies it is a dominant theme which is only slightly attenuated among subgroups. In the United States working-class and black families show slightly stronger tendencies toward joint households or at least residential proximity of the extended family. Women appear to take more responsibility for maintaining family ties beyond the nuclear unit. Overall, however, there is a very clear pattern in this country of separating the generations by place of residence, especially when marriages are intact. Even in bereavement, however, it is relatively uncommon for widowed older parents to move in with children. Siblings, too, maintain their distance in old age, except in the case of those who never married. Single older brothers and sisters often live together. Potential social space is used sparingly, for it seems that older parents are linked mostly to their children, but single older persons are close to similarly situated siblings. If anything, the breaking up of the family of origin into separate core family units as the children move into adulthood seems to affect sibling ties more than generational ties.

Within this limited space, however, the great majority of aging parents are in very regular contact with their children. This contact is characterized mainly by exchanges of affection and respect with tokens of mutual aid. Although there clearly are boundaries beyond which the separate households of aging parents and adult children do not overlap, this autonomy is described as mutually satisfactory by both generations. Independence is prized, yet the continuous interaction is highly valued, perhaps especially by older members. Most aging parents do not want to see their children, or for that matter their grandchildren, any more or any less than they do. Many older people in fact find their own marriages enhanced by the freedom from middle-age responsibilities. Married or not, there is a discernible tendency to enjoy pursuing one's own interests and living style. Parents and their adult children generally seem to adapt well to each other's needs. Although this model lacks the true intimacy of sharing all household joys and burdens, the other generation is there when wanted. There is dissatisfaction only in the minority of cases in which the adult child remains dependent, or in which the older parent finds it hard to accept "intimacy at a distance."

It is clear that older parents need not share a household or participate in all aspects of their adult children's lives in order not to feel abandoned. As parents grow relatively older and/or develop chronic disabilities, far from abandoning their elders, children tend to increase contact and services of various kinds. The care they offer, however, causes psychological stress because of role reversal. Aging parents find it difficult to be dependent on the offspring they taught to become independent. The relatively small family system with few resources, also suffers from heavy, continuous care demands. At this point, the children reluctantly may turn to long-term care institution.

Studies in this area to date are limited, but they consistently show that this transfer of care of the elderly to other hands is in many instances a last resort after every effort has been made for home care. It is very difficult to perceive this as abandonment. The state, however, may inadvertently abandon both older parents and their children by its unwillingness to intervene with community services.

As long as older parents are able to care for themsevles fairly well, the bond between the generations—which seems to be the closest family tie in old age and the one about which we know most—is characterized by an emphasis on continuity within certain norms of industrial society. By a continuing flow of contact, characterized by affection and respect, adult children honor their parents for a job well done in raising them to manage their own lives. By caring when chronic illness takes its final toll, they also demonstrate their commitment to the continuity of kinship identity across the generations. Both parties suffer from the role reversal that the very last phase of life often entails, when the parent becomes a child again and the child must assume the superior position of the parent. In trying to care and in coping as best they can, the younger recommit themselves to the essential idea of kinship loyalty: that human bondage, unchosen and unequal, entails the obligation of caring concern that no one has a right to discard. But as will be shown in the following chapters, one of the more poignant expressions of this commitment to the "structure of frailty" that describes the family of advanced age in modern society is its manifestation of guilt.

6 on dying: premature social abandonment

At first glance, our three theoretical perspectives would not seem to apply at all to the subject of dying and death. Should one think of dying as relative deprivation or a matter of relative privilege vis-a-vis living? Do we not all have to die? Does it make sense even to suggest thinking of dying as abandonment or liberation? Does death not obviously mean a final parting, relegating all thought of diachronic solidarity between the living and the dead to the realm of the absurd? The answer is no, however much one may regret it. Modern medicine, science, technology, social organization, and hospitals, have made dying a frightfully complicated business. The days when grandfather died at home, surrounded by family and friends, are long gone now. Men and women in modern society die in hospitals, organized *not* for caring for the terminally ill but for curing the recoverably ill. That makes our modern ways of dying very complex, which makes application of our theoretical perspectives a necessity rather than a luxury.

Perspectives

The perspective of diachronic solidarity applies best to the funeral and to bereavement, both subjects of the next chapter. What it means for dying, however, can be noted here and briefly discussed later. Diachronic solidarity would be reflected in keeping company with the dying and sharing the meaning of death with them. This involvement with the dying would be as part of a chain lasting from generation to generation so that each generation could expect a return of the loyalties they showed to their forebears. There is little we can relate to this perspective in the material on dying. Both abandonment and liberation have their uses when it comes to dying. Applied to dying persons, abandonment simply means letting go of them before they are ready to go. Treating a dying person as one with a status of privilege has an equally simple meaning. Such relative privilege of the dying refers to their receiving care, attention, and respect even after their ability to reciprocate has been significantly diminished or even extinguished. As long as the brain is still alive, human life may be said to exist, even in the absence of significant interaction with the dying (Maguire 1975). Honoring that life is a way of conveying concern to the dying while liberating them from the responsibility to reciprocate and share such concern. As will be seen shortly, liberation of the dying is rare, premature social abandonment more frequent.

Various Aspects of Death

Defining abandonment and liberation of the dying in this fashion links these concepts to the distinctions among various aspects of dying used by specialists in terminal care. Pattison (1977:56), for example, distinguished between sociological, psychological, and physical death. These concepts describe separate aspects of death, and they provide theoretical insight to a discussion of the dying older person in modern society. Sociological death is the withdrawal of that kind of social interaction from the dying person that characterizes him or her as a living member of the community. It is a way of relating to the dying as if they were nearly dead or dead. One example would be nurses who respond less often to call lights of the terminally ill than to those of the recovering patients (Kastenbaum & Aisenberg 1972); another would be even fewer visits to the hospital by family members of an older person who takes a long time dying (Kastenbaum 1977:167). Psychological death denotes the dying person's withdrawal of motivation for social interaction with the living. No longer wanting visits from family and friends illustrates this aspect of death (Kastenbaum 1977:177). Physical death is the determination of death of the organism by criteria of brain death or the cessation of heart and respiratory function. Distinguishing these separate aspects of dying is particularly useful because of some striking parallels in the subjective experience of the dying person, on the one hand, and that of bereavement of those suffering the loss, on the other. We shall describe these parallels later.

These different aspects of death inspired some professionals to think of "optimum dying" as a process of mutual disengagement between the living and the dying. It was thought that anticipatory grief work by the survivors would facilitate such a step-by-step process so that the living and the dying would let go of each other more or less at the same rate. That, so it was held, would be of psychological benefit to both parties. But this has proved to be a rather unrealistic view of dying in modern times. A mosaic of evidence, demographic, organizational, educational, and normative, suggests instead that, by and large, sociological death tends to precede psychological death. In that sense one can speak of a modal pattern in which the dying older person tends to be somewhat prematurely socially abandoned. To be sure, such abandonment neither entails any callousness nor, indeed, any premature withdrawal of physical care of the body in the typical case, though both do apply to some of the indigent. If anything, it is a relative surfeit of physical care and an impressive technical life-prolonging capability coupled with a relative absence of emotional support for dying that characterizes the encounter with death of an older person in industrial society. Unfortunately, much of the relevant evidence on premature social abandonment of the dying has been entangled with what appears to be a false issue: the denial of death in advanced society. Therefore, we shall have to address that issue, even though both the popularity of death and dying courses on the American campus scene and the burgeoning literature on death relegate it to the status of a fashion truly out of style.

DEATH IN MODERN SOCIETY

One central feature of the literature of death and dying has been the claim that people in industrial society have some extraordinary need to deny the reality of death. If one were to focus on mass death by violence and the possibility of the annihilation of all human life in a nuclear holocaust, much would recommend this perspective. But curiously, the actual experience of modern war has not influenced the literature. According to a cross-cultural and historical perspective, the term modern usually refers to the industrial social order in peacetime. There the thesis of the denial of death has little sociological merit, either in theory or in fact. Indeed, a better case can be made for the assertion that people in an industrial society, when at peace, are singularly unprepared to deal with the dying. It is unpreparedness in relating to the dying, not having learned how to feel and share emotion and what to say, rather than any extraordinary need to deny the reality of death which seems to be at the root of the premature social abandonment of the dying in modern times. If anything, that should make social change more difficult. In denial, reformers can draw on preformed and shared concerns, however hidden. But in unpreparedness, resting in part on indifference, reformers have to mobilize concern.

Whether one attributes social abandonment of the dying to unpreparedness and indifference or to denial is an issue important enough to deserve some attention. Accordingly, we first shall examine some claims and counterclaims about the denial of death. Then we shall turn to organizational and educational matters. They tell of impressive cures and a similarly impressive helplessness in providing emotional support and psychological care for the dying. Rebalancing the situation for more effective terminal care is the objective of the hospice movement. Should it succeed, premature social abandonment of the dying may decline.

Denial of Death

The notion that people in industrial society have some unusual propensity to deny the reality of death has gripped the recent literature on death and dying to such an extent that it operates like an article of faith, endlessly reiterated (Tillich 1959; Wahl 1959; Feifel 1963; Caughill 1976; Rossman 1977:5). Dramatizing the point, Gorer (1955) claimed that death had become so much a taboo topic as to find expression only in pornographic form, taking the place that sex enjoyed before. Fulton (1976) wrote an article entitled "On the Dying of Death."

The evidence supplied for such claims is quite varied as is, indeed, the meaning of the term "denial" which is not uniformly used in the psychoanalytic sense of repression or banishment from conscious thought. Gorer, for example, was struck by the finding that the deathbed scene, a regular feature of the Victorian novel, had simply disappeared from corresponding contemporary literature in Britain. The author of a best seller and critic of American funeral customs in the sixties, Jessica Mitford (1963), argued for a denial of death on the basis of two observations. One was reliance on euphemistic language in the funeral parlor where one refers to "the departed" or the "deceased" rather than to the dead. The other was embalming practices seeking to give a corpse a lifelike appearance. Evelyn Waugh's satirical account of Hollywood's cemetery Forest Lawn, as a "slumberland" may have given impetus to the denial of death thesis.

Others noted that people in industrial societies die in hospitals (Blauner 1968) which seems to indicate that death is managed bureaucratically by functionaries rather than by family members. If by the term denial one means the expenditure of effort to avoid facing the death of self *and*/or that of others *based on* fear or anxiety about death, none of this evidence is compelling. In each case one could easily imagine motives other than fear or anxiety about death.

Theoretically, this view of the modern denial of death seems to rest on a confluence of two streams of thought, one psychoanalytic, the other existential (Becker 1973). The assertion that the modern age is a secular one is a connective link between the two. Freud (1915/1959, 1917/1959, 1926/1959) asserted that people's unconscious totally rejects the idea of the death of the self. Indeed, the very discovery of psychoanalysis as a therapeutic technique owes its origin to a case involving death, the famous "Anna O" (Breuer & Freud 1895). Thus the link between death and identity has a venerable history, and we shall use it below.

Freud made a case only for the denial of one's own death. To extend this to the denial of the death of another and to Western culture generally, which "in the presence of death, has tended to run, hide, and seek refuge in euphemistic language . . . " (Feifel 1963:66-67) is a view that rests heavily on assertions that ours is a godless age. Though a little risky, the existential root of the alleged need to deny death can be stated in the following proposition. Because we have no religiously compelling interpretations that connect life with death, the death of another symbolizes the void of our own, one we cannot bear and so banish from sight. This is a much simplified characterization of sometimes sophisticated and complex arguments. But the generalized denial of death in industrial society has been denied itself by others (Parsons & Lidz 1967), though apparently without much impact. Our own grounds for not presenting the position in greater detail is quite simple: One, the idea itself is not new; two, it is not true; and three, it has no merit in sociological theory.

The notion that modern society denies death was a widespread intellectual concern in British society toward the end of World War I and already had created a "death awareness industry" that could, were it appreciated, easily evince a sigh of envy from any contemporary thanatologist (Lerner 1975). To this we add only one other consideration. Humans can entertain the idea of their own nonbeing only in terms of a hypothetical logical contrast to being. Compared to the information about being, that about nonbeing is very sparse and lacks compelling conviction. On grounds such as these, Goethe long ago asserted that "everyone carries the proof of his own immortality within himself" (Choron 1964:37). No doubt, in some form, the denial of death thesis is very ancient.

Next, neither claims of secularism nor data on death anxiety support the denial of death thesis. As for a belief in God or some supernatural being, God is not dead in America and seems alive and well in industrial Western society in general. For example, definitely committed agnostics or atheists make up less than 3 percent of the American adult population (Glock & Stark 1965). From fourteen thousand visitors to the 1967 Montreal World Exposition, described as representing the younger, better educated, elite sectors of Western industrialized societies, we learned that only 1 percent subscribes to the idea that God is dead (Cappon 1970). Beyond that, answers indicative of agnosticism or atheism amounted to 19 percent. For about a quarter of these people "God was alive and personally reachable"; for another third, God represented an ethical principle for which people strive. As for a belief in an afterlife, this too was found to be widespread. Over three quarters of Americans subscribed to such a belief as "completely" or "probably" true. Among the Montreal Expo visitors, two thirds registered some belief in an afterlife. In short, ours is not a godless age, and death does not signify a meaningless void that strikes terror in the hearts and minds of men and women.

Is the thought of death repressed? Two types of survey data show that it is not. One technique was to ask respondents directly about their thoughts on death, usually in the form of whether and how frequently they entertain such thoughts. That has the disadvantage of drawing the respondent's attention to the topic of death. So this approach can tell us only what a person recalls about himself or herself *when asked*. But it does not tell us about the actual level of thinking of death undisturbed by the stimulation provided by the investigator. "Actual consciousness sampling," the alternative approach, avoids that limitation. Here the interviewer simply asks, "What were you thinking about during the last five minutes?" thus avoiding stimulating the respondent in any direction. The interviewer suggests only that normal persons normally think about something. In addition, in order to avoid social contexts that may unduly either suppress or alert a person to the topic of death, one uses "situation sampling." The question, "What were you thinking about . . . " is asked of people at home, at work, in school, at church, and so on, covering all hours of the day, evening, and all days of the week. For estimates of the denial of death among the general population first, we report information based on the former technique. Here we rely on a survey of the Montreal Expo visitors and a national sample of thirty thousand "younger and better educated" Americans (Shneidman 1973). For information based on the second technique we rely on Cameron's (1973) survey of over four thousand people in four cities across the United States. What do we find?

Only 8 percent of the Expo visitors said that they "had never thought about losing" their lives. Among the Americans only 6 percent stated that they "rarely or never" thought about death. Suicidal thoughts are not rare either. Two thirds of the Expo visitors had had them, and just over one half of the Americans reported having "seriously contemplated suicide." From the results of actual consciousness sampling, we find that almost a quarter, 23 percent of American females had death on their mind when they were asked what they were thinking. Among males the proportion was less. Seventeen percent were thinking about death when the interviewer asked. If one contemplates, for just a moment, the wide range of topics these people could have thought about, given the enormous variety of contexts in which the question was raised, it would seem that awareness of death is high indeed. Further, comparing these results with actual consciousness data on sex, Cameron reported that death is less a taboo subject than sex. Finally, returning once more to Shneidman's sample of Americans, asked how they *feel* when thinking of their own death, only 30 percent answered in terms of "fearful" or "depressed," and the remainder gave answers not classifiable as indexing fear or anxiety. Ours does not seem to be an age unusually anxious about or repressive of death.

What about those who manage the dying and handle the dead, health professionals, and funeral home employees? Despite much literature on American physicians' attitudes toward death, we shall deal with the topic very briefly, for the following reason. It appears that much of the earlier research assumed too direct and simple a relationship between attitudes and corresponding behaviors. Recent psychological evidence shows that this assumption is out of date. For example, studies have shown that "authoritarian" attitudes are quite unrelated to "behavior seeking to dominate others" (Heaven 1977). We shall use studies that asked doctors and nurses more practical questions about how they cope with terminal patients. For attitudes we shall confine ourselves largely to more recent studies.

Three small sample studies using scales to measure fear of death and dying show the following: Funeral parlor employees have the same death and dying anxiety scores as those of the general population; nursing faculty and nursing students have generally lower scores; and registered nurses score in the middle or average range (Tampler and others 1976; Lester and others 1974; Shusterman 1973). One large survey of over fifteen thousand nurses practicing in the United States and Canada also indicated that the profession is not characterized by any unusual tendencies to deny death (Popoff 1975). For example, a question about the meaning of death proved quite illuminating because the answers obtained from nurses were comparable to those given by Cappon's Montreal Expo visitors to a question on a belief in life after death. Presumably, if death were seen as the end of all existence, a meaningless void, that would induce anxiety. But only one third of the Expo visitors and a mere 14 percent of the nurses thought of death in this way. Also, suicidal thoughts were more frequent among nurses than among the general population visiting the Expo. This seems significant in view of another finding. Working on a small sample, Denton and Wisenbacker (1977) demonstrated that having encountered situations "where one seriously thought one would die" *reduced* death anxiety among nurses. Finally, Popoff's large survey also indicated that a nurse's fear of his or her own death is not affected by the frequency of treating dying patients. In short, on death anxiety and fear, nurses came across as quite "normal," if not resilient, given their higher exposure to the dying and the dead. That is an important fact because hospital nurses have much more contact with patients, including the terminally ill, than doctors.

What about physicians? Do they display unusual levels of death anxiety resulting in extraordinary efforts to deny death? Earlier research seemed to affirm this (Oken 1961). This was inferred from two observations. Patients with terminal illness, it appeared, wanted to know the diagnosis and prognosis of their condition relating to impending death. Doctors, as a rule, however, did not tell them the truth. Doctors, so it seemed, could not face the facts of death. They apparently saw in a dying patient a threat to their professional competence. That had to be avoided at all costs, particularly because, "given the massive denial of death in modern society," it seemed reasonable to suppose that physicians had chosen their career in order to defeat death (Feifel 1965). Whatever the truth about this twenty years or so ago, more recent evidence offers a more complex and quite different picture. To put it into context, let us recall some of the facts that seemed so conclusive in the recent past.

Let us begin with the person dying in a hospital. If we ask: Does the terminal patient want to know that his or her life is ending?—the best answer seems to be the one that humans always encounter in a complex situation: "It depends. . . ." A famous early study tried to gauge how much patients want to know (Cappon 1962). Surveying healthy persons and patients with varying degrees of serious disease including terminal ones, it was found that desire to know *whether* one has to die declines from near 100 percent wanting to know among healthy persons to about two thirds among terminal patients. As for the time *when* one will die, only about 70 percent of the healthy persons desired that knowledge for their hypothetical case. Among the terminal patients 60 percent still wanted to know the time of death. But knowledge of *what* one would feel when dying was desired by only a half of all the respondents regardless of health condition. When asked whether that information was wanted if it were possible to give it "right now," less than half the terminal patients wanted to know.

A more recent review of literature in this area concluded that, so far as known, dying patients prefer knowledge to ignorance of their condition (Schulz & Aderman 1976). But available opinion surveys simply have not given us any adequate knowledge. The question posed is simplistic. Physicians with considerable experience in treating the terminally ill generally make two points. First, the desire of patients to know the truth takes many forms and varies over time, depending on their physical and psychological condition. Second, the dying learn about their condition whether or not they are directly told.

Various "awareness contexts" of dying have been described by sociologists. They protray the communication of knowledge of death in varying degrees and the many patterns of sharing such knowledge among patient, hospital staff, and family, reflecting the different needs of the dying, the grieving, and professionals (Glaser & Strauss 1965). Kalish (1970) listed no less than a dozen sources of knowledge available to a patient in the typical hospital situation. Kübler-Ross, an experienced psychiatrist, felt quite strongly that the question of whether or not a patient should be told is quite irrelevant. She asserted: "They all know the seriousness of their condition. *They* tell us, not the other way around" (1970: 160). This clinical experience was supported by Popoff's (1975) nursing survey. According to one half of the nurses, three quarters or more of the terminal patients knew of their death even when the doctor had not told them. Further, two thirds of these nurses found that only a small minority of the terminally ill, a quarter or less, denied the reality of their death until the very end.

DYING

Both the rate and the quality of dying vary greatly, depending on the disease. The pain experienced differs, the certainties of diagnosis and prognosis vary, and so does the condition of the patient. Such variations tell us that the simple questions "does the patient want to know" and "should the patient be told the truth" are absurd. A couple of examples should suffice to make the point. A "dying trajectory" (Glaser & Strauss 1968; Strauss & Glaser 1970) is a record of a patient's deterioration over time. Very uncertain trajectories typically occur in critical heart disease. Physicians often have no reliable prognosis. Very frequently, their patients die suddenly or recover miraculously. Among many types of cancer, on the other hand, prognosis of eventual death is frequently quite certain, and even the time of death often can be reliably predicted.

Let us take a "lingering" trajectory, say, an elderly patient expected to die within two to three months. In such a case, there may be good days and bad ones, and ups and downs during the days and nights. The level of pain and the moods of fear, hope, depression, and resurgence alternate. Whether, and in what sense such a dying person "knows" varies with these conditions. The best possible generalization seems to be Weisman's (1972): Most terminal patients have "middle knowledge"; they "know" about impending death in varying degrees of acknowledgment, with respect to varying aspects of their remaining life and varying amounts of attention paid to that knowledge. All of this changes over time.

Stages of Dying

In view of Pattison's (1977) adaptation of the Glaser-Strauss "dying trajectory," this generalization of "middle knowledge" strikes us as the only one possible. Pattison's is a *psychological* dying trajectory. He plotted anxiety level against physical deterioration, showing how both vary over time. This device yields successive stages of dying, though their length varies with the disease involved. Three stages can be distinguished. The first, "crisis knowledge," is acute anxiety with the potential of personality disintegration. It occurs at the discovery of dying. At this point, denial, as Kübler-Ross (1969) argued, is indeed typical. It may appear in such forms as "existential denial," not thinking of the self as finite; "psychological denial" as in repressing known facts; or "non-attention denial," simply focusing attention elsewhere than on the new knowledge (Pattison 1977:44-47).

Helping the patient implies efforts aimed at reducing anxiety rather than trying to defeat denial. During the second phase, that of "chronic living-dying," anxieties or fears focus on loss of body, loss of self-control, pain and suffering, the threat of regression, and loss of identity. Depending on the disease and prognosis, the phase may be short or last for years. Kübler-Ross's (1969) stages of dying, anger, bargaining, and depression, in whatever temporal order or admixture, would seem to belong to this phase.

Giving psychological support usually requires strategies for maintaining a sense of self. The terminal phase is signaled by a decrease in anxiety and an increase in apathy. The dying person often withdraws into himself or herself, not caring any more about social interaction. But such "psychological dying" cannot be diagnosed without full knowledge of the medical-physical data.

To illustrate this point, Pattison (1977:61-73) reported a study of DOPS patients (suffering from diffuse obstructive pulmonary syndrome or clinical emphysema). The DOPS syndrome often includes heart malfunction as well. Such patients exist in so precarious a cardiopulmonary balance that the slightest emotional excitation may lead to shortness of breath and death. It appears that maintaining life depends strictly on maintaining emotional equilibrium. It follows that what *may* look like the onset of "psychological death," withdrawing from social interaction, *may* be a self-protective response by the patient and not just in a DOPS case. The line between the struggle for life and the acceptance of death often is difficult to distinguish. One might agree with Feder (1965) that the questions of whether patients should know or do know are entirely too simplistic to deserve much attention. But psychological and communicative sensitivity to what a patient may be telling staff is not enough either, as Feder and Kübler-Ross indicated. Knowledge of the physiological state is required as well, if health professionals are to help persons in their dying.

Deciding When or If to Tell the Patient

Even though the general question, "should the patient be told," is meaningless, when considered somewhat differently, physicians have answered it. When asked "do you usually tell a dying patient?" about twenty years ago, two thirds or more of the physicians queried answered no (Oken 1961). By the middle sixties medical opinion already had changed considerably. Observations collected from weekly conferences about dying cancer patients revealed that one half of the doctors usually told their patients (Rich & Kalmanson 1966). Those who did tell their patients seemed to be more "autocratic" kinds of physicians who enjoyed their control over treatment plans and people, but those who usually withheld the information admitted that anxiety about death and their own feelings of insecurity were among the reasons for their behavior.

In the early seventies a questionnaire study of 150 physicians in ten specialties revealed a further advance in the practice of "telling the dying the truth" (Rea and others 1975). Focused on the physician's willingness to communicate a terminal prognosis in relationship to the patient's age, physical condition, and remaining life expectancy, this study also illustrated advances in research sophistication. Surely, many considerations enter a physician's decision to reveal this information, and just knowing whether a doctor "usually" tells or not is hardly significant. The effect on the patient is a consideration. Telling him or her means stripping that person of two attributes of the "sick role" which pertains to most hospital patients. That may have consequences difficult to control and difficult to foretell for the patient, other hospital staff, and his or her family. Let us see how.

According to Parsons (1951:428-73) being a patient means playing a social role with four characteristics. First, a patient is not regarded as personally responsible for the inability to perform normal role obligations while sick. Second, such a person is excused from performance, and his or her status in the corresponding social networks is protected until he or she returns. Illness, when certified by a doctor, is the best available excuse from work or any set of social obligations. Third, these privileges of sickness are granted on the condition of seeking competent medical help. Fourth, they also are granted only on the additional condition of the patient's active and willing cooperation with the medical staff to become healthy again.

When a physician decides that a patient is terminally ill because all available resources to cure have been exhausted, this attenuates the requirement to use competent medical expertise. The physician is seen as trained to cure illness, not to provide just comfort. As we shall see, the hospital is an organization designed for the cure of the sick, not the dying of the old. To decide that a patient is terminal is, therefore, a matter with many difficult consequences for the staff as well as for the patient. It amounts to declaring him or her unsuitable for hospitalization. Because that organization cannot do anything significant within its mandate for a dying person, the family may be under pressure to take the patient home. But a modern family also is not an organization designed for the dying process. Typically, it lacks the physical, technical, and emotional resources to provide comfortable care. Finally, upon the official declaration of terminal status, the role requirement of a normal patient to cooperate in regaining health is declared null and void. That may well produce reluctance to comply with "doctor's orders." Thus, deciding to tell a patient of his or her terminal status means transforming a normal patient with many rights and duties into a marginal figure with uncertain rights and questionable duties. It means changing his or her status from a member in good standing in the hospital community into a burden for the organization, whatever the doctor's own feelings may be. Such decisions are not easily made. Yet the physician is expected to know when someone is dying and must protect his or her reputation as a competent doctor. Hospital procedure is a third consideration. It requires placing the dying on the critical list; next of kin must be notified.

Little of the complexity of this decision-making process is known. Changes in "medical opinion" can at best indicate shifts in general orientations. At any rate, let us return to the research of Rea and others (1975). It tells us that doctors no longer "deny death" if, indeed, that ever was the case. Seventy-one percent of these physicians asserted that the patient must be told, quite a change from Oken's respondents. But the other matters revealed are more interesting. Just under one third of these physicians also said that the patient's age is not much of a consideration for "telling the truth." The remaining two thirds were split; one group found it harder to tell an elderly patient, the other found it harder to tell young people under eighteen. Three quarters took remaining life expectancy into consideration, and a third told the patient even if that remaining life could stretch on for more than a year. The majority of the physicians whose practice made the encounter with death very likely also reported that they did *not* view the death of a patient as a professional or personal failure.

Further, just over one half stated that spending extra time with a dying patient *was* their duty, and another 38 percent were "inclined" to accept it as one of their duties. Interestingly, it was the younger doctor with the greater encounter with death who was more willing to tell the patient. But spending extra time with a dying patient was more characteristic of older doctors. Finally, as one would expect, encountering death in medical practice varies with specialty. Cancer, kidney, and heart specialists, as well as surgeons encounter death more often than psychiatrists, gynecologists, and so on do. But among Rea's respondents, actual experience with having one's patients die was not related to considering such deaths as a professional or personal failure.

We conclude that there is no serious factual basis in either the general population or the health professions of modern society on which one could claim that modern people have any distinctive tendencies to deny death. As we shall see, there is no basis for such a claim in sociological theory, either. On the contrary, in preindustrial societies one theoretically would expect a greater need to deny death. Yet all this may make very little practical difference to the older person now dying in a hospital. Relying on the work of Hahn (1968) and elaborating a little, we can demonstrate that it is unpreparedness, normatively, organizationally, and educationally in relating to the dying person and the bereaved that leads to a relatively premature social abandonment of these people in distress in contemporary society.

BEING UNPREPARED FOR DEATH

The first source of unpreparedness for death by the general population in industrial societies is the rarity of personal encounters with death; the second is that dying usually occurs in the hospital rather than in the home (Blauner 1968). In all preindustrial societies death was part of everyday experience. For us, death has become a secondhand experience, something that happens to others. For most of us (Shneidman 1973), the first half of life contains no personal encounters with death. Although death struck in preindustrial societies literally at any moment, we live with a distinction unknown even to the generation of our grandparents. Normal death is death in some "ripe old age," certainly after age sixty-five. Everything else is premature death, something that should not happen, and something to which we direct our preventive efforts. In 1900, when a person reached the age of average life expectancy, which was about thirty-eight years in Germany and forty-nine years in America, he or she already had survived several epidemics and attended the funerals of children, siblings, and parents. A Swede born in 1800 who lived to age eighty which, although rare, could happen, had encountered a number of deaths in his or her family that would take a contemporary Swedish person a life span of two hundred years to match (Hahn 1968: 15-21). In contrast to our forebears then, it seems unreasonable that we should deny death more than they did. Throughout the first half of our life we frequently lack the opportunity to witness death, and we certainly do not expect it for ourselves.

Significance of Death

As Hahn made clear, the quality of the death encounter is different for people in contemporary society as well. Preindustrial societies varied greatly in their characteristics, such as religious and political organization or stratification. But all shared important differences in other respects notwithstanding, a type of social network in which most people spent most of their lives which differed greatly from that prevailing in all industrial societies. Sociologists use a variety of labels to describe that difference. Durkheim contrasted "mechanical" with "organic" solidarity. Toennies spoke of *Gemeinschaft* versus *Gesellschaft*. Redfield wrote about "folk" and "urban" ways of life. Whatever the terms used, they all agreed that the preindustrial social order was organized so as to permit people to have comprehensive knowledge of each other, touching on all the roles each played. In industrial society, whether in the factory or office, at church, bowling alley, or in the supermarket, people maintain relations with many others about whom they have only segmental knowledge, pertaining to one role played, not the whole person. Compared to us, even our grandparents had a socially more informed life with respect to personal knowledge. For interpersonal contacts outside the family, ours has become a highly information-poor social life. This difference is important to the impact that another's death has on one's own identity.

Central to the social theories of Mead and Cooley is the proportion that our conscious sense of self is, to a great extent, social. It is indeed a product of current social interaction. William James called the role-playing self the "empirical self." It is the self known and understood by us. The self that "does the knowing" is not accessible by common-sense experience; it is only inferred. The known self is always anchored in a social role. We know ourselves only as fathers or mothers, as factory workers or sales clerks, as golfers or baseball fans. In these roles we are known to others and so to ourselves as punctual or rarely on time, or as calm or temperamental. It is role playing that tells us what we have in common with others and how we are different from them. Finally, it is in relating socially to others that we find a reassuring sense of our individuality. We also have memories of roles played in our past. We also read books, enjoy art, and watch TV or listen to the radio. From these one-way flows of information we also learn something about ourselves, who we are and perhaps ought to be. But compared to these alternate sources of our self-knowledge, it is mainly the two-way process of interacting with others on which we must depend for really knowing who we are. *The* reality test of our identity is social, here and now.

That is why the first reaction to the realization that one is dying is a terrifying threat to oneself. The mind says one shall simply cease to play all the social roles that one ever played. But the heart refuses to go along because "it knows" that the social role-selves are the only real certainty in one's identity. The same is true for the initial reaction to bereavement. Loss of a role partner through death is a direct threat to intimate survivors if they depended much on the dead for their sense of self. As a first reaction, the denial of dying and that of the death of another is anchored in social life. It is a universal reaction regardless of the type of society to which one belongs. Still, who is affected and who can help whom in dying and bereavement vary enormously between preindustrial and industrial societies.

The social ties of preindustrial peoples were so intricately intertwined, in contrast to the more segmental ties for most of our relations, that we follow Hahn and use Parsons's (1951) "pattern variables" to describe this difference in greater detail. With this device Hahn provided a definitive theoretical refutation of "the denial of death" as a distinctive trait of industrial societies. The way he did it also illuminates the nature of the contemporary problem in relating to the dying and the dead. The pattern variables should show that the death of anyone in a preindustrial society was an immediate threat to the identity of all. But, for people in an industrial society, death, *outside* the circles of kinship and friendship, is a statistic and a statistic is "people with the tears wiped off." Although the bereaved person in preindustrial societies could rely on many others in coping with death, when death strikes kin or friends in industrial societies, two factors make the experience more difficult. First, the death of a "personally close" other is a greater threat to the identity of the bereaved because he or she has so few others serving as identity-assuring resources. Second, coping with the loss is more difficult since the circles of kinship and friendship are small and the members equally bereaved.

Clearly, the significance of the death of another to a person is in the kind of social relation between them. The kind of relations in preindustrial social orders were *particularist, diffuse,* and *affective.* But for people in industrial society, these types of social ties are confined to the family and friends, and practically all other relations, which make up the vast majority of interpersonal contacts, are *universalist, specific,* and *affectively neutral.*

Put simply, a particularist relation is one tailor-made for the individuals relating to each other. That implies a norm of irreplaceability. The other is treated as a unique person, not just a category of persons into which potentially many fall. The latter, treating the other in categorical role terms, as a fellow worker for example, describes the relation as universalist. That implies a norm of replaceability. If relating to one person in this fashion proves unsatisfactory, one is supposed to seek a more rewarding arrangement with another.

A relationship is diffuse when a comprehensive right to attention and the inclusion of any conceivable interest is the norm. One may bring up any topic or concern and have the right to be heard; it is the other person, if he or she does not want to be bothered, who has to offer an excuse. That means the identities of the partners have multiple points of anchorage in each others' conduct, beliefs, and interests. In a specific relation, on the other hand, the normally expected range of mutual relevance of the parties to each other is carefully circumscribed. In case of doubt about that relevance, it is the person demanding attention who has to make a case for it. That means that any mutual dependency for identity is reduced to one role sector or role. Specific relations imply a norm of limited liability, diffuse ones a norm of unlimited liability.

Finally, a relationship is affective when the securing of gratification from just being together is a rightful expectation. The social bond is *supposed to* satisfy emotions (including negative ones). But affective neutrality signals an instrumental relation in which one is supposed to delay emotional gratifications. To treat another as a kind of statistic in an affective relation is the first step to terminating it, but treatment in "statistical terms" is almost an obligatory norm in an affectively neutral association, such as in any large bureaucratic organization.

Living in a social world of particular, diffuse, and affective relations, death in a preindustrial society was a devastating blow to the whole community. It threatened the social identity of all. For this reason, as well as the frequency of encounters with death, traditional societies had generally more elaborate funeral practices than can be found in industrial societies. They were threatened by death far more; if anything, theirs was the greater need to deny the reality of death. They too *had* to spend more of their scarce resources on funeral rites to deal with death.

Comparatively, people in industrial societies encounter death as a statistic. When a fellow worker dies, it will occasion some talk. But the personnel department seeks a replacement, and its routines are not at all different from the case of someone who quit the organization to work elsewhere. After a few weeks, certainly some months, the dead person has been effectively forgotten. People can afford to forget because their identity depended so little on the one who died. That, too, produces unpreparedness and comparative helplessness when death strikes kin and friends on whom we depend so much for our identity as persons.

Conclusions

Socially we are unprepared for relating to the dying and the dead. We never have encountered death personally before the first one comes in the middle years of life. When it comes, we have learned none of the norms, the socially accepted, understood, and assumed procedures that our grandparents learned from childhood onwards. Comparatively, we have a massive normative deficit in relating to the dying and the dead. We do not know what to say to a dying person. We do not know really what we feel. We do not know how to express emotion, and we do not know how to share it with the dying person. These four forms of ignorance make up the burden of relative deprivation in relevant knowledge of and experience with dying for modern men and women. It is a deprivation relative to what our forebears knew and one caused by the demography of death in modern peacetime society.

The difference in the social bonds of preindustrial and industrial societies suggests that people in traditional societies had a greater need to deny death than men and women in modern society do. We found only one study that sheds some light on this point. Beshai and Templer (1978) measured death anxiety among a small sample of Egyptians and compared the results with those of American subjects. The Egyptian subjects were living in Cairo, a huge city and hardly a traditional social context. Still, Egypt remains to date an underdeveloped society in comparison to the United States. So, although it would have been preferable for our purposes to compare the death anxiety of Egyptian peasants from the hinterland with that of Americans, the findings are relevant. They show that Egyptians have a somewhat higher death anxiety than Americans, exactly what our theoretical speculations implied. Unfortunately, the difference in mean death anxiety scores between the two national groups was not statistically significant. That is a way of saying that given the size of the difference in death anxiety, on the one hand, and the small number of subjects that could be tested, on the other, the difference may have been caused by chance. All we can say, therefore, is that what little empirical evidence there is about the death anxiety and the need to deny death in different types of societies "suggests" the correctness of our theoretical argument.

But attitudes toward death and helplessness in relating to the dying are not the only preconditions leading to premature social abandonment of the dying by the living. The organizations in which most of us die, general hospitals, are not designed for dying. Nor are the medical professionals to whom we leave most of the burden of dealing with the dying, formally educated for that task.

THE HOSPITAL: ORGANIZATIONAL INADEQUACY FOR DYING

Surveying the literature on who took care of the dying and the dead, Hahn (1968) found many instances of special caretaker roles in preindustrial societies. But all the functionaries were religious. *Only* in industrial societies do people die in a secular organization, and we are not used to it, yet. Dying in the hospital in the United States is a recent custom. As late as 1949 still only under half of all deaths took place there. By 1970, 70 percent of all deaths occurred in hospitals (Feifel 1973:39). In medieval times a hospital was a place to *care* for the dying in Western culture. Today that is no longer the case. If anything, the history of disease and the changes in organizing efforts for dealing with it are rather ironic.

In 1900 most people died of some *acute* illness; by 1965 the majority died from some *chronic* condition. Yet 83 percent of all hospitals in the United

States are general hospitals, organizations designed for curing short-term, acute illness with all the life-saving technology that modern medical science has developed (Graham & Reeder 1972:66). These contrary trends of climbing death rates from chronic disease and declining chronic care facilities in the United States continued throughout the post-World War II period. From 1950 to 1973 the death rate from chronic conditions increased, and that from acute illness and accidents decreased. But the proportion of general hospitals in all medical settings keeps growing while that of chronic care facilities keeps falling (Coe 1978:57, 287). Largely because of the chronic nature of disease among older people and the fact that one now dies in a hospital, general hospitals always have a relatively high proportion of elderly patients, precisely those kinds of cases for which such places are not designed. Dying in a cure-oriented rather than a care-oriented environment is the fate of people in industrial societies. Although that may be a relatively light burden to bear when an all-out battle to preserve life is the consensus, for people dying in old age, there is no such consensus. For them and their attendants the burden seems heavy.

Dying in Hospitals

Competence in the modern world is held only by the specialist, a person who knows more and more about less and less. The general hospital in American society is an organization designed for the maximal utilization of medical expertise. That inevitably means the fractionalization of curative efforts spread over many specialists and, so, the fractionalization of the patient. In technical coordination of the specialists on a given case, it is agreed that fragmenting the staff is less of a problem to the hospital's curative efforts than to ambulatory treatment. Both physical proximity and the fact that all treatments are recorded on the patient's chart reduce errors and improve coordination among the specialists in the hospital. But that sheds little light on fragmenting the patient's emotional needs in terminal illness. Not only do relatively few physicians in the United States specialize for chronic care (Graham & Reeder 1972:99; Lasagna 1970: 92), the trend for medical specialization to cure remains unabated.

In 1923 only 11 percent of American physicians listed themselves as specialists. By 1950 that proportion had grown to 36 percent. In 1963 the general practitioner was already a small minority making up about a quarter of all active physicians. That proportion declined to 17 percent by 1972 and is expected to drop further to 12 percent by 1980 (Friedson 1972:345; Coe 1978: 353). As we shall argue, specialists in curative skills do not make good caretakers. Suffice it to say that the growing American interest in the "hospice movement," referring to specialization for terminal *care,* was inspired by that judgment.

Dying in hospitals is not just an American phenomenon. Two out of three people in West Germany also die in hospitals (*Der Spiegel,* May 8, 1978:39). Comparing the organization of the hospital in several nations, Glaser (1970) noted a converging trend in all technical departments as well as in conceptions of disease. This means that any general hospital anywhere, if it is modern, is an organization designed to cure acute illnesses manageable in the short term. But there are some cross-national differences in relevance to the dying patient. One is hospital size, the other the role of the family in hospital care. Both matter to the terminally ill who need psychological and emotional support, preferably from those familiar with the dying as whole persons.

It follows that the smaller the hospital is, the greater is the chance for the medical staff to get to know the patient. For size, the Netherlands seems to be in the best position to minister to the dying because a long history of denominational segregation produced small hospitals. Each community accordingly has three, a public, a Protestant, and a Catholic one. Allowing family members to participate at the hospital also allows a more personal atmosphere. Here the Japanese seem to do the best, for in Japan family members function as active participants in patient care. In the United States, we do not go that far, although the family has comparatively liberal visiting hours. In Britain, visiting privileges are highly restricted, dissociating the dying from their families the most (Glaser 1970:188-96).

Care for the Chronically Ill

Knowing that death in modern societies often is caused by chronic disease tells us that old persons usually do not die suddenly. Dying takes its time, but that may vary according to the disease. This knowledge permits us to gather more information about the American way of dying from a comparative study on long-term care in six countries (Kane & Kane 1976).

Comparing England, Scotland, Sweden, Norway, and Israel with the United States shows some similarities and differences. Among the similarities is that chronic care is everywhere identified as a serious social problem needing to be solved. Institutionalization of the elderly with chronic illness, for example, is seen everywhere as harmful, something to be delayed as long as possible. This underscores the inadequacy of the hospital as an organization for providing terminal care. Among the differences we find the following: Europeans provide more hospital beds for long-term care than Americans do. Physician and nursing care in convalescent and continuing care facilities by far exceeds that available in the United States. In none of the other countries does one find as much employee turnover as in American institutions for the old and the dying. This is probably because of the relatively steep income differentials in this country between medical and social service personnel in the curing as compared with the caring settings. In no other country are such obvious monetary incentives provided to induce professionals and paraprofessionals to opt for curing over caring. In general, then, the United States stands out as an underperformer in cross-national differences significant to elderly patients in terms of emotional support and comfort.

Yet the general aversion to institutionalization leads to a final comment on organizational inadequacy in providing care for the dying elderly. We can describe this empirically only for the United States, but the problem seems to exist to some degree everywhere. If adequacy reflects an ideology of "total patient care," one oriented to avoid any fragmentation of the dying by offering sustained emotional support by the same staff members to a dying person (Croog & VerSteg 1972), American society has very little practical experience with the deliberate organization of such tasks. The American medical complex has only four types of organizations: 1) general hospitals, 2) psychiatric hospitals, 3) physical rehabilitation facilities, and 4) high-risk research medical teams usually found in the university hospitals (Coe 1978:331-43; Fox 1959; Fox & Swazey 1974). None of these is designed for the terminally ill of advanced age.

In mental hospitals, where many elderly with chronic conditions were found not too long ago, they were given only poor custodial care. It meant that they were treated so as to maximize administrative efficiency and minimize costs for society. That was one reason for the recent attempt at deinstitutionalizing the elderly and for the policy of avoiding any institutionalization as long as possible. But whether the elderly fare better in fact on the outside, or even stay there very long, has yet to be established. For the end of life itself, which can take months to come, medical technology makes institutionalization unavoidable.

PHYSICIANS AND NURSES: LACK OF PSYCHOLOGICAL TRAINING FOR TERMINAL CARE

Since dying occurs so often in hospitals, let us ask whether doctors and nurses are formally trained to deal with the emotional problems of terminal patients. Does that task belong to prevailing conceptions of professional competence as reflected in professional education? Here the available evidence permits a conclusive answer. The majority of physicians and nurses practicing today did not receive any formal training in fulfilling the emotional and psychological needs of the terminally ill.

For Physicians

About twenty years ago only 5 percent of Chicago's physicians indicated that they had learned in medical school about this problem of telling the dying the truth (Oken 1961). The great majority claimed to have learned from clinical experience. But since such claims were in no way related to the length of a doctor's practice, Oken suspected that the alleged "clinical experience" actually stood for lay attitudes and considerations. Three more recent studies of medical education in America revealed that learning how to cope with the dying has not become part of the formal training program in either the pre-medical or the clinical years of training (Miller 1970; Mumford 1970; Busher & Stelling 1977). We found no evidence of formal lecture courses on the dying patient. During clinical training when future physicians learn by doing, the formal tracking of responsibility and accountability for their behavior is the patient's chart. The chart is a record of observations of the physical and physiological condition of the patient and what was done about it, however, not of what was said to the patient. All the evidence shows that becoming a physician in the sense of acquiring a professional identity as a doctor is a process geared to the mastery of curative skills and knowledge. Caring for the patient as a person, psychiatry aside, is something acquired incidentally, as for example, through an encounter with the intractable patient who, for whatever reasons, does not follow a doctor's orders. Available studies of medical education did not focus on coping with the dying (Becker and others 1972). Nevertheless, they did make one thing clear. Within the time now allocated to becoming a doctor and the present organization of that training, adding a few courses or seminars on how to cope with the dying would not be sufficient to counteract the primarily curing emphasis.

For Nurses

One might expect nursing education to be different. After all, first and historically, nursing is an extension of the female role with its emphasis on socioemotional skills (Glaser 1970). Second, one still speaks of nursing *care* as a profession. Third, to return to attitudes, using a cure-care index, Linn (1975) also found what one suspected: Medical faculty and their students are far more cure-oriented, and nursing faculty and their students are more care-oriented. For example, over three quarters of the medical faculty in the sample agreed with the statement that "getting a patient well is more important than keeping him comfortable," but less than one half of the nursing teachers subscribed to this belief.

But in caring for the dying patient, most nurses practicing today received just as little formal training in this area as physicians did. Quint (1967) related the widespread avoidance of the terminal patient among nurses she observed directly to inadequate education. Two questions in Popoff's (1975) extensive survey can be used here. Asked what had had the greatest influence on their present attitude toward the dying patient and what had been the most helpful source of advice on how to cope with the dying, there was no reference to seminars or classes in the answers to the first question, and formal teaching was mentioned by just under one quarter of the nurses in answers to the second question. In shaping attitudes, religious teaching ranked first (32 percent) and coping with the death of someone close to the nurse in family and friendship circles ranked second (20 percent). Nursing school was not listed at all. On learning how to cope with a dying patient, the terminal patient was the main teacher (38 percent); books and magazines, in effect reading one of Kübler-Ross's works (1969), ranked second (26 percent); and seminars and classes ranked third (23 percent). Over three quarters apparently learned nothing pertinent in their formal education.

In the nursing profession it is not just a lack of training that leads to the relative neglect of the dying patient. The nursing role has been under severe strain in recent decades. As Coe (1978:250-64) noted, the humanist service ideals that originally led many nurses into the profession are frustrated in contemporary nursing practice and in how rewards such as promotion are structured. There are only two channels of career advancement, and both mean further removal from direct patient contact and actual patient care. The ambitious nurse either can become a nursing supervisor or administrator in a hospital or can teach in a school of nursing. In either case, the path to ambition is away from the patient. Coe reported some studies showing that the more competent nurses also tended to be the more frustrated, the ones who showed more disillusionment and disappointment with the profession, and the ones more alienated from their work. A frustrated and alienated nurse does not make a good terminal caretaker.

As far as we know, the psychological *care* of the dying is not yet part of the accepted meaning of professional competence of doctors and nurses. As students they face many tests of their competence before they attain professional certification. But, the occasional seminar or discussion group aside, no one, it seems, faces the serious prospect of "flunking" examinations in courses on the psychological care of the terminally ill. At the beginning of the career that means the health professional encounter dying and death with as little preparation as the lay public does. But contrary to the public, they do encounter death far more frequently. Unprepared, we would expect them to avoid and to minimize that encounter as much as professionally respectable, not because of any denial of death but quite simply because they do not know what to say, how to feel, or what to do beyond the physical requirements of care.

THE CONSEQUENCE:
PREMATURE SOCIAL ABANDONMENT
OF THE DYING

General Care

Observational studies in hospital settings are characterized by one consistent finding. With some clarifying comments we can describe it in the words of Livingstone and Zimet (1965:223): "It is a commonly observed fact that on a hospital ward, except for minimal requisite care, the terminally ill patient is virtually abandoned." The work of Glaser and Strauss (1965, 1968), Sudnow

(1967), Quint (1967), Kastenbaum and Aisenberg (1972), and the findings of the psychological autopsy (Kastenbaum 1977) do show the truth of that statement when confined to the behavior of the health care professionals.

A qualification is that, except for the very poor and the old about whom nobody on the outside cares any more, minimal care does not mean inadequate physical care. Rather, abandonment means that the staff does not develop the kind of supportive and social interaction patterns with the dying older person that a psychologist would insist on as adequate support for the process of dying. Although most of these studies were done before the current concern with dying among professionals and the public, one cannot expect a small change in the climate of opinion to change behavior. Popoff's (1975) nursing survey supported this contention. It was made after Kübler-Ross's work had become a household word.

Asked whether the dying patient should be given extra care, 77 percent of the nurses replied in the affirmative. But preference hardly corresponds with practice. When asked whether they tended "to avoid" the dying patient, to treat him or her "like any other patient," or to provide "extra care," about one quarter (26 percent) admitted to avoiding, just under a half (45 percent) reported treating him or her "like any other patient," and only 28 percent said that they gave extra care. Lack of time and concern with neglecting other patients were the reasons given. Nurses told us that the hospital, as now organized, leaves little room to practice one's preference. Since caring for a terminal patient "like any other one" is a way of not responding to his or her special status and needs, we conclude that 71 percent of the nurses actually disregard the fact that a terminal patient is dying when they talk with him or her.

The picture does not seem to be very different in a geriatric hospital. Although older people are expected to die, talking with them about their dying is so stressful that it usually is avoided. Kastenbaum (1977) studied two hundred attendants and nurses in such a setting. When a dying person confronted the staff with thoughts about his death, inviting them to share these concerns, five patterns of response by the staff were noted. Four of these, 82 percent of the encounters, clearly avoided sharing the experience of dying with the terminally ill. Among these strategies of avoidance Kastenbaum found: 1) reassurance (you are doing well, you don't have to feel this way); 2) denial (you don't mean that, you don't have to die); 3) changing the subject; and 4) fatalism (we all have to die some time), which also rejects the invitation to talk about dying. Similar observations were supplied by Glaser and Strauss (1965:226-32) and Quint (1967).

Even in some American old-age homes with a permanent in-house nursing staff, and thus organizations intended for terminal care of the aged, the staff was found to avoid interaction with the more disabled. The term disabled included, for example, anal and bladder incontinence, and having to use a wheel chair, both common conditions in very old age.

Studying two such old-age homes, one for Jewish, the other for elderly black people, Watson and Maxwell (1977) found the following indices of avoidance. In both homes, the severely disabled were placed farther away from the nursing stations than the less disabled were. Thus, the more helpless the patients and presumably the greater their need for care, the greater was their isolation. Social segregation was measured by a systematic time sampling that recorded where a nurse was: at the station with staff peers, in the rooms of the more disabled or those of the less disabled. In both homes, again, the more disabled were found to be the more isolated. In addition, the Jewish home had various ranks among the terminal care staff. There were registered nurses, aides, and orderlies. Here the higher ranks, the registered nurses, interacted less with the severely disabled than the lower ranks did. Patterns of spatial segregation and avoidance of social interaction with the dying also were found in a large (360 beds), church-related old-age and nursing home (Gubrium 1976:197-208).

We have litle information about contact between family members and friends and the dying elderly in hospitals. What indications we do have suggest that relative social abandonment of the dying is not confined to the behavior of staff. Many of the dying in advanced age experience the "lingering death trajectory" in which death comes slowly, with many ups and downs in the patient's condition, stretching over months. Because of physical distances, perhaps, and the emotional strain that the dying of someone close imposes on us, visits from adult children seem to decline as time goes on (Kastenbaum 1977:167). As Strauss (1970:140) and Glaser termed it, relatives may be "grieved out" long before the actual death.

The mosaic of evidence we can use, then, points to social abandonment of the dying older person before the latter is ready to die. One last example from geriatric hospitals concludes this evidence. It used to be assumed that lapsing into a nonresponsive state was a sure indication that a terminally ill elderly was entering psychological death. Yet, after reviewing the available findings of the "psychological autopsy," Kastenbaum (1977:173-82) recently destroyed that assumption.

A psychological autopsy is detective work. It reconstructs all relevant information about a given death and dying process, including the patient's intentions, feelings, and experiences, and what the staff, family, and friends did, said, hoped, or feared. The procedure integrates medical, psychological, and social data. The data were gathered in a geriatric hospital. That is why one can use them to assert that for the older person dying today, it is the rule rather than the exception that sociological death precedes psychological death.

There are two important findings. First, most of the terminally ill aged maintained considerable awareness of themselves and their social environment until close to or right up to biological death. It seems a great mistake to treat nonresponsiveness to friendly remarks as a sign of genuine psychological death. Having been prevented from sharing what they care about, namely, their thoughts and feelings about dying, what looks like withdrawal of interest in social intercourse is certainly that. But it does *not* reflect genuine disinterest in relating to others, only resigned frustration of not being listened to on topics of central concern. Second, it takes detective work to discover how the dying elderly view the prospect of their death, right up to the last moment. The people who care for them do not know.

Four patterns were found. One of these, "acceptance," corresponds in part to Kübler-Ross's stage of acceptance. It describes the patient who refers to his or her own death in a dispassionate, objective way. "Apathy," described as a state of indifference to any event, approaches Pattison's concept of psychological death. These dying people are literally tired of the struggle for life. "Apprehension" is evident in the dying who display anxiety and fear. "Anticipation" is that ideal of a good death that most people wish for in old age: acceptance plus a definite wish to die (Kastenbaum 1977:176-77). All of these patterns appear to be common. But only one, apathy, *may* be the condition in which not relating to the dying is not perceived as frustrating by them. If "anticipation" also were included, despite the dying person's obvious need to share the wish for death, in one half the cases the living withdraw from the dying before they are ready to have them go. It seems safe to conclude that a majority, somewhere above 50 percent, is subject to social abandonment before psychologically dying.

Emphasizing that the distinctions between different forms of death are anything but satisfactory yet, this still is an important discovery. Such withdrawal from a dying person can contribute to death. It is likely indeed that it is even a form of killing. Ellison (1969) succeeded in demonstrating that social isolation does reduce the will to live. And this in turn can kill. Parkes (1969) compared death rates of bereaved and nonbereaved persons, and found that one can die of a "broken heart."

Over a decade ago Holsclaw (1965) observed that organizations designed to cure pose severe limits on caring for the dying. A curative organization is based on rules that presuppose the full patient role. The staff and the sick relate to each other in order to achieve recovery, which transcends and relegates to secondary importance whatever intrinsic satisfactions the staff and patients may find in their relationships. Dying, in contrast, requires a "social process" form of organization, a design for cooperation that addresses members as individuals and that seeks cooperation based on the satisfactions of the members in the relationship itself. Translated into Parsons's pattern variables, this means: The fault with the curative organization in dealing with the dying rests on its use of universalist and specific social relations. Dying, however, from the point of view of the dying person, requires interaction in particularistic and diffuse ways. This also was evident in Strauss's and Glaser's (1970) discussion of why a curative organization cannot satisfy the emotional needs of the dying person. The hospital as it is now is a very good place for recovery from acute illness, but it is a "soul-less dungeon" abandoning the dying. That is why the hospice movement is attracting so much attention.

THE HOSPICE:
ATTEMPTS TO INTEGRATE DYING
WITH LIVING

A hospice is a social organization designed to prevent premature social abandonment of the dying. Essentially, it provides professional care for the terminally ill, combining it with as much family participation as possible in the last phase of life (Saunders 1976; Rossman 1977; Stoddard 1978; Lack & Buckingham 1978). Finding its inspiration in the hospice of medieval times, the only significant differences are using the latest in pain control technology and adapting to the fluid, diverse, and relatively unstructured modern religious situation.

Their Organization

Still in its experimental stage, hospices vary in their physical forms. The founding institution, St. Christopher's in London, England, is a separate hospital for the dying with its own building and grounds. To date this form can only be found in America only at Branford Hospice (New Haven, Connecticut). In New York and Montreal there are wings in hospitals, set aside for specialization in terminal care. A roving hospice team taking care of the dying throughout a hospital is a third form. One hospital, in Harrisburg, Pennsylvania, has the smallest possible hospice organization, a one-nurse "hospice team." In California, the hospice staff are currently completing plans for a separate institution (Stoddard 1978).

Practically everywhere, caring for the dying combines home care and hospital care. The objective is to provide the technical advantage of an institution with the least amount of institutionalization. The dying are always treated as persons, never as cases. If dying at home becomes too stressful, not only the dying but their family and friends are brought into the hospice, becoming active participants in care.

The first objective is pain control. Here prevailing English practice seems far ahead of American practice. Not only is medical sophistication more developed, the law in England also is more favorable. Heroin and its derivatives can be used for medical purposes in England, but it still is prohibited in the United States. Whether heroin is the only really effective pain killer is a matter of controversy in America (see *American Pharmacy,* November 1978). At any rate, pain control aims at that point at which the dying have lost the fear of pain and have attained that level of tolerable suffering which *in their eyes* constitutes a good trade-off for the alternative of oblivion in the completely drugged state.

Their Care

Relations are deeply personalized. Genuine suffering from loss is not an infrequent experience of nurses, staff, and physicians. But no one considers weeping in itself unprofessional. Yet the descriptions of St. Christopher's are clear on one point: It is not a sad place. Having created a completely open atmosphere in which everyone is aware that this is a place for dying and is given continuous evidence that dying is not painful physically, participants emotionally accept death much better than was thought possible. Sociologically, this is not surprising. The hospice has developed a normative culture that tells persons how to express emotion, and where, when, and with whom to do so. As we shall see, this contrasts with grieving and bereavement in general.

The development and maintenance of personalized relations in these organizations is made possible by the division of labor. One way this is done is with a team ideology. Everyone belongs to the caring team, from doctors to cleaning persons. When the nurse, the physician, or the orderly at St. Christopher's are not needed for their special skills, "a patient may choose to discuss his needs with a hairdresser or cook, instead of a physician; a pastor may be asked to rub a back, a physician to pray" (Rossman 1977:101-10). Another mode of attenuating the normal division of tasks and thus avoiding tendencies to fragment the patient is through research and writing. At St. Christopher's, at Branford, and on the West Coast, nurses are expected as part of their usual duties not only to provide care, but also to teach and to write.

Research Medicine

A team ideology and similarly personalized relationships also can be found in high-risk American research medicine (Fox & Swazey 1974). There the terminally ill volunteer for experimental procedures. Hoping to contribute to the advance of useful knowledge, they make dying more significant in a quasi-sacrificial way. But the purposes of hospice and research medicine are very different. Attaining as peaceful and easy a death as possible is the aim of the hospice. Fighting for life as long as possible in order to learn about disease and dying is the main objective of research medicine. The terminally ill in research medicine are the most active patients, in Parsons's sense of collaborating with their doctors, that one can find in the literature. Aside from the management of pain control, the dying person in a hospice is not a patient at all. It is because of these differences that the similar mechanisms in the maintenance of personalized relations between staff and the dying are important.

In both places the effective use of different skills is preserved. Although in most formal organizations, skills are put in a hierarchical order of different worth, this is not permitted in hospice or in medical research settings.All roles are treated as equal. The contribution of each, however different from that of another, is regarded as equal to the purposes of the organization. Only people and their dedication matter, and some have more dedication and more strength to give. Personal esteem may vary, and on that score a nurse can outrank a physician. Specialized roles and their skills, however, are not subjected to ranking of differential worth. That, it seems to us, is a necessary condition for combining the advantages usually ascribed to bureaucratic organization with personal relationships.

Although interest in hospice organization as a solution to the social problem of dying in modern society is spreading in the United States, no one can know the outcome at this time. All sociologists can do is raise a few points worthy of observation. First, we have indicated that for the development and maintenance of personalized relations, preaching team spirit may not be enough. There also must be corresponding action. Teaching, research, and writing sustain the hospice movement at this time. But what will happen when others have been taught that there is a better way to die? In the hospice, it appears, these activities are instrumental in bringing acceptance. In research medicine, they are the way of life. Will a substitute for teaching and writing be found after the hospice has been better established?

Second, though research medicine has the character of a social movement in its social relations, it is not seen as such by its participants or by the general public. Research medicine can draw on familiar images of organization and purposes in legitimating itself to the public. The hospice personnel are a social reform movement in their own eyes as well as those of the public. What will happen here, once the charismatic founding figures of Cicely Saunders in England and Elizabeth Kübler-Ross in America are gone?

Third, research medicine seeks funds from the established organizations that support science. Their support may wax and wane as does that of science in general. We have all become used to the fact, however, that science is expensive. In its full-fledged form as a separate institution, a hospice also is an expensive way of dying. We are not used to that. At St. Christopher's the ratio of staff to dying is about 1.25 to 1 (Saunders 1976). For in-house care it takes more than one full-time, specially trained caretaker to make the dying of another peaceful. Of course, St. Christopher's relies heavily on volunteers. But such reliance has its limits. Volunteers there have a high turnover, which interrupts the maintenance of personal relations with the dying. What will happen here, once the novelty wears off?

Rather than asking more questions, let us stress in closing why any routinization of hospice activity that returned to more impersonal relations would signal defeat. From the point of view of the dying person, death is a threat to all known and understood dimensions of identity. That is why the struggle to maintain an integrous sense of self can be aided by caretakers only if they treat the dying as a whole person in all the relevant roles he or she played. That requires learning and coming to know what of the role repertoire is now, in the days and weeks of dying, significant to the person facing death. It is only a fairly good knowledge of the dying that enables their helpers to focus with them on the more sound, guilt-free structures of the self in order to strengthen the weaker parts. It is only by listening to, sharing with, and expressing one's strengths, weaknesses, successes, and failures, that the predicament which is life can be mobilized against the threat of identity loss. Beyond controlling pain, which is already a giant step, helping in dying demands diffuse relations. That makes it hard for the helper. The test of having shared in the dying is to be found in the pain of bereavement. This puts the staff under strain. They have to engage in the role of the comforter *and* in that of the bereaved at the same time (Wallace & Townes 1969). Finding an equivalent of what religious orders could do in the past seems to be the principal challenge of the hospice movement today.

In summary, there is not much sociological merit in believing that people in modern societies must deny the reality of death more intensely than people in preindustrial societies did. There may be more philosophical merit to such an idea. But most people are not philosophers and, as we shall see in the next chapter, neither death nor bereavement makes them more or less religious. Professionals in hospitals, where most die, avoid treating a dying person as one who is dying. But this results from a lack of organizational and educational qualifications to provide the kind of terminal care that a psychologist would define as adequate to the needs of those facing death. As indicated by the responses of nurses who answered Popoff's questionnaire, just changing the climate of opinion of death and dying would not be sufficient to alter behavior significantly. Many nurses believe that a dying person should be given "extra time," but few manage to do so. Organizations and professions entirely oriented to cure lack the resources for making dying more humane. There is no sign of diachronic solidarity. Both the staff and families shy away from the dying and avoid the whole topic of death, let alone its meaning. This is why we say that the fact that people die in institutions nowadays amounts to premature social abandonment. The dying are treated as dead or nearly so before they are ready to depart. The hospice movement has been created to counteract this treatment. It is an effort to mobilize the staff, families, and community volunteers to give the dying diffuse human concern, while at the same time liberating them from responsibility for reciprocity. The hospice is designed to specialize in terminal care, developing those resources of compassion for the dying that seem to be lacking in modern societies. Whether this movement will succeed in accomplishing that on a scale significant enough to affect the dying of the reader remains to be seen.

7

on death and bereavement: liberation and abandonment

Any social perspective on death treats the relations between the living, the dying, and the dead. These are curious relations. For the scientific observer, at least, the living are seen as relating to the dead, but the dead do not respond. Regardless of how people have treated their dead, historians, anthropologists, and sociologists alike always describe the dead as "significant others" to the living, oriented to by the living but not answering in kind. However sacred or important, however much "alive" the dead are in the eyes of their survivors, to the scientific observer the dead "do not speak." It has always been the living who spoke through them to each other.

It has been the same with the models of death and its meaning. They were the products of the living. Logically, the situation today is the same. Since one defines death as an irreversible exit from life, the dead cannot tell us about their experience, so social science circles believe. But more than logic influences how we think and the questions we ask.

Experiences of Near-Death

Today we have reports of the subjective experience of near-death. They come from people near death by drowning or falling while climbing a mountain.

Others come from the hospital. The "clinically dead," regarded as "gone" by physicians and nurses, have reported what they heard, felt, and saw while apparently dead. These latter reports, defying sound clinical judgment, have made concern with the subjective experience of death itself respectable in categories of meaning beyond psychiatry. Seen in this light, one can say quite definitely: As far as is known, the experience of death itself is one of joyous liberation, *not* one of terror or identity disintegration.

Their Interpretation

One might object to these reports on the grounds that they do not give us knowledge of death. Such objections might come from quite different interests, one scientific, the other religious. A scientific objection could be that reports of the subjective experience of death cannot be what they purport to be because the people furnishing them did, after all, not die. The best way to answer such reports, then, is to label them reports of close encounters with death, describing experiences with extreme life-threatening situations. However, such play with labels may have serious consequences for intellectual honesty. It is fair to guess that what is most attractive and interesting about these reports, for lay persons and *social* scientists alike, is what they purport to be, experiences with death. Defiance of logic does not necessarily reduce one's interest. One may relabel the reports as descriptions of life-threatening situations but one reads them nonetheless, as reflecting experiences with death.

It seems to us that this is an honest way out of this dilemma. We may simply accept the reports as imperfect knowledge of death with the full knowledge that imperfect knowledge is the only one we shall ever have. The choice would seem to be between imperfect knowledge and no knowledge. Taking the reports seriously, then, is simply a preference for some knowledge over none at all. We would call this way out an honest one because a preference for imperfect knowledge over none is merely the application of one of the two beliefs that underlie all scientific work. As Weber (1919b/1958) made eminently clear, a nonrational foundation of science is the twin beliefs that scientific knowledge is preferable to other kinds of knowledge *and* that knowledge in general is better than ignorance. One can assign respectability to these reports on the basis of the second belief underlying all scientific work.

The possible religious objection to such reports is not as easily resolved; in fact, we have no resolution to offer to this objection. From the religious point of view the trouble with these reports could be in their uniform content attesting to death as a joyous liberation from life. If one believes that, then, there is no room for the traditional possibility of hell after life on earth. Only hell in life and in the experience of the living remains. Although there is enough of that to satisfy even the masochists among us, the purported absence of hell after life poses vexing religious problems. The reason is simple. All salvation religions postulate that there are two possibilities for life after death: heaven or hell. One need not quibble here with the theological fine points as to the meanings of these terms. On a lay person's level of understanding, the concept of salvation involves doing something to attain some state of ultimate meaning and to avoid actions that threaten that goal. These two possibilities, heaven or hell, are particularly important to the salvation of Christians, to whom most of the literature on death and bereavement is directed. Not being theologians but merely social scientists, the only thing we can do is to identify the points of tension between secular knowledge and the ethical implications of the religious beliefs of those for whom we have data. On this point, then, we simply shall continue in the footsteps of the sociological tradition.

In the study of values and therefore also of religious belief and practice, so Weber (1919a/1958, 1919b/1958) held, sociologists can make a very modest contribution to human life at best. They can help clarify the ethical implications of the religious beliefs held by the people they study. But by using sociological inquiry only, they cannot determine the validity of either the religious ideas or their own values. Finding ethical implications for moral conduct in everyday life or pointing to tensions between salvation interests and social or secular interests can be sociological tasks; so is identifying tensions between the requirements of mental health, something understood in secular terms, and spiritual health, something to be understood in sacred terms. Clarity on problems of this kind are the *only possible* gains to be expected from sociological investigation of questions of faith. In reference to the funeral and bereavement, questions of faith cannot be avoided honestly, because modern men and women do bury their dead with a religious ritual.

Exploring Death

Relations today among the living, the dying, and the dead reveal a deep cleavage in the experience of the former two and the last. Dying, experiencing and witnessing it, and surviving in bereavement create social strain, threats to identity, and pain. As the previous chapter showed, dying is the experience of premature social abandonment by the living. In this chapter we shall indicate that relative social abandonment also is the common fate of modern men and women in mourning. Death, on the other hand, seems entirely stressless. However imperfect our knowledge of it, death is a liberation from the stress and tension of life. We shall start with the experience of death, because it takes little time to tell. Next, we shall survey the nature of grief, bereavement, or mourning, terms we shall use interchangeably. Then we shall analyze the problem of bereavement in modern society in terms of the four functions traditionally assigned to the funeral.

Ever since Durkheim and Malinowski, social scientists have argued that a funeral serves four purposes. These are: 1) assigning meaning to death and sharing that meaning with the survivors; 2) producing diachronic solidarity in a shared and continued identity between the living and the dead; 3) integrating the survivors into a community of mourners; and 4) regulating postfuneral mourning behavior so as to find a replacement for the dead person in fact, while acknowledging that the dead are irreplaceable in normative theory. Our examination of the literature will try to answer the questions of whether, how much, and how these functions of the funeral are realized by men and women in advanced society. Lastly, where these functions fail us today, with neither an old goal attained nor a new one found worthy of pursuit, thus turning that portion of the funeral into an empty ritual, we shall endeavor to find out why.

THE PERSONAL EXPERIENCE OF DEATH: LIBERATION

In *Life After Death,* Wheeler (1976) surveyed the literature on the experience of death. It may be that this information has not received serious enough consideration among academics. Wheeler, and most of the writers whose works he reviewed, consider that the available knowledge of the experience of death does attest to the fact of life after death, although they admit to the impossibility of scientific proof (e.g., Moody 1976:5). For example, Kübler-Ross is quoted as stating that she is totally convinced that there is life after death *because,* having seen more than one thousand people die, she has evidence of life after death and that she talks as if the dead can testify (Wheeler 1976:79). In addition, she, her co-workers, and others who agree with them, in caring for the dying, teach them how to have "afterlife experiences" while dying.

To disregard reports of the experience of being clinically dead solely because of such claims seems unwise. As we pointed out, the only knowledge the living can ever have about the subjective experience of death comes from those who stood at the door of death but did *not* pass through it. Those who disdain such information as mere hallucination in effect prefer ignorance to any kind of knowledge. Furthermore, teaching the dying how to attain alternative forms and states of consciousness to the ones they were used to throughout their lives may indeed serve their interests. *If* reducing fear of death, *and* this is not in conflict with other beliefs, why not use the only available knowledge we have?

The first striking feature of these reports of being dead is in the nature of the experience and its apparent uniformity. Being dead appears as an experience of unqualified bliss, a genuine liberation from life. There seem to be no exceptions. No one wanted to return to life. Second, it did not seem to matter who the person was in social life. The experience of death as always happy and devoid of fear, was reported by a variety of people. They included mountain climbers who fell, lower class males shot in city slums, upper class women entering clinical death (no breathing, no blood pressure) during child delivery in a hospital, middle-class males having heart attacks, and children as well as old people. In short, the consistent reports of a benign, if not indeed a "blissful" experience of being dead, are significant because they come from people in all walks of life, in several societies.

Three Aspects of Death

The encounter with death has three aspects. Sometimes they appear as successive stages. But the first does not appear in all accounts nor does the third always occur after the second and in clearly separable form. These three aspects are resistance, panoramic life-review, and transcendence. Usually the first reaction to thinking and feeling one is dying is the mobilization of the body and the mind to retain life. Feats of superhuman physical strength are sometimes reported, as is the heightened arousal of mental capacities beyond those the person had experienced before. Noyes and Kletti (1976) interpreted this as a biological defense of the organism against the threat of death.

Often as a second stage, but sometimes as the first reaction, was the panoramic life-review. People reported seeing specific experiences of their past lives in a speed and clarity of recall, once again, beyond anything in their previous experience. The kinds of events they recalled seldom were threatening; they tended to be pleasant or neutral. According to Noyes and Kletti (1976), this review of past life experiences serves to protect the self against the threat of disintegration as well as to facilitate the acceptance of death as real. The last experienced before. Noyes and Kletti (1976) interpreted this as a biological always so. Although the content of accounts varied, all had some religious connotation. By the latter we mean simply a sense of assurance of the preservation of self in a state liberated from all conceivable sources of frustration and constraint. The forms may be traditionally religious, meeting Christ, for example. Travel through a dark tunnel or valley from which the person came into a peaceful space with "beautiful music," "brilliant light" or "a huge eye that permits one to enter" are some of the recurring themes in the reports of "being dead." Another feature of the encounter with clinical death in a hospital is the "out of body experience" (OOBE). In this the survivors said that they had a sense of "floating on the ceiling" and could see their own body and those trying to revive it. Significant in these accounts is the near universal finding that "the dead" had no desire to return to life. On the contrary, they wanted the hospital staff to stop and let them die. Many said afterwards that they could hear and understand what staff were saying, which agrees with the fact that hearing is the last sense to give way.

Release from Social Life?

In reading the reports we were particularly interested in evidence of the experience of death as an appreciated release from *social* life. We looked for some direct indication of a sense of joyous release from some specific role obligation, whether that of parenthood, marriage, work, friendship, and so on. But we found nothing so social. In fact, the exprience of transcendentalism—in the words of Noyes and Kletti (1976) of "spiritualism" or "rebirth constructions"—was so utterly different from any common sense experience that the greatest difficulty of these near-dead was communicating what they had experienced in a way adequate to it. All felt their words failed them. Their experience was so "otherworldly," so radically different from ordinary social life and its language that attempts to translate the experience to the living always fell short in the eyes of those "who had come back."

"Death," then, is not experienced as a release from social life. Raising that question is natural for sociologists with their ideas of identity, however naive it may appear in hindsight. Death seems to be a joyous release from uncertainty. However varied in content, all the experiences were those of an ultimate order in harmony with itself. Perhaps, then, death is a release from personality in the sense of William James's "conscious self," the one that constructs our empirical social identities. These social identities are the only ones we really know. We know ourselves as fathers or mothers, as workers in office or factory, or as voters and friends. As parents we may be known as reticent in showing affection to our children; as workers we may be known as tardy or punctual; as voters highly informed or barely aware of candidates and issues; or as friends we may be known as reliable or undependable.

In short, it is through our social identities that we know what makes us like other people and what makes us different from them, giving us our individuality. But the mental agency that knows all this remains inaccessible to common-sense experience. Perhaps psychoanalysis can reveal it. But few of us have sufficiently compelling reason to try analysis. Although this agency remains hidden, we are dependent on it throughout life. Lying beyond our reach, we know of its efficacy only through its products, certainty about our social selves. How it operates is never understood, and whether it will continue to do so is always uncertain. The exceptionless experience of death as an apprehension of ultimate order appears to be a liberation from the possibility of ultimate chaos in life, one resting in turn on our inability to understand how the "conscious self" does its work.

Interpretations of Death

However tentative, our interpretation rests on the one other feature of these reports. All come from people in societies with religious cultures that Bellah (1964) described as historical, early modern, or modern. That means that they are deeply characterized by symbols of ultimate meaning. These are ideas of so perfect a truth or so total a deception, so perfect an order or so utter a chaos, so complete a vision of the beautiful or so horrible an ugliness that everything corresponding to them in real social life and its experiences remains a mere shadow, small, petty, ephemeral, and insignificant when one encounters death.

Conceptions of ultimate meaning are very abstract, but they do seem to bind emotions with a force that has no parallel elsewhere.

If the voices of those who "return from death to life" are any indication, ordinary men and women who lived in religious settings with symbols of ultimate meaning display an extraordinary yearning for positive meanings and a similar apprehension of negative meanings. Also, we know from these reports that such concerns have nothing much to do with how religious, in belief and practice, the person was before encountering death. Whether the person thought of himself or herself as religious or secular before, all reported that the encounter with death was an entry into a state of ultimate order. Presumably, this was a release from the possibility of ultimate chaos or meaninglessness for which culture as well as the psyche are models.

There is another interpretation, more mundane, which reduces this religious experience to a biological one. Sagan (1979) argued that the just-described "death" experience is nothing more than a reflection of the birth experience. Before presenting this view, let us first remember that the death experience has three aspects. First, there is a fierce struggle for life; then there is the panoramic life review; and finally, there comes the transcendental experience of ultimate harmony.

Our experience of birth has many parallels. The first stage here is analogous to the last days before labor begins. In the words of Sagan (1979:41), the first stage "is the blissful complacency of the child in the womb, free of all anxiety, the center of a small, dark, warm universe—a cosmos in an amniotic sac." Then comes labor, the uterine contractions, "with the fetus dreadfully compressed," without "hope of surcease, . . . in seemingly endless agony." Being pushed from the womb into life is parallel to the fierce struggle for life during our experience with death. The end of the birth process, when the head of the child is already outside but the rest still inside, is like the experience of going through a tunnel into light, even if the eyes are closed. According to Sagan (1979:41):

> The discovery of light for a creature that has lived its entire existence in darkness must be a profound and on some level an unforgettable experience. And there, dimly made out by the low resolution of the newborn's eyes, is some godlike figure surrounded by a halo of light—the Midwife or the Obstetrician or the Father. At the end of a monstrous travail, the baby flies away from the uterine universe, and rises toward the lights and the gods.

The transcendental experience of death is a mere recollection of our entry into life.

There are three reasons to treat Sagan's interpretation not as competing with but merely as complementing our own account of the death experience. First, the birth experience is a universal one. If it alone could produce the death experience, one should find accounts of the latter in reports from all cultures independently of whether or not they had salvation religions. Yet, although Sagan (1979:39) claimed that death experiences are to be found in all human societies, the only references he gives come from societies with salvation religions. Second, Sagan refused to treat people's religious beliefs as an independent and important source of these experiences, preferring instead a naturalistic account. The themes of birth and rebirth, however, are deeply embedded in religious culture. For example, in 1976 about one third of all Americans told the Gallup pollster that they had had "a born-again experience" (see Table 7.1). Finally, we would always prefer multi-causal interpretations to single-factor explanations simply because the latter have seldom been applicable to human life. Sooner rather than later they were found to be wrong. Thus, the birth experience may well be one contributing factor to the experience of death as liberation, and living in a religious culture of salvation is another. No doubt, more will be found before the uniformly liberating nature of death is more fully understood.

THE NATURE OF GRIEF AND ITS SOCIAL SETTING

In assessing how and to what extent the contemporary funeral serves any of the functions usually expected of it, we must rely in great part on three studies of widows (Lopata 1973; Glick and others 1974; Marris 1958). We shall refer to them as the Chicago, the Boston, and the London widows, designating where the studies were done. Most of these widows were under the retirement age of sixty-five. Besides these studies, there is little information about the funeral as experienced by the person closest to the dead. Unfortunately, the Chicago widows were interviewed a considerable time after the funeral, but the Boston widows were observed as they struggled with the experience of having their husbands die, through the funeral, and the first year of bereavement. So the reliability of the information varies as well. Some data are recollections of distant events, others of close ones. The fact that these are not elderly widows is less serious, however. Certainly, from the point of view of the significant determinants of grief (Parkes 1972), chronological age alone supplies at best two among a dozen such factors that should make suffering the loss of an intimate other in old age different from losing him earlier in life. As for the severity of grief, one of these may reduce it, the other may intensity it.

The timeliness of death in advanced age may diminish grief. Though there is no consensus as to when one has reached "a ripe old age," the encounter with death at age seventy or later is not seen as tragic, a designation reserved for the "untimely" death, occurring earlier in life. This means only that the elderly woman is not expected to react to the loss of her husband as an "unjust" event. Old age, after all, means heightened awareness of death. One's friends and siblings die. That is why one finds that older people think of death more often than young people do (Riley & Foner 1968; Jeffers & Verwoerdt 1966). Similarly, because death in old age is regarded as normal, older people also reported less fear of death than younger ones did (Jeffers, Nichols, & Eisdorfer 1961; Swenson 1961). But all these social expectations are of little help when death comes to the small family of the elderly. The smallness of the family itself intensifies the pain of grief.

When death strikes in old age, it strikes the family reduced to a couple. In most cases the children have left long before. They have established their own family, are leading separate lives, and presumably also have reduced their identity-conferring social ties with their parents. Thus, death in advanced age is for the widow or widower most often the loss of the only significant intimate left in life. Of course, friends may be other intimates. But friends in grief are not recognized in their bereavement status in prevailing American funeral customs, which focus on the surviving spouse as the central figure (Folta & Deck 1976). In its social aspect, then, the modern funeral is focused on the dissolution of a family. This is one of its drawbacks, compared to funerals in preindustrial societies.

Purely hypothetically (Parkes 1972:99), any social system encountering the death of one of its members may react to that loss in four ways: 1) the roles performed by the missing person remain unperformed, with some strain on the survivors as the consequence; 2) a substitute is found; 3) the tasks of the missing person are assumed by survivors; and 4) the social system breaks up. Using the evidence available then, Parkes listed two tasks of the missing person that remained unperformed for most widows in industrial societies. A widow becomes a desexualized woman, and no substitute for the companion-protector role of the dead husband usually is found. This is a long-term experience for widows who lose their husbands in the midst of life. For most elderly women, we suggest, it is an irreversible loss. It is the fourth outcome, however, the destruction of the social system, that dramatizes the significance of the funeral and of widowhood in old age.

The family is the only social system in modern society designed for a finite life span. From its start the family is destined to end in death or dissolution. With its social relations patterned almost exclusively, and certainly distinctively, in particularist, diffuse, and affective ways, the relationship of a married couple is the accomplishment of a tailor-made social tie. If we marry for love alone, something not done in preindustrial societies, we also can legitimate divorce when love disappears. As a reason for tying and untying the marital bond, love designates marriage as a voluntary tie. But in old age, most widows cannot remarry, and most maintain their own household rather than joining that of children.

Friendship aside, all other social systems are designed for an indefinite life span. In fact, we think of many as eternal. Corporations in the economy, government organizations, schools or universities, prisons, golf clubs, or churches all are social systems through which people pass. Some of these organizations fail, of course. But they are not social systems designed for particular people and so are not as finite as the latter. In its normative design only the modern family is constructed according to specifications dictating a finite life span. It starts as incomplete when two marry. With the arrival of children it becomes complete. With their departure to form their own families, it returns to the incomplete status of the couple. With the death of one partner, it dissolves. If it can be said that no preindustrial society officially permitted marriage on the grounds of love alone, it would follow that none wove the impermanence of human life as closely into the fabric of society as the modern society did. That affects both grief and the tasks of the funeral.

The Nature of Grief

The experience of dying and the experience of grieving over the death of another have remarkable parallels. According to Kübler-Ross, the dying experience the following: denial, anger and protest, bargaining (if I survive this, I will . . .), depression, and acceptance. Though labeling them stages, she did not intend to imply that they evolve in stage-like temporal succession as the person nears death. They do not occur in stage fashion either (Pattison 1977). Stages are somewhat more prevalent in grief or bereavement. The first reaction to death is numbing shock and disbelief. One denies it. The bereaved also react with anger and hostility. There is aggression. Sometimes it is directed at the self, arising from guilt of omission or commission. Sometimes the aggression is focused on others. Doctors and health personnel often are targets of criticism as the bereaved struggle with the question of the cause of death. Idealization of the dead person often occurs. In fact, at some stage in grieving most wives convince themselves that they had an unusually good husband. This belief appears regardless of the quality of the marriage (Glick and others 1974:140). It also is a sign of reconciliation with the loss and of the return to the gradual resumption of normal emotions, and social activities (Engel 1961).

The same elements of denial, anger and hostility, depression and despair, guilt, and idealization of the dead appear in Parkes's (1972) review of the evidence of grief and its nature. His account was a very detailed description organized in terms of "the state of organismic alarm," "searching for the dead," strategies to "mitigate the pain of loss," and, eventually, "gaining a new identity." The subjective experiences of dying and bereavement share all essential elements save one: There is no bargaining about death once it has occurred.

Direct or not, these parallel experiences probably were at the root of some of the recent concern with "anticipatory grief." This holds that the more grief work could be done before the actual event, the less shattering the impact would be (e.g., Ujhely 1963). But this idea is too simple. The study of the Boston widows shows that grieving takes years rather than weeks. Anticipatory grieving also means regarding the dying as near dead or already dead. Inadvertently many do so but not consciously, for that would mean hastening death, killing the other. The Boston widows almost deliberately avoided anticipatory grieving. However similar the subjective experiences of dying and bereavement, normally bereavement comes afterwards. It is a *delayed* mutuality in disengagement between the dying and the grieving. One study showed that anticipatory grief in fact increased the pain of the actual experience of loss (Clayton and others 1973).

None of this is surprising when viewed from a perspective on the social nature of identity. It takes time to become a wife. So it should take time to become a widow. Just as becoming a wife is begun only on the wedding day, so the latter process starts only with the funeral. One does not acquire an identity in the same way that one buys toothpaste in a shop. Neither does one discard an identity like a dirty shirt. Acquisition of an identity occurs through interaction with another, a process that takes time, concluding with the internalization of a membership role with that other person.

Similarly, letting go of identity, that other in oneself, requires interaction with others in turn and time. For an elderly woman, after a long marriage mourning is somewhat like a courtship process in reverse (Marris 1974:23-27), one that has to alter something acquired over many years. We do not want to argue against crisis-intervention centers for widows. But we should *not* expect them to speed up grieving significantly. The widows may tell us that they found the aid helpful (McCourt and others 1976). Yet that aid probably was most useful for matters other than reshaping identity and reducing the pain associated with it. In this area it is difficult to find a substitute for family cohesion and resilience (Polack and others 1975).

Although scales to measure grief suitable for large numbers of people in bereavement still are being developed (Faschingbauer and others 1977), the length of normal grieving in a statistical sense remains unknown. Clinical data tell us that "normally" grief in its acute initial stage is a very incapacitating and painful condition (Parkes 1972). Although the question of whether grief is a genuine cause of physical illness remains to be settled, one can die of a broken heart (Parkes, Benjamin, & Fitzgerald 1969). Suffering from depression seems to be the main cause.

This has another parallel to the subjective experience of dying in old age. Clinical evidence shows that when time is running out, many older persons become preoccupied with a review of their lives, certainly the major events in it (Butler 1964). If such reminiscences focus on "the chances missed," "the wrongs done," or "the years misspent in some futile pursuit of unattainable ends," all matters that can no longer be corrected, severe depression may result (McMahon & Rhudick 1967). Being depressed may well lead an elderly person to give up in the face of illness. That in turn can speed dying (Schmale & Engel 1967). Depression also is the core syndrome in acute grief, and here Parkes (1972) described its debilitating effect as practically indistinguishable from many psychiatric disorders characterized by depression. The findings of Clayton and others (1974) support his contention.

Although depression has many forms, it suffices here to describe it in terms of the four "don'ts": "you don't know what you want any more"; "you don't play any more"; "you don't bring yourself to work any more"; and "you don't care any more." In the beginning, the pain of loss is too sharp for the body to sustain that mood constantly over hours and days. Episodes of pain, crying, and reexperiencing the discovery of loss alternate with denial. It is the body that saves many from confinement to bed. Otherwise, it is a psychological sickness, as painful and debilitating as many physical diseases. The status of bereavement, aside from the immediate occasion of the funeral, does lack social recognition in modern society. This will be demonstrated below. At this point we note that because bereavement is not recognized as a social status, grief in modern times amounts to being ill but without the usual privileges granted those with other physical or mental illnesses. With this as a background, let us turn to the funeral.

THE MODERN FUNERAL: SOME FUNCTIONS MISSED, SOME FULFILLED

What of the first function of the funeral: How much does the funeral serve to assign meaning to death, and how much sharing of that meaning is realized among the survivors? For the meaning of death as experienced at the funeral, all the observations on which we must rely are limited by three facts. First, both in the United States and West Germany the great majority of the dead were buried in a religious ceremony (Pine and others 1976; Dirschauer 1973). Second, both in the United States and European societies God is not dead. Practically all people said that they believe in God. Third the vast majority of people participating in the funerals on which we have information were Christians. These three facts persuade us to examine the meaning of death from the perspective of the Christian faith.

Death and Christianity

We showed in the previous chapter that our age is not secular, at least not in the simple absence of belief. In surveys conducted in the 1950s and early 1960s most people in advanced societies said that they believe in God. In Europe that belief runs like a mighty river from North to South and from East to West. It was the same in the United States (Swanson 1968). As far as we know, faith did not lose its hold over people in the 1970s (see Table 7.1). Belief in God is clearly a mass phenomenon. The majority still believes in a literal interpretation of the Bible. Although a majority still believe in an afterlife in the United States, barely one half the Germans and even fewer British do. This is important to our subsequent analysis. The religious beliefs of modern men and women do not hold together very well; they do not form a system of beliefs. In the Christian meaning of death, these unsystematic, modern belief patterns are significant.

Although we shall have to rely entirely on American data for these patterns, it will be seen that there is little consensus on more specific questions of the meaning of death. If Americans lack consensus in this area, it is very likely that this is a general condition in modern societies, because the United States remains the most religious country among the Western industrialized nations (see Table 7.1). Let us note that Americans are quite firm believers. Almost one half cared enough about God to encourage someone else to believe in Jesus Christ. About one third told the Gallup pollster that they had had a mystical or a "born again" experience. True, so intense a religious experience was characteristic of only one third, but we would suggest that as an index of religious concern these answers reflect more the tip of an iceberg than the whole reality of religious belief in the lives of these people. The Gallup surveys listed in Table 7.1 also tell us that the elderly in American society are more religious on practically all dimensions than younger people are. What then is the meaning of death in the Christian religion?

Denominational differences and theological details aside, a "rock bottom minimalist belief requirement" to call oneself a Christian at all in this area contains the ideas of sin, guilt, and sacrifice. In Christ, God became human and suffered death in order to save humans from otherwise inescapable meaninglessness. They who do not experience themselves as sinful cannot see meaning in this self-sacrifice of God's Son. Christ's dying was, of course, a biological event. But in the call "my God, my God, why hast Thou forsaken me?" he alluded to the fear of death as eternal banishment from God's presence. Whatever else may be said about the New Testament's definition of death, for a lay person, *any* Christian burial rite is a confrontation with the resurrected Christ figure whose death was a transfer to eternal life, or into the company of God. Death is supposed to mean salvation from the meaninglessness inherent in human existence, one that humans on their own cannot overcome (Dirschauer 1973). It would appear to follow that belief in the resurrected Christ and his God-status as well as the sinful nature of humans are the minimum requirements for the generation and sharing of the significance of death at a burial ceremony.

Although ours is not a "godless" age, in the United States there is little consensus on these two points (Glock & Stark 1965). For example, for just over a quarter of Congregationalists and a fifth of American Methodists, Christ was only a man "and no more the son of God than all of us are the children of God." Glock and Stark showed that the inevitability of sin is also not believed widely. Over a third of the members of two Protestant groups and 43 percent of American Catholics regard this idea as "probably or definitely not true." In addition and worse yet for the clergy, only just a half of the Catholics and less than that among several Protestant denominations still believe that faith is an

Table 7.1
Some Religious Beliefs in Western Industrialized Countries
(Percent of "Yes" Answers in National Samples)

	U.S. 1976	U.S. 1968	U.K. 1975	France 1967	France 1973	West-Germany 1967
Believe in God?	94	77	72	72	82*	68
Believe in afterlife?	69	38	—	—	—	48
Believe in literal meaning of the Bible?	83	—	69**	—	—	65
Ever had a mystical religious experience?	31	—	—	—	—	—
Ever had a "born again experience"?	34	—	—	—	—	—
Ever encouraged someone to believe in Jesus?	47	—	—	—	—	—

*Nearest comparable question was: Do you consider yourself a Christian?
**Nearest comparable question was: Do you believe in prayer?

Sources: G. H. Gallup, The Gallup Poll 1972-1977 (Wilmington, Del.: SR Scholarly Resources Inc., 1978), pp. 859-61, 627-29. G. H. Gallup, The Gallup International Public Opinion Polls: France 1939, 1944-1975 (New York: Random House, 1976), pp. 639-962. G. H. Gallup, The Gallup International Public Opinion Polls: Great Britain 1937-1975 (New York: Random House, 1976), pp. 995-1418. "Was Glauben die Deutschen?" Der Spiegel, December 18, 1967, pp. 28-55.

absolute requirement for salvation. On the other hand, "works" are regarded as important to salvation. In short, for the funeral, the contemporary religious situation is not promising. On the absolute minimum of details in belief required to share the Christian meaning of death at a funeral, Americans suffer from inadequate consensus. At the funeral site, Berger's (1967) claim of the privatization of religious belief would seem to hold. According to his vision, Americans no longer form a living community of faith. Instead, each person must construct his or her own beliefs. Presumably, the same situation prevails in Europe.

Having stressed the *social* nature of identity throughout this chapter, let us add one more consideration. *Any* transcendental religion requires a deep emotional commitment to ultimate symbols, radically different from those of common-sense social reality. In the Christian case with its focus on eternal life, this *requires* commitment to continued existence in a form radically different from social identities. No matter how a minister may adapt himself or herself to the emotional needs of the bereaved at the grave site, since the resurrection of Christ means no less than overcoming sin *and* death themselves, he or she has to represent the "radical otherhood" of God *and* the dead. Eternal life cannot be really understood in terms of categories familiar to social life in this world.

Faith demands a comprehension of the status of the dead transcending the realm of society and its role playing. But the bereaved wife in her state of acute grief at the funeral still carries within her identity the husband in nothing but social terms. Because her identity as wife is under assault by the death of her partner, defending the integrity of her own identity requires clinging to the *social* nature of her husband and thus of herself. If she is not to fall apart, her psychological needs will require focusing on her dead husband in his human, social nature. The requirements of psychology and Christian theology are in deep tension. This is a difficulty that no consensus in matters of faith can diminish. Only a very strong faith, highly disciplined, constantly honed throughout life, and so rationalized in the relations of its credal components as to eventuate in a cultural identity stronger than our secular social-role identities could mitigate that tension. Precisely this, however, is absent from modern religion, certainly in America and West Germany (Glock & Stark 1965; *Der Spiegel,* December 18, 1967), and probably elsewhere too. Although not secularized heathens in any simple way, modern men and women are helpless in confronting the meaning of death because their beliefs lack sufficient inner coherence and sufficient information, if not indeed sufficient intellectual honesty in facing up to the implications of their faith.

How does the American clergy adapt? An earlier survey and some articles in the journal *Pastoral Psychology* (Fulton 1961; Fulton & Geis 1968; Irion 1963, 1973; Gealy 1963; Forest 1963; Bonnel 1971; Rogers 1973a, 1973b) suggested the following: The Catholic priest tends to follow the traditional requirements of faith. His funeral objectives are: 1) to pray for the salvation of the soul; 2) to honor the body and the memory of the dead; and 3) to teach the living to prepare for their own death, in that order of importance. He tends to leave comforting the bereaved to the funeral director and his or her staff or to the family. Protestant ministers have different funeral priorities. Comforting the bereaved comes first, generating a hope for future life comes second. Also, Protestant ministers see themselves in serious competition with morticians in comforting the bereaved. However indirectly, priests are directed more to the demands of God, ministers more to the demands of humans in distress.

We also have some indication that clergy and their congregations agree on the purposes of the funeral. Recently bereaved Catholics tend to see the funeral as serving the dead rather than the living, a matter on which Protestants were split half and half (Khleif 1976). Among the seven essays on the funeral, mostly by Protestants, five advised their clerical colleagues how to comfort the bereaved. Only one discussed the inevitable tension between the Christian's duty to God and the dead on this occasion, on the one hand, and the psychological needs of the bereaved, on the other. One writer revealed theological ambivalence. Because *only* the immediately bereaved attend the funeral, he found it an unsuitable opportunity for the teaching mission of the church. In short, relative to the demands of faith, the Christian clergy finds itself in a dilemma.

If the clergy were to turn for help to scientists specializing in the study of death, the most notable among contemporary thanatologists, they probably would be wrong to expect much constructive aid for spiritual problems of the contemporary funeral. One study of the scientific experts on death showed clearly that thanatologists have little interest in the funeral as a ceremony and little sympathy with religous concerns in general. In their own personal attitudes and values, the modern specialist of death is not a religious adherent (Burton 1978).

Further, as Hoge (1976), among others, stressed, American values are quintessentially pragmatic. One believes in God *in order to* have a better family life, to be a better person, to be a good and steady worker, and to improve oneself. This instrumental orientation to beliefs has been reported for Protestants, but Catholics also are American. We would be wrong in describing them as less pragmatic but probably would be right in finding among them a greater willingness to go along with traditional rituals. The situation seems to be one of mutual adjustment to social reality by the churches and their members. But it is deceptive. Pragmatic values are directed to life in its social terms. If the information from the widows is an indication, they fail us in the confrontation with death in every respect other than the social exigencies of the situation.

The Boston widows saw ministers and priests as wholly marginal figures during the funeral. They were there, they did their duty. But nothing they said was of any significance to the widows. The Chicago widows found nothing notable in this experience to remember later. Among the London widows, religion had little if any importance. But the Boston widows viewed the funeral director and the staff as significant figures and had nothing but praise for them. Their story is clear: Protestant ministers appear to have lost the competition to comfort the bereaved. The available evidence points to a failure of the funeral in its first function to generate and to share the meaning of death.

If we had meanings of death alternative to religious ones with sufficient structure for sharing, the situation might be different; but we do not. With a lack of consensus about the religious meanings, yet using a religious service, the situation still could be different if confrontation with death could make people more religious than they otherwise are. But the demands of Christianity are far too complex for that, and one cannot invent alternative beliefs instantly. Dying fails to make us more, less, or differently religious than we were before (Pattison 1977:76). From the widows in Chicago, Boston, and London we know that bereavement, neither before, at the funeral, nor afterwards affects one's religious beliefs and practices. In rural or small towns the funeral may still serve to mobilize and to share the meanings of death. In cities it seems to be no longer the case.

The experience of the meaning of death for survivors differs from that of the dying. From the clinically dead we learned about a release from life in terms radically different from the common-sense meanings of social life. It also appears that most in life yearn for such alternative patterns of meaning. But such yearnings seem to be realized only in death. Originally, the message of the Christian funeral was aimed at letting the living partake of these meanings. Today it no longer achieves that aim. One can surmise only that the Puritans succeeded where contemporary Americans fail. The Puritans had a strong faith, one rationalized in a lifetime of effort. Theirs too was a religious life, obsessed with the problem of the meaning of death (Stannard 1973). For a Christian, still burying the dead and grieving death in a Christian way, there is no substitute for faith. So far rituals different from those of the church have not been developed. Unless they are developed or unless there is a return to a more rationalized faith, the contemporary funeral will remain an empty ritual in respect to its first function: the generation and sharing of the meaning of death.

Funerals and Diachronic Solidarity

What about the second function of the funeral, the production of diachronic solidarity in which the living maintain a shared social identity with the dead? In this task the contemporary funeral succeeds. One is tempted to say even that it excels in this function. The available evidence indicates that the social identity of the dead is maintained and that the funeral is important to that maintenance. Aside from the death of a hero such as a slain president or a great statesperson, however, only the intimates of the dead person maintain identities with the dead, as we shall see.

In West Germany investigators asked the recently bereaved why they had a funeral and whether and why they tended the grave (Hahn 1968). The answers of all, independently of age, sex, social class, and family status relationship to the dead, clearly indicated that all of these bereaved persons believed in the continued existence of the person who just died. According to Hahn, those who responded spoke in the following terms. "But that is the least I could do for my mother, who cared for me all my life," so a son affirmed his identity as son; "Seeing how my husband slaved all his life to maintain the family, not having a proper funeral would be a gross form of ingratitude," so said a bereaved wife. For children, for the wife and widow-to-be, and for friends, the German data show that the funeral is a rite through which one reaffirms one's threatened social identity, signaling at the same time the inevitability of its change.

It is the same in the United States. But here we can show the contrast in terms of a demand for ritual before the actual event and the expressed satisfaction with the ritual when it occurs. That more than any other single factor highlights how deep, indeed how inescapable is the need of the bereaved to cling to the dead. When the question about a funeral and its form is asked in reference to a hypothetical situation as Shneidman (1973) did to younger Americans, most of whom had not yet attended a funeral, the demand of ritual was quite low. Only 42 percent of his respondents described themselves as "somewhat" or "very" religious. Even among the very religious, one fifth said that they did not want funerals. That proportion steadily increased as one went down the religiosity scale. Hypothetically, then, the majority of Americans repudiate the need for ritual.

Funeral Costs

The situation is similar for funeral costs. As long as the question was hypothetical, and therefore one divorced from the psychological reality of loss, most Americans preferred a modest funeral. About two thirds of Shneidman's young Americans, for example, preferred a funeral costing under $300. Only 2 percent considered $600 "reasonable." At about the same time, in 1971, the amounts actually paid by Americans to the funeral home alone, exclusive of cemetery plot, monument or marker, and flowers, was for most more than twice this amount. Only about 7 percent spent under $500; just about one half spent between $500 and $1,000; and the remainder, about 43 percent, spent over $1,000 (Shibles, 1974:425-28).

Some people argue that this discrepancy reflects exploitation by the funeral industry (Bureau of Consumer Protection 1978). We shall treat this with extreme caution, for the following reasons. First, the advocates of consumer protection in this area had an extraordinary insensitivity to the psychological significance of the funeral for the widow. They tended to think of buying a coffin as similar to buying a car and trading in the old one. If they considered grief at all, it was only to indicate the presumed vulnerability of the widow in her role as "a consumer." That an expensive funeral could be a last gift to a dead husband and one that serves to fortify the most critical components of the identity of the widow-in-becoming, her identity as wife, simply did not occur to these critics of the American way of death. Second, many facts refute simple exploitation. For example, in 1961 bad debts made up a paltry 2 percent of accounts receivable by the American funeral industry (Gidden 1963). Unless one were to believe that funeral homes rely on significantly more ruthless or efficient collection agencies than other industries this would indicate a far higher than usual willingness to pay the bills. Further, the funeral industry is not among the nation's "inflation pushers." From 1963 to 1972 the general cost of living index rose by 41 percent, but "funeral services, adult" rose by only 32 percent (Shibles 1974:447). None of these facts is likely to convince the critic of American funeral expenses, contemplating reasonable expenditures from a position of false psychological security available to anyone who considers such matters in purely hypothetical terms. One may doubt that reports of satisfaction with funeral arrangements from persons in bereavement will convince such critics. We add such reports here only because, when all is said and done, the available evidence is more against the exploitation argument than for it. The issue is too complex, though, to be resolved here.

Satisfaction with Funerals

In two studies the recently bereaved expressed satisfaction with the funeral at a rate of 80 percent and above. In one the bereaved did not prefer the cheaper disposal service (no viewing of the body, minimal services) and claimed that the funeral "had helped ease their grief." In the other, the funeral was seen as "a meaningful way to express love" for the dead (Hutchens 1976; Khleif 1976). All the widows in Boston had a religious service and a cemetery ritual, and about three quarters had arranged for an open-casket viewing with a restored body. In response to viewing the body, just under half found it a "helpful" experience, but the majority reacted with increased distress. All found the cemetery ritual the hardest to bear. But here, too, just under one half found that "helpful," pain and anguish notwithstanding. Neither at the time of the funeral nor later did any of the widows express that they had been exploited by the funeral director.

One gains an impressive portrait of the importance attached to the funeral by widows in industrial societies. Making sure of having "a proper funeral" emerges as the first and foremost concern among the newly bereaved. Practically all the Boston widows wanted a proper funeral very much. They got it, and they appreciated the practical advice, the actual arrangements and services, and the emotional support they received from their funeral directors in terms that can be described as "enthusiastic." Significantly, both the desire for a proper funeral and the deep gratitude for the management of it prevailed among these widows completely independently of the quality of their marriages. The wives who were aware of having had a poor marriage evidently needed to have their identity as wives confirmed just as much as those with a satisfying marriage did. According to findings by Khleif (1976), widowers in Boston were less enthusiastic about the funeral director. That confirms the social nature of identity. Though it may change, the role of wife is more central to the identity of women than is the husband role to that of most men.

The Boston widows also told us why the funeral director was so important and the clergy were so marginal at the funeral. The funeral director showed the bereaved wife what she could do in a manner than reassured her in her identity as a competent and responsible wife confronting her last duties as a wife. He was important because, above all else, he assisted the bereaved wife in doing something. He conveyed information, assisted in letting the wife decide what was a proper arrangement, given the financial situation of the family, communicated that the difficulty of making decisions was normal, tolerated patiently her frequent changes of mind, and supplied sympathy and emotional support. All this yielded viable results, structured the situation, reduced uncertainty, and, above all else, continually reassured the wife on the point most in peril at this time, that she *is* a wife. Compared to this reliance on the funeral director, all that the clergy could offer were instructions on how to feel. But the funeral director provided action that channeled emotion. When the Boston widows recalled who it was that sustained them in their most vulnerable hours of grief, they remembered the funeral director, sometimes doctors and nurses, then members of their own family, and, last and indeed least, the clergy. A card, flowers, or the rare experience of attendance at the funeral by medical personnel was more significant than the presence of the other family members. For if they, comparative strangers, cared so much, that said something unusual about the value of the man and so of the value of his wife.

The funeral does provide an opportunity to reaffirm and share social identities among the closest survivor, the spouse, the surviving family members, and the dead. What psychological consequences this has for grief remain largely unknown. Fulton (1976), for example, found better adjustment (less alcohol and tranquilizer use) among a group of bereaved who had had a full "traditional" funeral than among another group with only a disposal service. But the funeral is only one among a dozen determinants of grief (Parkes 1972:121). It can hardly be so powerful a factor as to affect the duration of grief. One study did support this contention (Schwab and others 1976).

Lower socioeconomic strata were somewhat more preoccupied with the importance of a "proper" funeral, were more willing to consider the costs encountered as reasonable and were even more satisfied with what they obtained from it all (Salomone 1968; Pine & Phillips 1970). Apparently, social disprivilege means living with a more brittle set of social identities. Reassuring oneself of one's identity on the occasion of the burial, therefore, should register more strongly. Thus, disproportionately greater funeral expenditures among lower class groups in society were hardly a surprising finding.

As for the third function of the funeral, let us ask whether the contemporary funeral integrates the bereaved into the family and into circles of friends. The answer is a qualified yes.

What little we know is based almost entirely on reports by widows of help received from relatives and friends at the funeral. If helping is an indicator of social cohesion, we can distinguish two aspects. The source of help tells us about social cohesion within the widow's own family, or between her and the husband's family, or among friends of the couple. Second, whether or not the widow perceived the aid received as "helpful" or "stressful," imposing more burdens on her, tells us something about the ability to empathize and to be sensitive to the needs of the bereaved person, and so something about the quality of closeness in the relationship.

The family of the husband is not a common source of help for the bereaved wife. Almost two thirds of the Chicago widows recalled receiving no help whatever from in-laws. They "were just there" at the funeral. Among the London widows, two thirds received help from their own kin at the funeral and just over a third also from in-laws. In Boston 70 percent of the widows found their own family far more helpful at the funeral than were the relatives of their dead husbands. Even at the funeral then, most of the bereaved persons in industrial societies have to rely on the small modern nuclear family, which family sociologists have described as a group weak in emotional resources because of its small size and extreme mutual dependence of all members on each other. The ones who share the loss most directly, the nearly equally distressed, have to help each other. For elderly widows this pattern would seem to have weakened. Having left the home a long time before, the children may suffer less from the loss of their father than their mother does.

There is one exception to the relative social distance of the in-laws as experienced by the bereaved wife. In Boston as well as in London, if there was a brother-in-law, he was singled out as particularly helpful with funeral arrangements. If one can speak of a temporary substitute for the dead husband, he would be the candidate. The Boston study also indicated that there was a sexual division of labor in helping. Help from men tended to be instrumental, that from females more emotional. Men helped with the financial and organizational aspects of the funeral arrangements. Women who helped tended to be partners in compassion, sustaining the bereaved when they broke down, helping them regain control. Whatever the form of help, the question of whether it was perceived as helpful or as making matters worse hinged on two factors. If the help received permitted the widow to express grief and share it, it was helpful. If the helpers failed to sense the proper moment to offer help, it imposed additional demands on self-control. That made help harmful. If the help reassured the bereaved in her role as wife, it was helpful; if it threatened her identity as a responsible wife, treating her as if she were a child, it was harmful.

We found only one quantitative study of helping patterns using both sources and quality of helpfulness (Maddison & Raphael 1975). The findings painted a dismal picture, highlighting the vulnerability of small families in distress. Once again members of the dead husband's family were not often helpful. They accounted for a tenth of all "helping interchanges." But they also accounted for just under a fifth of all "unhelpful" aid received. The widow's own mother was part of only 6 percent of the helping relations and accounted for 7 percent of the "unhelpful" ones. Help from the widow's own children made up under one half of the total received. From sons it was instrumental aid. The help from daughters was emotional but subjected the widow to role strain. A mother is supposed to comfort children. Having that normative definition of the situation reversed through attempts to give emotional support to her apparently threatened the bereaved in her identity as wife-mother. Finally, friends accounted for one half of all helping patterns. But their help also accounted for one half of all "unhelpful" aid. That means that practically all their help was frustrating to the bereaved wife. It seems indicative of a drastic normative deficit of the role of friends at the funeral.

Our lives while someone is dying in a hospital and at the funeral seem to be regulated by "next of kin" rules (Folta & Deck 1976). That makes friends relative outsiders. This strikes us as of particular importance to dying and death among the elderly. Friends at that stage in life may well be closer intimates of the dying and of those who suffer that loss than are children who long ago left their parents' household. Friends may grieve more than the children who have made their own lives do. But the prevailing rules, if there are any governing who is expected to suffer grief and therefore is entitled to consideration, all focus on family members. Rather than augmenting the emotional resources of the modern elderly family, small and weak in any case, the situation leaves friends to themselves, a wasted resource for coping with grief.

In sum, the available information indicates that the funeral is an occasion for increased social cohesion among the bereaved. But this seems confined to members of the immediate family of the dead person. The emotional resource base is small, and the quality of aid is presumably much less helpful than it would be if friends and in-laws figured more prominently at this time. But we know so little about the role of social networks in the experience of becoming a widow that the presumption here may well be quite naive. Maddison and Raphael (1975) found some evidence for competition for the star role at the funeral between the widow and her mother-in-law. "You, my dear, lost a husband, but I lost a son!" All a sociologist can say here is the obvious: The increase in helping at the time of the funeral by friends and in-laws, in the absence of rules specifying rights to pain, grief, and obligations to help, is not likely to produce more "helpful" help for anyone involved.

The last function of the traditional funeral is mourning, a set of behaviors that does succeed in replacing the dead among the survivors while acknowledging the idea of their irreplaceability.* Viewing mourning as a funeral function rests on funeral rites in some preindustrial societies which had multi-stage ceremonies stretching over a year or more. Contemporary funerals are accomplished within a few days, usually in not more than three. In stark contrast, all three widow studies showed that bereavement in contemporary society tended to stretch well beyond the first year after the loss. For the elderly widow, of whom we know so little, perhaps one should expect that such bereavement symptoms as preoccupation with the dead, feeling his presence, idealizing him in memory, and asking oneself what he might think in decision making would last about one year. Given also the more "timely" nature of death in advanced age, the experience of the younger widow during the first year of bereavement in terms of family relations should apply also to an older widow-in-becoming. It may apply even more so, since death at a later age is seen as normal.

Although bereavement lasts a year or so, mourning in industrial society is not recognized as a status nor is it respected much beyond the occasion of the funeral itself. The Boston widows told us that nearly all found themselves abandoned by their family members more or less right after the funeral. Among the London widows, postfuneral family relationships, in terms of helping and visiting, either stayed the same as before the experience of loss or suffered a decline. Household economics also were important. Losing a husband often means a loss of disposable income. The London widows felt that they could not reciprocate offers of social visiting, indicating that the status of mourning was not seen as a privileged one. The Chicago widows also suffered similar social isolation. Mourning could be a privileged status legitimating inequality in exchange. One could receive more than one is expected to give. But on the bases of visiting, helping, and gift giving, none of the widow studies indicated that mourning was a clearly defined and respected status.

All three widow studies showed another pattern. During the first year of bereavement, widows avoided contact with men who could be seen as sexual

*One should keep in mind that the analysis of funeral functions in contemporary society with its focus on the couple's relation assumes that the death of the partner is a psychologically and socially significant loss to the surviving spouse. Empirically, this varies with the intensity, extensiveness, dependency, and so on, of the marital tie. However obvious, one usually does not think of the case in which the significance of the partner has shrunk to zero in what looks like an intact marriage. But a couple may be one *only* in the sense of sharing a mailing address. In one study of the elderly widowhood resulted in no observable changes in behavior (Heyman & Gianturco 1973). They were found to be "adjusted" because, already having lived separate lives long before death took away the partner, there was little to adjust to. In so extreme a case of marital attrition prior to the loss, probably quite rare, there is no threat to identity; the funeral is nothing but a disposal, whatever the degree of going along with custom, and life for the surviving spouse goes on much as before.

partners. Still in grief, such association was seen as a betrayal of the dead husband and so a threat to the identity as wife. Knowing that elderly widows seldom remarry, this means that two roles are never resumed. One is that of provider, the other is the sexual one. Whatever else coming out of mourning may entail, among the elderly, permanent widowhood seems to be a common fate. In terms of the irreplaceability norms governing intimate relations, this gives industrial societies the edge over preindustrial societies. Poor in resources, the latter *had to* manage replacing the dead while acknowledging their irreplaceability. In contrast, the impressive surplus generated in modern economies make it quite feasible to "mourn forever." But even short-term mourning, when the bereaved still struggles with regaining a new identity without totally relinquishing the older one, is not a normatively regulated status.

It is probably this absence of norms for mourning that accounts for the small effect that social isolation has on the experience of grief. Asking whether bereavement causes social isolation or whether isolation delays the grief process, Clayton (1975) compared the depressive moods of widows in their late fifties and early sixties who either lived alone or with their children. Unfortunately, those who lived alone also were the older ones. At one month after the loss, the groups did not differ in psychological or physical symptoms of grief. A year later, those who lived by themselves showed more depressive symptoms, and those living with their children suffered more from physical ailments. There was a similar pattern among the London widows. Greater contact with relatives and friends was associated with a lower incidence of psychological disturbance. But as Parkes (1974:142) pointed out in reviewing the knowledge of this area, we do not know which is chicken and which egg.

Mourning Behavior

The normative deficit of the status of mourning is perhaps nowhere more evident than in the opinions of the "proper" waiting time for remarriage after widowhood. In considering the results of some opinion research in Los Angeles (Kalish & Reynolds 1976:33) and in West Germany (Hahn 1968:116-25), let us keep in mind that the bereaved widow abhors the very idea of sexual contact at least during the first year of bereavement. The nonbereaved think otherwise. Varying by ethnic group, about a fifth of the Americans considered any waiting for remarriage "unimportant." But not one among the German respondents regarded immediate remarriage as morally justifiable. About another tenth of the Americans thought that one could remarry within less than a year, but another third or so deemed a year's waiting proper. The rest insisted on periods longer than a year. Among Germans, just about one half indicated a waiting period of one year as correct, but the other half made the whole issue dependent on circumstances mostly pertaining to the children's needs for a father and economic considerations. Still, although none of the Germans felt as easy as some of the Americans did about immediate remarriage, about a third of the Germans could not give one reason for having a mourning period.

As for wearing black or any distinctive mourning clothing after the funeral, about one half of the respondents in both countries attached no significance to it. This was true of the elderly in Los Angeles as well (Kalish & Reynolds 1976: 212). We also know from the studies of widows that the actually bereaved do not wear mourning clothing for any length of time. Here then one finds relative consensus that "advertising" one's bereavement status is undesirable. A norm for about half the population is that grief should be real *and* private. Those who know a person suffered a loss, need not be told with clothing; those who do not know should not be burdened. But this does mean that the encounter with loss is withdrawn from public view. Recalling that most of us usually live to middle age before we encounter death in the family, that privacy of grief also means a lack of stimulation and training in relating to the bereaved person. When grief does come, when bereavement befalls, we do not know how to feel, how to talk, or what to do. Such helplessness also is evident among college students when encountering a fellow student who recently experienced a death (Vernon 1970: 166). Asked their opinion about what they would do in such a situation, a tenth did not know, they had never thought about it; a quarter would not mention the death; another quarter would acknowledge the other's bereavement status by bringing it up; and 40 percent thought it might be best to let the mourner mention it.

What conclusions can we draw from such lack of consensus on proper mourning behavior, on the one hand, and from such tendencies for the privatization of the pain of loss, on the other? We suggest that the status of the bereaved after the funeral in urban industrial societies amounts to almost an institutionalized anomie, a condition in which normlessness is the norm. We have seen that loss of an intimate associate is a severe threat to the survivor. Further, when compared to other cultures, people in industrial societies have few intimates. Thus, when they lose one, the threat to their identity should be more severe because of their deep involvement with the lost partner and the unlikelihood of finding a replacement.

We may not know much about the mechanisms of internalization or how a person does come to be the bearer of another's identity through long-term intimate interaction. But we do know that emotions are *learned* orientations, as is our ability to express emotion in a manner understandable to others and, therefore, to ourselves. Emotions are a manageable part of social life only to the extent that they are obligatory role obligations. One learns to love in courtship. In that relation the learning and the loving are duties. Spouses are supposed to love each other and, as we have seen, the survivor is expected to suffer from the loss of the partner. The pain of grief sets in automatically, because it comes from an obligation to love and to depend (Hahn 1968:126). Not to suffer is a form of deviance. Yet, in the period following the funeral, the modern situation insists on the experience of pain but provides no means to express, share, and, therefore, know it. Since it is relating to others that tells us who we are in happiness and sadness, having never learned how to share the emotion of loss, the grief of losing another appears only as a psychiatric disorder, one manageable at best by the expert in mental health. Outside the clinical setting, the mourner cannot be acknowledged in his or her bereavement status because no one knows how to express it in a socially approved manner. We learn to love one another. But a discounting of death rituals as somehow "unbecoming" has deprived us of opportunities for learning to lose each other. For the elderly widow suffering her grief it is a private hell, one that fades, eventually, but not a role that orders life. If mourning is like a story of courtship read backwards, then the script of modern society is poorly written, and the characters are badly depicted.

SUMMARY

A deep gulf separates the subjective experience of death and the accomplishment of the funeral to assign meaning to death. As experienced by those near death, "being dead" is a form of consciousness devoid of concrete social symbolism. One is liberated, but not so much from the constraints of society; instead one encounters a structure of meaning radically different from anything experienced in social reality. That is, for the one encountering death of the self, it is an experience at least in one respect conforming to the minimum requirements of the Christian faith. In the figure of the resurrected Christ, that faith demands a commitment to an order of meaning radically other than that experienced by humans in the temporal realm. Among the survivors at the grave the situation is profoundly different. Their social identities are threatened by the loss of an intimate other. They suffer from another loss. Still believers in God, and still burying their dead in a Christian ceremony, they nonetheless have lost sufficient consensus on matters of their faith relevant to death. That effectively defeats the funeral's first function, the assignment of meaning to death and the ability to share that meaning. If the Boston widows are any guide to the funeral experience of modern men and women everywhere, that purpose of the funeral has died. Apparently, it perished when religious belief in modern times became a private matter. That is why the clergy have become marginal at the funeral, of little if any significance to the central figures of the modern funeral drama, the widowed.

Only the overtly nonreligious aspects of the funeral succeed "classically" in the production and sharing of diachronic solidarity between the survivors and the dead. The funeral is a family ritual, assuring the widow-in-becoming of her identity as a wife and letting sons and daughters and relatives and friends, stripped of their other selves of occupation and the like, appear only as associates of the dead. Beyond this, the immediate reassurance of social identities, the contemporary funeral fails. Even social integration among the survivors in terms of helping that "really helps" seems weak. And the postfuneral period of bereavement is a condition in which normlessness approaches the norm. We insist that those who undergo a loss do suffer, but we provide no rules for how that is to be expressed and with whom it is to be shared. Not recognizing bereavement as a social status, the widow is, in effect, abandoned before she has worked through her grief.

growing old:
bonds
8 that break,
bonds
that hold

In the previous chapters we described some features of the lives of older people that were quite similar in all industrial societies. Engagement with political roles, for example, was one of these, as was the prominence of the aged in positions of political leadership. Modern political life everywhere has gerontocratic elements. We also discussed national differences. The aged in the Netherlands, for example, are more engaged in family roles and much more engaged in their church and club obligations than their American counterparts are. Japan, as others have discovered before us, is very different from practically all other industrialized countries in social respects. Japanese institutions and practices make generalizations about the fate of being old in modern times exceedingly difficult. Nonetheless, there were a number of cross-national similarities, pertaining to a majority of the modern societies for which we found information. The pervasive similarities permit us to describe and interpret the meaning of old age in modern times.

The fate of old age can be delineated as a particular pattern or constellation of diachronic solidarity with the aged, their abandonment, and their liberation. In some spheres of life our social bonds with older people not only hold but also the way their belonging into society is managed preserves continuity of inter-generational solidarity from generation to generation. In other spheres of life industrial societies abandon the aged. The ties of belonging are broken. In still other spheres or institutional domains old age is a privileged status. While rare and also temporary, here the social bonds not only hold but are changed so as to accord rights to persons toward the end of life which are not commensurate with obligations. What we have found, then, is a multi-dimensional syndrome of the fate of being old in modern times. What is this syndrome, or what is the meaning of old age in modern society? Describing it is our first task. Our second is to evaluate how Americans treat their older people. Here we rely on differences in the lives of older people in various nations to delineate the particular American pattern. That should tell us in what respects this country does better or worse in caring for its elderly. Finally, we turn to the interpretation of the principal constellation of the fate of old age across nations, seeking to understand why some bonds break and others hold.

THE SYNDROME OF OLD AGE: A DESCRIPTIVE SYNTHESIS

Briefly stated, the modern fate of being old is a fourfold experience of: 1) diachronic solidarity in economic or material care; 2) diachronic solidarity in political bonds of citizenship; 3) abandonment in the area of spiritual care; and 4) death as a liberation from the uncertainties inherent in the human condition. This is the main constellation of the meaning of old age in modern times in the countries we studied. It needs to be qualified, to be sure, when one examines more closely such spheres of life as the economy, polity, or family.

Seen in historical perspective, the material and physical care given to older people in modern societies is very impressive. In preindustrial societies, being old almost always meant suffering severe economic deprivation. Indeed, the lives of most older people were truly nasty, brutish, and short. As shown in chapter 4, the abandonment of older people by the younger was characteristic of the relations between the generations throughout most of human history. Only with the full establishment of industrial society did this end.

The Aged in Preindustrial and Modern Societies

The history of neglect of the aged has had very little to do with any pronounced lack of love or caring concern for them. Instead, economic abandonment of the elderly was necessary for the very survival of preindustrial societies. They simply could not afford to feed and sustain social members when old age took its toll of the body and the mind. No matter how small a proportion of the population, when the old became economically useless members of society, they became unsupportable. For the good of the group as a whole, old people had to be removed or at the very least be reduced to short rations. The inability of most preindustrial societies to produce any appreciable economic surplus was the main cause of abandonment. Preindustrial societies were unable to dominate either physical or human nature. They were "double structures of frailty," constantly threatened by the vicissitudes of climate and the unpredictable forces of people.

In contrast, modern society is a frail creature primarily vis-à-vis human nature. The economy may go into a deep depression, or war may break out and end the human condition. These are inescapable possibilities. But as long as neither happens, a huge economic surplus is routinely produced, making the fabled riches of Oriental empires pale in comparison. Wealth is characteristic of modern society, just as poverty and scarcity governed the lives of most people is preindustrial social orders.

Even the very short step into the economic history of old age that we took in chapter 4 should suffice to make one point. The idea that abandoning older people into economic misery is peculiar to modern societies is simply wrong. If one must make historical comparisons to gain a foothold for one's grasp of the contemporary situation, an alternative statement is much closer to the truth. Older people have never before enjoyed the level of prosperity that modern society provides for most of them. True, if we define an adequate old age income as one that maintains that standard of living attained during the last working years before retirement, many people in the last phase of life are not adequately supported. Also, if retirement incomes are compared with those earned by cohorts in the middle years of life, old age means relative deprivation. But it must be kept in mind that even standards such as these were beyond the reasonable imagination of reasonable people throughout most of human history before the rise of industrialism. The critic of modern society may justifiably prefer to assert the validity of contemporary standards and the irrelevance of history in judging contemporary reality. We shall come to that later. What is important here is that however inadequate old age income may be for many, it is a fact that older people are better off than they ever were before. But saying that is not saying enough. Materially, everybody is more affluent. This way of telling the story, then, hides rather than reveals its moral aspect. Let us examine the morals at play before adopting a critical stance, one we contend is better handled with comparisons among modern societies.

As was emphasized in the first two chapters of this book, taking care of older people in modern society is a collective national effort. Old age income is financed to an important degree by a social security system that transfers income from the younger and still working to the older in retirement. Though data on various countries telling just what proportion of old age income comes from this source may elude us, there is no doubt that social security is very important to the economic security of old age everywhere.

This means that retirement in old age is a gift, one presented to the elderly by younger men and women. Just because the younger and working pay their taxes and obey the law in caring for their elderly does not prevent us from speaking of the gift of retirement. To give a gift in ordinary life is a duty as is, indeed, receiving it. Even in the circles of kinship or friendship, we usually do not give gifts out of the blue. Gifts are given and accepted on prescribed occasions be that a birthday, an anniversary, or Christmas. Nonetheless, the norms of gift giving contain a voluntary element. If giving and receiving were only duties, we would not consider the things that change hands as gifts. Yet this voluntary element, even when spontaneity and altruism are stressed, does not negate the obligatory nature of gifts and the relations that they nurture. Marcel Mauss (1925) reminded us of this essential aspect of gift giving. We shall see in a moment that what is true on the level of interpersonal relations is even more true in the public sphere in which the impersonal nature of the law regulates the relations between the generations.

Let us recall that, however sparse, the relevant data we could find revealed considerable intergenerational political support for social security, on the one hand, and for retirement as a social right earned by growing to old age, on the other. In chapter 3 we considered the influence of the age-based lobbies in the United States, the United Kingdom, and Sweden. In membership these special interest organizations are huge, dwarfing in all three countries the largest and most powerful labor unions. Yet, no matter how the numbers are put together in the voting data, in none of the three countries could the political support for social security systems be attributed to the clout of age-based lobbies.

Age-based organizations are simply not influential enough to explain the increased attention and contribution to the needs of the elderly as the century grows older and there are more and more old people among us. So far, chronological age clearly has not become a political cleavage in industrial societies. In estimating whether retirement has become an accepted social right, something to which a person becomes entitled just by attaining a certain age, we had to rely on American data. Once again, we found strong cross-generational support for retirement as an earned end phase in the human life cycle.

That retirement is acceptable is also indirectly borne out by the evidence that there is a retirement role, although its content may vary from country to country. Old people are simply not social outcasts. They continue, sometimes even at an accelerated pace, to be active in other social spheres when the work life is over.

Diachronic Solidarity and Social Security

For the task at hand, estimating the duty of giving the gift of retirement to the elderly, the available data are hardly ideal. Clearly, it would be important to know just who and how many in the general population are aware that social security is insurance. Many may harbor the illusion that a social security check merely represents the money that has been paid in during the working years. Perhaps many believe that some get more out than they paid in because some contributors die prematurely and thus leave more for the rest or because interest accumulates on retirement contributions made over the years. We simply do not have that kind of information. Thus, although our present knowledge leaves much to be desired, available data send us consistently one simple message. That message is that social security and retirement as a social right are supported by all age groups in society.

We pay taxes to care for the elderly. But that is no argument against the fact that taking care of them is a form of gift giving. Using once again a historical perspective, the voluntary character of the gift of retirement can be emphasized further. As we earlier pointed out in discussing social security, only people in modern societies feel entitled to create and impose obligations on each other as perceived needs dictate. Only modern society creates law where there was none before. All preindustrial societies understood "law" as no more than sanctified custom. They could not invent legal obligations; they could only pretend to rediscover them. But modern men and women can *make* law, and they also can change again what they made. They are capable of creating obligations and then undoing them. That phenomenon provides a voluntary character to social security, and it makes retirement a gift precisely because it is one that can be rescinded.

So far there is widespread support for social security. Not the least significant source of this support is the expectation that retirement is a social right that is here to stay. Those who pay expect to receive when their time comes. It is this expectation of an endless chain of obligations to care, connecting successive generations one after another, that led us to suggest that support for old people serves far more than just the needs of our elders. Caring for the aged provides the caretakers with a sense of continuity of rights to belong to society, rights that have become independent from performance defined as doing one's own fair share in contributing to economic productivity.

But no rights are absolute. That is one reason why one finds all social security systems based on the twin principles of welfare and equity. The equity principle directs the flow of transfer payments from the younger to the older in a manner that preserves income differences. The welfare principle reduces such differences. Both contribute to continuity of the norms of distributive justice. More detailed evidence on this point was confined to American data. Let us pause a moment and review our findings.

Our examination of the distribution of pre- and postretirement income in the United States revealed a high level of fidelity to the American norms of distributive justice. As described in chapter 2 on the basis of empirical evidence provided by Rainwater (1974), the predominant normative imperative that

Americans profess is the "merit principle": differential reward for differential contribution to society. Americans believe, even when they themselves do not benefit from the rule, that those whom they see as working harder or more effectively *should* get more. Americans' moral convictions on this point are radically different from the egalitarianism inherent in the Marxian principle "from each according to his abilities, to each according to his needs." Proclaiming the ideal of the classless society, the latter is official doctrine in Eastern European societies. For Americans the notion of a classless social order simply lacks morality. A national sample survey of distributive justice in America showed that the merit principle is not the only norm pertaining to judgments of fairness in income differences, but that it is the overriding consideration and the one on which there is impressive consensus in all social classes (Alves & Rossi 1978).

Americans are not completely capitalists in their beliefs. They also subscribe to the "principle of disalienation," according to which no one should be deprived of *any* claim to the resources of society. Some minimal income level is recognized below which no one should be permitted to fall. Similarly, fairness standards also dimly recognize some maximum income level above which no one should be permitted to rise. In addition, as stressed by Rainwater (1974), Americans deem the merit principle justifiable only under conditions of equal opportunity for all. Current complaints focus on inadequate provision of equality of opportunity, but otherwise Americans regard the actual distribution of income as essentially fair.

In reference to old age income, let us recognize that the merit principle finds its place in social security under the label "equity": Differential earnings before retirement should be preserved into retirement. Also, the disalienation principle reappears in social security and the related Supplementary Security Income program in terms of welfare provisions that redistribute income from the better off to the needy. The intent is the provision of minimum levels below which no one should sink.

Nonetheless, given the predominance of the merit principle and the idea of retirement as a just desert for a lifetime of work, we have argued that a just and fair distribution of old age income in the United States would be one as unequal as that just before going into retirement. Such a condition would signify that a place earned in the distribution of rewards would be a place maintained until death. Caring for the elderly in a manner that assures justice in this sense is then a way of producing diachronic solidarity in commitments to the predominant merit principle. Because old age income is to a large extent transfer income from the younger and working to the elderly in retirement, each transfer creates obligations to honor the merit principle again in the future when those who give the gift of retirement today become themselves the recipients of it.

As we saw in chapter 2, Americans do care for their elderly in this fashion quite well. They do less well than some European countries, but that is a point to be considered later. At this stage in our argument let us emphasize that this mode of caring for the economic needs of the elderly in society has an importance far beyond the more mundane and simple matters of human decency commanding us to be nice to our elderly.

Norms of distributive justice give identity to society. They tell Americans what the American way of life is. They tell Belgians what it means to be Belgian, and so on. Therefore, the gift of retirement is far more than just the expression of some nice sentiment vis-à-vis the elderly. Providing that gift in a way that perpetuates norms of distributive justice from generation to generation welds continuity into the fabric of history and change. Insofar as such norms are specific to nations, continuity of one element of national identity is preserved as long as these particular bonds between the generations hold. In America the young and the old, cohort after cohort assure each other of belonging in a continuous stream of the American community.

Yet the fact that retirement is a gift also makes it a risky one. What the law gave at one time, the law may take away again later. The benefit levels currently in effect in most modern societies were set before the elderly became a very substantial group in society. Further, in recent decades the benefit levels have been continually adjusted upward. But this was done during periods of economic growth and before it was realized that high economic growth rates were not a very stable feature of modern life. That is why experts worry and speak of a crisis in social security. They may well sense that more is at stake than merely disappointing the expectations of some individuals. After all, Americans live also by so individualist and utilitarian a set of standards that they are led to expect that people will constantly try to get more out of any bargain than they themselves put in. Having survived the Great Depression of the 1930s without a breakdown in democracy, they may well be confident of dealing with a few individual disappointments. But seriously retrenching on social security would cause a breakdown in a mechanism that contributes to continuity of the American way of life. Seen in this light, the current and future tax load required to continue old age social security benefits leaves one far less sanguine.

Experts tell us that social security has been a good buy so far but that it is also rapidly becoming a poor bargain for many people (Munnell 1977:41). Seen from the point of view of the individual paying the tax, all those currently receiving social security benefits could not have done much better with alternative investments and savings, if indeed they could have done as well. That is so, we have seen, because they receive transfer income from the younger and not what they invested or saved. But facts are one thing, beliefs another. And it is currently available facts rather than mere belief that tell us that in the United States social security today is not a good buy for a young and enterprising man (Munnell 1977:41). The young man today does have reasonable alternatives to provide for his own retirement in ways that promise a better return. Once he and the many in his position find that out, political support for social security may well diminish.

Our task, however, is not to speculate about the future but to report facts and reasons why they take the form they do. Thus, we can conclude that so far the promises made to the elderly have been kept. So far the bonds of loyalty and obligation that bind successive generations into one continuous community have held. They have served a larger purpose than those who paid the gift of retirement and those who received it intended.

Caring for the elderly in America has been one way of producing diachronic solidarity in commitments to prevailing norms of distributive justice. This raises the question of whether caring for the elderly serves a similar purpose elsewhere. Although we do not have access to sufficient data on income inequality for various age groups in other societies, a few observations suggest that diachronic solidarity in commitments to norms of distributive justice is not peculiarly American. Let us turn to other Western European countries first and then consider the case of Eastern Europe.

Parkin (1971) reported that the merit imperative "differential reward for differential contribution" pertains to other countries besides the United States. Citing various studies and emphasizing the accommodative nature of the outlook of working-class people to the values of the more dominant strata, he asserted that similar norms of distributive justice can be found in Western European society more generally (Parkin, 1971:79-86). What may vary in Western capitalist societies, is the amount of emphasis on the merit principle relative to the disalienation principle.

We do know that Western European social security systems are based on the principles of equity and welfare just as the American system is (Kaim-Caudle 1973). Therefore, it seems reasonable to suggest that caring for the elderly also produces diachronic solidarity in the norms of distributive justice in Western Europe. Indeed, since fewer of their elderly are economically abandoned, as we saw in chapter 2, one may suggest that the capitalist countries in Europe produce a higher level of diachronic solidarity than does the United States.

Whether the Japanese eventually will adopt a similar strategy remains to be seen. So far, the Japanese support retirement significantly less than do other modern societies. But as we noted in chapter 3, there is a debate about caring for the elderly in Japan that may well change their arrangements in the near future.

The official norms of distributive justice under Communism in Eastern Europe are quite different from those in the West. In fact, they have a pattern of priority that is the reverse of that prevailing in the West. Although the Western countries give priority to the merit principle over that of disalienation (no one should be entirely excluded from the wealth of the nation), the "socialist democracies" of Eastern Europe give priority to the egalitarianism inherent in the principle of disalienation and acknowledge merit only grudgingly as a concession to sluggish human nature. The Communist ideology attempts to marry a deep yearning for the eventual attainment of genuine equality among all members of society with the meritocratic principle, but the latter serves only as a tool for the former (Parkin 1971:137-59). Focused on the classless society in which "the free development of each is the condition for the free development of all" (Marx 1848:57), Communism proclaims the ideal of real equality among all members of society. But reaching the future demands not only immense effort, it also requires compromising with imperfect human nature. Therefore, according to the official doctrine, during the transition stage of socialism, one serving the goal of Communism, meritocratic considerations must be given their due. But these meritocratic considerations amount to nothing less than the capitalist merit principle "differential reward for differential contribution to society." One may suspect that such a marriage of incompatibilities must be an unstable one when it is government itself that administers inequalities in society. Parkin documented the instability quite well. Soviet and other Eastern European government policies have been characterized generally by swings of a pendulum. Periods emphasizing income inequalities and incentives have been followed by periods of reducing inequalities again. Waves of criticism of "equality mongering" follow waves of suspicion about "bourgeois revisionism."

Still when the principle of merit is but a tool for its own abolition, one can specify one clear implication for the distribution of retirement income in society. Presumably, the ideal of the Communist future of equality can be realized more easily among those in retirement than among those still at work. The reason is simple. Economically, people in retirement make no contribution to the construction of the Communist future, but total equality of retirement income would not be politically advisable. It would undercut incentives during the working years, particularly in the preretirement period. This is recognized in the pension rules in Communist countries. As shown in chapter 2, pensions are set as a percentage of preretirement earnings. That tends to perpetuate income inequalities into retirement.

Three facts tend to offset this effect, however, reducing income inequality in old age (Trojan 1972). First, there are more job opportunities for elderly people who were in unskilled, low paid jobs before reaching retirement age, and they tend to continue working at a disproportionately higher rate than persons in higher paid jobs. Second, higher pension rates are in effect for physically taxing labor, raising the retirement income of the lower paid strata relative to that of the better paid employees. Third, in contrast to the United States where continuing work after age sixty-five comes at the cost of retirement benefits, workers in several Communist countries receive extra pension increments for each additional year in the labor force after reaching retirement age (U.S. Social Security Administration 1975). Thus, continuing to work after one becomes entitled to a pension is economically rewarded rather than punished. The net effect of these arrangements is a somewhat lower income inequality among the elderly than that prevailing during the preretirement period.

Thus, caring for the elderly in Communist societies also takes the form of creating obligations that implement their norms of distributive justice. Once again in contrast to the United States, since fewer of their elderly seem to be economically abandoned, diachronic solidarity in commitments to these norms is produced to a higher extent than in America. With the probable exception of Japan, as far as we can tell, no other industrial society abandons as much as almost a quarter of its older people to a retirement income of less than forty percent of preretirement earnings as does the United States.

Beyond social security we found three additional instances in which the relations between generations produce diachronic solidarity. Only one of these also includes obligations for material care. Children, often near old age themselves, hardly ever shirk responsibility to care for their parents when failing health turns the latter into creatures dependent on their own offspring. The other two instances are the aging political leadership circles in modern societies and the bereaved clinging to the social identities of the dead. Let us take these in turn.

Diachronic Solidarity in the Family

There is a phase in the family life of older people that entails a classic role reversal between parents and children. As we showed in chapter 5, when there are severe health decrements, making it impossible to continue living alone, older people move in with their adult children. All the evidence at hand suggests that this is an extremely frustrating experience for both parties. The parents, apparently, simply cannot accept dependency on their own children whom they raised to be independent. Not being able to accept their loss of independence, they react with anger and hostility to help from their children. Apparently, the value commitments to individualism and independence have been developed to the point at which loss of the latter means loss of being human. But in the West this holds entirely in the interpersonal sphere of the family. Dependency on the impersonal apparatus of the state does not result in any comparable sense of finding oneself dehumanized. Nonetheless, the children really make an effort; they continue taking care, even though the quality of the relation deteriorates so much that caring in the sense of loving effectively ends. Encountering nothing but frustration, the younger generation nevertheless does not shirk the responsibility to keep their elderly out of public institutions as long as humanly possible. They do so, we suggested, out of a deep sense of loyalty and in the expectation that should the same horrible fate befall them, their own children in turn will save them from becoming institutionalized.

The pattern seems to produce diachronic solidarity in commitments to a form of absolute filial loyalty, but one reduced to physical care. At the beginning of life, nature dictates our extreme helplessness and total dependency on a mother figure. Growing up to mature adulthood means for Western modern men and women becoming independent. After a lifetime of effort in this direction, the fact that nature once again dictates extreme dependency leaves us without any commensurate cultural resources to cope with it. Fetishists of independence, we cannot accept the fact that the ending of life often makes us children again, as helpless and dependent as we were when entering life.

Most of our evidence on this came from American data. But we have some indications that the same dilemma exists in Western Europe, only probably more poignantly since Europeans maintain more chronic care facilities than do Americans (Kane & Kane 1976:174-86). It should be emphasized that this is only one phase in the family life of older people. In effect, the diachronic solidarity phase in the family is sandwiched between the phase of liberation preceding it and that of abandonment following it. We shall return to the family later.

Diachronic Solidarity in Politics

Diachronic solidarity between the generations also characterizes the political institutions of modern societies. Everywhere advanced societies are run by aging politicians. The polities of modern societies have a distinctive gerontocratic element. Since this is true in many countries, one would find it difficult to argue for some cohort effect. The political histories of the societies in which we found this pattern are so different that attributing the presence of older people in positions of political leadership to some particular generation of voters appears impossible. Neither can one attribute the predominance of older people in political life to Michels's (1911) famous "iron law of oligarchy."

Briefly, the iron law of oligarchy assumes that incumbents necessarily have the edge over contenders for their office. The "ins" have not only superior experience with political realities than the "outs," but they also have superior control over resources relevant to the political competition. Yet these considerations do not withstand the test of reality very well. Such a law should apply with equal if not greater force to the private sector of the economy and its large corporations. Henry Ford II and similar leaders of the business world simply do not have to compete as much to retain their positions as do politicians in elected positions. Consequently, the oligarchic control of upper level managers in the corporate world over resources in keeping their jobs would seem to be far larger than that at the disposal of public officials, routinely subjected to elections. Yet one finds the leaders of the economy routinely relinquishing their offices and going into retirement.

In contrast, the "gerontocrats" of the public sphere are reelected again and again by the people. The difference may well be due to quite different role expectations in political as compared to economic leadership. Politics is an arena in which people seem to prefer the generalist rather than the narrow technical specialist. This, it has been said, is one reason why one finds so many lawyers in political life (Czudnowski 1975).

We suggest that preferring older people in positions of political leadership to younger ones simply reflects the same preference for the generalist. The older person has lived longer; therefore, he or she has seen and experienced more than younger people have. Let us recall, in this connection, the positive stereotype of the elderly endorsed by Americans of all ages. They were seen as "wise from experience." Accordingly, other things being equal, a long life itself makes us generalists. So, to the extent that the public prefers the generalist in positions of political leadership, longevity is an asset in running for office and staying in it. In contrast, running a business corporation is seen as requiring the latest in technical and specialized knowledge. Since that kind of knowledge is constantly changing, the older executive is expected to step down to make room for younger people with the latest training.

But why the preference for the generalist in political leadership roles? Apparently the answer is to be found in the old adage that politics is the art of the possible. Making political decisions on the national level does amount to choosing among competing values and using the powers of the state to make people care more about some values than about others. The national leader always has to appear as the promulgator of some national interest. His or her persuasive powers to convince the multitudes that they have a common interest is his or her most important tool for leadership. The need for that tool gives the person who appears to be a generalist the edge over the one who looks like a specialist.

Thus, the prominent role of the elderly in positions of political leadership throughout the modern world may well indicate that there is a place for wisdom after all in modern societies. For when it comes to the use of power to extract sacrifice for national objectives, people prefer to subject themselves to the elderly rather than to younger persons, however much more formally educated the latter may be. Putting younger people into high office smacks too much of "technocracy," apparently.

Older people, on the other hand, because of their longer life, have been part of the crucial experience of all the age cohorts in society and the formative events that shaped their varied outlooks. Being in a position to span in experience all the generations in society and having shared and witnessed whatever affected any one given cohort still alive are what make us trust older people. An elderly senator in the United States Senate, for example, would have experienced the Great Depression of the 1930s, President Roosevelt's New Deal, World War II, the Senator McCarthy period which stifled civil liberties, the Korean War, the Vietnam War, and a president's resignation from office. Only an older person has such range of experience. He or she, far more than any younger person, can claim to understand and to respond to what formed the political consciousness of different cohorts. That is why the younger find it easier to subjugate themselves to the authority of the elderly rather than to that of their age peers.

This pattern too is a form of diachronic solidarity, though not one based on creating obligations handed from generation to generation. No one has a duty to cast his or her ballot for the older of two competing candidates, obviously.

But if there is a place for wisdom in modern life and that place is concentrated in political leadership on the national level, as we suggest, then the rule of the elderly may well be a persistent feature. It will be repeated again and again, bringing successive cohorts in their old age to positions of prominence and thus preserving at each juncture in the twisting road of national priorities the experience of the past sixty years or so as a relevant input into current decision making.

Diachronic Solidarity and Funerals

The last instance of diachronic solidarity we discovered was a part of the contemporary funeral, as described in chapter 7. The funeral excels in maintaining a sense of continued identity between the dead and their survivors in bereavement. The identity that is maintained is strictly social. Our discussion of the modern funeral revealed a very simple fact of modern life. Only when suffering the loss of another close to us are we so much our brother's keeper in a true psychological sense. Above all others on this occasion, this applies particularly to the widow-in-becoming. Having been a wife for many years, the death of the husband poses a direct threat to her identity because, in the wife role, she truly carries her husband within herself. Threatened in her identity by the death of her partner, a truth that the head accepts while the heart refuses it, she can use the funeral to do wifely duties one more time. The funeral is a last gift to her husband and herself. It reassures the person in bereavement on her most fragile point of being, her wife-identity, while also signaling that that identity must change.

The impact on adult children suffering the loss of a parent may be less. Having lived in "intimacy at a distance" with the parent, the father or mother is less a central part of son or daughter. Even so, it is really only the death of a parent that emancipates us finally from childhood and the family of our origin. Only when they die do we cease to be sons and daughters. Only when that happens does the torch of family identity pass entirely into our hands and into our care. And in response, at the graveside, we stand as nothing but sons or nothing but daughters, reaffirming the continuity between the generations. However "distant," intimacy means carrying the other in ourselves. At the funeral we affirm that identity one last time. Knowing that we must change, our mode of taking leave takes the form of sharing our identity with the dead. Though not as wrenching an experience as for the wife who cannot be more than a widow-in-becoming, children also are only adults-in-becoming on that occasion. Only when their grieving ends have they entirely let go of their parents in themselves.

For the wife and her relation to her dead husband, we cannot speak of diachronic solidarity in a technical sense. The relation is between members of the same generation, and no obligation to share the dead is handed on directly to the next generation. Still, this pattern too repeats itself endlessly. It does so for no other reason than that the marital tie is the most intimate for older people in modern times. For the children there is a duty to mourn the death of a parent. Although intimacy at a distance occurs before death, it does not extinguish that duty, though it may diminish the actual pain of loss considerably. Here the sharing of identity is between the generations.

In short, as long as we are born and raised in families, and as long as we shall continue to form our own, there will be diachronic solidarity in commitments to the same family-identity between the living and the dead. We experience that identity, more so than at any other time in our lives, when we bury our dead. On that occasion all members of the family are each other's keepers. As long as the family persists, the laws of social psychology themselves guarantee diachronic solidarity in family-identity across the generations.

This exhausts what we could discover about the production of diachronic solidarity in connection with the aged in modern societies. All other aspects of growing old indicate patterns of abandonment or liberation. Let us turn to abandonment next.

Phases of the Elderly in Family Life

Abandonment is concentrated in areas of spiritual care. Abandonment of the elderly occurs when they are dying. It also is the common fate of the widow in acute grief. These are matters confined to the family life of the old and their children.

As shown in chapter 5, it is almost taboo in modern society for an elderly couple to live with any of their married children. The exceptions to this pattern of separate households are to be found in Yugoslavia and especially in Japan. Everywhere else, as long as the marriage is intact, and failing health does not force the aged under the roof of children, the generations live apart from each other.

Loneliness, however, is not a fate of older people at this stage. There is frequent visiting. Parents and children exchange affection, and genuine caring characterizes the relations between the generations. Nonetheless, costly decisions and the responsibilities they entail are made by the couples of each generation for their own separate households. That is why the relationship has been labeled "intimacy at a distance." That term rather aptly captures a sense of liberation from the demands of parenthood for older people and from the duties of childhood for the younger ones.

In early retirement both the old and the young seem to enjoy a new relationship with each other, one that has been freed from the constraints of parenting. Having put the children on their own feet, the parents can relax. Having been put on their own feet, children can stop worrying about pleasing their parents in decisions such as where to work and live, when to have their own children, and what style of life to adopt. Some American data also indicate that the quality of the marriage among the elderly improves during that period. Thus, it seems that family status itself becomes a relatively privileged one in early retirement, not only for the parents but also for their adult children. The family ties of intimacy at a distance are more voluntary. They are freed from burdens that characterized them before and that will return to them soon again. Perhaps it is this liberation phase in intergenerational relations that builds up motivation for the children to care materially for their parents in the next phase when illness returns the latter to the terror of childlike dependency.

That phase, as we have described above, is one of diachronic solidarity, although caring for the elderly in the family is confined to their material and physical well-being. One may think of this phase as the onset of the abandonment period that follows. Failing health and growing incapacities turn into terminal illness, often a matter of lengthy suffering from chronic disease. This is the phase of dying in which the older are abandoned. Dying is not a well-regulated social status in modern society. This has been a very clear finding in all the studies we used in chapter 6. Neither the professional staff in general hospitals, where most of us do our dying, nor family members know how to feel, how to share their emotions, and what to say to the dying. As a result, the dying are socially abandoned before they are ready to let go of life. As documented in chapter 7, the same pattern of abandonment distinguishes the older widow in bereavement. Hers too is not a well-regulated social status. Grief is a psychiatric disorder. Though obviously "normal," grieving is not a role that orders life. That is why attempts to help and share the burden of loss so often fail.

Growing old in modern times means a family life that unfolds in three phases, one following the other. First comes a phase of liberation. Still married, still healthy, the elderly couple and their married children confront each other in a privileged status they never had before. They are now equals. Throughout life before, parents and children were always unequals. Parents had responsibility for the life chances of their offspring, and children had a duty to listen to and honor their parents.

Only early in the retirement years of the parents does this pattern come to an end. Then for a while, both parties are liberated from the burdens of inequality, of superior responsibility on one side and dependency on the other. But when health seriously fails the parent or death comes near and nearer, the parent experiences the loss of independence and both parties lose their liberation. Moving in with adult children to avoid institutionalization begins a diachronic solidarity phase between the generations. The younger, often already nearing their own retirement, genuinely sacrifice themselves for their ailing and aging parents. But neither party can adapt to the role reversal between parent and child. Interpersonal dependency of an older on a younger person in the modern family seems unbearable for both. But because dying looms in the near future, and because dying calls for emotional care, both parties hesitate as long as possible before recourse to an institution becomes acceptable. The quality of the relation between the generations deteriorates. Still, the younger keep on struggling to provide physical care, and they cope, somehow, with the fact that caring and loving gradually elude the powers of both parties. This phase serves as anticipatory socialization for abandonment in dying, though hardly intended and indeed resisted. Nonetheless, the bonds of family belonging become thinner and thinner. When terminal illness comes they finally break. Among the survivors in bereavement, once the funeral has passed, the bonds of family solidarity break as well. Toward the end of life, in dying and in mourning, home may still be the place where they have to take us in. But being taken care of is all we can expect; for caring, nurturing, and loving are matters beyond the powers of modern men and women when the body collapses and the mind begins to dim.

Death as Liberation

Finally, we also found that the modern subjective experience of death is one of joyous liberation from life. Clearly, this is not an instance of liberation as a social status of privilege, the meaning of the term liberation in other respects. The dead can, of course, have a social status. That is simply a matter of how the living view their dead. But aside from the funeral, this remains an open question. The subjective experience of being dead can be labeled a cultural status. That conforms to the religious interpretation we gave to it in chapter 7.

Modern men and women, so we have seen, experience death not as a liberation from any social role but rather from the uncertainty of ever finding in human life what humans strive for: comprehensive meaning. We based this interpretation on two facts. First, as far as we could estimate, belief in God is a very widespread characteristic of people in advanced societies. Our data on this point covered North America and Western Europe. Later we shall add data on Eastern Europe. That leaves Japan as a possible exception. Second, all the reports of death experiences come from people who lived in cultures with salvation religions. Together these two facts tell us that people in most advanced societies are aware, however subliminally, of symbols of ultimate meaning, very different from anything experienced and understood by common social sense.

With the exception of Japan again, at this moment in history advanced societies are mostly found in the orbit of Christian civilization. In the Christian religion, regardless of denomination, the mystery of God's nature is an explicit part of dogma. Mystery simply means something radically different from what is known to us through common sense. Many people may not be concerned with any of the details of the nature of God. They may leave that problem to theologians, or, with the decline of church religion in modern society, they may not even concern themselves with that question, a matter to which we will return. At this point it is enough to suggest that Western modern men and women somehow are aware of the nature of symbols of ultimate meaning. However inarticulate, this means that striving for a comprehensive meaning of life, the religious impulse, is one not to be satisfied with the more readily understood symbols of social life. We suggest that a sense of inadequacy of social common sense as a means for finding any comprehensive meaning in life is a widespread fact of life. That is why Western modern men and women experience death as a release from the profound uncertainties caused by their striving for comprehensive meaning in life. However implicitly, having lived in a Christian culture, they know that religion is a burden on human beings and not just a convenient tool to explain the otherwise inexplicable such as individual misfortune, injustice, and suffering. Somehow men and women sense that an image of God as a nice father may be appropriate for children and the troubles of childhood. It may serve us as adults on occasion. But when all is said and done there remains the realization that such an image remains too childish and, therefore, unbecoming to modern people who can, after all, end the human condition and with that the very question of God.

But what that different nature of God is and what it implies for human life are questions to which we have never found a satisfying answer. Death, so it appears, means no longer having to seek one. Whatever the challenge here to more traditional beliefs in afterlife with their options of heaven and hell, if we take seriously the reports of the near dead, death implies having found the answer that eluded us throughout life. According to these reports, death is nothing less than a release from our existence as doubters.

This completes our description of the dominant patterns of the fate of modern old age according to cross-national similarities. An interpretation of its meaning will be the concluding part of this chapter. But before that, we need to explore cross-national differences in the lives of older people in order to evaluate the American fate of being old. Let us turn then to comparative data and examine the relative strengths and weaknesses of the American experience of growing old.

CONTRASTS BETWEEN THE NATIONS: EVALUATION OF THE AMERICAN WAY OF GROWING OLD

The configuration described above has major themes with some variations. Many of the variations are relatively minor, differing only in the degree to which a particular pattern is implemented. But there are a few exceptions. The approach taken to evaluation is a relative one. No attempt is made to apply absolute standards as to what constitutes a good or a poor performance. We assume that the pattern that has just been described is somehow rooted in the organization of social life in industrial societies, a matter to be discussed in our interpretation. Nevertheless, the configuration does give us the basis upon which some decisions can be made as to which countries are doing better or worse with respect to particular aspects of the management of old age. And, here and there, a modern society seems to ignore the "rules" entirely, a matter to give us pause when we try to make generalizations. Even our limited standards for evaluation, then, run into complications.

Retirement

It has been seen that both Western and Eastern European industrial societies produce diachronic solidarity from economic support in retirement, according to their particular norms of distributive justice. Westerners reproduce inequalities of preretirement income in the last years of the working life quite faithfully in retirement. Easterners come a little closer to their ideal of equality of condition with their old people than they have been able to manage with the population in general.

Relatively, as far as can be determined, Americans are outperformed by European countries in economic terms. This country lives up to its norms of distributive justice fairly well but abandons relatively more of its old people according to prevailing values of what they deserve. As we saw in chapter 4, the middle class, absolutely better off in economic circumstances, complain just as much as the working class whose income is objectively less adequate. But the middle class as a group is more likely to suffer from lower income replacement after retirement. Thus the relative deprivation felt by some members of the middle class can be elevated to a moral level. The complainant says in effect: "I worked harder than others to get to where I was at the end of my working life, yet I am supported in retirement on a level that suggests that much of that effort was in vain." Social recognition for differential contribution has been denied, and the offended person is left to question the justice of the American system of rewards. Since this country disappoints relatively many more social members precisely on its own value grounds, it is "doing worse" than other industrial societies in handling postretirement income. And what it is doing worse violates the deeply held commitments of the population at large to the American way of life. The damage therefore is not simply economic; it strikes at the very heart of our beliefs about what is right and about what constitutes social justice.

It is a peculiar property of the American approach to retirement that most older people accept income loss without complaint. They certainly do not like it nor overtly encourage it as a policy, but they perceive it as just. The nonworker must take the backseat as compared with the worker. But Americans enjoy retirement more than people in other societies do. As long as they are able, they play the retirement role to the hilt, and the role suits them often more than they anticipate.

In other countries, with some exceptions that will be explored, most people enjoy retirement too, but not quite as much. Is this simply attributable to the fact that the United States is a wealthy country and that, although relatively impoverished, older people here are in real terms usually better off and in better health at age sixty-five? This is no doubt part of the reason but not all. An elderly person can be as healthy and as wealthy as circumstances permit but can find that social outlets are not available. The United States, in its typical activist fashion, has worried just as much about keeping its old people involved in social life as long as possible as it has about caring for them when their capacities fail. This may be a misplaced emphasis on activity when the needs of the "frail elderly" are so obvious, but American retirees who are in good health and above the poverty level seem to thrive on it.

Satisfaction with retirement does seem to be higher in the United States than elsewhere. Further, although we found no adequate comparative data on this, Americans manage to accept retirement relatively well, provided only that they find sufficient opportunities to remain active, a matter which has no apparent relationship to continued employment on any level. With two exceptions, in European countries, satisfaction with retirement also had nothing to do with whether or not the person was still participating in work. Some, always a minority, were still working although almost always on a reduced basis, and they were usually satisfied with their life conditions. Others who were not working at all were equally likely to be satisfied. What made Americans different is that they were finding a little more to do and liking retirement just that much better. We can only suggest that Americans, having legitimated retirement as a status, also used their activist orientations to consider how one manages such a status. Retirees in this country seem to have more preparation for the postretirement social life and apparently with good results. This observation brings us to the two exceptions.

First, among the European countries, available information suggests that only in Poland does inability to continue working affect adversely life satisfaction. There are economic reasons for this finding. Apparently, Poland is not affluent enough to satisfy recent desires of consumers of all ages. But there is another reason. In other countries, economically disadvantaged older workers may have to continue working as best they can in order to survive, but they need not feel that they *should* work for the welfare of the nation. The Polish men who were studied by Havighurst and others (1969) did feel that they should work. Yet the majority of them were unemployed. One might conclude then that the nation was morally abandoning its old men or at least subjecting them to profound alienation. Pension laws say that one is entitled to retire, and the state will give one as much equity as it can afford. But prevailing social norms reject retirement, stipulating that every person ought to continue working as long as possible. Dilemma on dilemma, the economy has insufficient space for the older worker, even when he or she is willing to "retire" into cultivating his or her own garden plot and selling the produce in the market. Neither jobs nor small plots of land are available for most Polish would-be, older workers. The retirement role is obviously not fully legitimated, but neither is continued productivity normally permitted.

The Japanese case is even more complicated. Up until 1970 at least, it was almost impossible for the Japanese worker to withdraw from employment with sufficient means to support old age. We again confine the discussion to men since they are the most affected by retirement policies. (Women work for pay in Japan, to be sure, but they are likely to be in and out of the marketplace over the adult life cycle and therefore not entitled to even the level of support granted to male workers.) That level of support by the standards of most industrial countries has been pitiful. The worker with an industrial firm is pensioned off in the private sector at age fifty-five with a small lump sum. Until he is sixty years of age, the government or public sector gives him nothing at all. The Japanese older worker is placed in a sort of social limbo. On the one hand, he cannot retain his old position with his accustomed firm. On the other, the pension that that firm gave to him will allow him to subsist for, at the most, two years without other means of support. This leaves public-pension eligibility, a bare floor for his existence in any case, still three years in the future.

At the same time, Japanese social norms disapprove of leaving work. It is regarded as a national duty to continue. So what do Japanese men do? Caught in an economic and an ethical bind, the majority of them find a "second career," either in a lower status position in the same economic sector or in another economic sector. Either way, they are cut off from reaping benefits from either continued work or from acceptable retirement. As we have seen, the majority of Japanese males do go on working, thereby accepting their devaluted but still "contributory" status. But after age sixty-five, a very significant minority are out of the labor force. What happens to them, we do not know. Palmore (1975) did not tell us. Perhaps they have other means of support; perhaps they feel too ill to work any longer; perhaps they cannot find another job.

Whatever the reasons, we can easily see that the Japanese have not accepted retirement as a legitimate phase of life. One reason is that Japan is very poor in natural resources. Relative to the United States, for example, Japan supports a very large population on a small land base. The Japanese must cultivate, often by hand, every inch of available land. It is into such efforts that many older "retired" workers go. But intensive farm labor is strenuous work for the body. If it were not for the aging of the body, there might be unlimited employment for the displaced older worker. As it is, however, Japan is the country that most clearly demotes and so devalues its older workers. Without viable opportunities for work, many must depend on their savings or their families to survive at all.

Yet, according to their own words, Japanese men believe deeply that work is the central duty in their lives. Still, only a bare majority of older men can engage in work after age sixty-five. This discrepancy between belief and practice may be related to the unusually high and rising rate of suicide among the elderly of Japan. All Japanese men throughout their lives seem to be exhorted to work and genuinely feel they ought to do so as a service to the nation. Yet many of the elderly are either physically unable to work or lack opportunities, and even those who manage to continue to work experience a considerable loss in status.

This surely must be a crushing blow to self-esteem. The effect of such a blow could hardly be confined to men; their wives too must suffer from it. The rising suicide rates among older men and women in Japan thus may be attributable to the lack of acceptance of retirement combined with the economic misery that comes with old age.

Retirement and Public Financing

For the acceptance of retirement as an institution, on the one hand, and the public financing of old age income, on the other, the countries we examined yielded the following picture. On both counts, the Japanese rank in the lowest position. There is not any genuine legitimation of retirement as a reward for a life of work, and the state has not assumed any real responsibility for old age income. In Poland the state provides a pension, but retirement still is not really acceptable. Consequently, although the public pensions in Poland, as in Eastern Europe generally, are on levels that do not abandon as large a proportion of retirees economically as is the case in the United States, having to go into full retirement has a direct negative impact on life satisfaction among the Polish elderly. In this respect, the Poles rank second lowest after Japan. The United States is in third position.

In this country, one finds a definite acceptance of retirement as a last phase of life just as in most of the other countries for which data were available. But in contrast to several countries in Western Europe, the United States condemns almost one quarter of its elderly to economic abandonment when retirement income is 40 percent or less of preretirement earnings. As shown in chapter 2, this shows social security to be comparatively underdeveloped in this country.

In addition, medical expenditures place a considerable burden on the American elderly. Our Medicare provides only for some minimum floor of protection against extraordinary expenses; it is not designed for complete coverage. When one realizes that this country's neighbor to the North, Canada, can afford a national health care plan, the onus of proof that the United States cannot afford to care better for its elderly falls squarely on the defenders of the status quo. Again, when one realizes that adoption of the West German or Swedish social security system would drastically lower economic abandonment of the elderly in the United States, few convincing excuses for American underperformance come readily to mind. In fact, American underperformance appears inexcusable even by the relatively less demanding criteria we have invoked for evaluation.

The Elderly and Public Support

The United States may no longer be the country with the highest living standards in the world. But even twenty or thirty years ago when that was indisputably the case, a larger proportion of the American elderly were economically abandoned than of those in Europe. In more recent times, this difference cannot easily be attributed to observable differences in public support for social security and for retirement as an institution. Perhaps the surprisingly high level of subjective satisfaction with old age income in this country provides a clue. As we have seen, despite a significant drop in income for most after retiring, very few Americans complain. We have three facts.

In the population as a whole both retirement and social security enjoy widespread support, at least verbally. Americans are no different from Western Europeans on this point. Secondly, the economic performance of the United States in caring for the elderly is definitely second rate. But, thirdly, older people do not complain as much as one might expect. Together, these facts suggest that older people are less in demand in the United States than they are in Europe with its recent history of war, coup, and revolution. Perhaps the fact that America was spared the political upheavals of the European continent means that the stability of the government serves to give Americans assurance of their national identity. In living memory, there has always been a Congress and an executive branch, the Presidency, a Supreme Court, and the principle of the divisions of power. No revolutionary party has ever seriously threatened American democracy from within. Although there have been threats from without, no foreign power has ever invaded this country in modern times. A coup by colonels may be played out in movies, but few if any Americans believe it can ever happen in their country. But today's elderly in most European countries have experienced dramatic changes in their national histories. For a sense of continuity as to who they are and will continue to be as Poles or Frenchmen, Germans or Italians, Russians or Yugoslavs, people in Europe can hardly look for assurance with anything like the confidence of Americans to their governmental institutions. Thus, the people of continental Europe may well have a far greater need than Americans to care for their elderly in a way that assures continuity of the norms of distributive justice. For them social security has been one of the few, if not the only, institutions with real stability in recent history. And this alerts us once again to the case of Japan, where the family has been a highly stable institution in society, one that can be looked to as a source of continuity for thousands of years.

The Elderly and Family Support

In the family life of older people we also found considerable national differences. Here the quality of Japanese life can be seen best in contrast to the common industrial pattern on the one hand, and the Yugoslav pattern on the other. In chapter 5, much time was spent in documenting the family style of "intimacy at a distance" as the accepted way of life across the generations in modern societies. From Shanas and others (1968), it was learned that the Danes were the most distant in their intimacy across family generations, the British the least, and the

Americans somewhere in between. Yet the dominant pattern across social classes in all three industrial nations was the same. Parents and adult children do not live in the same household, especially if there are intact couples in both generations. More leeway is allowed for intergenerational "doubling up" if a spouse is missing in either generation. Even in such cases, however, the strong preference is for separate households.

Shanas and Sussman (1977) added more national cases with very similar results. Give or take a few percentage points from country to country, the modal and also the preferred pattern was independent living arrangements for parents and their adult children. Both older and younger generations agreed that this was the way it should be. Living in separate households, within which the major decisions and responsibilities of life are managed, is just what people of all ages and family statuses in most industrial societies said they wanted. It is almost as if some "invisible hand" is at work to sort out the rules of family life in modern society. Presumably, Americans and Danes, British and Dutch, and Israelis and Austrians do not confer among each other as to how they should behave in the family. Yet somehow they all manage in approximately the same way.

The "new" form of the extended family is cemented by felt attachments and obligations. One may, nowadays, be able to exchange a marital partner if unsatisfied with the bond that has been established. But one still clearly feels tied to the family line of both parents. Still, that highly popular and widespread family constellation in modern society is not viable for some purposes, no matter how tenacious and loyal the attachments.

The more traditional form of the extended family had a built-in continuity and a more comprehensive caring structure, whatever its other limitations. At first glance, Yugoslavia seems to have preserved this type, but in fact it may be performing less well in terms of family arrangements than other countries that have adopted "intimacy at a distance." The Yugoslav family seems to be in a transitional stage between the stem extended family and the modern conjugal version. Modernizing Yugoslavia has required many of its able-bodied workers to relocate from rural to urban areas. Like all Communist countries, "workers" are not only all physically fit males but females as well. As we noted in chapter 5, women traditionally have and still do involve themselves far more than men in caring for the family. But in Eastern Europe, the middle generation of women is as much a part of the labor force as men are, although women are allowed to retire several years earlier.

The Yugoslav data give us a contemporary glimpse of the transition from a basically agricultural into an essentially industrial economy. Although seventy percent of older parents are recorded as living with an adult child and usually a married one, far fewer actually live with such a child in any day-to-day sense. Yugoslavs recently have become extremely concerned with a new modal family condition: Old people and grandchildren live on the old homestead, and the middle generation, male and female, is off working in the city. For most practical purposes, there often is a missing link in the generational chain. Family consultants on the federal level fear, with some supporting evidence, that the grandparents are being exploited and given more responsibility both to produce on the farm and to care for their grandchildren than they want or can manage. Old people, under these circumstances, are being left behind in the least productive sphere of society. They are being abandoned but so are their grandchildren who must somehow try to survive under these very inadequate circumstances. This picture resembles the preindustrial era with its need of getting the last ounce of productivity out of the aged, but it is found in a country undergoing industrialization.

It also seems very clear that when the middle generation departs, Yugoslav elders have even less of a chance than aging parents in most industrial societies do to be given comprehensive family care. It seems, as Karl Marx effectively argued about Great Britain, that incipient industrialism is the most brutal of all phases in human history. To know that one would be treated as socially detrimental if one should happen to grow old is bearable. But to live to old age under one set of rules that is understood and accepted and then to find that an upset in the social order has destroyed all known social principles must be disillusioning, indeed. The Yugoslav family scene, therefore, is a contemporary example of what must have happened to some degree in the course of industrialization everywhere, except in Japan.

In the family, the Japanese have managed to adapt the traditional to the modern in a manner unmatched by any other industrialized society. We do not know why this is so; we know only that it is the case. Before industrialization the stem family prevailed in Japan as it did in Europe. Through all their political vicissitudes and despite rapid industrial development, the extended family still is not only statistically highly prevalent but also consensually socially supported in Japan.

During the U.S. occupation after World War II, General Douglas MacArthur insisted that the Japanese democratize their family obligations and modify the stem structure. Consequently, it is no longer the first-born son who both inherits all property and undertakes all responsibility for the care of aging parents. But all MacArthur really accomplished was to enlarge the Japanese family structure beyond the fragile stem. Today, or at least in the early seventies, 80 percent of aging parents live with their children, and almost everyone prefers such living arrangements. True, there is some erosion of this preference for joint households among those in urban areas and among the youngest adults. But the consensus is still so strong, and the attribution of changing attitudes to emerging urban and youth cohorts so uncertain, that the Japanese stem family seems here to stay from generation to generation, as it has been for thousands of years.

The Japanese also recognize some need for separating "nuclear" households. By that, we mean that as far as is spatially feasible, the older couple is given their own living quarters or at least dining times separate from those of their adult children and grandchildren. But this concession to independent households is small in comparison with the overriding shared responsibility for the welfare of the joint household.

No matter how equal or unequal the partnership between the generations, and this doubtlessly varies from household to household, the fact that "one roof" is the center for all certainly strengthens solidarity. Keeping at least two adult generations under one roof makes it more difficult to erect barriers to complete intimacy and to establish selective intimacy as modern family arrangements have done elsewhere. Being together by sharing a household keeps bonds visible, comprehensive, and alive in all areas of life. Probably this also means that "role reversal" between parents and their adult children is less stressful for both parties when failing health makes the old more and more dependent on their offspring. Most likely love and respect for the elderly can be maintained until death. Earlier we said that Japan supports its stem family through its unique employment pattern in industry in which a worker tends to stay with a company for life. As long as permanent employment with one firm lasts, the continued validity of the stem family in this modern society seems assured.

In comparison to the rest of the modern world, in Japan growing old assures that all family bonds will hold, very firmly, to the end of life. In most modern societies one finds that "intimacy at a distance" includes some loosening in the bonds of family life, but nowhere before death is there a real break. Americans are typical in this respect. The Danes appear somewhat more brittle in their ties to their children. In Denmark, there is a real reluctance to exchange support and care between the generations. In Yugoslavia, in contrast, one finds patterns of exploitation of the elderly. They are used for child custody and, apparently, are relatively deprived of the amenities of modern life. But the variations usually are slight. In general, the family bonds of older people in modern society are far greater than what they would be if we had the bare "nuclear" family unit as outlined in chapter 5. For all that, there comes a phase in family relations when the bonds between the generations break. Once again Japan is the exception, but wherever we find intimacy at a distance in one phase we also find that the bonds break later when death comes.

Families and Dying

Modern families do very well as long as the older members remain in reasonably good health. In the very last phase of life, when death becomes imminent, family failure is very poignant, for all members suffer. Here we have very little to distinguish among nations in the handling of aging. We suspect that most industrial nations do very poorly because of the similarity of the medical care institutions which are simply not geared, anywhere, to deal with patients who cannot be expected to recover.

If anything, our organizations for the chronically ill and the dying may be the "worst of a bad lot." More than in most other countries, in the United States medical personnel are rewarded disproportionately for entering the curing complex. Those who accept service in chronic care facilities will receive far lower salaries and lower status. The inevitable outcome is high staff turnover and low morale. Other countries provide more equalized rewards and also more beds reserved for chronic care. But the United States is only probably doing a little less well. Americans are more liberal in their visiting hours than has been found in some other countries, but they also tend to emphasize the "efficiency" of large institutions for medical care, although these are, as we argued in chapter 6, probably not suitable for the dying patient.

Tentatively, it looks as if Japan provides the most continuity in care for the elderly, a matter of the survival of the stem family and its cooptation by hospitals. In Japan, families are not only allowed to visit but are also invited into the institution to participate in patient care. Given the family structure, this means that the dying elderly person probably feels less abandoned in that country. He or she lives in the household of a child as long as possible, and the younger family members can follow the aging person right into the medical care facility if institutionalization becomes necessary. Thus family members care for the Japanese elderly until death. Accordingly, the sense of abandonment should be far less. In the absence of specific data, however, this likely outcome in the Japanese case has to remain speculative.

Institutions and Death

If dying in general is handled poorly in modern societies because for most it takes place in general hospitals, Americans are underperformers in a triple sense. Not only do they provide less public medical cost coverage for the elderly, not only are there fewer chronic care facilities than in Europe, but also our medical system has been quite unresponsive to persistent criticism from one of the helping professions. Social work, with which one of the authors of this book is identified, has long attempted in this country to plead for more emphasis on caring in a holistic, personalized sense for the ailing old person (Morris 1969; Lowy 1976). But the medical complex has proved extraordinarily resistant to pleas to relax its insistence of specialization in health care which deals primarily with segmented bodily functions.

The fact that this approach does not serve the needs of a growing number of "incurables" has fallen pretty much on deaf ears. A recent study of nursing homes for the elderly, for example, showed that the smaller homes indeed were more capable of offering emotional support along with physical care (Glasscote and others 1976). Patients were more likely to be treated as persons rather than simply as bodies to be tended. But these are the very institutions that this society is now attacking through bureaucratic rules that specify the numbers of exits and firedoors, the required area around and between beds, and the number of different medical specialists who must be on the premises. However necessary these safety provisions may be, many of these rules have little to do with the personal caring functions that seem so important to the dying, but they can put out of business the small homes that do provide such care.

Bereavement and Death

In death and bereavement, we have found hardly any national differences. Only the Japanese may be somewhat more acceptant of death, which seems to ease mourning. Bereavement leaves the widowed with a sense of lost identity for which there is little means of assuagement, since the meaning of the death of another is shrouded in mystery. As a partial consequence the person in mourning "searches" for the dead, mostly unconsciously but sometimes consciously. In the West, becoming aware of searching leads to high anxiety. Fifty percent of the London widows in the Marris study (1958), for example, reported a "felt presence" of the departed spouse, but thought that this sensation was an indication of incipient insanity. In Western religious systems, the dead do not come back.

But in Japan, by contrast, a small study of widows showed that almost all felt that presence, and none worried about her sanity in consequence (Yamamoto and others 1969). This difference is probably explained by the fact that most of the Japanese widows were practicing Buddhists and had family altars in their homes where ancestor worship was still maintained. The Japanese, in contrast to westerners, are, on this slim evidence, probably better at accepting death and coping with bereavement. One does not really "lose one's dead"; in spiritual terms they still are present among the living. Again, it is possible only to suggest that Americans do about as well or as badly in the management of bereavement as most modern countries. But the Japanese demonstrate an astonishing capacity to manage the whole process of aging, dying, death, and bereavement through the central institution of the family, bolstered by the support of unique industrial arrangements on the one hand and religious traditions which make sacred the family heritage on the other.

Comparing the Fate of Old Age

The fate of growing old shows more cross-national similarities in modern societies than differences. Perhaps that is one reason why critics of the pattern of modern aging have to use purely normative standards in evaluating how well or how poorly a given society treats its older people in some area of concern. The configuration of growing old in modern times described in the first part of this chapter shows only minor variations in the nations examined.

There is one point at which cross-national differences do come to the aid of the critic. In terms of relative economic deprivation, *only* the United States abandons as large a proportion as almost one quarter of its elderly into economic misery. Most modern nations also have national health care plans for the elderly. If Western Europe, similar socially, economically, and politically to the United

States, can provide significantly better economic and medical securities for older people, then it is *not* naive idealism to demand improvement in America. If Eastern Europe, politically different but economically less developed than the United States, can afford to abandon fewer of their elderly than the United States does then it is obviously difficult to argue that America cannot afford better care for its elderly. Japan, in contrast, provides very little public economic care to the elderly but excels in providing emotional security both through its stem family and the way the family cooperates in the operation of the hospital.

The case of Japan therefore tells us that the principal constellation of the fate of older people in modern society which we found is *not* a necessity, unavoidable and therefore to be borne without hope for change everywhere. A cross-national perspective clearly suggests that Americans could do better in caring for their elderly in income and in the cost of illness. No similar claim, however, can be made in the area of emotional care in dying and bereavement. In these two areas Americans are very similar to other Western nations.

In the United States and in European countries, industrialization has been accompanied by the increased allocation of citizen support to the public sector. The family structures are inadequate to provide terminal care. Therefore, we have to assume that public policies will continue to stress the medical complex with its emphasis on size, efficiency, and specialization. Though there is always room for some innovation, such as the hospice, essentially it appears that the delivery of dying persons into impersonal public care is part and parcel of the essential developmental pattern, by now strongly rooted in most modern societies. In the management of bereavement in industrialized countries, deeply ingrained religious attitudes in the West interfere with any sense of continuity uniting the dead with the living. Here, too, our negative evaluation leads to an interpretation that will be dealt with in more depth in the next section, but there is little hope of change. In short, with Japan as the only exception, the configuration described earlier holds for modern societies in its essential outlines. Modern societies present generally consistent patterns. The implementation of those patterns is only a matter of degree. The next and final task is to interpret the configuration which has emerged.

THE MODERN FATE OF GROWING OLD

Only cross-national uniformities or similarities can tell us what is peculiarly modern about the fate of older people in modern society. Patterns that hold across several societies cannot be attributed to one feature of a given country which would describe the American or French, the West German or Polish fate of being old. The demands of interpretation of cross-national similarities are similarly straightforward. If one is to understand them, one must relate them to features that all societies have in common. Let us now consider the main cross-national similarities of this study as a set and attempt an interpretation.

To recapitulate, with the exception of Japan, we found a fourfold constellation characterizing the relations between older people and others in society. This constellation is made up of, first, diachronic solidarity in economic and material social ties of caring for the elderly. Second, we found diachronic solidarity in the political bonds of citizenship. Both of these sets of relations are managed in a fashion that perpetuates the bonds of loyalty and caring between the generations from one set of cohorts to another. Both clearly indicate that there is a demand for older people in modern society. The aged and the way we care for them perform important functions for younger people.

In economic support, caring for the aged produces diachronic solidarity in commitments to norms of distributive justice in society. Thus, caring for the elderly contributes to continuity of one important element among those factors that make up our national identity. That is a finding in direct contradiction to Burgess's (1960) general claim of the "role-less" role of the aged in modern times.

In national political life, we found a preference for older people in positions of national leadership. Being the most general of generalists available in society, older people in positions of national leadership function as a fiduciary trust. Because of old age, the elderly can claim to have been a party to all those crucial political events in a nation's recent history that forged out of its populace different political generations. Spanning in experience all the formative experiences prevalent in the body politic, older people have the edge over younger ones in the competition for trust.

This finding directly contradicts Cowgill's and Holmes's (1972) central assertion that old age necessarily amounts to status loss in modern society. Whatever the merit of the status-loss thesis of older people elsewhere in social life, in national politics it does not hold true. Similarly, the fact that the bonds of political citizenship continue into old age in patterns not significantly different from those earlier in life does lay to rest both hopes (Rose 1965) and apprehensions (Cutler & Bengston 1976) about the use of chronological age to form political subcultures. Up to now, there have been no signs of new political confrontations pitting age-cohort centric groups or variant political generations, each with its own anger, own vision, and specific leaders and followers, against all others.

The bonds with the elderly break toward the end of life. In dying, on the one hand, and in mourning, on the other, we abandon the elderly. These are occasions for spiritual care, and here the capacity for caring fails modern men and women everywhere. Neither dying nor mourning are recognized social statuses with rights and duties attached to those involved. It is a fact of modern life that the ending of human life and the suffering of loss of another close to us condemn most of us to precisely as role-less a role as Burgess (1960) claimed.

On this point he proved to be an investigator who saw with unusual clarity a truth about the modern condition that still evades some later writers. Contrary to Atchley (1977:183), who simply claimed that a terminal diagnosis automatically assigns "the social role of dying person," role playing as ordinarily understood demands a little more than just the recognition that someone is dying. Unless we learn then how to behave, what to do, to say, to feel, and how to share these things with the person dying, there is no role. Simply expecting that younger people who die should struggle more against death and be more concerned with unfinished business in their lives than older people does not suffice to structure roles for dying persons or their caretakers. That is why taking care rather than caring is all one finds when it comes to dying and mourning.

Finally, we also found that the subjective experience of death in modern times is one of blissful liberation from life. Death is experienced, as best one can tell, not as a release from social life and its burdens but rather from human existence in general. However imperfect our knowledge of it, death as liberation is the only message we receive from those who came back to us from encounters with extreme life-threatening situations.

The question is, what does this fourfold constellation of the fate of old age mean? Why is it that our bonds hold before terminal illness occurs and break afterwards?

Diachronic Solidarity

Drawing on the work of Eisenstadt (1964) in chapter 1 we claimed that the solidarity of a modern complex society demands at least two mechanisms. First, there must be modes of assuring the supremacy of collective over individual interests in society; otherwise the complexity of the division of labor produces so many varied groups or specialized interests in conflict with each other as to lead to the breakdown of social order. In modern society it is the state that both creates collective or national interests that constrain the pursuit of individual interests and regulate the patterns of conflict among special interests.

Second, solidarity in a modern society also has a temporal dimension. Modern men and women live with the notion that the lives of their parents—the roles they played—were different from their own, and they also expect that their children in turn will live under different conditions, playing different roles and facing different problems with different tools to solve them. This consciousness of social change creates the specter of a complete break between the past, the present, and the future. But many programs of the modern state are long-range ones. They take more than one generation to complete. A generation is usually reckoned as thirty years. Whether one thinks of economic development in the Common Market countries of Western Europe or in their counterparts in Eastern Europe, of urban planning or the integration of blacks into society in the United States, it is more typical than exceptional to encounter national goals that require much time to achieve. The need to assume responsibility for long-term projects and the specter of constant social change then combine to generate a need for diachronic solidarity. There also must be mechanisms to ensure the supremacy of continuity over change in citizenship identities. Otherwise any office or bureau in modern society could assume responsibility only until the next turnover of personnel.

If this much be granted on purely abstract terms, our study will have shown that caring for the elderly and preferring their leadership on the national level provide two such mechanisms of diachronic solidarity. More specifically, the first assures continuity in prevalent norms of distributive justice, and these, belonging to a set of norms that sociologists call stratification codes, comprise one very important element of national identity. Placing the elderly disproportionately into positions of national political leadership, in turn, produces a sense of trust that current decision making is informed by recent historical experience.

Underlying both of these patterns of diachronic solidarity are two very general roles, that of the citizen and that of the retiree. Let us emphasize two related characteristics of these roles: their highly general nature and the fact that they cut across all other roles in society that are stratified and/or involved in political cleavages. Both the citizen and the retiree in modern society can be found everywhere: in the middle class or the working class, among northerners or southerners, people of Irish or Italian background, of the Roman Catholic or some Protestant faith. Thus the citizen role and that of the retiree cross-cut the cleavages in society. That is related to their very general nature. Both are characterized more by certain rights than by any detailed specification of duties. As a citizen one has the right to vote. One also may have some moral duty to do so. But with very few exceptions there is no legal obligation to vote or to exercise one's right as a citizen. Beyond casting a ballot, there are no legally enforced duties connected with the citizen role at all. The vote of the decidedly uninformed about public issues counts as much in legitimating power in modern society as does the vote of the assiduous student of politics.

This emphasis on rights and a *laissez-faire* attitude toward duties also pertains to the role of the retiree. He or she is entitled to a pension, always a public one, and sometimes also a private one. But except for rules that may prohibit substantial employment as a condition for receiving the pension, what he or she does with it is not prescribed in any great detail. Indeed, how a pension is consumed is less and less prescribed. Not too long ago an old-age pensioner had to reside within the country granting the pension in order to preserve eligibility. Now he or she may not only reside where he or she likes, visa regulations permitting, but also North American and Western European countries have made more and more bilateral arrangements that permit older people to draw social security in more than one country, gathering benefits from all the countries in which they worked. These are policies deliberately designed to maximize income for the elderly. They further enlarge the sphere of rights without commensurate duties.

In short, general roles such as these are based primarily on rights and only secondarily, if at all, on any particular duties. That has given unusual freedom to the persons in these roles. But it is a freedom with a burden. Not being told by anyone in any detail what to do, the citizen and the retiree alike can decide for themselves but also must bear by themselves the consequences of their decisions. If it turns out that they voted for the wrong politician or that he or she was elected because they did not go to the polls, they have only themselves to blame. If they do not know what to do after retirement with leisure on their hands, they only have to blame themselves, unless it was compulsory retirement that forced them into the position.

Diachronic solidarity then involves very general roles, those that emphasize rights and minimize duties. For the citizen role this is true both before and during old age. The retiree role only begins with old age. The fact that modern societies provide for continuity in national identity through roles emphasizing rights and few duties is scarcely accidental. It is instead related to three of our other findings: 1) the kinds of dependencies in old age that we find tolerable or unbearable; 2) the morality of caring for the elderly by public means; and 3) our helplessness in caring spiritually for each other in dying and in suffering the loss of each other. Let us see how.

We know that growing to old age inevitably means an encounter with dependency again. Whether lengthy or short, depending on the dying trajectory, we leave this world as we entered it: in complete dependency on others who must care for us. Though dictated by nature and more or less unavoidable, becoming childlike again in old age before death does us part is so unbearable a condition for modern men and women that they part in fact before death comes. Such loss of independence is unbearable only in the interpersonal sphere. We cannot bear to become dependent on our children or our friends.

Yet long before terminal illness comes, the pensioner is dependent on the state. So it is in general for the citizens of modern nation states at all ages. But dependency on the state is not experienced as dependency. We treat ourselves instead to a self-definition as bearers of social rights. Rights tell us that we are entitled to services. We are not charity wards. Experiencing dependency as a matter of right therefore does not diminish us in our own eyes or in those of our fellow citizens. The contrast, suffering from interpersonal dependency but not even perceiving dependency on public agents as dependency, is rooted in the modern form of individualism.

Modern Individualism

The origin and nature of modern individualism were brilliantly analyzed by Emile Durkheim (1873/1947) in his famous book, *The Division of Labor*. He argued for a direct connection between the ever increasing centralization of the powers of the state and the concomitant growth of individualism and individual freedom. With an advanced division of labor in society the state becomes the main coordinating agency. Laws proliferate; more and more activities are subjected to state regulation, and men and women come to depend more and more on impersonal bureaucratic administrative agencies. That process, too, makes us less and less dependent on our families, friends, and neighbors. The growing freedom from constraints of the interpersonal sphere comes with the growing dependency on impersonal others in the bureaucracies of the state, the economy, and the educational and health complexes. The result, so it seems, has been the conviction that individual freedom, and the responsibility to stand on one's own feet associated with it, means primarily freedom from the constraints of interpersonal relations outside the bureaucratic organizations in which we work. That puts a premium on independence as a valued attribute of individuals only when it is independence from other people with whom we have personal relations. Dependence on bureaucracy is not seen as real dependence; it is perceived as a social right. Receiving social security or tax or health care advantages in old age all can be seen as social rights, precisely because the recipient is merely a statistic, a cipher in a computer printout. What one then does with the receipt is still one's own decision.

Receiving physical care and help from one's own grown children when one can no longer stand on one's own feet in old age, on the other hand, is experienced as unbearable dependency precisely because the source from which the help comes is personal, involving helper and helped in a personal nexus dramatically different from that to which they were accustomed. Whether it is a role reversal as occurs when children take care of their ailing and dying parents or just a change, as when friends try to care for each other, personalized dependency relations cause nothing but pain. They make us subject again to detailed instructions. We are told, once more, what we can and cannot do. We are subjected, once again, to personalized authority ties, something we have not experienced since early childhood. And to add insult to injury, there is the suggestion that, because everything is done for our own good interest as understood by the caretakers, we should be grateful for the burdens of authority and responsibility assumed by them. All this makes us unbearably childlike because it deprives us of the most cherished aspects of mature adulthood, the ability to decide for ourselves and to bear the consequences by ourselves.

Throughout our adult years when working in bureaucratic organizations, we were rewarded for taking responsibility. That indeed formed us into what we have come to understand as mature adulthood. Taking individual responsibility is so much an aspect of working in large bureaucratic organizations, where most modern men and women spend their work lives, that it should be described. The message of the following account of organizational life is very simple. Taking responsibility, self-reliance, and independence from personalized authority bonds, these characteristics of modern individualism all are rooted in the experience of bureaucratic work settings.

For most modern men and women the world of work is that of the bureau-cratic organization. That is where we spend our adult lives. That has an importance far surpassing the time we spend at work. With the forty-hour work week we do spend less than half our waking time at work. But the experience is formative because it determines so much the life styles we have and what we can or cannot do for our children. To be sure, not everyone works in a bureaucracy. There are niches in the network of bureaucratic life where the small family business of old survives. The gas station, the shirt laundry, the small grocery store around the corner, the family farm, and, in America, the funeral home are among the most notable nonbureaucratic work settings left in the modern world. But only a minority of the adult population works in such places. For most of us work life means organization life, and being a worker means being an organization man or woman.

Working in a complex bureaucratic organization demands of each individual an unusually high level of individual responsibility, a matter often overlooked because of the hierarchical nature of bureaucratic organizations with its levels of management and chains of command from the president down to the worker on the shop floor or to the typist in the steno pool. Yet the very nature of large and complex organizations makes their normal functioning directly dependent on workers assuming responsibilities for their tasks without the need for detailed supervision at each step in the work process, in each department, work group, and work station. No factory or office could operate even with modest efficiency if detailed supervision were necessary. If we had to have as intense a supervision as a police officer in each corner of a factory floor constantly watching over individuals and monitoring their behavior every moment, the costs of administration would far outweigh the advantages of complex organization.

In short, a bureaucratic organization is tolerably efficient only as long as the workers subject themselves to impersonal rules more or less voluntarily. Impersonal rules of procedure are the key words here. Impersonal rules are not only the hallmark of burearcracy, they provide the most important element for organizational survival, which is that subordinates enforce the rules on each other. The routine operation of an organization rests directly on individual responsibility of subordinates who work with each other without the need of a supervisor constantly breathing down their necks. Just how much individual responsibility and mutual control of behavior is required becomes apparent immediately when we realize that any bureaucracy breaks down into chaos as soon as the employees decide "to go by the rule book." That well-known fact of modern life tells us how impossible it is to prescribe in detail what workers in large complex organizations are supposed to do. The very fact that "going by the rule book" brings chaos emphasizes how much the routine operation and indeed the survival of complex organizations depend on individual responsibility and initiative.

High individual responsibility is only one aspect of modern individualism.

Equality in the relationships is another. Both are related to the nature of impersonal rule in bureaucratic life. A distinction between the two roles that we all play in any organization may help clarify these matters. Swanson (1978:256) reminded us of another simple fact of all social life. We are participants in organizations for what we get out of them. That part of our behavior in them can be called our usership role through which we realize our self-interest. On occasion, we must be able to strip off the usership role and start acting for the organization itself, its interests rather than our individual self-interest.

Then we enter the agentship role, acting on behalf of the organization and caring about its aims, prosperity, and survival. Assuming the agentship role among subordinates is a matter most easily appreciated in conditions of crisis. For example, every union member knows that in a strike there usually comes the time when the survival of the union itself is at stake. At that point the call to stand up for the union is a call to take on the agentship role. Similarly, elsewhere in the office or factory life, it is in crises that we exert ourselves, going the extra mile. But that should not mislead us into believing that assuming the agentship role is confined to crises. Whenever subordinates make each other toe the line, subordinating themselves to impersonal rules or procedures, they perform their agentship role, acting responsibly on behalf of the organization. And calling on each other to act responsibly in concert is a mode of calling on each other as equals. Men and women who rule each other by bowing to the demands of impersonal rules subordinate themselves under a principle that binds all equally to a common purpose, one they share above and beyond whatever divides them in their various usership roles. Aside from bringing home the paycheck, one man may use work to escape a shrewish wife, another to kid with buddies, a third may like to daydream, a fourth enjoy the air conditioning. The sources of pleasure and of pain at work are many. But agentship brings us all together under one common purpose larger than ourselves and in most cases outlasting our own lives. Just as any role, agentship too becomes part of ourselves, our sense of who we are, and so part of our identity.

Modern men and women are used to identifying with larger collective purposes, not as underlings to an overlord but as equals sharing responsibility for purposes larger and more permanent than their own lives. If the ability to identify with the larger purposes of some corporate actor like a firm is part of everyday life for most adults, this raises the question of whether such an ability extends to identification with society at large. However speculative our answer must remain, we think an affirmative one is justified. Objectively, as we have seen on the basis of income inequality for several generations in America, caring for the elderly does ensure continuity of the norms of distributive justice. That is, of course, a form of caring for a larger purpose than our own individual lives. But the widespread political support for retirement and old-age social security programs that we have noted also raises the questions of whether this caring for the elderly is indeed caring, that is, a form of nurturance and love? Since survey data do not tell us with any sufficient detail just what the understandings of social security are in the population at large, one cannot answer definitely.

Nonetheless speculating about it is important for two reasons, one practical, the other theoretical. First, if it seems likely that caring for the elderly is an expression of our agentship roles as citizens, the prospects for our ability to maintain the benefit levels into the near future are enhanced. If it is really caring for others, rather than just looking out for ourselves, the young and enterprising person who is told by Munnell (1977:41) that a better deal awaits in the private market may hesitate to go there. Theoretically, our interest is in the discovery of a connection between our impressive ability to care for older people before terminal illness and the end of life and our impressive failure to provide spiritual care for the dying and mourning. There are three facts that *suggest* that caring for the elderly is caring rather than mere caretaking.

Caring and Loving

First, as we noted in the last two chapters, it is a characteristic of modern men and women to profess a belief in God. Ours is not a secular age if by secular one means a widespread absence of belief among the population of modern societies. Second, recognizing each other as citizens and as retirees is a way of addressing fellow social members as persons. We care for the elderly through engaging in our citizenship roles. That role is an exceedingly general one, filled with rights and little burdened with detailed obligations. The receiver of the gift of retirement is a retiree, once again an exceedingly general role, full of rights and saddled with few if any detailed obligations. Relating to each other in such general roles then is relating to each other as persons. Thus, we suggest, the very nature of the roles that modern men and women everywhere use to care for the elderly turns this caretaking into caring.

When persons care for each other as persons, what each gives and the other receives amounts to giving and receiving nurturance. Nurturance is love. Since love is so central a theme in the Judaeo-Christian tradition, this of course raises the question of whether caring for the elderly also has a religious connotation. Is the modern way of caring and loving in the public sphere one that *has* to be channeled through bureaucracy, one that has to take the form of social rights? Although the question cannot be answered here, there is one additional fact indicating such a religious role for social security.

Using different material and basing their case on different observations, Bellah (1964), Swanson (1968), and Parsons, Fox, and Lidz (1972) all argued for a fundamentally democratic relationship between God and humans as typical in the modern religious situation. This suggestion of a typically modern relation between God and humans has three features that parallel the mode of caring for the elderly. First, the relationship is contractual. God and humans work together in a compact or contract, an element preserved from the parent religion of

Chrstianity, the covenant of the people of Israel. And social security is a contractual relationship. Second, the relationship between God and humans has become one in which near equal or equal partners meet each other in a common undertaking, each party sharing the role of agentship. And we all are equal to each other in the role of citizenship, which is the one through which we channel social security support to the aged. Third, the common undertaking between God and humans has become an exceedingly abstract enterprise. Neither in original Protestantism nor in its modern version could one insist on assigning direct sacred significance to any concrete action. Only one's whole life was to be a test for salvation. In Bellah's opinion that abstract feature provides religious sanction for endless social reform and endless attempts at self-improvement by individuals, and in neither area can one assign success to any particular step or any particular instance of change. This emphasizes the necessarily abstract and almost "invisible" nature of the modern religious situation. But again there is a parallel to caring for the elderly. We also care for the elderly by channeling support through the abstract language of social security laws and by depersonalizing what we do for each other.

Dying and Mourning

If it is true that a modern way of caring in the public sphere demands a contractual relationship, in which people meet each other as equals and channel support through the impersonal rules of bureaucracy, it should not come as much of a surprise that we fail to give spiritual care to the dying and those in bereavement. Dying and grieving are assaults on the social identity of persons. The parallels in the subjective experience of dying and mourning noted in the last two chapters all attest to the fact that dying and mourning are struggles fought to preserve identity, despite the recognition that identity must change. Death signals to us that we no longer shall be any of the role-selves through which we know and understand ourselves. Mourning means taking leave of one part of ourselves, the part that belongs to the dead whom we carried in ourselves.

We also showed that such threats to our identity are very painful, and pain reduces us to the status of helpless children once more. Necessarily, in dying and in suffering the loss of someone dear and near, we become unequal to others not so afflicted. On these occasions, ours is a life of inner turmoil, of profound insecurity as to who we are and who we are to become. That not only makes us less than equals, it also makes us dependent on particular others for help and modes of helping which are personalized. There is simply no way to help someone with a change in identity that is not wanted and indeed is feared with the tools of bureaucracy and its impersonal relations. Chinese brainwashing techniques can force such change. But these are not techniques of helping. If we are to help each other with problems of identity change we must come to depend on each other as persons. Yet as unequals we can bear that only in a situation of illness, as when psychiatrist and patient work with each other. Only in illness can modern people still accept inequality in a personalized, helping relationship. That makes our attempts to help each other in dying and mourning so difficult and, in essence, unmanageable. Our only acceptable model for inequality and dependency is *illness and cure.* But when we die in old age, there is no cure, and when we mourn the loss of another that is normal and not pathological. Both the model of illness and the secular knowledge that it summons are misapplied. Let us elaborate a little more.

Both dying and mourning are occasions on which we have to come to terms with the finitude of human life. If the modern religious situation has even remotely the features described above, it is immediately apparent that all the relevant value commitments are commitments to life. They serve to improve life, something accomplished mostly through collective effort. If there is a religious content in caring for the elderly, if that is how we have come to understand what it means to care for one another, then all of it is no more than an extension of the old familiar theme of "domination over the world" which ushered in the modern age.

These values of life fail us when we face its end. All the *modern* helping professions share the commitments to master life; none has been organized yet to manage ending human life.

The directly relevant professions for the management of change in identity are psychology and psychiatry. The scientific disciplines here are composed entirely of meanings directed to the mastery over life, not to the management of death. Such concepts as denial or repression, indeed the very notion of defense mechanisms as well as the pervasive concern with the normal and the pathological, all of these are tools for *curing* illness. None of these concepts was originally designed for terminal *care.* It is very difficult, if not impossible, for professionals trained in skills of mastering the problems of life to understand that there are problems that simply have no solutions. The very meaning of the term problem is associated in the minds of modern men and women with the duty to find a solution. Nothing illustrates this better than the common-sense meaning of the phrase used by a doctor when a patient is declared a terminal one. "Nothing can be done for him anymore" is a statement true *only* in terms of the goals of a curative discipline. But it sounds far more general, indicating our helplessness in the face of problems that we cannot master.

That much indeed can be done, caring for the dying, being there and sharing however unequally in the agony of death, is a matter that has almost vanished from the world of the emotionally significant in our lives. More and more we realize our fundamental unpreparedness to cope with dying in a human way, both organizationally and as individuals. The general hospital where most of us are dying currently is not designed for ending human life. That is why the hospice movement is spreading so quickly in contemporary America. Only time can tell whether acceptance of the finitude of life will be learned once again.

Only the future can show whether we can relearn to accept these dictates of nature which are inevitable: Our fate of interpersonal dependency as unequals at the end of life.

That we cannot now accept the return to the helplessness of childhood at the end of life and in suffering the loss of another is the main reason why we abandon the dying and those in bereavement once the immediate period of the funeral is over. Our bonds to the dying and the grieving break. That is partial confirmation of both disengagement and socialization theory.

Contrary to Cumming and Henry (1961), it is not mutual disengagement with mutual psychological benefit that characterizes the modern dying scene. Rather, it is the living who disengage from the dying and usually before the dying are ready for it. Consequently, disengagement does not serve a mutual psychological benefit. It serves, at best, a one-sided one. The living may spare themselves the agony of facing a problem that has no solution. That is certainly true for most nurses in general hospitals who tell us that they either treat terminal patients "just like any other one" or avoid contact with them (Popoff 1975). As we saw in chapter 6, it also is true of many family members when the dying trajectory is one of a lingering death. There is a similar, one-sided disengagement from the widow in mourning once the funeral is over. These facts tell us that we are not socialized for dying and for mourning. Rosow's (1974) assertion of inadequate socialization for old age in general may be exaggerated and perhaps even misconceived regarding the role of the retiree. But for persons in lingering death and for people who typically grieve the loss of another for years, his propositions hold.

Religion and Death

Finally, there is something poignant, if not indeed tragic, in the contemporary religious situation with its stress on the mastery of life and the abstract mode we have found to exert ourselves in its service. Having committed ourselves to the realization of some religious imperative in social reform through the application of impersonal law, the cooperation among equals, and the insistence that no sacred significance can be attached with certainty to any particular action, we have left ourselves as mortal individuals in a state of religious anxiety. That anxiety seems clearly reflected in the essentially escapist nature of the modern death experience as a liberation from human life. We have given it a religious interpretation, claiming that death as liberation indicates release from the human search, from the yearning for some comprehensive meaning in life. Finding a meaning that is strong enough to carry us through the door of death does belong, so it would seem, to that part of the religious life of modern men and women that has been effectively "privatized" (Berger 1973). In coping with the impending death of oneself or with the loss of another, each person must search for religious meaning himself or herself.

The "privatization" of anything simply means its withdrawal from role playing, from social control, and so from the forces that order our lives. To cling to beliefs about the nature of God that pertain to the questions of the experience of death in a private fashion is, after all, a way of withdrawing judgment of their validity from the opinion of others. As Weber (1919b/1958) long ago told us, these are the questions of how we should have lived and how we should die. No forms of secular knowledge, the only ones we still recognize as knowledge, can supply answers to such questions. Relegating the answers to a private realm of fantasy, as long as death and loss did not touch us personally, leaves us inevitably utterly alone when death comes. Having never seriously played the role of religious believers under conditions of control by others in matters touching on the finitude of life, we encounter death and loss in a state of helpless anomie. We do not know what to do with each other, what to say, what to feel, and how in all of that to share and bear each other.

For those who remember rather than forget recent history, there is another source of anxiety. The social science speculations about the modern relationship between humans and God clearly imply that modernity means humans' arrogance in choosing and fashioning their own image of God as a partner. That, as George Orwell said, confronts us with "the real problem of our time" which "is to restore a sense of absolute right and wrong when the belief that it used to rest on . . . has been destroyed" (Fleishner 1974:72). Perhaps this may restore dignity to the idea that there are other forms of knowledge besides merely science or common sense, which cannot tell us how to live and how to die.

If the experience of death as liberation tells us that we have lived spiritually like adolescents who never grew up, it might be wiser not to scorn such conduct and to try instead to restore the dignity of adulthood and adult responsibility to the search for comprehensive meaning in our lives. For our moral situation is very different from that of Max Weber's time. This can be illustrated with the ending of his famous lecture on science as a vocation. There he referred to the Jewish people as one who kept yearning for meaning throughout its history. He said of them:

> The Jewish people . . . has enquired and tarried for more than two millenia, and we are shaken when we realize its fate. From this we want to learn the lesson that nothing is gained by yearning and tarrying alone, *and we shall act differently.* We shall set to work and meet "the demands of the day," in human relations as well as our vocation. This, however, is plain and simple, each finds and obeys the demon who holds the fibers of his very life. (Weber 1919b/1958:156, italics added)

That was said in Germany at the end of the First World War. We who lived during the Second World War and the Holocaust know that we acted differently indeed, in Germany as well as elsewhere. Later, still living, we can draw a different conclusion, which is that nothing is gained by the privatization of that which makes humans quintessentially human—their yearning for meaning in life and in death.

references

ADAMS, B.N. 1970. "Isolation, function, and beyond: American kinship in the 1960's." Journal of Marriage and Family 32:575-97.

ADAMS, JAY E. 1976. Competent to Counsel. Nutley, N.J.: Presbyterian and Reformed Publishing Company.

ALVES, WAYNE M. and PETER H. ROSSI. 1978. "Who should get what? Fairness judgments of the distribution of earnings." American Journal of Sociology 84:541-64.

ANDERSON, MICHAEL. 1977. "The impact on the family relationships of the elderly of changes since Victorian times in governmental income-mainte-nance provision." Pp. 36-59 in Ethel Shanas and Marvin Sussman (eds.), Family, Bureaucracy, and the Elderly. Durham, N.C.: Duke University Press.

ARIES, PHILLIPE. 1962. Centuries of Childhood. New York: Knopf.

ASH, P. 1966. "Pre-retirement couseling." The Gerontologist 6:97-99.

ATCHLEY, ROBERT C. 1971. "Retirement and leisure participation: Con-tinuity or crisis?" The Gerontologist 2:13-17.

_____ 1976. The Sociology of Retirement. Cambridge, Mass.: Schenk-man.

_____. 1977. The Social Forces in Later Life: An Introduction to Social Gerontology. Second Edition. Belmont, Calif.: Wadsworth.

BARRON, MILTON L. 1961. The Aging American. New York: Thomas Y. Crowell.

BARTLEY, DOUGLAS. 1977. "Compulsory retirement: A reevaluation." Personnel 54(2):62-66.

BECKER, ERNEST. 1973. The Denial of Death. New York: Free Press.

BECKER, HOWARD S. 1972. "Medical education." Pp. 191-205 in Howard E. Freeman, Sol Levine and Leo G. Reader, (eds.), Handbook of Medical Sociology. Englewood Cliffs, N.J.: Prentice-Hall.

BELL, DANIEL. 1973. The Coming of Post-Industrial Society. New York: Basic Books.

BELLAH, ROBERT N. 1964. "Religious evolution." American Sociological Review 29:358-74.

BENGSTON, VERN L. 1969. "Differences between sub-samples in level of present role activity." Pp. 35-52 in Robert J. Havighurst, Joep M. A. Munnichs, Beatrice L. Neugarten and Hans Thomae, Adjustment to Retirement. Assen, Netherlands: Van Gorcum.

————. 1971. "Inter-Age differences in perception and the generation gap." Gerontologist, Part II:85-90.

BENGSTON, VERN L. and NEAL E. CUTLER. 1976. "Generations and intergenerational relations: Perspectives on age groups and social change." Pp. 130-59 in Robert H. Binstock and Ethel Shanas (eds.), Handbook of Aging and the Social Sciences. New York: Van Nostrand Reinhold.

BERGER, PETER L. 1967. The Sacred Canopy: Elements of a Sociological Theory of Religion. Garden City, N.Y.: Doubleday.

BERGER, PETER L., BRIGITTE BERGER and HANSFRIED KILLNER. 1973. The Homeless Mind. New York: Random House.

BERKNER, LUTZ. 1972. "The stem family and the developmental cycle of the peasant household: An eighteenth century Austrian example." American Historical Review 77:398-418.

BESHAI, JAMES A. and DONALD I. TEMPLER. 1978. "American and Egyptian attitudes toward death." Essence 2:155-58.

BINSTOCK, ROBERT H. 1972. "Interest group liberalism and the politics of aging." Gerontologist 12:265-80.

————. 1974. "Aging and the future of American politics." Annals of the American Academy of Political and Social Sciences 415:201-12.

BINSTOCK, ROBERT H. and MARTIN A. LEVIN. 1976. "The political dilemmas of intervention politics." in Robert H. Binstock and Ethel Shanas (eds.), Handbook of Aging and the Social Sciences. New York: Van Nostrand Reinhold.

BLACKWELL, R. 1974. "Political generation and attitude change among Soviet Obkum elites." Paper presented at the annual meeting of the American Political Science Association, Chicago.

BLAU, ZENA. 1961. "Structural constraints on friendship in old age." American Sociological Review 26:429-39.

————. 1973. Old Age in a Changing Society. New York: New Viewpoints.

BLAUNER, ROBERT. 1968. "Death and social structure." Pp. 531-40 in Bernice L. Neugarten (ed.), Middle Age and Aging. Chicago: University of Chicago Press.

BLENKNER, MARGARET. 1965. "Social work and family relationships in later life with some thoughts of filial maturity." Pp. 46-59 in Ethel Shanas and Gordon Streib (eds.), Social Structure and the Family: Generational Relations. Englewood Cliffs, N.J.: Prentice-Hall.

BLOOD, ROBERT O. 1967. Love Match and Arranged Marriage: A Tokyo-Detroit Comparison. New York: Free Press.

BLOOD, ROBERT and DONALD WOLFE. 1960. Husbands and Wives. New York: Free Press.

BLUMER, HERBERT. 1954. "What is wrong with social theory?" American Sociological Review 19:3-10.

BONNEL, GEORGE C. 1971. "The pastor's role in counseling the bereaved." Pastoral Psychology 22:27-36.

BOSKIN, MICHAEL J. 1977. "Social security: The alternatives before the U.S." Pp. 173-88 in Michael J. Boskin (ed.), The Crisis of Social Security. San Francisco: Institute of Comparative Studies.

BREUER, J. and S. FREUD. 1895. Studien über Hysterie. Leipzig: Deuticke.

BROTZ, EDWARD S. 1968. "Retirement and the individual." Journal of the American Geriatrics Society 16:1-15.

BROWN, R.G. 1970. "Family structure and social isolation of older persons." Pp. 270-77 in Erdman Palmore (ed.), Normal Aging. Durham, N.C.: Duke University Press.

BUCHER, R. and J. G. STELLING. 1977. Becoming Professional. Beverly Hills, Calif.: Sage Publications, Inc.

BUREAU OF CONSUMER PROTECTION, FEDERAL TRADE COMMISSION. 1978. "Funeral Industry Practices." Final Staff Report to the Federal Trade Commission. Washington, D.C.: U.S. Government Printing Office.

BURGESS, ERNEST W. 1960. Aging in Western Societies. Chicago: University of Chicago Press.

BURTON, ARTHUR. 1978. "Attitudes toward death of scientific authorities on death." The Psychoanalytic Review 65:415-32.

BUTLER, D. and D. STOKES. 1971. Political Change in Britain. New York: St. Martins Press.

BUTLER, R.N. 1964. "The life review: An interpretation of reminiscence in the aged." Pp. 265-80 in R. Kastenbaum (ed.), New Thoughts on Old Age. New York: Springer-Verlag.

BUTLER, ROBERT N. and MYRNA LEWIS. 1977. Aging and Mental Health: Positive Psychosocial Approaches. St. Louis: C.V. Mosby.

CAMERON, PAUL, L. STEWART and H. BIBER. 1973. "Consciousness of death across the life span." Journal of Gerontology 28:92-95.

CAMPBELL, A. 1971. "Politics through the life cycle." Gerontologist 11:112-17.

CAPPON, D. 1970. "Attitudes on death." Omega 1:103-8.

CAUGHILL, RITA E. 1976. The Dying Patient. Boston: Little Brown.

CHORON, JACQUES. 1964. Death and Modern Man. New York: Collier Books.

CLARK, MARGARET. 1972. "An anthropological view of retirement." In Frances Carp (ed.), Retirement. New York: Behavioral Publications.

CLARK, MARGARET and BARBARA ANDERSON. 1967. Culture and Aging. Springfield, Ill.: Chas. C Thomas.

CLAYTON, PAULA. 1973. "Anticipatory grief and widowhood." British Journal of Psychiatry 122:47-51.

_____. 1974. "Mourning and depression: Their similarities and differences." Canadian Psychiatric Association Journal 19:309-12.

_____. 1975. "The effect of living alone on bereavement symptoms." American Journal of Psychiatry 132:133-37.

CLEMENTE, FRANK. 1975. "Age and the perception of national priorities." Gerontologist 15:61-63.

COE, R.M. 1971. Sociology of Medicine. New York: McGraw-Hill.

CONOVER, P.W. 1975. "An analysis of communes and intentional communities with particular attention to sexual and genderal relations." Family Coordinator 24:453-64.

CONVERSE, P.E., W. MILLER, J. RUSK and A. WOLFE. 1969. "Continuity and change in American politics: Parties and issues in the 1968 election." American Political Science Review 63:1083-105.

COTTRELL, FRED and ROBERT C. ATCHLEY. 1969. Women in Retirement: A Preliminary Report. Oxford, Ohio: Scripps Foundation for Research in Population Problems.

COWAN, EDWARD. 1977. "Background and history." Pp. 1-15 in Michael J. Boskin (ed.), The Crisis in Social Security. San Francisco: Institute of Contemporary Studies.

COWGILL, DONALD O. and LOWELL D. HOLMES (Eds.). 1972. Aging and Modernization. New York: Appleton-Century-Crofts.

CROOG, S.H. and D.F. VER STEG. 1972. "The hospital as a social system." Pp. 274-318 in H.E. Freeman, Sol Levine, & Leo G. Reeder, (eds,), Handbook of Medical Sociology. Englewood Cliffs, N.J.: Prentice-Hall.

CUMMING, ELAINE. 1963. "Further thoughts on the theory of disengagement." UNESCO International Social Science Bulletin 15:377-93.

CUMMING, ELAINE and WILLIAM E. HENRY. 1961. Growing Old: The Process of Disengagement. New York: Basic Books.

CUMMING, ELAINE and DAVID M. SCHNEIDER. 1961. "Sibling solidarity: A property of American kinship." American Anthropologist 63:498-507.

CZUDNOWSKI, MOSHE. 1975. "Political recruitment." Pp. 115-242 in Fred I. Greenstein and Nelson W. Polsby (eds.), Handbook of Political Science. Volume 2. Reading Mass.: Addison-Wesley.

deBEAUVOIR, SIMONE. 1972. The Coming of Age. New York: Putnam's.

DENTON, J.A. and V.B. WEISENBACKER. 1977. "Death experience and death anxiety among nurses and nursing students." Nursing Research 26:61-64.

DEUTSCH, KARL W. 1970. Politics and Government. New York: Houghton Mifflin.

DIRSCHAUER, K. 1973. Der totgeschwiegene Tod. Bremen, West Germany: Schüneman Universitäts-Verlag.

DONAHUE, WILMA, HAROLD L. ORBACH and OTTO POLLAK. 1960. "Retirement: The emerging social pattern." In Clark Tibbetts (ed.), Handbook of Social Gerontology. Chicago: University of Chicago Press.

DRUCKER, PETER. 1971. "What can we learn from Japanese management?" Harvard Business Review 49:110-22.

DURKHEIM, EMILE. [1893] 1947. The Division of Labor, Glencoe, Ill.: Free Press.

DYER, L.D. 1973. "Implications of job displacement at mid-career." Industrial Gerontology 17:38-46.

EISDORFER, CARL. 1972. "Adaptation to loss of work." Pp. 245-46 in Frances Carp (ed.), Retirement. New York: Behavioral Publications.

EISENSTADT, SHMUL N. 1964. From Generation to Generation. New York: Free Press.

————. 1971. Social Differentiation and Stratification. Glenview, Ill.: Scott, Foresman.

ELLISON, DAVID L. 1969. "Will to live: A link between social structure and health among the elderly." Sociological Symposium (Spring):37-47.

ENGEL, G.L. 1961. "Is grief a disease? A challenge for medical research." Psychosomatic Medicine 23:18-22.

ERIKSON, ERIK H. 1959. "Identity and the life-cycle." Psychological Issues 1, Monograph No. 1.

FASCHINGBAUER,T.R., RICHARD A. DEVARL and SIDNEY ZISCOOK. 1977. "Development of the Texas inventory of grief." American Journal of Psychiatry 134:1696-98.

FEDER, S. 1965. "Attitudes of patients with advanced malignancy." Group for the Advancement of Psychiatry, Symposium 11.

FEIFEL, H. 1963. "The taboo on death." American Behavioral Scientist 6:66-67.

————. 1965. "The function of attitudes toward death." Group for the Advancement of Psychiatry, Symposium 11.

————. 1973. "Death and dying in Contemporary America." Pp. 37-47 in Tom Hick (ed.), Grief: Its Recognition and Resolution. University Park, Penn.: Pennsylvania State University.

FELDMAN, HAROLD. 1964. Development of the Husband-Wife Relationship. Department of Child Development and Family Relationships, New York State College of Home Economics, Cornell University.

FINER, S.E. 1958. "Interest groups and the political process in Britain." Pp. 117-44 in H.W. Ehrmann (ed.), Interest Groups on Four Continents. Pittsburgh: University of Pittsburgh Press.

FISHER, P. 1973. "Major social security issues: Japen, 1972." Social Security Bulletin 36:26-38.

FLEISHNER, EVA (Ed.). 1974. Auschwitz: Beginning of a New Era? New York: KTAV.

FLUGEL, J.C. 1945. Man, Morals, and Society. New York: International Universities Press.

FOLTA, J.R. and E.S. DECK. 1976. "Grief, the funeral, and the friend," Pp. 231-40 in V.R. Pine et al. (eds.), Acute Grief and the Funeral. Springfield, Ill.: Chas. C Thomas.

FONER, ANNE. 1972. "The polity." Pp. 115-59 in Matilda White Riley, Anne Foner, Mary E. Moore, Beth Heso, and Barbara K. Roth (eds.), Aging and Society. Volume 3. New York: Russell Sage Foundation.

FOREST, JACK D. 1963. "The major emphasis of the funeral." Pastoral Psychology 14:19-24.

FOX, ALAN. 1974. "Earnings replacement from social security and private pensions: Newly entitled beneficiaries, 1970." U.S. Department of Health, Education, and Welfare, Social Security Administration, Office of Research and Statistics, Report No. 13, Washington, D.C.

_____ 1976. "Work status and income change, 1968-1972: Retirement history study preview." U.S. Department of Health, Education, and Welfare, Social Security Administration, Retirement History Study Report No. 10, Washington, D.C.

FOX, RENÉE C. 1959. Experiment Perilous. Glencoe, Ill.: Free Press.

FOX, RENÉE C. and J. P. SWAZEY. 1974. The Courage to Fail: A Social View of Organ Transplants. Chicago: University of Chicago Press.

FREE, L. and H. CANTRIL. 1968. The Political Beliefs of Americans: A Study of Public Opinion. New York: Simon & Schuster.

FREEDMAN, EUGENE and ROBERT J. HAVIGHURST (Eds.). 1954. The Meaning of Work and Retirement. Chicago: University of Chicago Press.

FREIDSON, ELIOT. 1970. Profession of Medicine. New York: Harper & Row, Pub.

_____ 1973. "The organization of medical practice." Pp. 343-58 in H.E. Freeman, Sol Levine and Leo G. Reader, (eds.), Handbook of Medical Sociology. Englewood Cliffs, N.J.: Prentice-Hall.

FREUD, SIGMUND. [1915] 1959. "Thoughts on war and death." P. 275 in James Strachey (ed.). Standard Edition. Volume 14. London: Hogarth Press.

_____ [1917] 1959. "Mourning and melancholia." P. 239 in James Strachey (ed.). Standard Edition. Volume 12. London: Hogarth Press.

_____ [1926] 1959. "Inhibitions, Symptoms, and anxiety." P. 87 in James Strachey (ed.). Standard Edition. Volume 20. Hogarth Press.

_____ [1927] 1964. The Future of an Illusion. Garden City, N.Y.: Anchor Books.

FRIIS, H. 1969. "Issues in social security policies in Denmark." Pp. 129-50 in Shirley Jenkins (ed.), Social Security in International Perspective. New York: Columbia University Press.

FROMM, ERICH. 1950. Psychoanalysis and Religion. New Haven, Conn.: Yale University Press.

FULTON, ROBERT L. 1961. "The clergyman and the funeral directory: A study in role conflict." Social Forces 39:317-23.

_____ 1967. "On the dying of death." Pp. 31-47 in E. Grollman (ed.), Explaining Death to Children. Boston: Beacon Press.

_____ 1976. "The traditional funeral and contemporary society." Pp. 23-31 in V.R. Pine et al. (eds.), Acute Grief and the Funeral. Springfield, Ill.: Chas. C Thomas.

FULTON, ROBERT L. and GILBERT GEIS. 1968. "Social change and social conflict: The rabbi and the funeral director." Sociological Symposium 1:1-9.

GEALY, FRED G. 1963. "The Biblical understanding of death." Pastoral Psychology 14:33-40.

GERSHUNY, J. 1978. After Industrial Society: The Emerging Self-Service Economy. Atlantic Highlands, N.J.: Humanitarian Press.

GIBSON, ROBERT M.   1977.   "Age differences in health care expenditures, fiscal year 1976." Social Security Bulletin 40:3-14.

GLASER, BARNEY and ANSELM L. STRAUSS.   1965.   Awareness of Dying. Chicago: Aldine.

———.   1968.   Time for Dying. Chicago: Aldine.

GLASER, WILLIAM A.   1970.   Social Settings and Medical Organization. New York: Atherton Press.

GLASSCOTE, RAYMOND.   1976.   Old Folks At Home. Washington, D.C.: Joint Information Service of the American Psychiatric Association and the National Association for Mental Health.

GLENN, NORVAL.   1974.   "Aging and conservatism." Annals of the American Academy of Political Science 415: 176-86.

GLENN, NORVAL and M. GRIMES.   1968.   "Aging, voting, and political interest." American Sociological Review 33: 563-75.

GLENN, NORVAL and T. HEFFNER.   1972.   "Further evidence on aging and party identification." Public Opinion Quarterly 36: 31-47.

GLICK, IRA O., ROBERT S. WEISS and C. MURRAY PARKES.   1974.   The First Year of Bereavement. New York: Wiley Interscience.

GLICK, P.   1975.   "A demographic look at American families." Journal of Marriage and Family 37: 15-26.

GLICK, PAUL and ARTHUR J. NORTON.   1973.   "Perspectives on the recent upturn in divorce and remarriage." Demography 10: 301-14.

GLICK, P.C. and R. PARKE, Jr.   1965.   "New approaches in studying the life cycle of the family." Demography II: 187-202.

GLIDDEN, THOMAS.   1963.   "The American funeral." Pastoral Psychology 14:9-18.

GLOCK, C.Y. and R. STARK.   1965.   "Is there an American Protestantism?" Transaction 3:8-13.

GOLDSTEIN, SIDNEY.   1965.   "Changing income and consumption patterns of the aged, 1950-1960." Journal of Gerontology (October):453-61.

GOODE, WILLIAM J.   1963.   World Revolution and Family Patterns. Glencoe, Ill.: Free Press.

———   1964.   The Family. Englewood Cliffs, N.J.: Prentice-Hall.

GOODY, JACK.   1976.   "Aging in nonindustrial societies." Pp. 117-29 in Robert H. Binstock and Ethel Shanas (eds.), Handbook of Aging and the Social Sciences. New York: Van Nostrand Reinhold.

GORDON, MARGARET.   1963.   "Income security programs and the propensity to retire." Pp. 436-58 in Richard H. Williams, Clark Tibbetts and Wilma Donahue, (eds.), Processes of Aging. New York: Atherton Press.

GORER, G.   1955.   "The pornography of death." Encounter 5:49-52.

GRAHAM, S. and L.G. REEDER.   1972.   "Social factors in chronic illness." Pp. 63-107 in H.E. Freeman, Sol Levine, & Leo G. Reeder, (eds.), Handbook of Medical Sociology. Englewood Cliffs, N.J.: Prentice Hall.

GREENOUGH, WILLIAM and FRANCIS KING.   1976.   Pension Plans and Public Policy. New York: Columbia University Press.

GUBRIUM, JABER F.   1974.   "Review of Streib and Schneider, retirement in American society, Carp, retirement." Contemporary Sociology 2: 79-82.

_____. 1975. Living and Dying at Murray Manor. New York: St. Martin's Press.

HAHN, ALOIS. 1968. Einstellungen zum Tod und Ihre Soziale Bedingtheit. Stuttgart, West Germany: F. Ehke Verlag.

HARRIS, LOUIS and ASSOCIATES. 1975. The Myth and Reality of Aging in America. Washington, D.C.: National Council on Aging.

HAVIGHURST, ROBERT J. 1960. "Life beyond family and work." Pp. 299-353 in Ernest W. Burgess (ed.), Aging in Western Societies. Chicago: University of Chicago Press.

HAVIGHURST, ROBERT J., JOE M.A. MUNNICHS, BERNICE L. NEUGARTEN and HANS THOMAS (Eds.). 1969. Adjustment to Retirement. Assen, Netherlands: Van Gorcum.

HAVIGHURST, ROBERT J., BERNICE L. NEUGARTEN and SHELDON S. TOBIN. 1968. "Disengagement and patterns of aging." Pp. 161-72 in Bernice L. Neugarten (ed.). Middle age and Aging. Chicago: University of Chicago Press.

HAUSER, PHILIP M. 1976. "Aging and world-wide population change." Pp. 59-86 in Robert H. Binstock and Ethel Shanas (eds.). Handbook of Aging and the Social Sciences. New York: Van Nostrand Reinhold.

HEAVEN, P. L. 1977. "Do authoritarians hold authoritarian attitudes?" Journal of Psychology 95: 169-71.

HECLO, H. 1974. Modern Social Politics in Britain and Sweden: From Relief to Income Maintenance. New Haven, Conn.: Yale University Press.

HEGEL, GEORG W. F. [1837] 1956. The Philosophy of History. New York: Dover.

HEIDBREDER, ELIZABETH. 1972. "Factors in retirement adjustment: White collar/blue collar experience." Industrial Gerontology 12: 69-79.

HEILBRONER, R.L. 1962. The making of Economic Society. Englewood Cliffs, N.J.: Prentice-Hall.

HENDRICKS, JON and C. DAVIS HENDRICKS. 1977. Aging in Mass Society, Myths and Realities. Cambridge, Mass.: Winthrop.

HENRETTA, JOHN C. and RICHARD T. CAMPBELL. 1976. "A study of stratification in old age." American Sociological Review 41: 981-92.

HENRY, WILLIAM F. 1963. "Theory of intrinsic disengagement." Paper delivered at the International Gerontological Research Seminar, Markaryd, Sweden.

HEYMAN, D.K. and D.T. GIANTURIO. 1973. "Long term adaptation by the elderly to bereavement." Journal of Gerontology 28: 359-62.

HIRSCH, D., D.P. KENT and S.L. SILVERMAN. 1972. "Homogeneity and heterogeneity among low-income negro and white aged." Pp. 484-500 in D.P. Kent, R. Kastenbaum, and S. Sherwood (eds.), Research Planning and Action for the Elderly: The Power and Potential of Social Sciences. New York: Behavioral Publications.

HOSCHSCHILD, A.R. 1975. "Disengagement theory: A critique and a proposal." American Sociological Review 40: 553-69.

HOGE, DEAN R. 1976. Division in the Protestant House. Philadelphia: Westminster Press.

HOLSCLAW, P.A. 1965. "Nursing in high emotional risk areas." Nursing Forum 4:36-45.

HOMANS, GEORGE C. 1961. Social Behavior: Its Elementary Forms. New York: Harcourt Brace & World.

HORLICK, MAX. 1974. "National expenditures on social security in selected countries, 1968 and 1971." U.S. Department of Health, Education, and Welfare, Social Security Administration, Office of Research and Statistics, Research Note No. 29, Washington, D. C.

HUDSON, ROBERT B. 1978. "Politics and aging." The Gerontologist 18: 428-40.

HUDSON, ROBERT B. and ROBERT H. BINSTOCK. 1976. "Political systems and aging." Pp. 369-400 in Robert H. Binstock and Ethel Shanas (eds.), Handbook of Aging and the Social Sciences. New York: Van Nostrand Reinhold.

HUTCHENS, GENE. 1976. "Grief therapy." Pp. 155-68 in Pine, V.R. et. al (eds.), Acute Grief and the Funeral. Springfield, Ill.: Chas. C Thomas.

INGLEHART, R. 1971. "The silent revolution in Europe: Intergenerational change in post-industrial societies." American Political Science Review 65: 991-1017.

INKELES, ALEX and DAVID H. SMITH. 1974. Becoming Modern. Cambridge, Mass.: Harvard University Press.

IRELAN, SOLA M. and KATHLEEN BOND. 1974. "Retirees of the 70's." Paper presented at Southern Conference on Gerontology (March).

IRION, PAUL. 1963. "In the midst of life . . . Death." Pastoral Psychology 14: 25-32.

————. 1973. "The church and the bereaved." Pp. 83-90 in Robert B. Reeves, Robert E. Neale, and Austin H. Kutscher, (eds.). Pastoral Care of the Dying and Bereaved. New York: Health Sciences Publications.

JACKSON, JACQUELYNE. 1972. "Marital life among aging blacks." Family Coordinator 21: 21-27.

————. 1973. "Family organization and ideology." In K. Miller and R. Dreger (eds.), Comparative Studies of Blacks and Whites. New York: Academic Press.

JAFFE, A. J. 1972. "The retirement dilemma." Journal of Industrial Gerontology 14: 1-89.

JEFFERS, F. C., C. R. NICHOLS and C. EISDORFER. 1961. "Attitudes of older persons toward death: A preliminary study." Journal of Gerontology 16: 53-56.

JEFFERS, F. C. and A. VERWOERDT. 1966. "Factors associated with frequency of death thoughts in elderly community volunteers." Proceedings of the Seventh International Congress of Gerontology 6: 149 (Vienna).

JENSEN, CLAYNE R. and GORDON W. SCHULTZ. 1970. Applied Kinesiology; The Scientific Study of Human Performance. New York: McGraw-Hill.

KAIM-CAUDLE, P. R. 1973. Comparative Social Policy and Social Security: A Ten-Country Study. New York: Dunnellen.

KALISH, R. A. 1970. "The onset of the dying process." Omega 1: 57-69.

KALISH, RICHARD A. and SHARON MORIWAKI. 1973. "The world of the elderly Asian American." Journal of Social Issues 29 (2): 187-209.

KALISH, R.A. and D.K. REYNOLDS. 1976. Death and Ethnicity: A Psychocultural Study. Los Angeles: University of Southern California Press.

KANE, R.L. and R.A. KANE. 1976. Long Term care in Six Countries. Washington, D.C.: U.S. Dept. of Health, Education and Welfare Publication No. (NIH) 76-1207.

KASTENBAUM, ROBERT J. 1977. Death, Society, and Human Experience. St. Louis. C.V. Mosby.

KASTENBAUM, ROBERT J. and R. AISENBERG. 1972. The Psychology of Death. New York: Springer-Verlag.

KATONA, GEORGE, JAMES N. MORGAN, and RICHARD E. BARFIELD. 1969. "Family patterns and morale in retirement." Pp. 173-94 in Ida H. Simpson and John E. McKinney (eds.), Social Aspects of Aging. Durham, N.C.: Duke University Press.

KERCKHOFF, ALAN C. 1966a. "Family patterns and morale in retirement." in Ida Simpson and John McKinney (eds.), Social Aspects of Aging. Durham, N.C.: Duke University Press.

_____. 1966b. "Husband-wife expectations and reactions to retirement." Pp. 160-72 in Ida Simpson and John McKinney (eds.), Social Aspects of Aging. Durham, N.C.: Duke University Press.

KHLEIF, B. 1976. "The Sociology of the mortuary: religion, sex, age, and kinship variables." Pp. 55-91 in Pine V.R. et al. (eds.), Acute Grief and the Funeral. Springfield, Ill.: Chas. C Thomas.

KING, A. 1971. "Ideologies as predictors of public opinion patterns: A comparative analysis." Paper delivered at the annual meeting of the American Political Science Association, New York.

KOMAROVSKY, MIRRA. 1964. Blue Collar Marriage. New York: Random House.

KRAUSS, IRVING. 1975. Stratification, Class and Conflict. New York: Free Press.

KREPS, JUANITA. 1976. "The economy and the aged." Pp. 272-85 in Robert H. Binstock and Ethel Shanas (eds.), Handbook of Aging and The Social Sciences. New York: Van Nostrand Reinhold.

_____. 1977. "Intergenerational transfers and the bureaucracy." Pp. 21-35 in Ethel Shanas and Marvin B. Sussman (eds.) Family, Bureaucracy and the Elderly. Durham, N.C.: Duke University Press.

KÜBLER-ROSS, ELIZABETH. 1969. On Death and Dying. New York: Macmillan.

_____. 1970. "The dying patient's point of view." Pp. 156-70 in O.G. Brim, Jr., Howard E. Freeman, Sol Levine, and Norman Scotch (eds.), The Dying Patient. New York: Russell Sage Foundation.

KUYPERS, JOSEPH A. and VERN L. BENGSTON. 1973. "Social breakdown and competence: A model of normal aging." Human Development 16: 181-201.

KUZNETS, SIMON. 1966. Modern Economic Growth: Rate, Structure, and Spread. New Haven, Conn.: Yale University Press.

LACK, S. and ROBERT BUCKINGHAM. 1978. The First American Hospice. New Haven, Conn.: Department of Public Information, Hospice Inc.

LAROQUE, PIERRE. 1975. "The age of retirement: Social and economic aspects." Vie Sociale 8: 480-503.

LASAGNA, L. 1970. "Physicians' behavior toward the dying patient." Pp.

83-101 in O.G. Brim, Jr., Howard E. Freeman, Sol Levine, and Norman Scotch, (eds). The Dying Patient. New York: Russell Sage Foundation.

LASLETT, PETER. Forthcoming. The European family pattern and socialization process.

———— 1977. "Societal development and aging." Pp. 87-116 in Robert A. Binstock, and Ethel Shanas (eds.), Handbook of Aging and the Social Sciences. New York: Van Nostrand Reinhold.

LAUFER, ARTHUR C. and WILLIAM M. FOWLERS, Jr. 1971. "Work potential of the aging." Personnel Administration (March-April): 20-25.

LEE, GARY R. 1977. Family Structure and Interaction: A Comparative Analysis. Philadelphia: Lippincott.

LERNER, JEFFREY C. 1975. "Changes in attitudes toward death: The widow in Great Britain in the early twentieth century." Pp. 91-117 in B. Schoenberg, Irwin Gerber, Alfred Wiener, Austin H. Kutscher, David Peretz and Arthur C. Carr (eds.), Bereavement, Its Psychological Aspects. New York: Columbia University Press.

LESTER, D. and GENE W. BROCKOPP. 1974. "Attitudes of nursing students and nursing faculty toward death." Nursing Research 23: 50-53.

LEVY, MARION. 1969. Colloquium on the Family, University of Toronto, Toronto, Canada.

LINDER, STAFFAN B. 1970. The Harried Leisure Class. New York: Columbia University Press.

LINN, S. 1975. "A survey of the 'care-cure' attitudes of physicians, nurses, and their students." Nursing Forum 14: 145-59.

LIPSET, SEYMOUR M. 1959. Political Man: The Social Bases of Politics. New York: Doubleday.

LITMAN, T. J. 1971. "Health care and the family: A three-generational-analysis." Medical Care 9: 67-81.

LITVAK. 1960. "Geographical mobility and extended family cohesion." American Sociological Review 25:385-94.

LIVINGSTONE, P. B. and C. N. ZIMET. 1965. "Death anxiety, authoritarianism, and choice of specialty in medical students." Journal of Nervous and Mental Disease 140: 220-30.

LOPATA, H.Z. 1973. Widowhood in an American City. Cambridge, Mass.: Schenkman.

LOWENTHAL, MARJORIE F., PAUL L. BERKMAN, and GERALD G. BRISSETTE. 1967. Aging and Mental Disorder in San Francisco. San Francisco: Jossey-Bass.

LOWENTHAL, MARJORIE F. and C. HAVEN. 1968. "Interaction and adaptation: Intimacy as a critical variable." American Sociological Review 33: 20-30.

LOWENTHAL, MARJORIE F. and BETSY ROBINSON. 1967. "Social networks and isolation." Pp. 432-56 in Robert H. Binstock and Ethel Shanas (eds.), Handbook of Aging and the Social Sciences. New York: Van Nostrand Reinhold.

LOWY, LOUIS. 1979. Social Work with the Aging: The Challenge and the Promise of the Later Years. New York: Harper & Row.

MAAS, H.S., and J.A. KUYPERS.   1974.   From Thirty to Seventy. San Francisco: Jossey-Bass.

MADDISON, D. and B. RAPHAEL.   1975.   "Conjugal bereavement and the social network." Pp. 26-40 in B. Schoenberg, and Irwin Gerber (eds.). Bereavement, Its Psychological Aspects. New York: Columbia University Press.

MADDOX, GEORGE L.   1966.   "Persistence of life-style among the elderly." Proceedings of the Seventh International Congress of Gerontology 6: 309-11 (Vienna).

_____.   1968.   "Persistence of life-style among the elderly." Pp. 181-83 in Bernice L. Neugarten (ed.). Middle Age and Aging. Chicago: University of Chicago Press.

_____.   1970.   "Themes and issues in sociological theories of human aging." Human Development 13 (1): 17-27.

_____.   1974.   "Is senior power the wave of the future?" Paper delivered at the annual meeting of the American Association of the Advancement of Science.

MAGUIRE, DANIEL C.   1975.   Death by Choice. New York: Schocken Books.

MARRIS, PETER.   1958.   Widows and Their Families. London: Routledge & Kegan Paul.

_____.   1974.   Loss and Change. London: Routledge & Kegan Paul.

MARSHALL, T.H.   1965.   Class, Citizenship, and Social Development. Garden City, N.Y.: Doubleday.

MARTIN, W., V. BENGSTON and A. ACOCK.   1973.   "Alienation and age: A context specific approach." Social Forces 54: 67-84.

MARX, KARL.   [1848] 1954.   The Communist Manifesto. Chicago: Henry Regnery.

MAUSS, MARCEL.   [1925] 1967.   The Gift. New York: W.W. Norton & Co., Inc.

McCOURT, WILLIAM F. et al.   1976.   "We help each other: Primary prevention for the widowed." American Journal of Psychiatry 133: 98-100.

McEWAN, PETER J.M. and ALAN P. SHELDON.   1969.   "Patterns of retirement and related variables." Journal of Geriatric Psychiatry 3: 35-54.

McKAIN, WALTER.   1972.   "A new look at older marriages." Family Coordinator 21: 61-69.

McKENZIE, R. and A. SILVER.   1968.   Angels in Marble: Working Class Conservatives in Urban England. Chicago: Chicago University Press.

McMAHON, A.W., Jr. and P.J. RHUDICK.   1967.   "Reminiscing in the aged: An adaptational response." Pp 64-78 in S. Levin and R.J. Kahana (eds.), Psychodynamic Studies on Aging: Creativity, Reminiscence, and Dying. New York: International Universities Press.

McTAVISH, D.   1971.   "Perceptions of old people: A review of research methodologies and findings." Gerontologist 11(Part II): 90-101.

MENG, HEINRICH and ERNST L. FREUD.   1963.   Psychoanalysis and Faith. New York: Basic Books.

MICHELS, ROBERT.   [1911] 1949.   Political Parties. Glencoe, Ill.: Free Press.

MILLER, STEPHEN J. 1965. "The social dilemma of the aging leisure participant." Pp. 72-92 in Arnold M. Rose and Warren A. Peterson (eds.), Older People and Their Social World. Philadelphia: F.A. Davis.

MILLER, S. 1970. Prescription for Leadership. Chicago: Aldine.

MITFORD, JESSICA. 1963. The American Way of Death. New York: Fawcett Books Group-CBS Publications.

MOODY, R.A. 1976. Life After Death. New York: Bantam Books.

MONRONEY, ROBERT M. 1977. The Family and the State. London-New York: Longman.

MORRIS, ROBERT. 1969. "Aging and the field of social work" in Matilda Riley, Anne Foner, Mary E. Moore, Beth Hess and Barbara K. Roth, (eds.), Aging and Society, Volume 2. New York: Russell Sage Foundation.

MUMFORD, E. 1970. Interns: From Students to Physicians. Cambridge, Mass.: Harvard University Press.

MUNNELL, ALICIA. 1977. The Future of Social Security. Washington, D.C.: Brookings Institution.

MUNNICHS, JOEP M.A. 1977. "Linkages of old people with their families and bureaucracy in a welfare state, the Netherlands." Pp. 92-116 in Ethel Shanes and Marvin B. Sussman (eds.), Family, Bureaucracy, and the Elderly. Durham, N.C.: Duke University Press.

MURDOCK, GEORGE P. 1949. Social Structure. New York: Macmillan.

————. 1967. Ethnographic Atlas. Pittsburgh: University of Pittsburg Press.

MURRAY, ROGER F. 1967. "Economic aspects of pensions: A summary report." In U.S. Joint Economic Committee, Old Age Income Assurance, Part 5. Washington, D.C.: U.S. Government Printing Office.

MYERS, ROBERT J. 1975. Social Security. Homewood, Ill.: Richard D. Trush.

NADELSON, THEODORE. 1969. "A survey of the literature on the adjustment of the aged to retirement." Journal of Geriatric Psychiatry 3: 3-20.

NELSON, BENJAMIN. 1949. The Idea of Usury: From Tribal Brotherhood to Universal Otherhood. Princeton: N.J.: Princeton University Press.

NEUGARTEN, BERNICE L. 1974. "Age in American society and the rise of the young-old." Annals of the American Academy, September: 187-98.

NEUGARTEN, BERNICE L. and KAROL K. WEINSTEIN. 1964. "The changing American grandparent." Journal of Marriage and the Family 26: 199-204.

NIE, N., S. VERBA and J. KIM. 1974. "Political participation and the life cycle." Comparative Politics 6: 319-40.

NORTH, R. and J. POOL. 1966. "Kuomintang and Chinese communist elites." Pp. 319-455 in Harold Lasswell and Daniel Lerner (eds.), World Revolutionary Elites: Studies in Coercive Ideological Movements. Cambridge, Mass.: M.I.T. Press.

NOYES, RUSSELL, Jr. and ROY KLETTI. 1976. "Depersonalization in the face of life-threatening danger: An interpretation." Omega 7: 103-14.

OKEN, D. 1961. "What to tell cancer patients: A study of medical attitudes." Journal of the American Medical Association 175: 1120-128.

OLSEN, MARVIN E. and J.C. TULLY. 1974. "Socio-economic ethnic status inconsistency and preference for political change." American Sociological Review 37: 560-74.

ORBACH, HAROLD L., CLARK TIBBETTS and WILMA DONAHUE. 1969. Trends in Early Retirement. Ann Arbor: University of Michigan, Wayne State University Institute of Gerontology.

PAILLAT, P. 1977. "Bureaucratization of old age: Determinants of the process, possible safeguards, and reorientation." Pp. 60-74 in Ethel Shanas and Marvin B. Sussman (eds.), Family, Bureaucracy and the Elderly. Durham, N.C.: Duke University Press.

PALMORE, ERDMAN. 1964. "Retirement patterns among aged men: Findings of the 1963 survey of the aged." Social Security Bulletin 27(8): 3-10.

————. 1972. "Compulsory versus flexible retirement: Issues and facts." Gerontologist 12: 343-48.

————. 1975. The Honorable Elders. Durham, N.C.: Duke University Press.

PALMORE, ERDMAN B. and KENNETH MANTON. 1973. "Ageism compared to racism and sexism." Journal of Gerontology 38: 353-69.

PARKES, COLIN MURRAY. 1972. Bereavement. New York: International Universities Press.

PARKES, C.M., B. BENJAMIN and A. FITZGERALD. 1969. "Broken heart: A statistical study of increased mortality among widowers." British Medical Journal 1: 740.

PARKIN, FRANK. 1971. Class Inequality and Political Order. New York: Praeger.

PARSONS, DONALD O. and DOUGLAS R. MUNROE. 1977. "Intergenerational transfers." Pp. 65-86 in Michael J. Boskin (ed.), The Crisis in Social Security. San Francisco: Institute of Contemporary Studies.

PARSONS, TALCOTT. 1951. The Social System. Glencoe, Ill.: Free Press.

PARSONS, TALCOTT and ROBERT F. BALES. 1955. Family Socialization and Interaction Process. Glencoe, Ill.: Free Press.

PARSONS, TALCOTT and RENÉE FOX. 1952. "Illness and the modern American family." Journal of Social Issues 8: 31-34.

PARSONS, TALCOTT, RENÉE C. FOX and VICTOR LIDZ. 1972. "The gift of life and its reciprocation." Social Research 39: 367-415.

PARSONS, TALCOTT and VICTOR LIDZ. 1967. "Death in American Society." Pp. 133-70 in Edwin S. Shneidman (ed.), Essays in Self-destruction. New York: Science House.

PARSONS, TALCOTT and GERALD PLATT. 1972. "Higher education and changing socialization." Pp. 236-291 in Matilda White Riley, Marilyn E. Johnson, Anne Foner, Aging and Society. Volume 3, A Sociology of Age Stratification. New York: Russell Sage Foundation.

PATTISON, E. MANSELL. 1977. The Experience of Dying. Englewood Cliffs, N.J.: Prentice-Hall.

PINE, V.R. and D.L. PHILLIPS. 1970. "The cost of dying: a sociological analysis of funeral expenditures." Social Problems 17: 405-17.

PINE, V.R. et al. (eds.).   1976.   Acute Grief and the Funeral. Springfield, Ill.: Charles C Thomas.

PIOTROWSKI, JERZY.   1977.   "Old people, bureaucracy, and the family in Poland." Pp. 158-73 in Ethel Shanas and Marvin B. Sussman (eds.), Family, Bureaucracy, and the Elderly. Durham, N.C.: Duke University Press.

PLATH, D. W.   1972.   "Japan: The after years." Pp. 130-50 in D.O. Cowgill and L.D. Holmes (eds.). Aging and Modernization. New York: Appleton-Century-Croft.

POLACK, P.R.   1975.   "Prevention in mental health: A controlled study." American Journal of Psychiatry 132: 146-48.

POPOFF, D.   1975.   "What are your feelings about death and dying?" Nursing '75, 5 (August): 15-25; (September): 55-62; (October): 39-50.

PRATT, H.J.   1974.   "Old age associations in national politics." Annals of the American Academy of Political and Social Science 415: 106-19.

_____. 1976. The Politics of Old Age. Chicago: University of Chicago Press.

PUTNAM, J.K.   1970.   Old-Age Politics in California: From Richardson to Reagan. Stanford, Calif.: Stanford University Press.

QUINT, JEANNE C.   1967.   The Nurse and the Dying Patient. New York: Macmillan.

RADCLIFFE-BROWN, A. R.   1952.   Structure and Functions in Primitive Society; Essays and Addresses. Glencoe, Ill.: Free Press.

RAINWATER, LEE.   1974.   What Money Buys: Inequality and the Social Meaning of Money. New York: Basic Books.

RAMEY, J.W.   1975.   "Intimate groups and networks: Frequency consequences of sexually open marriage." Family Coordinator 24: 515-30.

REA, M.P.   1975.   "Physicians and the terminal patient: Some selected attitudes and behavior." Omega 6: 291-301.

RICH, T. and G.M. KALMANSON.   1966.   "Attitudes of medical residents to the dying patient in a general hospital." Postgraduate Medicine 40: 127-130.

RILEY, MATILDA WHITE.   1971.   "Social gerontology and the age stratification of society." The Gerontologist 11: 79-88.

RILEY, MATILDA WHITE and ANNE FONER.   1968.   Aging and Society. Volume 1. New York: Russell Sage Foundation.

ROGERS, WILLIAM F.   1973a.   "The pastor's work with grief." Pp. 91-97 in R.B. Reeves, Robert E. Neale, and Austin H. Kutscher, (eds.), Pastoral Care of the Dying and Bereaved. New York: Health Sciences Publications.

_____.   1973b.   "The relationship of the funeral to counseling the bereaved." Pp. 99-104 in R.B. Reeves, Robert E. Neale and Austin H. Kutscher, (eds.), Pastoral Care of the Dying and Bereaved. New York: Health Sciences Publications.

ROLLINS, BOYD and HAROLD FELDMAN.   1970.   "Marital satisfaction over the family life cycle." Journal of Marriage and the Family 32: 20-28.

ROSE, ARNOLD M.   1965.   "The subculture of aging: A framework of research in social gerontology." Pp. 3-16 in Arnold M. Rose and Warren R. Peterson (eds.), Older People and Their Social World. Philadelphia: F.A. Davis.

ROSE, CHARLES L. and **JOHN M. MAGEY.** 1972. "Aging and preference for later retirement." Aging and Human Development 3: 45-62.

ROSEN, SHERWIN. 1977. "Social security and the economy." Pp 87-106 in Michael Boskin J. (ed.), The Crisis in Social Security. San Francisco: Institute of Comparative Studies.

ROSENBERG, GEORGE and **DONALD ANSPACH.** 1973. Working Class Kinship. Lexington, Mass.: Lexington Books.

ROSENMAYER, L. and **E. KOCKEIS.** 1965. Unwelt and Familie Alter Menschen. Berlin: Luchterland-Verlag.

ROSOW, IRVING. 1967. Social Integration of the Aged. New York: Free Press.

_____. 1974. Socialization to Old Age. Berkeley and Los Angeles: University of California Press.

ROSSMAN, PARKER. 1977. Hospice. New York: Association Press.

ROSTOW, W.W. 1960. The Stages of Economic Growth. Cambridge, Mass.: Harvard University Press.

SAGAN, CARL. 1979. "The amniotic universe." Atlantic Monthly 243 (April): 39-45.

SALOMONE, J. 1968. "An empirical report on some controversial funeral practices." Sociological Symposium (Fall): 47-56.

SAUNDERS, CICELY. 1976. "St. Christopher's hospice." Pp. 516-23 in Edwin S. Shneidman (ed.), Death: Current Perspectives. Palo Alto, Calif.: Mayfield Publishing.

SCHLESINGER, J.A. 1967. "Political careers and party leadership." Pp. 266-93 in L. Edinger (ed.), Political Leadership in Industrial Societies. New York: John Wiley.

SCHMALE, A.H., Jr. and **G.L. ENGEL.** 1967. "The giving up-given up complex illustrated on film." Archives of General Psychiatry 17:135-45.

SCHULZ, JAMES et al. 1974. Providing Adequate Retirement Income. Hanover, N.J.: Dartsmouth University Press.

_____. 1976a. The Economics of Aging. Belmont, Calif.: Wadsworth.

_____. 1976b. "Income distribution and the aging." Pp. 561-91 in Robert H. Binstock and Ethel Shanas (eds.), Handbook of Aging and the Social Sciences. New York: Van Nostrand Reinhold.

SCHULZ, R. and **D. ADERMAN.** 1976. "How the medical staff copes with dying patients: A critical review." Omega 7: 11-21.

SCHWAB, KAREN. 1974. "Early labor force withdrawal of men: Participants and non-participants aged 58-62." Social Security Bulletin (August).

SCHWAB, J.J. 1976. "Funeral behavior and unresolved grief." Pp. 241-48 in V.R. Pine, A.H. Kutscher, D. Aeretz, A.C. Shater, A. DeBellis, A.J. Volk, and Daniel J. Cherio (eds.), Acute Grief and the Funeral. Springfield, Ill.: Charles C Thomas.

SHANAS, ETHEL. 1962. The Health of Older People: A Social Survey. Cambridge, Mass.: Harvard University Press.

_____. 1967. "Family help patterns and social class in three countries." Journal of Marriage and the Family 29: 257-66.

SHANAS, ETHEL and MARVIN B. SUSSMAN. 1977. Family, Bureaucracy, and the Elderly. Durham, N.C.: Duke University Press.

SHANAS, ETHEL, et al. 1968. Old People in Three Industrial Societies. New York: Atherton Press.

SHELDON, H.D. 1960. "The changing demographic profile." Pp. 27-61 in Clark Tibbitts (ed.), Handbook of Social Gerontology. Chicago: University of Chicago Press.

SHEPPARD, HAROLD L. 1972. Where Have All the Robots Gone?— Worker Dissatisfaction in the 1970's. New York: Free Press.

————— 1976. "Work and retirement." Pp. 286-309 in Robert H. Binstock and Ethel Shanas (eds.), Handbook of Aging and the Social Sciences. New York: Van Nostrand Reinhold.

SHIBLES, W. 1974. Death: An Interdisciplinary Analysis. Whitewater, Wis.: Language Press.

SHIMKIN, D.B. and E.M. SHIMKIN. 1975. The Extended Family in United States Black Societies: Findings and Problems. Unpublished paper, Department of Anthropology, University of Illinois, Urbana-Champaign.

SHNEIDMAN, EDWIN S. 1973. "A national survey of attitudes toward death." Pp. 201-24 in Edwin S. Schneidman (ed.), Deaths of Man. New York: Quadrangle/The N.Y. Times.

SHUSTERMAN, L.R. 1973. "Attitudes of registered nurses toward death in a general hospital." International Journal of Psychiatry in Medicine 4: 411-25.

SIKLOVA, JIRINA. 1974. Gerontology Centre, Thomayer Hospital. Prague: CSSR. MS.

SIMMONS, LEO W. 1945. The Role of the Aged in Primitive Society. London: Oxford University Press.

SIMPSON, IDA H., KURT W. BACK, and JOHN C. McKINNEY. 1966. "Orientation toward work and retirement, and self-evaluation in retirement." Pp. 75-89 in Ida H. Simpson, Kurt W. Back and John C. McKinney (eds.), Social Aspects of Aging. Durham, N.C.: Duke University Press.

SLATER, S., M.B. SUSSMAN, and M.W. STROUD, III. 1970. "Participation in household activities as a prognostic factor in rehabilitation." Archives of Physical and Medical Rehabilitation 51: 605-11.

SMOLIC-KRKOVIC, NADA. 1977. "Aging, bureaucracy and the family." Pp. 75-91 in Ethel Shanas and Marvin B. Sussman (eds.), Family, Bureaucracy and the Elderly. Durham, N.C.: Duke University Press.

SOMERVILLE, R.M. 1972. "The future of family relationships in the middle and older years." Family Coordinator 21: 487-98.

STANNARD, DAVID E. 1973. "Death and dying in Puritan New England." American Historical Review 78: 1305-30.

STEINER, PETER O. and ROBERT DORFMAN. 1957. The Economic Status of the Aged. Berkeley and Los Angeles: University of California Press.

STINNETT, N., LINDA CARTER and J.E. MONTGOMERY. 1972. "Older persons' perceptions of their marriages." Journal of Marriage and the Family 34: 665-70.

STODDARD, SANDOL. 1978. The Hospice Movement. Briarcliff Manor, N.Y.: Stein & Day.

STRAUSS, ANSELM L. and BARNEY G. GLASER. 1970. Anguish: A Case History of a Dying Trajectory. Mill Valley, Calif.: Sociology Press.

STREIB, GORDON F. 1977. "Bureaucracies and families: Common themes and directions for further study." Pp. 204-15 in Ethel Shanas and Marvin B. Sussman (eds.), Family, Bureaucracy and the Elderly. Durham, N.C.: Duke University Press.

STREIB, GORDON and C.J. SCHNEIDER. 1971. Retirement in American Society. New York: Cornell University Press.

SUDNOW, D. 1967. Passing On. Englewood Cliffs, N.J.: Prentice-Hall.

SUSSMAN, MARVIN B. 1960. "Intergenerational relationships and social role changes in middle age." Journal of Gerontology 15: 71-75.

_____. 1976. "The family life of old people." Pp. 218-43 in Robert H. Binstock and Ethel Shanas (eds.), Handbook of Aging and the Social Sciences. New York: Van Nostrand Reinhold.

_____. 1977. "Family, bureaucracy and the elderly individual: An organizational/linkage perspective." Pp. 2-20 in Ethel Shanas and Marvin B. Sussman (eds.), Family, Bureaucracy and the Elderly. Durhman, N.C.: Duke University Press.

SWANSON, GUY. 1968. "Modern secularity: Its meaning, sources, and interpretation." Pp. 801-34 in Donald R. Cutler (ed.), The Religious Situation: 1968. Boston: Beacon Press.

_____. 1978. "Trance and possession: Studies of charismatic influence." Review of Religious Research 19: 253-78.

SWEETSER, DORIAN A. 1963. "Asymmetry in intergenerational family relationships." Social Forces 41: 346-52.

SWENSON, W.M. 1961. "Attitudes toward death in an aged population." Journal of Gerontology 16: 49-52.

TAKENAKA, KAZURO. 1974. "The problems of the aged and community development in Japan." Paper read at the Eighth Congress of the International Sociological Association, Toronto, Canada.

TECHNICZEK, DOROTA. 1969. "The Warsaw teachers and steelworkers." Pp. 86-94 in Robert J. Havighurst, Joep M. A. Munnicks, Beatrice L. Neugarten and Hans Thomas, (eds.), Adjustment to Retirement. Assen, Netherlands: Van Gorcum.

TEMPLER, D. et al. 1976. "The death anxiety of those who work in funeral homes." Pp. 174-78 in Pine V.R., et al. (eds.), Acute Grief and the Funeral. Springfield, Ill.: Chas. C Thomas.

THOMLINSON, RALPH. 1965. Population Dynamics: Causes and Consequences of World Demographic Change. New York: Random House.

THOMPSON, GAYLE B. 1973. "Income of the aged population: 1971 money income and changes from 1967." U.S. Department of Health, Education and Welfare, Social Security Administration, Research and Statistics Note No. 14, Washington, D.C.

THOMPSON, WAYNE E., GORDON F. STREIB and JOHN KOSA. 1960. "The effect of retirement on personal adjustment: A panel analysis." Journal of Gerontology 15: 165-69.

THORSON, J.A., L. WHATLEY and K.G. KANCOCK. 1974. "Attitudes toward the aged as a function of age and education." Gerontologist 14: 316-18.

TILLICH, PAUL.   1959.   "The eternal now." Pp. 30-38 in H. Feifel (ed.), The Meaning of Death. New York: McGraw-Hill.

TOFFLER, ALVIN.   1970.   Future Shock. New York: Random House.

TROJAN, J.A.   1972.   "Attitudes toward older employees working ·in industry." A Report of the Gerontology Centre, Thomayer Hospital, Prague, Czechoslovakia.

TROLL, LILLIAN E.   1970.   "Issues in the study of generations." Aging and Human Development 1: 199-218.

————.   1975.   Early and Middle Adulthood: The Best Is Yet to Be—Maybe. Monterey, Calif.: Brooks/Cole.

UJHELY, G.B.   1963.   "Grief and depression: Implications for preventive and therapeutic nursing care." Nursing Forum 5: 23-35.

UNITED NATIONS.   1962.   Sex and Age Patterns of Participation in Economic Activities. New York: United Nations, Department of Economic and Social Affairs, Demographic Aspects of Manpower.

————.   1971.   The World Population Situation in 1970. New York: United Nations, Department of Economic and Social Affairs, Population Studies, No. 49.

UNITED STATES BUREAU OF THE CENSUS.   1965.   Current Population Reports, No. 143. Washington, D.C.: U.S. Government Printing Office.

————   1973.   "Some demographic aspects of aging in the United States." Current Population Reports, Series P-23, No. 43. Washington, D.C.: U.S. Government Printing Office.

————.   1974.   Statistical Abstract of the United States: 1974. Washington, D.C.: U.S. Government Printing Office.

UNITED STATES DEPARTMENT OF HEALTH, EDUCATION and WELFARE. 1975.   Minority Health Book. Washington, D.C.: U.S. Government Printing Office.

————.   1965.   The Older American Worker: Age Discrimination in Employment.

————.   1969-70.   National Survey of Attitudes Toward Retirement. Ann Arbor: University of Michigan Survey Research Center.

UNITED STATES DEPARTMENT OF LABOR.   1974.   Manpower Report of the President.

UNITED STATES SOCIAL SECURITY ADMINISTRATION.   1972.   Social Security Bulletin: Annual Statistical Supplement. Washington, D.C.: U.S. Government Printing Office.

————.   1975.   Social Security Programs Throughout the World. Washington, D.C.: U.S. Government Printing Office.

VERNON, GLENN M.   1970.   The Sociology of Death. New York: Ronald Press.

VISCUSI, W.K. and R.J. ZECKHAUSER.   1977.   "The role of social security in income maintenance." Pp. 41-64 in Michael J. Boskin (ed.), The Crisis in Social Security. San Francisco: Institute for Comparative Studies.

VOGEL, EZRA.   1967.   Japan's New Middle Class. Berkeley and Los Angeles: University of California Press.

WACHTEL, H.   1966.   "Hard-core unemployment in Detroit: Causes and remedies." Pp. 233-41 in Proceedings of Eighteenth Annual Meeting of Industrial Relations Research Association. Madison, Wis.: Industrial Relations Research Association.

WAHL, C.W. 1959. "The fear of death." Pp. 16-29 in H. Feifel (ed.), The Meaning of Death. New York: McGraw-Hill.

WALLACE, E. and B.C. TOWNES. 1969. "The dual role of comforter and bereaved." Mental Hygiene 53: 327-32.

WATANUKI, J. 1967. "Patterns of politics in present day Japan." Pp. 447-66 in Seymour M. Lipset and Stein Rokkan (eds.), Party Systems and Voter Alignments: Cross-National Perspectives. New York: Free Press.

WATSON, WILBUR H. and ROBERT J. MAXWELL. 1977. Human Aging and Dying. New York: St. Martin's Press.

WEBER, MAX. [1904-5] 1958. The Protestant Ethic and the Spirit of Capitalism. New York: Scribner's.

_____. [1915] 1958. "Religious rejections of the world and their directions." Pp. 323-59 in H.H. Gerth and C. Wright Mills (eds.), From Max Weber. New York: Oxford University Press.

_____. [1919a] 1958. "Politics as a vocation." Pp. 77-128 in H.H. Gerth and C. Wright Mills (eds.), From Max Weber. New York: Oxford University Press.

_____. [1919b] 1958. "Science as a vocation." Pp. 129-56 in H.H. Gerth and C. Wright Mills (eds.), From Max Weber. New York: Oxford University Press.

_____. [1922] 1968. Economy and Society. New York: Bedminster Press.

WEISMAN, A.D. 1972. On Dying and Denying. New York: Behavioral Publications.

WEITZMAN, MURRAY S. 1974. "Family (money) income 1947-1971: Summarizing twenty-five years of a summary statistic." U.S. Department of Commerce, U.S. Bureau of the Census, Technical Paper 35, Washington, D.C.

WHEELER, DAVID R. 1976. Life After Death: Journey to the Other Side. New York: Ace Books.

WILLIAMS, RICHARD H. and CLAUDINE WIRTHS. 1965. Lives Through the Years. New York: Atherton Press.

WINCH, ROBERT F. 1971. The Modern Family. Third Edition. New York: Holt, Rinehart & Winston.

YAMMOTO, J. 1969. "Mourning in Japan." American Journal of Psychiatry 125: 1660-65.

YOLAHEM, MARTHA R. 1977. "Employee benefit plans, 1975." Social Security Bulletin 40: 19-28.

YOSHIDA, SUMIO. 1974. "Media for socio-medical services between home and institution in transitional Japan." Osaka, Japan: Osaka University Publication.

YOUMANS, E.G. 1963. Aging Patterns in a Rural and Urban Area of Kentucky. Lexington: University of Kentucky Agricultural Experimental Station.

index